Marine Algal Bioactives

Marine Algal Bioactives

Editor

Luigi Salvay

scitus
academics

Marine Algal Bioactives
Edited by **Luigi Salvay**

ISBN: 978-1-68117-700-7
Library of Congress Control Number: 2016958860

SCITUS Academics LLC,
616, Corporate Way, Suite 2, 4766,
Valley Cottage, NY 10989

www.scitusacademics.com

Notice

Reasonable efforts have been made to publish reliable data and views articulated in the chapters are those of the individual contributors, and not necessarily those of the editors or publishers. Editors or publishers are not responsible for the accuracy of the information in the published chapters or consequences of their use. The publisher believes no responsibility for any damage or grievance to the persons or property arising out of the use of any materials, instructions, methods or thoughts in the book. The editors and the publisher have attempted to trace the copyright holders of all material reproduced in this publication and apologize to copyright holders if permission has not been obtained. If any copyright holder has not been acknowledged, please write to us so we may rectify.

Printed in United States of America on Acid Free Paper

Preface

Marine organisms are potentially prolific sources of highly bioactive secondary metabolites that might represent useful leads in the development of new pharmaceutical agents. Algae can be classified into two main groups; first one is the microalgae, which includes blue green algae, dinoflagellates, bacillariophyta (diatoms) etc., and second one is macroalgae which includes green, brown and red algae. Marine algal species produce a variety of compounds that are ultimately beneficial to human health. The wide diversity in the biochemical composition of seaweeds provides an excellent choice to explore a variety of biologically active components in their bodily composition with a broad range of physiological and biochemical characteristics, many of which are rare or absent in other taxonomic groups. Marine algae are a famous fragility in some parts of world, and also a well-known source of important food phlorotannins, pigments and sulfated polysaccharides. Compared to the terrestrial plants and animal-based foods, seaweed is rich in some health-promoting molecules and materials such as, dietary fiber, ω-3 fatty acids, essential amino acids, and vitamins A, B, C, and E.

The marine world, due to its phenomenal biodiversity, is a rich natural resource of many biologically active compounds. Many marine organisms live in complex habitats exposed to extreme conditions and, in adapting to new environmental surroundings, they produce a wide variety of secondary (biologically active) metabolites which cannot be found in other organisms. Furthermore, considering its great taxonomic diversity, investigations related to the search of new bioactive compounds from the marine environment can be seen as an almost unlimited field.

Marine Algal Bioactives enlightens readers on the numerous bioactives of marine algae in drug discovery and development, ranging from the preliminary research to clinical trial. The importance of marine algae, the isolation of bioactives, their significance in biological effects, and their biomedical and industrial applications are presented.

Increasing knowledge regarding the impact of diet on human health along with state-of-the-art technologies has led to significant nutritional discoveries, product innovations, and mass production on an unprecedented scale. Specifically, naturally occurring bioactive extracts or single compounds thereof, that are believed beneficial to human health, have produced an important and dynamic new extent of research resulting in significant developments in nutritional familiarity. The marine environment signifies a relatively untapped source of functional ingredients that can be useful to various aspects of food processing, storage, and fortification. Furthermore, in this text, several marine-based compounds have been recognized as having varied biological activities, with some reported to interfere with the pathogenesis of diseases.

Table of Contents

Chapter 1

Antitumor and Antimicrobial Potential of Bromoditerpenes Isolated from the Red Alga, *Sphaerococcus coronopifolius*

Daniel Rodrigues [1,2,†], Celso Alves [1,†], André Horta [1], Susete Pinteus [1], Joana Silva [1], Gérald Culioli [2,3], Olivier P. Thomas [2,4] and Rui Pedrosa [1,5,*]

[1]*Marine Resources Research Group (GIRM), ESTM, Polytechnic Institute of Leiria, 2520-641 Peniche, Portugal*

[2]*Nice Institute of Chemistry-PCRE, UMR 7272 CNRS, University de Nice-Sophia Antipolis, Parc Valrose, 06108 Nice, France*

[3]*MAPIEM, EA 4323, Université de Toulon, 83957 La Garde, France*

[4]*Mediterranean Institute of Biodiversity and Ecology, Marine and Continental, Rue de la Batterie des Lions, 13007 Marseille, France*

[5]*Centre of Pharmacology and Chemical Biopathology, Faculty of Medicine, University of Porto, 4200-319 Porto, Portugal*

ABSTRACT

Cancer and infectious diseases continue to be a major public health problem, and new drugs are necessary. As marine organisms are well known to provide a wide range of original compounds, the aim of this study was to investigate the bioactivity of the main constituents of the cosmopolitan red alga, *Sphaerococcus coronopifolius*. The structure of several bromoditerpenes was determined by extensive spectroscopic analysis and comparison with literature data. Five molecules were isolated and characterized which include a new brominated diterpene belonging to the rare dactylomelane family and named sphaerodactylomelol (**1**), along with four already known sphaerane bromoditerpenes (**2–5**). Antitumor activity was assessed by cytotoxicity and anti-proliferative assays on an *in vitro*model of human hepatocellular carcinoma (HepG-2 cells). Antimicrobial activity was evaluated against four pathogenic microorganisms: *Escherichia coli*, *Pseudomonas aeruginosa*, *Staphylococcus aureus* and *Candida albicans*. Compound **4** exhibited the highest antimicrobial activity against *S. aureus* (IC_{50} 6.35 μM) and compound **5** the highest anti-proliferative activity on HepG-2 cells (IC_{50} 42.9 μM). The new diterpene, sphaerodactylomelol (**1**), induced inhibition of cell proliferation (IC_{50} 280 μM) and cytotoxicity (IC_{50} 720 μM) on HepG-2 cells and showed antimicrobial activity against *S. aureus* (IC_{50} 96.3 μM).

Keywords: red algae; *Sphaerococcus*; diterpenes; sphaerane; dactylomelane; HepG-2; pathogenic microorganisms

1. INTRODUCTION

Cancer and infectious diseases continue to be one of the major public health concerns, and consequently, there is a perpetual need for new chemotherapeutics to fight new diseases and drug resistance. In the last few decades, nature has played a significant role as a source of new drugs, and recent trends in drug research emphasize that the marine environment has a high potential for the discovery of new pharmaceuticals [1,2,3]. Marine ecosystems are among the richest and most complex ones in terms of biodiversity. Original chemical and physical conditions in such an environment provide conditions for the production of quite specific and potent active molecules. Among other reasons, marine organisms have been found to produce original and bioactive substances because they are living in an exigent, competitive and aggressive environment [4,5]. These characteristics render marine organisms ideal candidates as novel sources of both preexisting and unrecognized high value-added biomolecules with potential for providing sustainable economic and human benefits [6]. Marine algae have been one of the richest and promising sources of bioactive specialized metabolites that probably have diverse simultaneous functions for their producer and can act, for example, as antimicrobial, antifouling and herbivore deterrents or as ultraviolet-screening agents [7,8,9]. These defensive strategies can result in a high level of structural and chemical diversity for the metabolites, originating from different metabolic pathways with great pharmaceutical and biomedical potential [10,11]. Marine algae-originated compounds have been found to be associated with numerous health-promoting effects, including, in particular, anti-oxidative, anti-inflammatory, antiviral, antimicrobial or anticancer effects [10,12]. Well-documented bioactive metabolites of marine algae include mainly brominated phenols, polysaccharides, but especially, a large variety of terpenoids, several of them being halogenated [13,14,15,16].

Since its first chemical analysis in 1976, the cosmopolitan red alga, *Sphaerococcus coronopifolius*, has yielded a large number of interesting brominated cyclic diterpenes, most of them containing one or two bromine atoms [17,18,19,20,21,22,23,24,25,26,27,28,29,30,31,32,33,34,35,36,37,38,39,40]. Concerning the biological activities of these compounds, some of them have already demonstrated antibacterial activity against Gram-positive bacteria [33], and others have been assayed for their cytotoxicity against human lung cancer cell lines [37] or their antibacterial activity against multidrug-resistant and methicillin-resistant *Staphylococcus aureus* strains [38,39]. Several bromoditerpenes have also been screened against the model organism, *Amphibalanus amphitrite*, in order to evaluate their antifouling properties.

The aim of the present study was to address the antitumor and antimicrobial bioactivity characterization of the major brominated diterpenes isolated from samples of *S. coronopifolius* collected in the Atlantic, while most of the chemically-studied specimens of this algal species were collected from the Mediterranean or the Adriatic seas.

2. RESULTS AND DISCUSSION

2.1. In Vitro Bioactivity-Guided Fractionation

The screening of antitumor and antimicrobial activities of compounds isolated from *S. coronopifolius* was performed for the methanol (MeOH) and dichloromethane (CH_2Cl_2) extracts of this alga. The CH_2Cl_2 extract exhibited the highest anti-proliferative and antimicrobial activities (Table 1 and Table 2, respectively). Consequently, in order to isolate and identify the compounds responsible for these biological activities, this extract was further studied. It was first fractionated by normal phase vacuum liquid chromatography (VLC) on silica with eluents of increasing polarities (from cyclohexane to EtOAc), yielding five fractions (F1–F5 through a 25% step). In the first bioassay, fraction F2 exhibited the strongest cytotoxicity (IC_{50} 104 μg/mL) and anti-proliferative (19.8 μg/mL) activity (Table 1). On the other hand, fractions F1, F3, F4 and F5 demonstrated much more potency in the inhibition of HepG-2 cell proliferation than in the reduction of their viability. In antimicrobial assays (Table 2), the highest growth inhibition was measured against *S. aureus* for fractions F2 and F3 with IC_{50} of 5.10 and 5.39 μg/mL, respectively. In the antifungal assay, the highest activity was exhibited against *C. albicans* by fraction F2 with an IC_{50} of 53.9 μg/mL.

Table 1. Cytotoxicity and anti-proliferative (IC_{50}) effects induced on HepG-2 cells by crude extracts and VLC fractions of *S. coronopifolius*. IC_{50} values are expressed as the means of eight independent experiments with 95% confidence intervals.

		IC_{50} (µg/mL)	
		Cytotoxicity	**Anti-Proliferative**
Crude extracts	MeOH	470.6 (310.7–712.6)	646.5 (398.4–1049.0)
	CH_2Cl_2	14.13 (8.12–24.60)	32.32 (22.37–46.70)
VLC fractions	F1	>1000	102.5 (68.08–154.2)
	F2	104.3 (81.82–132.9)	19.78 (13.79–28.38)
	F3	>1000	70.17 (38.78–127.0)
	F4	>1000	36.68 (23.37–57.55)
	F5	>1000	39.32 (25.89–59.71)

According to these results, several VLC fractions showed interesting effects against different targets, and it was decided to purify and structurally characterize the main components of fractions F2 and F3, due to their high anti-proliferative and antimicrobial effects, respectively.

Table 2. Antimicrobial activities (IC_{50}) against *E. coli*, *P. aeruginosa*, *S. aureus* and *C. albicans* of crude extracts and VLC fractions obtained from *S. coronopifolius*. IC_{50} values are expressed as the means of eight independent experiments with 95% confidence intervals.

		IC_{50} (µg/mL)			
		E. coli	*P. aeruginosa*	*S. aureus*	*C. albicans*
Crude Extracts	MeOH	>1000	>1000	73.65 (58.52–92.69)	>1000
	CH_2Cl_2	267.1 (231.5–308.1)	363.1 (207.0–637.1)	25.15 (13.47–46.96)	435.9 (285.6–665.5)
VLC Fractions	F1	107.0 (92.02–124.5)	338.7 (248.3–461.9)	16.49 (10.19–26.66)	78.61 (58.12–106.3)
	F2	228.4 (188.7–276.4)	141.5 (117.6–170.4)	5.10 (4.50–5.78)	538.9 (308.4–941.6)
	F3	>1000	599.9 (307.4–1171.0)	5.39 (4.19–6.93)	>1000
	F4	433.9 (358.5–525.1)	436.4 (184.1–1035.0)	6.45 (5.16–8.05)	>1000
	F5	757.0 (614.5–932.6)	422.8 (291.9–612.4)	13.16 (9.98–17.35)	>1000

2.2. Isolation and Structure Elucidation of the Major Compounds of Fractions F2 and F3

The HPLC purifications of the selected VLC fractions, F2 and F3, followed by the structural identification of the major compounds by NMR and MS led to the identification of five diterpenes belonging to two distinct families: one new dactylomelane (**1**) and four known sphaeranes (**2**–**5**) (Figure 1). It was not surprising to find compounds belonging to the sphaerane class of diterpenes in our samples. In comparison with literature data, we were thus able to identify, unambiguously, bromosphaerol (**2**) [31], 12*S*-hydroxybromosphaerol (**3**) [34], 12*R*-hydroxybromosphaerol (**4**) [34] and sphaerococcenol (**5**) [31] as additional major metabolites of the CH_2Cl_2 extract of *S. coronopifolius* harvested on the Portuguese coast.

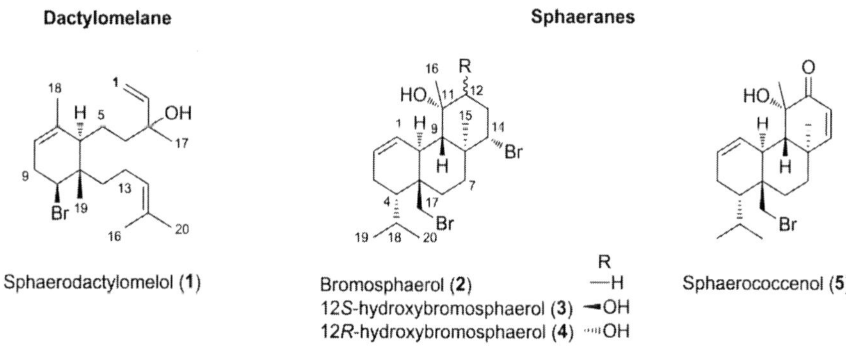

Figure 1. Chemical structure of the five bromoditerpenes, **1**–**5**, isolated from *S. coronopifolius.*

Compound **1** was isolated as an optically-active oil, and its (+)-HRESIMS spectrum (see Supplementary Information) revealed an isotopic pattern characteristic of the presence of one bromine atom at *m/z* 351.17117 and 353.16891 (intensities 1:1) that was consistent with the molecular formula $C_{20}H_{32}Br^{+}$. The ^{1}H NMR spectrum (see Supplementary Information) confirmed the presence of a diterpene with five characteristic methyl signals at δ_H 0.89 (s, H_3-19), 1.30 (s, H_3-17), 1.63 (s, H_3-16), 1.69 (s, H_3-20) and 1.70 (s, H_3-18), the chemical shifts of the last three revealing three methyls substituted on olefinic double bonds (Table 3). A terminal monosubstituted double bond was evidenced by the vinylic signals at δ_H 5.92 (dd, *J* = 17.2 and 10.8 Hz, H-2), 5.22 (dd, *J* = 17.2 and 1.2 Hz, H-1a) and 5.09 (dd, *J* = 10.8 and 1.2 Hz, H-1b). Two additional trisubstituted double bonds were inferred from the NMR signals at δ_H 5.22–5.17 (m, H-8), δ_C 120.5 (CH, C-8) and 137.2 (qC, C-7) and at δ_H 5.12–5.08 (m, H-14), δ_C 124.3 (CH, C-14) and 131.8 (qC, C-15).

Table 3. ^{1}H (500 MHz) and ^{13}C (125 MHz) NMR data of sphaerodactylomelol (**1**).

Atom n°	δ_H in ppm, mult. (*J* in Hz)	δ_C in ppm, mult.
1	5.09, dd (10.8, 1.2) 5.22, dd (17.2, 1.2)	112.3, CH_2
2	5.92, dd (17.2, 10.8)	144.9, CH
3	-	73.6, qC
4	1.83, td (13.1, 4.7) 1.46 m	44.2, CH_2
5	1.63, tdd (13.1, 4.7, 2.0) 1.38–1.29, m	23.3, CH_2
6	2.11–2.06, m	45.0, CH
7	-	137.2, qC
8	5.22–5.17, m	120.5, CH
9	2.62–2.49, m	35.3, CH_2
10	4.31, dd (10.2, 6.2)	61.5, CH
11	-	41.4, qC
12	1.57, ddd (14.4, 12.4, 5.1) 1.43 m	38.6, CH_2
13	2.03, dd (12.9, 5.8) 1.90–18.1, m	21.5, CH_2
14	5.12–5.08, m	124.3, CH
15	-	131.8, qC
16	1.63, s	17.9, CH_3
17	1.30, s	27.9, CH_3
18	1.70, s	22.4, CH_3
19	0.89, s	16.8, CH_3
20	1.69, s	25.9, CH_3

It appeared that the terminal double bond was connected to a quaternary carbon, as evidenced by the absence of further scalar coupling from the vinylic protons. The H-1 and H-2/C-3 HMBC correlations indicated that the chemical shift of the quaternary carbon was δ_C 73.6 (qC, C-3), which was characteristic of an allylic alcohol (Figure 2a). The conclusion on the presence of an alcohol and not a bromine atom at this position was also given by the observation of a second heteroatom-substituted carbon at δ_H 4.31 (dd, J = 10.2 and 6.2 Hz, H-10), δ_C 61.5 (CH, C-10), with chemical shifts fully consistent with a brominated methine. Consequently, the isotopic pattern obtained by HRESIMS was the result of dehydration of the allylic and tertiary alcohol at C-3 $[M - H_2O + H]^+$, and the molecular formula of **1** was then determined to be $C_{20}H_{33}BrO$. In view of the NMR data, from the four unsaturations corresponding to this molecular formula, the last one was assigned to a cycle. As described in Figure 2a, full analysis of ^1H-^1H COSY and HMBC spectra (see Supplementary Information) allowed the establishment of the carbon skeleton of compound **1**. More precisely, the closing of the precursor geranylgeranyl chain through the C-6/C-11 bond was ascertained by the key H_3-19, H-10, H_2-12/C-6 and H_3-19, H-10, H-9/C-11 HMBC correlations, thus leading to the six-membered ring. The key H_2-12/C-6, C-11, C-19 HMBC correlations placed the last H-12/H-13/H-14 spin coupled system at C-11, thus revealing the full planar structure of **1**. We relied on the NOESY spectrum (see Supplementary Information) for the elucidation of the relative configuration of **1**. H-10/H-6 nOe placed the bromine on the same side as the linear alkyl chain at C-6, while the second alkyl chain was placed on the other side, thanks to H_3-18/H_2-4 and H-10/H_2-13 nOes (Figure 2b). The absolute configuration was not determined, due to the lack of simple assessment. However, we assume the same stereochemistry as the one determined for the known analogues, **2**, **3** and **4**.

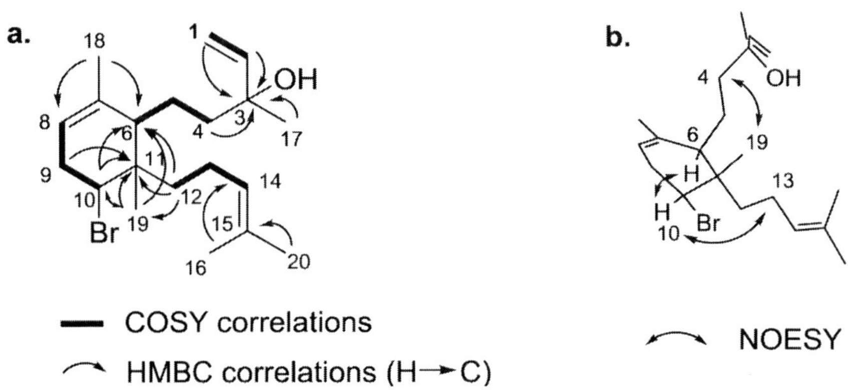

Figure 2. Key COSY, HMBC (**a**) and NOESY (**b**) correlations for sphaerodactylomelol (**1**).

This compound does not belong to the usual sphaerane family found in this species, but it is another rare example of the dactylomelane family (Figure 1) [41]. To date, there are nine compounds of this class of diterpenes described in the literature. Eight of them are characterized by a bridged oxide between

C-7 and C-10, thus leading to a 7-oxabicyclo[2.2.1]heptane moiety. These compounds were isolated from sea hares of the genus *Aplysia*, but also from a red alga of the genus *Laurencia*, thus confirming the diet of the sea hare [41,42,43]. The last compound of this chemical class was isolated from the same species, *S. coronopifolius*, harvested also along the Atlantic coast [33]. Its chemical structure is very similar to that of compound **1**, differing by the presence of an allylic alcohol at C-14 instead of a dimethyl-substituted double bond. Interestingly, all of the compounds isolated from samples of *S. coronopifolius* collected in the Mediterranean and Adriatic seas belong to the sphaerane family, suggesting that the presence of dactylomelanes would be restricted to Atlantic specimens.

2.3. Antitumor and Antimicrobial Activities of Purified Compounds

The results of the anti-proliferative experiments demonstrated that all isolated compounds have anti-proliferative activity on HepG-2 cells at sub-toxic concentrations (Table 4). The highest inhibition of cell proliferation was exhibited by compound **5** and then compound **4** with IC_{50} of 42.9 and 105 μM, respectively. Sphaerococcenol A (**5**) has already demonstrated high cytotoxic activities against A549, OE21, PC-3 and LoVo cell lines, with LC_{50} of 3.7, 3.0, 3.7 and 2.8 μM, respectively [37]. However, this is the first report of activity against HepG-2 cells. In the same report, 12*R*-hydroxybromosphaerol (**4**) also showed cytotoxic activity against the four cell lines with LC_{50} of 28, 25, 26 and 26 μM, respectively. The absence of cytotoxicity was verified in the case of NSCLC-N6 (L16) and A549 cell lines [34]. On the other hand, the major reduction of HepG-2 cell viability was induced by the new compound **1** with an IC_{50} of 720 μM, which also showed an anti-proliferative activity (IC_{50} 280 μM).

Table 4. Cytotoxicity and anti-proliferative effects (IC_{50}) induced on HepG-2 cells by bromoditerpenes **1–5** isolated from *S. coronopifolius* and drugs (positive controls). IC_{50}values are expressed as the means of eight independent experiments with 95% confidence intervals.

		IC_{50} (μM)	
		Cytotoxicity	**Anti-Proliferative**
Bromoditerpenes	**1**	719.85 (519.79–996.81)	279.93 (206.78–378.74)
	2	>1000	203.33 (90.65–456.18)
	3	>1000	291.42 (206.22–411.83)
	4	>1000	104.83 (55.27–198.89)
	5	>1000	42.87 (22.76–78.88)
Drugs (+)	Cisplatin	454.6 (388.9–531.3)	75.41 (61.78–92.05)
	Tamoxifen	>1000	45.68 (31.84–65.57)

Regarding antimicrobial activity (Table 5), the highest growth inhibition against *S. aureus* was obtained for compounds **4**(IC_{50} 6.35 μM), **2** (IC_{50} 22.4 μM) and **1** (IC_{50} 96.3 μM). This is the first report for an antimicrobial activity of 12*R*-hydroxybromosphaerol (**4**). For sphaerococcenol A (**5**), a previous report showed an antimalarial activity against the chloroquine-resistant *Plasmodium falciparum* FCB1 strains with an IC_{50} of 1 μM, but no results has been published on antimicrobial activities [33].

3. EXPERIMENTAL SECTION

3.1. General Experimental Procedures

UV and CD spectra were measured using a Jasco J-810 spectropolarimeter. Optical rotation was measured on a Perkin-Elmer 343 polarimeter, using a 100-mm microcell. IR spectra were recorded on a Bruker Tensor 27 spectrophotometer. NMR spectra were measured on a Bruker Avance 500-MHz spectrometer. Chemical shift values (δ) were reported in parts per million (ppm) relative to the appropriate internal solvent standard, and coupling constants (*J*-values) are given in Hertz and referenced to residual solvent signals ($CDCl_3$ at δ_H 7.26 and δ_C 77.16). HPLC purifications were carried out on a Jasco LC-2000 system equipped with a PU-2087 Plus preparative pumping system and a UV-2075 Plus detector. HRESIMS data were conducted on an LTQ Orbitrap mass spectrometer (Thermo Fisher Scientific, Waltham, MA, USA).

Table 5. Antimicrobial activities (IC_{50}) against *E. coli*, *P. aeruginosa*, *S. aureus* and *C. albicans* of bromoditerpenes **1–5** isolated from *S. coronopifolius* and drugs (positive controls). IC_{50} values are expressed as the means of eight independent experiments with 95% confidence intervals.

		IC_{50} (μM)			
		E. coli	*P. aeruginosa*	*S. aureus*	*C. albicans*
Bromoditerpene	1	>100	>100	96.30 (84.60–109.61)	>100
	2	>100	>100	22.42 (15.44–32.57)	>100
	3	>100	>100	>100	>100
	4	>100	>100	6.35 (4.78–8.42)	>100
	5	>100	>100	>100	>100
Drugs (+)	Ampicillin	6.42 (1.86–22.26)	-	0.11 (0.08–0.15)	-
	Bacitracin	>100	-	2.85 (2.36–3.44)	-
	Chloramphenicol	>100	-	80.49 (58.99–109.86)	-
	Oxytetracycline	1.12 (0.65–1.89)	2.13 (1.65–2.76)	0.87 (0.59–1.32)	-
	Amphotericin b	-	-	-	>100
	Flumequine	-	-	-	>100

3.2. Sampling, Identification and Treatment of Algal Material

Sphaerococcus coronopifolius samples were collected freshly from Berlenga Nature Reserve (39°24'44.8"N 9°30'29.5"W), Peniche (Portugal), in June 2012, and immediately transported to the laboratory. The alga was then cleaned and washed with sea water to remove epiphytes, detritus and encrusting material, and the resulting algal material was freeze-dried (Scanvac Cool Safe, LaboGene, Lynge, Denmark). The dry algal material was ground and stored at −80 °C until further use.

3.3. Extraction and Fractionation of Algal Extract by Vacuum Liquid Chromatography (VLC)

Freeze-dried samples of *S. coronopifolius* (470 g) were sequentially extracted in a 1:4 biomass:solvent ratio with MeOH and then CH_2Cl_2 at constant stirring for 12 h. Liquid-liquid extraction was additionally performed for the MeOH extract, using*n*-hexane to remove fats. The CH_2Cl_2 extract (5.2 g) was further concentrated and subjected to normal phase vacuum liquid chromatography on silica gel 60 (0.06–0.2 mm), using cyclohexane with increasing amounts (25%) of ethyl acetate (EtOAc) as the mobile phase (5 fractions, each one with 400 mL of eluent). The dried fractions were stored at −20 °C until further use (F1 287 mg, F2 412 mg, F3 796 mg, F4 442 mg, F5 159 mg).

3.4. Purification of Bromoditerpenes

Fraction F2 (412 mg) was further purified by preparative reversed-phase HPLC (XSelect CSH Phenyl-Hexyl 19 mm × 250 mm, 5 μm, Waters) at a flow rate of 12 mL/min and with a mixture of eluents H_2O/CH_3CN: isocratic from 0 to 5 min (25:75) and then a linear gradient from 5 to 20 min (from 25:75 to 15:85). This first purification afforded 6 subfractions, F2f1–F2f6, from which only compound **2** (F2p6, t_R 18.8 min, 23 mg) was pure. Fraction F2f1 (t_R 12.6 min, 80 mg) was subjected to a second purification step on a semi-preparative reversed-phase column (Synergi Fusion-RP 80 A, 10 mm × 250 mm, 4 μm, Phenomenex, Torrance, CA, USA) with an isocratic mode H_2O/CH_3CN (27:73) and a flow rate of 4.5 mL/min to afford pure compounds **3** (F2f1p1, t_R 17.5 min, 10 mg) and **5** (F2f1p2, t_R 19.0 min, 26 mg). Subfraction F2f3 (t_R 14.2 min, 9 mg) was purified on the same column with an isocratic mode H_2O/CH_3CN (20:80) at a flow rate of 5 mL/min to yield new compound **1** (F2f3p1, t_R 18.0 min, 4.5 mg).

The purification of fraction F3 (796 mg) was performed with the same procedure previously used for fraction F2, starting with a preparative reversed-phase HPLC separation. The elution was performed using mixtures of H_2O/CH_3CN under the following conditions: isocratic step from 0 to 5 min (30:70) and then a linear gradient until 25 min (from 30:70 to 15:85). This purification afforded pure compound **4** (F3p1, t_R 13.4 min, 19 mg), along with the four compounds previously purified from fraction F2.

3.5. Sphaerodactylomelol (1)

Colorless oil; $[\alpha]_D^{20}$ −33.3 (*c* 0.15, $CHCl_3$); UV (DAD) λ_{max} 255 nm; ECD (*c* 2.68 × 10^{-4} M, CH_2Cl_2) λ_{max} ($\Delta\varepsilon$) 228 (0.95), 277 (−0.13) nm; IR (neat) σ 2968, 2927, 2855, 1457, 1437, 1377 cm^{-1}; ^{1}H and ^{13}C NMR data, see Table 3; HRESIMS *m/z*351.17117 and 353.16891 $[M - OH]^+$ (50:50, calcd. for $C_{20}H_{32}Br^+$, 351.16819 and 353.16614, Δ −8.5 and −7.8 ppm).

3.6. Biological Activities

3.6.1. Cytotoxicity and Anti-Proliferative Activities

The anti-proliferative activities were performed on an *in vitro* carcinoma model of a human hepatocellular cancer (HepG-2), acquired in the American Type Culture Collection (ATCC). HepG-2 cells were cultured in RPMI 1640 (Sigma, Saint-Louis, MO, USA) medium supplemented with 10% fetal bovine serum (FBS) (Gibco, Grand Island, NY, USA) supplemented with 100 U/mL penicillin G, 0.25 µg/mL amphotericin B and 100 µg/mL streptomycin (Sigma, USA). The cells medium was changed every 3 days, and the cells reached confluence after 5–6 days of initial seeding in plates of a 25-cm^2 growth area at a concentration of 42.2 × 10^6 cells/ plate. For the subculture, cells were dissociated with trypsin-EDTA (Sigma, Saint-Louis, MO, USA), split into a 1:3 ratio and subcultured in Petri dishes with a 25-cm^2 growth area. Cells were maintained in controlled conditions: 95% of humidified atmosphere, 5% of CO_2 and 37 °C. Cells were seeded in 96-well plates, at a concentration of 4.4 × 10^4 cells/well, for the cytotoxicity and anti-proliferative assays.

Cytotoxicity was evaluated after the cells reached total confluence and anti-proliferative activity after 36 h of initial seeding. Cells were incubated with crude extracts, VLC fractions and purified compounds, previously sterile filtered (0.2 µm, Whatman, Little Chalfont, UK), during 24 h at 1 mg/mL. For the samples with the highest activity, dose-response assays were done (10–1000 µg/mL; 24 h). Cisplatin (Sigma, St. Loiu, MO, USA) and tamoxifen (Sigma, Shanghai, China) were used as positive controls. The effects were estimated by the colorimetric assay based on the conversion of tetrazolium dye (MTT) (Sigma, Seelze, Germany) into a blue formazan product by living mitochondria [44]. After the treatment with bromoterpenes compounds, the cells medium was removed, and cells were washed with Hank's medium (medium composition, in mM: NaCl 137, KCl 5, $MgSO_4$ 0.8, Na_2HPO_4 0.33, KH_2PO_4 0.44, $CaCl_2$ 0.25, $MgCl_2$ 1.0, Tris HCl 0.15 and sodium butyrate 1.0, pH = 7.4). Cells were then incubated with MTT (1.2 mM), previously dissolved in Hank's medium, during 4 h at 37 °C. The formazan products were dissolved in isopropanol (Panreac, Barcelona, Spain), contained 0.04 N HCl and were determined by the absorbance at 570 nm.

Results were expressed as IC_{50}, defined as the concentration causing a 50% reduction or inhibition of cell viability and cell proliferation, respectively.

3.6.2. Antimicrobial Activities

Antimicrobial activities were evaluated by the capacity to inhibit *E. coli* (ATCC 25922), *P. aeruginosa* (ATCC 27853), *S. aureus* (ATCC 25923) and *C. albicans* (ATCC 10231) growth (OD 600_{nm}). The crude extracts, VLC fractions, purified compounds and positives controls (ampicillin, bacitracin, chloramphenicol, oxytetracycline, amphotericin b and flumequine, from Sigma Aldrich, Canada) were prepared with sterile-filtered dimethylsulfoxide and stored at −20 °C. Tests were performed in 96-well plates at 37 °C for bacteria and 30 °C for fungi. Antimicrobial activity was expressed as IC_{50}, defined as the concentration causing a 50% reduction of microorganism growth.

3.6.3. Data Analysis

IC_{50} were calculated from the analysis of non-linear regression using GraphPad Prism program even $Y = 100/(1 + 10 (X - \text{Log } IC_{50}))$ equation.

4. CONCLUSIONS

In the present study, the chemical characterization of the major brominated diterpenes isolated from samples of *S. coronopifolius* collected in the Atlantic revealed five major compounds, including a new brominated dactylomelane diterpene, named sphaerodactylomelol (**1**), and four already known sphaerane bromoditerpenes, **2–5**. These molecules exhibited interesting high antimicrobial and antitumor activities against different targets and open new therapeutic potential. To the best of our knowledge, this is the first study on the isolation, identification and bioactive screening of bromoditerpenes isolated from *S. coronopifolius* collected from the Atlantic. Nonetheless, future studies will deeply describe the antitumor and antimicrobial activities and the mechanisms of action of the isolated compounds.

ACKNOWLEDGMENTS

This work was supported through funding provided by the European Commission Collaborative Project FP7 number 265896-www.bammbo.eu). One of the authors (G.C.) was partially supported by CNRS (Côte d'Azur delegation-DR 20). J.-M. Guigonis from the Plate-Forme Bernard Rossi of Nice is acknowledged for recording HRMS spectra.

AUTHOR CONTRIBUTIONS

The authors Daniel Rodrigues and Celso Alves contributed equally to this work and did the main experiments (purification, identification, cytotoxicity, anti-proliferative, antimicrobial assays and drafted the manuscript). Joana Silva, André Horta and Susete Pinteus have been involved in the antimicrobial, cytotoxicity and antiproliferative assays. Gérald Culioli and Olivier Thomas designed and coordinated the purification and identification of compounds. Rui Pedrosa designed and coordinated the antimicrobial, cytotoxicity and anti-proliferative experiments and conceived the study.

CONFLICTS OF INTEREST

The authors declare no conflict of interest.

REFERENCES

1. Xiong, Z.-Q.; Wang, J.-F.; Hao, Y.-Y.; Wang, Y. Recent advances in the discovery and development of marine microbial natural products. Mar. Drugs 2013, 11, 700–717.

2. Sawadogo, W.; Schumacher, M.; Teiten, M.-H.; Cerella, C.; Dicato, M.; Diederich, M. A survey of marine natural compounds and their derivatives with anti-cancer activity reported in 2011. Molecules 2013, 18, 3641–3673.

3. Simmons, T.L.; Andrianasolo, E.; McPhail, K.; Flatt, P.; Gerwick, W.H. Marine natural products as anticancer drugs.Mol. Cancer Ther. 2005, 4, 333–342.

4. Aneiros, A.; Garateix, A. Bioactive peptides from marine sources: pharmacological properties and isolation procedures. J. Chromatogr. B 2004, 803, 41–53.

5. Rocha, J.; Peixe, L.; Gomes, N.C. M.; Calado, R. Cnidarians as a source of new marine bioactive compounds—an overview of the last decade and future steps for bioprospecting. Mar. Drugs 2011, 9, 1860–1886.

6. Murray, P.M.; Moane, S.; Collins, C.; Beletskaya, T.; Thomas, O.P.; Duarte, A.W. F.; Nobre, F.S.; Owoyemi, I.O.; Pagnocca, F.C.; Sette, L.D.; et al. Sustainable production of biologically active molecules of marine based origin. N. Biotechnol. 2013, 30, 839–850.

7. Paul, V.J.; Puglisi, M.P. Chemical mediation of interactions among marine organisms. Nat. Prod. Rep. 2004, 21, 189–209.

8. Ianora, A.; Boersma, M.; Casotti, R.; Fontana, A.; Harder, J.; Hoffmann, F.; Pavia, H.; Potin, P.; Poulet, S.A.; Toth, G. New trends in marine chemical ecology. Estuar. Coast. 2006, 29, 531–551.

9. De Almeida, C.L.F.; de S. Falcão, H.; de M. Lima, G.R.; de A. Montenegro, C.; Lira, N.S.; de Athayde-Filho, P.F.; Rodrigues, L.C.; de Souza, M.d.F.V.; Barbosa-Filho, J.M.; Batista, L.M. Bioactivities from marine algae of the genus Gracilaria. Int. J. Mol. Sci. 2011, 12, 4550–4573.

10. Pangestuti, R.; Kim, S.-K. Neuroprotective effects of marine algae. Mar. Drugs 2011, 9, 803–818.

11. Joana Gil-Chávez, G.; Villa, J.A.; Fernando Ayala-Zavala, J.; Basilio Heredia, J.; Sepulveda, D.; Yahia, E.M.; González-Aguilar, G.A. Technologies for extraction and production of bioactive compounds to be used as nutraceuticals and food ingredients: an overview. Compr. Rev. Food Sci. Food Saf. 2013, 12, 5–23.

12. Thomas, N.; Kim, S.-K. Beneficial effects of marine algal compounds in cosmeceuticals. Mar. Drugs 2013, 11, 146–164.

13. Viano, Y.; Bonhomme, D.; Ortalo-Magné, A.; Thomas, O.P.; Hattab, M.E.; Piovetti, L.; Blache, Y.; Culioli, G. Dictyotadimer A, a new dissymmetric bis-diterpene from a brown alga of the genus Dictyota. Tetrahedron Lett. 2011,52, 1031–1035.

14. Lee, J.-C.; Hou, M.-F.; Huang, H.-W.; Chang, F.-R.; Yeh, C.-C.; Tang, J.-Y.; Chang, H.-W. Marine algal natural products with anti-oxidative, anti-inflammatory, and anti-cancer properties. Cancer Cell Int. 2013, 13, 55.

15. Li, Y.-X.; Himaya, S.; Kim, S.-K. Triterpenoids of marine origin as anti-cancer agents. Molecules 2013, 18, 7886–7909.

16. Cabrita, M.T.; Vale, C.; Rauter, A.P. Halogenated compounds from marine algae. Mar. Drugs 2010, 8, 2301–2317.

17. Fattorusso, E.; Magno, S.; Santacroce, C.; Sica, D.; di Blasio, B.; Pedone, C.; Impellizzeri, G.; Mangiafico, S.; Oriente, G. Bromosphaerol, a new bromine-containing diterpenoid from the red alga Sphaerococcus coronopifolius. Gazz. Chim. Ital.1976, 106, 779–783.

18. Fenical, W.; Finer, J.; Clardy, J. Sphaerococcenol A, a new rearranged bromo-diterpene from the red alga Sphaerococcus coronopifolius. Tetrahedron Lett. 1976, 731–734.

19. Cafieri, F.; de Napoli, L.; Fattorusso, E.; Impellizzeri, G.; Piattelli, M.; Sciuto, S. Bromosphaerodiol, a minor bromo compound from the red alga Sphaerococcus coronopifolius. Experientia 1977, 33, 1549–1550.

20. Cafieri, F.; de Napoli, L.; Fattorusso, E.; Piattelli, M.; Sciuto, S. Presphaerol, a new rearranged diterpene from the red alga Sphaerococcus coronopifolius. Tetrahedron Lett. 1979, 20, 963–966.

21. Cafieri, F.; Fattorusso, E.; di Blasio, B.; Pedone, C. Diterpenes from the red alga Sphaerococcus coronopifolius. Structure of sphaerodiene and reassignment of structure for presphaerol. Tetrahedron Lett. 1981, 22, 4123–4126.

22. Cafieri, F.; Ciminiello, P.; Fattorusso, E.; Santacroce, C. 12S-hydroxybromosphaerol, a new bromoditerpene from the red alga Sphaerococcus coronopifolius. Experientia 1982, 38, 298–299.

23. Cafieri, F.; Ciminiello, P.; Santacroce, C.; Fattorusso, E. (1S)-1,2-Dihydro-1-hydroxybromosphaerol, a minor bromoditerpene from the red alga Sphaerococcus coronopifolius. Phytochemistry 1982, 21, 2412–2413.

24. Cafieri, F.; Ciminiello, P.; Santacroce, C.; Fattorusso, E. Three diterpenes from the red alga Sphaerococcus coronopifolius.Phytochemistry 1983, 22, 1824–1825.

25. Cafieri, F.; Fattorusso, E.; Santacroce, C. Bromocorodienol, a diterpenoid based on a novel bicyclic skeleton from the red alga Sphaerococcus coronopifolius. Tetrahedron Lett. 1984, 25, 3141–3144.

26. Cafieri, F.; Fattorusso, E.; Mayol, L.; Santacroce, C. Coronopifoliol, a diterpene based on an unprecedented tetracyclic skeleton from the red algae Sphaerococcus coronopifolius. J. Org. Chem. 1985, 50, 3982–3984.

27. Cafieri, F.; Fattorusso, E.; Mayol, L.; Santacroce, C. Structure of bromotetrasphaerol, a further irregular diterpene from the red alga Sphaerococcus coronopifolius. Tetrahedron 1986, 42, 4273–4276.

28. Bavoso, A.; Cafieri, F.; de Napoli, L.; di Blasio, B.; Fattorusso, E.; Pavone, V.; Santacroce, C. Isolation and structure determination of norsphaerol, a bis-nor-diterpene from the red alga Sphaerococcus coronopifolius. Gazz. Chim. Ital. 1987,117, 87–89.

29. Cafieri, F.; De Napoli, L.; Fattorusso, E.; Santacroce, C. Diterpenes from the red alga Sphaerococcus coronopifolius.Phytochemistry 1987, 26, 471–473.

30. Cafieri, F.; De Napoli, L.; Fattorusso, E.; Santacroce, C. Sphaeropyrane, a diterpene from the marine red algaSphaerococcus coronopifolius. Phytochemistry 1988, 27, 621–623.

31. De Rosa, S.; De Stefano, S.; Scarpelli, P.; Zavodnik, N. Chemical studies of north Adriatic seaweeds. Part 3. Terpenes from the red alga Sphaerococcus coronopifolius of the north Adriatic Sea. Phytochemistry 1988, 27, 1875–1878.

32. Cafieri, F.; Ciminiello, P.; Fattorusso, E.; Mangoni, A. Two novel bromoditerpenes from the red alga Sphaerococcus coronopifolius. Gazz. Chim. Ital. 1990, 120, 139–142.

33. Etahiri, S.; Bultel-Ponce, V.; Caux, C.; Guyot, M. New bromoditerpenes from the red alga Sphaerococcus coronopifolius.J. Nat. Prod. 2001, 64, 1024–1027.

34. Smyrniotopoulos, V.; Quesada, A.; Vagias, C.; Moreau, D.; Roussakis, C.; Roussis, V. Cytotoxic bromoditerpenes from the red alga Sphaerococcus coronopifolius. Tetrahedron 2008, 64, 5184–5190.

35. Smyrniotopoulos, V.; Vagias, C.; Rahman, M.M.; Gibbons, S.; Roussis, V. Brominated diterpenes with antibacterial activity from the red alga Sphaerococcus coronopifolius. J. Nat. Prod. 2008, 71, 1386–1392.

36. Smyrniotopoulos, V.; Vagias, C.; Roussis, V. Sphaeroane and neodolabellane diterpenes from the red algaSphaerococcus coronopifolius. Mar. Drugs 2009, 7, 184–195.

37. Smyrniotopoulos, V.; Vagias, C.; Bruyère, C.; Lamoral-Theys, D.; Kiss, R.; Roussis, V. Structure and in vitro antitumor activity evaluation of brominated diterpenes from the red alga Sphaerococcus coronopifolius. Bioorg. Med. Chem. 2010,18, 1321–1330.

38. Smyrniotopoulos, V.; Vagias, C.; Rahman, M.M.; Gibbons, S.; Roussis, V. Ioniols I and II, tetracyclic diterpenes with antibacterial activity, from Sphaerococcus coronopifolius. Chem. Biodivers. 2010, 7, 666–676.

39. Smyrniotopoulos, V.; Vagias, C.; Rahman, M.M.; Gibbons, S.; Roussis, V. Structure and antibacterial activity of brominated diterpenes from the red alga Sphaerococcus coronopifolius. Chem. Biodivers. 2010, 7, 186–195.

40. Piazza, V.; Roussis, V.; Garaventa, F.; Greco, G.; Smyrniotopoulos, V.; Vagias, C.; Faimali, M. Terpenes from the red alga Sphaerococcus coronopifolius inhibit the settlement of barnacles. Mar. Biotechnol. 2011, 13, 764–772.

41. Fernandez, J.J.; Souto, M.L.; Gil, L.V.; Norte, M. Isolation of naturally occurring dactylomelane metabolites as Laurencia constituents. Tetrahedron 2005, 61, 8910–8915.

42. Estrada, D.M.; Ravelo, J.L.; Ruiz-Pérez, C.; Martín, J.D.; Solans, X. Dactylomelol, a new class of diterpene from the sea hare Aplysia dactylomela. Tetrahedron Lett. 1989, 30, 6219–6220.

43. Findlay, J.A.; Li, G. Novel terpenoids from the sea hare Aplysia punctata. Can. J. Chem. 2002, 80, 1697–1707.

44. Yuan, Y.V.; Walsh, N.A. Antioxidant and antiproliferative activities of extracts from a variety of edible seaweeds. Food Chem. Toxicol. 2006, 44, 1144–1150.

Chapter 2

Antibacterial Activities of a New Brominated Diterpene from Borneon *Laurencia*spp.

Charles Santhanaraju Vairappan [1,*], Takahiro Ishii [1], Tan Kai Lee [1], Minoru Suzuki [1] and Zhan Zhaoqi [2]

[1]*Laboratory of Natural Products Chemistry, Institute for Tropical Biology and Conservation, Universiti Malaysia Sabah, 88999 Kota Kinabalu, Sabah, Malaysia*

[2]*Shimadzu (Asia Pacific) Pte Ltd, 16 Science Park Drive, #01-01, The Pasteur Singapore Science Park, 118227, Singapore*

ABSTRACT

In our continuous interest to study the diversity of halogenated metabolites of Malaysian species of the red algal genus *Laurencia*, we examined the chemical composition of five populations of unrecorded *Laurencia* sp. A new brominated diterpene, 10-acetoxyangasiol (**1**), and four other known metabolites, aplysidiol (**2**), cupalaurenol (**3**), 1-methyl-2,3,5-tribromoindole (**4**), and chamigrane epoxide (**5**), were isolated and identified. Isolated metabolites exhibited potent antibacterial activities against clinical bacteria, *Staphylococcus aureus, Staphylococcus* sp., *Streptococcus pyogenes, Salmonella* sp. and *Vibrio cholerae.*

Keywords: *Laurencia* sp.; halogenated metabolites; antibacterial activity

1. INTRODUCTION

Red algae of the genus *Laurencia* (Rhodomelaceae, Ceramiales) are known to be prolific sources of a wide variety of halogenated secondary metabolites, such as C_{15}-acetogenins and C_{15}-, C_{20}-, and C_{30}-terpenoids [1]. In the course of our chemical and biological investigation of *Laurencia* species from the coastal waters of Borneo (Malaysia), we reported the chemical composition of *L. snackeyi* (Weber-van Bosse) Masuda [2], *L. similis* Nam et Saito [3], and *L. majuscula* (Harvey) Lucas [4,5]. As part of the chemical analysis of the undescribed *Laurencia* species, we examined five populations of unrecorded *Laurencia* sp. collected from the coastal waters of North Borneo Island, Sabah. Each specimen contained one halogenated metabolite, a total of five halogenated metabolites were isolated and identified. These specimens yielded one new 10-acetoxyangasiol (**1**) and four known halogenated metabolites; aplysiadiol (**2**), cupalaurenol (**3**), 1-methyl-2,3,5-tribromoindole (**4**), and chamigrane epoxide (**5**). The structure of the new compound 10-acetoxyangasiol (**1**) was elucidated by spectral data. The structures of the known metabolites (**2–5**) were determined based on the comparison of spectral data to that of the published reports of Ojika *et al.* [6,7], Ichiba and Higa [8] and Carter and Rinehart [9]. In this paper, we describe the isolation and structure elucidation of these compounds and their antibacterial activities against clinical bacteria.

2. RESULTS AND DISCUSSION

The partially dried specimens of algae *Laurencia* sp. were extracted in MeOH (1:1, v/v). The concentrated extracts were partitioned between H_2O and EtOAc. The EtOAc soluble fraction was dehydrated over Na_2SO_4 anhydrous, filtered, concentrated and purified by a combination of silica gel column chromatography and High Performance Liquid Chromatography (HPLC) separation, to yield compounds **1–5** (Figure 1).

Compound **1** was obtained as white powder, $[\alpha]^{25}_{D}$ +6.4 (*c* 0.9, $CHCl_3$). The IR spectrum indicated the presence of OH group (3532 cm^{-1}), γ-lactone carbonyl group (1773 cm^{-1}) and acetoxy functionality (1734 and 1236 cm^{-1}). The positive ESI-MS exhibited a characteristic molecular-ion cluster at *m/z* 535/537/539 in a ratio of 1:2:1, suggesting the presence of two bromine atoms. The molecular formula was determined to be $C_{22}H_{32}Br_2O_5$ by HR-ESI-TOFMS, indicating six degrees of unsaturation. The ^{13}C NMR spectrum (Table 1) along with the DEPT experiments showed the presence of 22 carbons including four methyls, seven methylenes, five methines and six quaternary carbon atoms. In addition, the ^{1}H and ^{13}C NMR spectral data

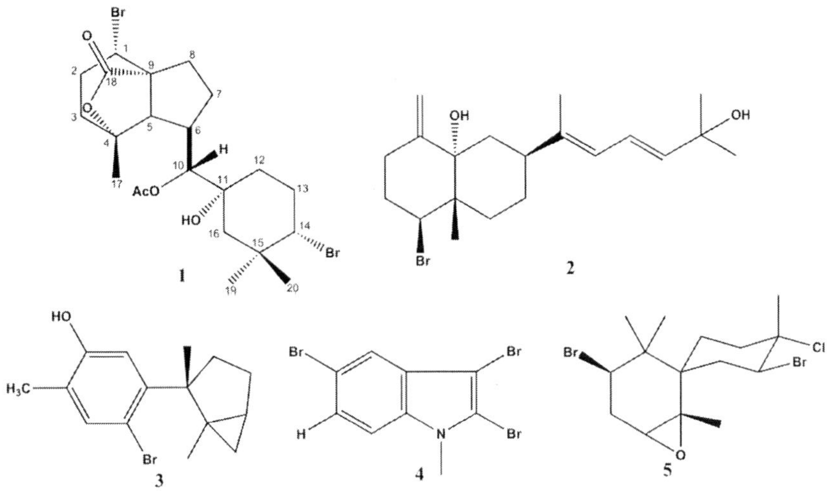

Figure 1. The structure of compounds **1–5** from specimens of algae *Laurencia* sp.

(Table 1) indicated the presence of a γ-lactone carbonyl group [δ_C 174.3 (s)] and an associated tertiary alkoxy group [δ_C 83.0 (s)], an acetoxy group [δ_C 169.4 (s), 20.2 (q); δ_H 1.58 (3H, s)], an acetoxymethine [δ_C 83.0 (d); δ_H 4.31 (1H, d, J = 8.9 Hz)], a tertiary alcohol [δ_C 73.7 (s)], two bromomethines [δ_C 64.4 (d); δ_H 3.52 (1H, dd, J = 13.1, 4.1 Hz) and δ_C51.0 (d); δ_H 3.33 (1H, dd, J = 11.7, 6.2 Hz)] and three tertiary methyls [δ_H 1.25, 1.15 and 0.93 (each 3H, s)]. According to the molecular formula and the functionalities mentioned above, compound **1** is suggested to contain one γ-lactone and three carbocyclic rings. Furthermore, the ^{13}C-NMR spectra of **1** closely resembled those of the known compound angasiol [10], except for the absence of one acetoxy group. It clearly suggested that **1** possesses the same skeleton and substituent.

Assignments were carried out based on ^{1}H-^{1}H COSY, HSQC and HMBC spectra data. ^{1}H-^{1}H COSY experiments revealed the sequences of the correlations depicted by the bold lines in Figure 2. Key HMBC correlations as shown in Figure 2 were consistent with the proposed structure of **1**. Furthermore, the relative stereochemistry of **1** was elucidated by NOESY experiments as well as the coupling constants in the ^{1}H-NMR spectrum. The coupling constant ($J_{6,10}$ = 8.9 Hz) indicated the*anti* conformation for the H-6/H-10. The configuration at C-10 was assigned as R* on the basis of the

Table 1. ^{1}H-NMR and ^{13}C-NMR spectral data of compound **1** (recorded at 600/150 MHz in $CDCl_3$; δ in ppm, *J* in Hz).

C	^{13}C (δ)	^{1}H (δ)	Multiplicity (*J* in Hz)
1	51.0	3.33	(dd, 11.7, 6.2)
2	32.6	2.00	m
		1.82	m
3	38.1	1.32–1.39	m
		0.81	(ddd, 13.7, 12.4, 5.5)
4	83.0		
5	60.1	1.34	(d, 8.3)
6	38.0	2.32	(dddd, 11.0, 8.9, 8.3, 4.8)
7	29.6	1.50–1.57	m
		1.05	(dddd, 14.5, 10.3, 4.8, 2.0)
8	32.7	2.54	(ddd, 13.1, 8.3, 2.0)
		1.43	(ddd, 13.1, 10.3, 10.3)
9	61.8		
10	83.0	4.31	(d, 8.9)
11	73.7		
12	34.3	0.90–0.95	m
		0.56	(ddd, 13.1, 13.1, 4.1)
13	29.7	2.25	(dddd, 13.1, 13.1, 13.1, 3.4)
		1.78	(dddd, 13.1, 4.1, 4.1, 4.1)
14	64.4	3.52	(dd, 13.1, 4.1)
15	36.1		
16	47.2	1.29	(dd, 13.7, 3.4)
		0.92	(d, 13.7)
17	21.9	1.15	s
18	174.3		
19	22.7	1.25	s
20	32.3	0.93	s
Ac	169.4		
	20.2	1.58	s

NOESY correlations observed between H-5/H-10, H-7β/H-10, H-10/Hax-12, H-10/Hax-16 and H_3-17/H_3-Ac. In addition, the remaining stereochemistry of **1** was determined by NOESY correlations as shown in Figure 3 and assigned to be the same as for angasiol and its related compounds, irieols A–G [10–12]. In consequence, the structure of 10-acetoxyangasiol (**1**) must be represented by structure **1**.

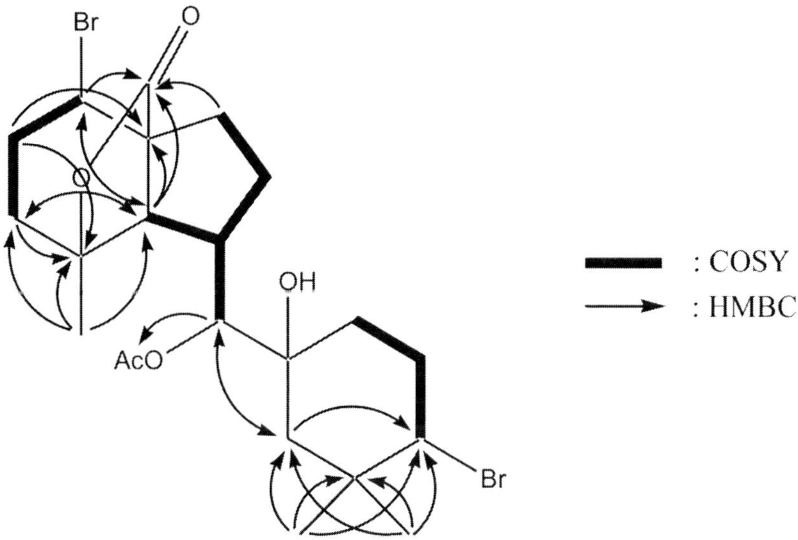

Figure 2. ^{1}H-^{1}H COSY correlations (bold lines) and key HMBC correlations (H→C) of**1**.

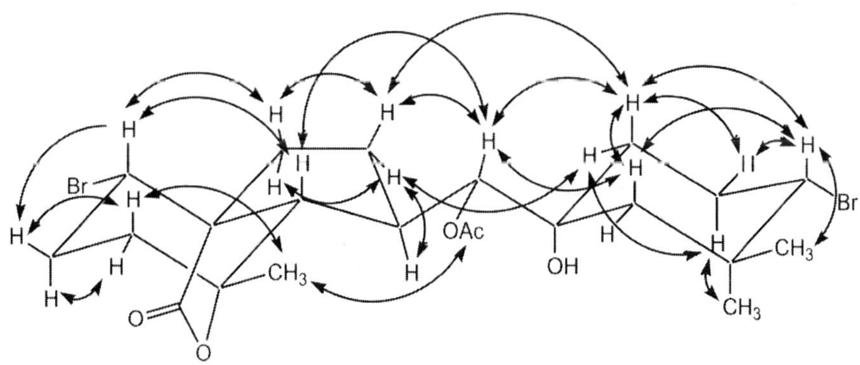

Figure 3. NOESY correlations of **1**.

All five metabolites were subjected to antibacterial bioassay against five species of clinical bacteria, and their antibacterial activities at 30 mg disc^{-1} are shown in Table 2. Compounds **1**, **2** and **3** exhibited potent inhibition against three of the tested bacteria. The lowest MIC value was observed for compound **1** against *Vibrio cholerae* at 100 µg mL^{-1}. Compounds **4** and **5**only exhibited weak inhibition against *Staphylococcus* sp. with a MIC value of 300 µg mL^{-1}. Vancomycin, used as a positive control, exhibited a >23 mm inhibition zone against all the tested microbes at 30 mg disc^{-1}. Based on our findings, these halogenated metabolites could be considered as possible candidates for further investigation against clinical microbes in our endeavor to combat the rise in antibiotic resistant microbes.

Table 2. Diameter of inhibition zone (DIZ) and minimum inhibitory concentration (MIC) of halogenated metabolites from *Laurencia* sp against five bacteria.

Tested Bacteria	Halogenated Metabolites				
	1	2	3	4	5
INHIBITION AT 30 mg/disc (mm)					
Staphylococcus aureus	10	8	15	-	-
Staphylococcus sp.	12	10	15	9	9
Streptococcus pyogenes	-	-	-	-	-
Salmonella sp.	-	9	15	-	-
Vibrio cholerae	18	-	11	-	-
MINIMUM INHIBITION CONCENTRATION (MIC) (μg/mL)					
Staphylococcus aureus	250	200	125	-	-
Staphylococcus sp.	200	125	125	300	300
Streptococcus pyogenes	-	-	-	-	-
Salmonella sp.	-	250	125	-	-
Vibrio cholerae	100	-	200	-	-

Note: Bioassay were done in triplicate, SD <10%, and not shown.

3. EXPERIMENTAL SECTION

3.1. General

Optical rotations were measured on an AUTOPOL IV automatic polarimeter (Rudolph Research Analytical). ^{1}H-NMR (600 MHz) and ^{13}C-NMR (150 MHz) spectra were recorded with a JEOL ECA 600, with TMS as internal standard. HR-ESI-TOFMS spectrum was obtained with LCMS-IT-TOF (Shimadzu). Silica gel (Merck, Kieselgel 60, 70–230 mesh) was used for column chromatography. Separation of the eluted fraction were carried out using Shimadzu HPLC with Phenyl Hexyl (Phenomenex, USA) 10 × 250 mm eluted with 70% MeCN/H_2O, and detected at 210 nm using SPD 20A Shimadzu UV-Vis detector. Analytical TLC was performed on Merck Kieselgel 60 F_{254}. Spots were visualized by UV light or by spraying with a 5% phosphomolybdic acid-ethanol solution.

3.2. Algal material

Specimens of *Laurencia* sp. were collected from Lohok Butun (4°27’23”N, 118°41’12”E), Selakan Island (4°35’00”N, 118°42’04”E), Layangan Island

(5°46'63"N, 115°53'39"E), and Gaya Island (6°00'47"N, 116°03'14"E). The specimens (voucher nos. 37604, 37610, 37665, 37767, 37774) are deposited in the Herbarium (BORH) of Institute for Tropical Biology and Conservation, Universiti Malaysia Sabah.

3.3. Extraction and isolation

The partially dried alga specimens (100 g) were extracted with MeOH. The MeOH solution was concentrated *in vacuo* and partitioned between EtOAc and H_2O. The EtOAc fraction was washed with water, dried over anhydrous Na_2SO_4, and evaporated to leave dark green oil. The extract was then fractioned by Si gel column chromatography with a step gradient (hexane and EtOAc). The fractions eluted with hexanes-EtOAc (9:1) and hexanes-EtOAc (8:2) were further purified by HPLC to give 10-acetoxyangasiol (**1**) (2.4%) from specimen BORH 37610, aplysidiol (**2**) (3.2%) from specimen BORH 37665), cupalaurenol (**3**) (0.9%) from specimen BORH 37774, 1-methyl-2,3,5-tribromoindole (**4**) (2.8%) from specimen BORH 37767, and chamigrane epoxide (**5**) (3.6%) from specimen BORH 37774. Yield was calculated based on the extracted methanol crude.

3.4. Characterization of 10-acetoxyangasiol (1)

White powder; $[\alpha]^{25}_{D}$ +6.4 (*c* 0.9, $CHCl_3$); HR-TOFMS *m/z* 535.0661 $[M + H]^+$ (calculated for $C_{22}H_{33}Br_2O_5$, 535.0689); ^1H-NMR and ^{13}C-NMR spectral data: see Table 1.

3.5. Bioassay

The antibacterial bioassay for the isolated metabolite was carried out against 5 species of clinical pathogens obtained from Department of Pathology, Queen Elizabeth Hospital, Kota Kinabalu, Sabah, Malaysia. These bacteria are*Staphylococcus aureus* (UMS01-08), *Staphylococcus* sp. (UMS02-08), *Streptococcus pyogenes*(UMS03-08), *Salmonella* sp. (UMS04-08) and *Vibrio cholerae*(UMS05-08). One loopful of each organism was precultured in 20 mL of peptone water overnight. The turbidity of the culture was adjusted to an optical density (OD) of McFarland 0.5 [13]. Then 0.1 mL of the precultured bacterial suspension was used to seed Nutrient Agar plates. Paper discs (Whatman, 6 mm) impregnated with 30 mg disc^{-1}of the respective isolated compounds were placed on the seeded agar plates and the diameter of the inhibitory zones measured after incubation at 28 °C for 24 h. Antibacterial activity was evaluated by measuring the diameter of inhibition zone of the tested bacteria. Vancomycin (Sigma, Germany) was used as positive control. Minimum Inhibitory Concentration (MIC) determination for the positive inhibitions was carried out via microdilution broth method as described by Shan *et al.*(2008) with slight modifications [14].

4. CONCLUSIONS

This is our first report on the composition of halogenated metabolites and their activities in unrecorded *Laurencia* sp. from the coastal waters of North Borneo Island of Sabah, Malaysia. Our initiative pertaining to the isolation and identification of halogenated secondary metabolites from Borneon *Laurencia* continues to excite us, with the isolation of a wide diversity of structurally interesting metabolites. To date, we have isolated a total of 42 halogenated metabolites from*L. snackeyii*, *L. majuscula*, *L. similis*, *L. nangii* and these five species of undescribed *Laurencia* spp.

ACKNOWLEDGEMENTS

We are grateful to the Sabah Parks for the support and assistance during field survey. This study was funded by the "International Foundation for Science (IFS)" and Committee for the Prohibition of Chemical Weapon, Hague, The Netherlands (IFS), Grant No: AF/4286-2). The authors would also like to acknowledge Hiroshi Matsuura for his kind assistance during data comparison.

REFERENCES

1. Erickson, KL. Scheuer, PJ, Ed.; *Marine Natural Products: Chemical and Biological Perspectives*; Academic Press: New York, NY, USA, 1983; Volume V, pp. 131–257.

2. Vairappan, CS; Tan, KL. Halogenated secondary metabolites from sea hare *Aplysia dactylomela*. *Malaysian J. Sci* **2004**,*24*, 17–22.

3. Vairappan, CS; Ang, MY; Ong, CY; Phang, SM. Biologically active polybrominated indoles in the red algae *Laurencia similis* from the coastal waters of Sabah (*Rhodomelaceae, Ceramiales*). *Malaysian J. Sci* **2004**, *23*, 119–126.

4. Vairappan, CS. Potent antibacterial activity of Malaysian red algal halogenated metabolites against human pathogenic bacteria. *Biomol. Eng* **2003**, *20*, 255–259.

5. Vairappan, CS; Phang, SM. Morphology and halochamigrene metabolite content of Laurencia majuscula (Rhodomelaceae, Ceramiales) from the Spratly Islands. *Malaysian J. Sci* **2005**, *24*(2), 29–36.

6. Ojika, M; Shizuri, Y; Yamada, K. A halogenated chamigrane epoxide and six related halogen containing sesquiterpenes from the red alga *Laurencia okamurai*. *Phytochemistry* **1982**, *21*, 2410–2411.

7. Ojika, M; Yoshida, Y; Okumura, M; Ieda, S; Yamada, K. Alysiadiol, a new brominated diterpene from the marine mollusc *Aplysia kurodai*. *J. Nat. Prod* **1990**, *53*, 1619–1622.

8. Ichiba, T; Higa, T. New cuparene derived sesquiterpenes with unprecedented oxygenation patterns from the sea hare*Aplysia dactylomela*. *J. Org. Chem* **1986**, *51*, 3364–3366.

9. Carter, GT; Rinehart, KL, Jr; Li, LH; Kuentzel, SL; Connor, JL. Brominated indoles from *Laurencia brongniartii*.*Tetrahedron Lett* **1978**, *46*, 4479–4482.

10. Pettit, GR; Herald, CL; Einck, JJ; Vanell, LD; Brown, P; Gust, D. Isolation and structure of angasiol. *J. Org. Chem* **1978**,*43*, 4685–4686.

11. Howard, BM; Fenical, W. Structures of irieols, new dibromoditerpenoids of a unique skeletal class from the marine red alga *Laurencia irieii*. *J. Org. Chem* **1978**, *43*, 4401–4408.

12. Ji, NY; Li, XM; Cui, CM; Wang, BG. Terpenes and polybromoindoles from the marine red alga *Laurencia decumbens*(Rhodomelaceae). *Helv. Chim. Acta* **2007**, *90*, 1731–1736.

13. Vairappan, CS; Suzuki, M; Ishii, T; Okino, T; Abe, T; Masuda, M. Antibacterial activity of halogenated sesquiterpenes from Malaysian *Laurencia* spp. *Phytochemistry* **2008**, *69*, 2490–2494.

14. Shan, B; Cai, YZ; Brooks, JD; Corke, H. Antibacterial properties of *Polygonum cuspidatum* roots and their major bioactive constituents. *Food Chem* **2008**, *109*, 503–537.

Chapter 3

Bioactive Compounds from Bacteria Associated to Marine Algae

Irma Esthela Soria-Mercado[1], Luis Jesús Villarreal-Gómez[2], Graciela Guerra Rivas[1] and Nahara E. Ayala Sánchez[3]

[1] *Facultad de Ciencias Marinas, Universidad Autónoma de Baja California, Ensenada, BC., México*

[2] *Centro de Ingeniería y Tecnología, Universidad Autónoma de Baja California, Tijuana, BC., México*

[3] *Facultad de Ciencias, Universidad Autónoma de Baja California, Ensenada, BC ., México*

1. INTRODUCTION

Since ancient times, humans have sought to satisfy their needs, one of which is, without a doubt, to stay alive. The fear of getting sick and dying, led man to study the organisms that surround him, discovering that the chemicals compounds present in some of them could be beneficial for treating illness. Thus; began the chemistry of the natural products; biotechnology area for human welfare. Several of these organisms produce secondary metabolites, which are part of a wide variety of natural compounds used by humans to combat diseases. Secondary metabolites are defined as organic compounds formed as bio products in organisms, not directly related to growth, development and normal reproduction of thereof. Some examples are fibers (cotton, silk, wool); fuels (oil and natural gas), and medicines (antibiotics, hormones, vaccines).

The importance of finding and using these secondary metabolites can be justified in two ways (1) to know the natural substances that can be beneficial for man and (2) to identify the organisms that produce these substances in order to make a rational exploitation of them, because they may be the only carriers of useful compounds to combat pathogenic microbes.

Marine organisms possess an inexhaustible source of useful chemical substances for the development of new drugs; among these organisms we find marine algae that are capable of biosynthesizing a broad variety of secondary metabolites and bacteria that live in the oceans and that are crucial organisms used in biotechnology in the discovery of new compounds from marine origin.

The discovery of new bioactive compounds necessarily involves previously diversity studies, because by knowing the type of microorganisms that reside in a certain environment, it is possible to design cultivation techniques adapted for all the microbial communities present in a certain ambience. That is why it is very important to identify the organisms that produce bioactive secondary metabolites, and to be able to structure a plan of use and preservation of those species that represent a potential source for new drug development, especially those obtained from bacteria, because of their own cultivation characteristics, have attracted attention on either a big quantity of investigators on a global scale in the search of new natural products with anticancer and antibiotic activity principally.

2. ANTICANCER ACTIVITY

Cancer is an illness that comprises more than hundred types. This disease appears when old cells are not replaced by new cells and are accumulated in a mass of tissue known as tumor (Figure 1).

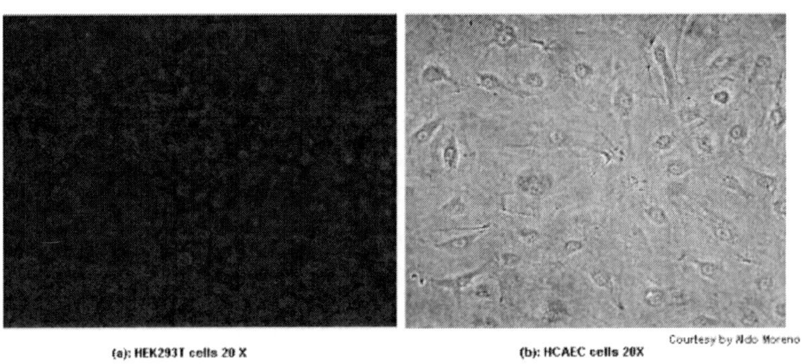

Figure 1. Pictures of immortalized cells that resemble carcinogenic cells and cells of a normal tissue (20X). (a): immortalized cells of Human Embryonic Kidney Cells (HEK293T) visualized with 20X amplification. (b): Human Coronary Artery Endothelial Cells (HCAEC) visualized with 20X amplification. (A courtesy of Aldo M.Ulloa, UCSD, School of Medicine).

The incidence of cancer increases constantly constituting an enormous challenge for health institutions, in many of the cases, the medicines used in chemotherapy treatment provoke secondary toxicity or resistance (Isnard-Bagnis et al., 2005). For all of the above, there is an urgent need to discover new anticancer compounds from natural sources. Compounds like taxol, camptothecin, vincristine and vinblastine, are obtained from superior plants (Cragg & Newman, 1999), recently some medicines obtained from marine organisms have showed promising results when administered at different cancer stages.

The metabolic and physiological capacity that allows marine organism to survive in extreme conditions provides an enormous potential for the production of unique compounds that are not present in the terrestrial organisms. That is way marine organisms are an attractive source of compounds with pharmaceutical activity, (Faulkner, 2002). Seaweeds are recognized as one of the richest sources of new bioactive compounds of which reviews have been published recently on the biological activity of their derivative compounds (Blunt et al., 2006).

3. RESISTANCE TO ANTIBIOTICS

The resistance to antibiotics is a phenomenon by which a microorganism stops being affected by an antimicrobial compound to which previously it was sensitive. It is a consequence of the capacity of certain microorganisms (bacteria, virus and parasites) to neutralize the effect of the medicine. The resistance can come from the mutation of the microorganism or from the acquisition of resistance genes. The infections caused by resistant microorganisms do not answer to the ordinary treatment, which result in a long illness and the risk of death (WHO, 2011).

Approximately 440 000 new cases of multiresistant tuberculosis produce at least 150 000 deaths every year. In South East Asia infections of *Plasmodium falciparum* that are late in disappearing after the beginning of the treatment with artemisinins are arising, which indicates resistance of the parasite to this specific medicine. Resistance has been found also to the antiretroviral medicines that are used in the treatment of the HIV's infection (WHO, 2011).

A high percentage of the infections contracted in the hospitals are caused by very resistant bacteria, like Methicillin Resistant *Staphylococcus aureus* (MRSA), *Enterococcus faecium* and several microorganisms Gram negative resistant to Vancomycin (WHO, 2011). New mechanisms can appear that can cancel completely the ability of antimicrobial drugs to act against bacteria. This could represent the last defense against multiresistant microorganism's strains. For example, a new β-lactamase, enzyme of the group of the carbapenemases that nowadays are named like NDM-1, gives resistance to the majority of the β-lactams medicines. The enzyme is linked to genes that are easily transferred between the common bacteria, and the infections caused by NDM-1's producer bacteria have no treatment or, if they have it, the therapeutic options are few (WHO, 2011).

4. FACTORS THAT ENHANCE THE RESISTANCE APPEARANCE TO THE ANTIMICROBIAL EFFECTS

According to the World Health Organization (WHO) several factors exist that enhance the resistance to antibiotics. One problem is the lack of commitment of the government towards solving the problem, the bad definition of the responsibilities of the interested parts and the scarce participation of the consumers those results in the lack of coherent and coordinated methods to anticipate and to contain the resistance to the antimicrobial compounds. The improper and irrational use of antimicrobial drugs promotes conditions for the appearance of resistant microorganisms, which at once propagate. This happens, for example, when the patients do not take the complete treatment of a prescribed antibiotic or when the above mentioned medicine is of bad quality.

The nonexistence or weakness of the systems of alertness determines the lack of information that can guide politicians to make recommendations and to closely continue to monitor the resistance to the existing antimicrobial compounds. Also, the scarcity of diagnosis means more medicines and vaccines for the prevention and treatment of illness, also, the shortcomings on the subject of research and development, debilitates the aptitude to combat the problem (WHO, 2011).

Right now, the WHO is focusing their efforts towards the regulation of the normatively by means of alertness, technical assistance, generation of knowledge and alliances, prevention and control of certain illnesses like tuberculosis, malaria, HIV, proper illnesses of the infancy, sexually transmitted diseases and hospitable infections; the quality, the supply and the rational use of essential medicines; the safety of the patients; and the guarantee of certified laboratories.

On the other hand, the struggle against the resistance to the antimicrobial compounds was the issue of the World Day of the Health of 2011 (April 7). On this occasion, the WHO called to contain the spread of the resistance to the antimicrobial compounds by means of a set of politics that were recommended so that the governments can start to solve the problem (WHO, 2011).

5. DISTRIBUTION AND ECONOMIC IMPORTANCE OF MARINE ALGAE

Marine algae are not only used in the discovery of new drugs, they are also used extensively as food on the Asian east coast (Japan, China, Korea, Taiwan and Vietnam), Indonesia, Peru, Canada, Scandinavia, Ireland, Wales, the Philippines and Scotland, among other places. From the economic point of view the marine algae represent an important resource of food and industrial input. The Caribbean Sea coast of Colombia contains innumerable species that have an economic value and are used as human food, medicinal products, fertilizers, fuel, and play an important role in the extraction of phycocolloids and hydrocolloids (Teas, 2007). All these products have a big industrial application. In spite of the speculation on the seaweed potential as a direct source of proteins and pharmaceutical products, the demand for phycocolloids will be the factor that will influence the future development of the marine algae world resources.

Many species have been exploited, but others like the genus *Sargassum* and *Codium* have been considered to be invasive for their capacity of adaptation and their high growth rate. Due to the fact that it has been established that marine algae are a potential source for new drugs their study should become a priority. The chemical screening of all the seaweeds and their related organisms is necessary in order to establish which species can be exploited without consequences and those that must be protected.

6. MARINE ALGAE AS PRODUCERS OF SECONDARY METABOLITES

In 2010, Mexican investigators found that the marine algae *Codium fragile, Sargassum muticum, Endarachne binghamiae, Centroceras clavulatum* and *Laurencia pacifica* possess compounds that inhibit the growth of Gram negative bacteria *Proteus mirabilis* (Villarreal-Gómez et al., 2010), which provokes 90 % of the infections caused by *Proteus*. The bacteria causes the production of big levels of urease that hydrolyze the urea to ammonia increasing the pH and therefore the formation of glazing of struvite, carbonate of calcium and/or apatite, causing the formation of kidney stones.

In the South-west coast of India, a group of scientists studied 13 groups of marine algae to evaluate the cytotoxic, larvicide, nematicide and ichthyotoxic activities on *Artemia salina* larvae. This Indian region is the only marine habitat with great marine algae diversity. 13 algae extracts between them*Dictyota dichotoma* and *Hypnea pannosa* showed lethal effect against the root nematode *Meloidogyne javanica. D. dichotoma* and *Valoniopsis* *pachynema* showed an ichthyotoxic activity. *A. orientalis, Padina tetrastromatica* and *Centeroceras clavulatum* showed activity against the urban mosquito larvae*Culex quinquefasiatus* (Manilal et al., 2009). Another study done in the same country, found marine algae that belonged to the family *Chlorophyceae* (*Caulerpa racemosa* and *Ulva lactuca*) and Rhodophyceae (*Gracillaria folifera* and *Hypneme muciformis*) that showed antibacterial activity against the Gram negative bacteria *E. faecalis, K. pneumoniae* and *E. aerogens,* as well as in the Gram positive bacteria *S. aureus* (Kandhasamy & Arunachalam, 2008). In a work done in the Iberian Peninsula with 82 marine algae (18 Chlorophyceae, 25 Phaeophyceae and 39 Rhodophyceae) the antibacterial and antifungal activity was analyzed to evaluate their application as natural preservatives for the cosmetic industry. The raw extracts of every taxon, prepared from fresh material as well as from lyophilized one, proved to have the opposite effect on three Gram positive bacteria, two Gram negative bacteria and yeast, by means of the agar diffusion technique. Sixty seven % of the studied seaweeds did not show antimicrobial activity against opposite the tested microorganisms. The biggest percentage of active taxon were presented in the group of the Phaeophyceae (84 %) followed by the Rhodophyceae (67 %) and finally the Chlorophyceae (44 %). The red seaweed presented the highest activity, with the widest spectrum. Inside this group, the most active species were *Bonnemaisonia asparagoides, Bonnemaisonia hamifera, Asparagopsis armata* and *Falkenbergia rufolanosa (Bonnemaisoniales).* As for the microorganisms, *Bacillus cereus* was the most sensitive and*Pseudomona aeruginosa* the most resistant. Three taxonomic groups showed seasonal change in the production of antimicrobial substances, being autumn the station with major percentage of active taxon for the Phaeophyceae and Rhodophyceae, while for the Chlorophyceae it was summer (Salvador et al., 2007).

Now a day there is a database that contains all the known natural compounds derived from marine algae, creating a crucial tool in the scientific community dedicated to the search of new useful compounds for medicinal purposes. This database provides the user with more than 3,600 released articles that describe 3,300 secondary metabolites originated from seaweeds, and it is still considered to be insufficient even though is growing every day. According to the database, Phaeophytas and Rhodophytas present significantly more quantity of bioactive compounds than Chlorophytas. The red seaweed *Laurencia (Ceramiales, Rhodomelaceae*) is one of the most prolific algae in the production of secondary metabolites derived from the sea. Sesquiterpenes, diterpenes, triterpernes and acetogenins (characterized by the presence of halogens atoms in their chemical structures) have been found present on this seaweed (John Davis & Vasanthi, 2011).

7. BACTERIA ASSOCIATED WITH MARINE ALGAE

The marine ambience is a complex ecosystem with an enormous plurality of forms of life that are associated between themselves, the most common associations found are between eukaryotic cells and microorganisms (Egan et al., 2008). The surface of all the marine eukaryotic organism are covered by microbes that live adherent to diverse communities often immersed in a matrix or forming a bilayer (Pérez–Matos et al., 2007). Also, the specificity of the guest organism also has been demonstrated in studies that show the presence of the only adherent stable communities to organisms of the same species through that they live on geographically distant regions (Webster & Bourne, 2007).

In the recent years, the bioactive properties of marine algae and marine microorganisms have been analyzed, and in both cases positive results have been obtained. Many of the marine algae species often come accompanied by several bacterial strains which have been taken of the sea together with the algae cells, or have been the result of a contamination in the algae culture. These mixed populations that are present in the culture and in the sea, show that the bacteria use organic substances secreted by living or dead algae cell. It has been observed that many types of seaweeds present a major growth in the presence of bacteria than in their absence. Some seaweed species need vitamins for their growth and possibly the bacteria are partially responsible for the production of these substances; some of them produce antibiotics (Jasti et al., 2005; Penesyan et al., 2010).

The number of natural products, discovered from several organism that include plants, animals and microorganisms, overcomes millions of compounds. Forty to sixty percent derives from terrestrial plants, from which twenty to twenty five % possesses bioactive properties such as antibacterial, anticancer, antifungal, antiviral and anti-inflammatory activity (Berdy, 2005).

Bacteria exist only in some seaweed species, as it is the case of *Leucobacter sp.*, collected in the Todos los Santos bay, BC. Mexico; which only was present in one out of six seaweeds analyzed (*Egregia menziessi)*, (Villarreal-Gómez et al., 2010). This member of the *Actinobacteria* family, has also been associated to the nematode *Caenorhabditis elegans*(Muir & Tan, 2008). *Micrococcus* is another actinobacteria strain that has been associated only to *Egregia menziessi.* This strain is usually found in soil and water. It is catabolically versatile, with the skill of using unusual substrates like pyridine, herbicides, polychloric biphenyl's and oil. It can also biodegrade many environmental pollutants (Zhuang et al., 2003). The bacterial strain*Kocuria palustris* (Sm32), it is exclusively present in the brown seaweed *Sargassum muticum* that is considered to be an invasive species in many countries. This strain has industrial applications in the degradation of organic matter (Kovacs et al., 1999). The*Alcaligenes* found exclusively in the seaweed *Endarachne* *binghamiae*, are used for the industrial production of not standard amino acids (Madigan et al., 2005). Finally, the bacterial strain member of the genus *Alteromona,* was associated only with the seaweed *Laurencia pacifica*, generally isolated in sea water; this *Proteobacteria* has industrial use, since they produce polysaccharides of high molecular weight. Several of the bacterial strains phylogenetically related, have industrial application; therefore, it is necessary to study the chemical interactions seaweed - bacteria for a better understanding of the process of production of the different secondary metabolites, which produce these species.

8. MARINE BACTERIA AS PRODUCERS OF SECONDARY METABOLITES

The marine microscopic communities are responsible of the change in the distribution of certain chemical elements in the sea. The autonomous aptitude of the marine organisms to produce substances biologically active that possibly accumulate, modify, kidnap and use toxins of other organisms, is a test of it (Mebs, 2000). For example, the lomaiviticins *a* and *b*, substances with antitumor potential were isolated for the first time from squids, and they contain the bacteria *Micromonospora lomaivitiensis*. In later experiments, this bacterium was isolated and cultivated in fermentation reactors, to finally determine that the bacteria were the real producers of lomaiviticin (He, 2001). Marine bacteria have often been considered to produce antibacterial and anticancer substances, allowing the ecological stability of the multiple marine ecosystems, the interrelations between epiphytic microorganism's ambiences, inhibiting the rival organisms and pathogenic microbes. The sharing or competition mechanisms that are known between these microorganisms are diverse, including antibiotic production, bacteriocines, siderofores, lysosomes, proteases and even the pH alteration through the production of organic acids (Avendaño-Herrera et al., 2005).

In recent studies done in Todos Santos Bay, B.C. to bacteria associated to the seaweed surface it was found that bacteria of the family *Firmicutes, Proteobacteria* and *Actinobacteria* produce compounds capable of inhibiting the growth of HCT-116 colorectal cancer cells (Villarreal-Gómez et al., 2010). Also, it was found that the bacteria *Microbulbifer thermotolerans*, and *Pseudoalteromonas sp*, are capable of producing biofilms and produce chemical compounds that protect them from the other protozoans. An example of these compounds is violacein, an alkaloid that it is synthesized predominantly in biofilm, it has been found that in nanomolar concentrations violacein inhibits protozoan cells and induces programmed cellular death in eukaryotic cells. This bacterial producing biofilm secretes specific chemical substances for defense purposes and contribute to the persistence of these bacterial strains in different environments and provide an ecological and evolutionary context for the discovery of bacterial metabolites against eukaryotic cells (Matz et al., 2008).

Bacillus sp species have been found to possess chemical compounds with anticancer activity. Although this type of bacteria can grow in almost any substrate, it is possible to suggest that this species seems to have acquired the skill to synthesize compounds capable of inhibiting HCT-116 colorectal cancer cells (Villarreal-Gómez et al., 2010).

Selective response mechanisms exist against certain organisms, as shown in marine biofilms of*Bacteriodetes, Planctomycetes, a,c* – and *d Proteobacteria*, where the production of chemical substances as violacein has been observed. This compound works as a defense mechanism against certain specific predators like the protozoa consuming bacteria. This allows the successful persistence of the bacterial biofilm in several marine environments (Matz et al., 2008). Studies done in seaweed collected in the same coastal area, share similar defense mechanisms and inhibit the growth of Gram negative bacteria *Proteus mirabilis* and *Klebsiella pneumoniae* (Villarreal-Gómez et al., 2010), creating an interesting ecological and biotechnological role, and becoming a great subject for the search of marine natural products.

The ethanolic extracts *of Grateloupia doryphora, Ahnfeltiopsis durvillaei, Prionitis decipiens, Petalonia fascia* and *feathery* Bryopsis of the central coast of Peru, presented antibacterial effect against the clinical strains *Staphylococcus aureus* ATCC 25923 and *Enterococcus faecalis* ATCC 29212 and not clinical strain *Staphylococcus aureus* ATCC 6633. The ethanolic extract of *B. plumosa*presented the biggest antibacterial effect against two strains of *S. aureus*, being evident in their inhibition halos, while the extract of *P. fascia* showed major antibacterial activity, acting on 3 mentioned above strains (Magallanes et al., 2003)

Studies done on bacteria associated with the marine worms of the *Polychaetes* species show a strong antimicrobial activity that can be used as a potential resource for the development of new medicines (Sunjaiy-Shankar et al., 2010).

The following table shows some examples of bacterial strains with bioactivity and the sources where they were obtained. It is possible to appreciate the diseases that can be fought utilizing the secondary metabolites from different types of bacteria. This emphasizes the importance of microorganisms as an ideal source of bioactive compounds.

Bacteria	Gram (+ or -)	Activity	Target organism	Disease	Source	Bibliography
Pseudomonas bromoutilis	-	Anticancer	*Staphylococcus aureus*, *Streptococcus pneumoniae*, *Streptococcus pyogenes*	Pneumonia, osteitis, arthritis, endocarditis, localized abscesses	Puerto Rico	Burkholder et al., 1966
Chromobacteria marinum	-	Antibacterial	*Escherichia coli*, *Pseudomona aureginosa*, *Staphylococcus aureus*	Pneumonia, osteitis, arthritis, endocarditis, localized abscesses	Seawater Of North Pacific	Anderson et al., 1974
Flavobacteria uliginosum	-	Anticancer	Sarcoma-180 cells	Viral tumor	Macroalgae (Sagami Bay Japan)	Okami, 1986
Bacillus sp.	+	Anticancer	HCT-116 cells	Colorectal Cancer	Mud near the Arctic Pole	Zhang et al., 2004
Lactococcus lactis	+	Anticancer	Human papilloma virus type 16 (HPV-16)	Cervical Cancer	Designed	Bermúdez-humarán et al., 2005
Staphylococcus aureoverticillatus	+	Anticancer	Tumor cells	Tumors	Marine sediments	Blunt et al., 2005
Marinobacter hydrocarbonoclasticus	-	Antibacterial (siderofore)	*Mycobacteria tuberculosis*, *Bacillus anthracis*	Tuberculosis, carbuncle (anthrax like)	Seawater	Pfleger et al., 2008

Table 1. Microorganism's producers of bioactive substances.

9. INTERACTIONS BETWEEN BACTERIAL SPECIES

Studying the diversity of bacterial species and knowing their inter and intraspecific interactions, makes the search for secondary metabolites in bacteria easier. For many years, researchers have managed to use different culturing methods that allow them to create dense bacterial populations that yield a great amount of extracts that can be used to investigate their bioactive properties.

Not only the seaweed - bacteria interactions can influence the secretion of bioactive substances, but also the interactions that exist between bacterial species that inhabit the same ecosystem. There are different types of interactions between bacterial species and other organisms; these can be positive (metabiosis and symbiosis) or negative (parasitism, predation and competition). For their high population density, nitrogen content and their relative incapability to escape from predators, the bacteria have served as food for diverse groups of organisms (Schlegel & Jannasch, 2006).

As a rule, bacteria have been considered to be the prey of many organisms, including other bacteria species or other types of microbes. This is the case of the genes involved in producing Pilli type IV which were identified in the periplasmic strain B of *Bdellovibrio bacteriovorus* 109J and in the epibiotic strain *Bdellovibrio sp.* JSS, both Gram negative proteobacteria, which are forced predators of other Gram negative bacteria (extracellular). Using immune fluorescence microscopy the presence of the pilli was observed in the phase of cellular attack, confirming that the Pilli type IV plays a role in the invasion of other Gram negative bacteria on the part of *Bdellovibrio* (Qin et al., 2010).

Another type of interaction between the bacteria is the competition. Some bacteria are eliminated by different species when the environmental resources are limited; therefore they produce compounds that impress negatively in their competitors. Generally, these antimicrobial compounds that are produced in the environment are difficult to detect, for example the bacteria incapable of producing antibiotic compounds must reproduce very fast compared to those that do. It has been found that in actinomycetes, bacterial species that have the slowest reproduction rates are the greatest producers of antibiotic compounds (Mahmoud & Koval, 2010).

In some cases, the seaweeds dissolve organic substances that are used as nutrients by the bacteria; nevertheless some of the bacteria do not obtain nutrients this way or from any other animals. They adhere to them only for physical support and obtain their nutrients directly from the surrounding environment (Rheinheimer, 1992).

Bacteria can have interactions among themselves in order to find mutual benefits. Such is the case of*Escherichia coli* and *Proteus vulgaris;* these two species can coexist in a rich in lactose and urea medium. In this case, *Escherichia coli* degrade lactose while *Proteus vulgaris* degrades urea. The final products of these degradations can be used by another organism as a carbon and nitrogen source (Rheinheimer, 1992).

10. TECHNIQUES USED FOR BACTERIA IDENTIFICATION

To this date, several bacterial identification methodologies are known to have contributed a great deal of information for the study of their diversity. Traditionally, the studies to characterize the bacterial diversity in environments are based on the assumption that the cultivation techniques allow the recovery of most of the microorganisms in a sample [39]. Nevertheless, in the database analysis of DNA sequences, it has been observed that the bacteria obtained by standard microbiological techniques represent just a limited proportion of samples from natural sources (Escalante-Lozada et al., 2004).

It has been proposed that non-cultivable bacteria are microorganisms phylogeneticaly related to the cultivable ones, but in a physiological state that makes them recalcitrant. The explanation is that some cultivable bacteria can turn in viable, but not cultivable when exposed to adverse environmental conditions and reverse to the cultivable state after the favorable conditions for their growth are restored (McDougald et al., 1998).

To study bacterial diversity, it is important to use molecular techniques that include the amplification of the 16S ribosomal gene using the polymerase chain reaction technique (PCR) in order to isolate and characterize their genetic material (Prieto-Davó et al., 2008).

11. MICROBIAL DIVERSITY CULTIVATION DEPENDENT TECHNIQUES

To go as far as knowing all the chemical compounds produced by bacteria extracted from different environmental samples, their isolation and cultivation, is necessary to prepare organic extracts that could be evaluated chemically and biologically. The techniques used are generally known as microbial diversity cultivation dependent techniques or traditional methods of cultivation (Joint et al., 2010). These techniques are based on the need that the microorganisms have of taking from the environment a series of compounds that are used as energy source and synthesizing the cellular constituents necessary for their survival, like C, N, S, P, Ca, K, Na, Mg, Mo, Cu and Zn. Some microorganisms need to take the light energy or to oxidize chemical compounds; others need to obtain their carbon source from CO_2 or through carbonated organic compounds. Some microorganisms need a nitrogen source, for which they fix the atmospheric nitrogen, or take it from NH_4^+. Others are capable of reducing NO_3^- or NO_2^- to use it as an ammonium source, or, to use free amino acids. All these characteristics, as well as temperature, pH and salinity, have demonstrated to create a propitious ambient, for the isolation and purification of microorganisms originated from environmental samples (Rheinheimer, 1992).

Therefore, the collected environmental samples are exposed to different conditions and forms of cultivation that help to obtaining microorganisms capable of adapting to the established conditions. This allows to study the microorganism's diversity, as well as to cultivate them from different environmental samples.

12. MOLECULAR TECHNIQUES FOR BACTERIA IDENTIFICATION

The molecular characterization of bacteria has had an enormous impact on the safety of microbiological industrial processes like the bio pharmacology and food industry as well as public health, since it establishes the source of contamination in a much more precise form and therefore to identify the strains involved in the process and to establish their trajectory.

The most used gene for bacterial molecular identification is the 16S ribosomal RNA gene, nevertheless, there have also been used other genes that can codify for 5S ribosomal proteins, and 23 S ribosomal RNA.

The ribosomes and ribonucleic acids (ribosomal RNA) are proteic complexes with the only function of synthesizing proteins. The ribosomes structure is preserved between the different life kingdoms (Plantae, fungi, animaleae, etc.). In the prokaryotes, the ribosomes are composed by two subunits: a big 50S, and small 30S subunits. The subunit 50S contains a 23S, one 5S rRNA and more than 30 different proteins. The subunit 30S contains one 16S rRNA and 20 additional proteins. Since the rRNA gene function is limited by the structure, certain regions in the rRNA genes that are in contact with other components in the ribosome must be preserved; the sequences between the preserved regions have major mutation valuations. The preserved regions are useful to determine distant relations (genus), while the regions with higher mutation rate or variable regions are useful to distinguish organism closely related (species) (Eickbush & Eickbush, 2007). These characteristics of rRNA genes are excellent molecular chronometers for phylogenetic analysis and taxonomic classification of cellular organisms.

In general, the phylogenetic trees based on the 16S and 23S rRNA genes can be used in parallel (De Rijk et al., 1995), while the 5S rRNA gene it is considered not to contain sufficiently long sequences to do significant statistical comparisons. The detailed phylogenetic studies based on the genetic sequences 16S and 23S provide comparisons in three primary domains Bacteria, Archaea and Eukarya (Woese et al., 1990). Nevertheless, one of the disadvantages of the 23S rRNA gene on 16S rRNA in the phylogenetic studies is the rare use of the taxonomic classification for the absence of primers that amplify a considerable length sequence and the difficulty of genes sequences too long for the current technologies.

Previously the 16S rRNA and 23S rRNA genes have been compared and the results show that the 16S rRNA gene has more closely related typical sequences, with major length, insertions and/or deletions and possibly a better phylogenetic resolution for their high genetic change (Blunt et al., 2005). Nevertheless, recent studies indicated that the 23S rRNA gene also contains conserved regions for the design of primers capable of amplifying a wider length with one grade similar to the primers used in the of 16S rRNA genes (Hunt et al., 2006; Pei et al., 2009).

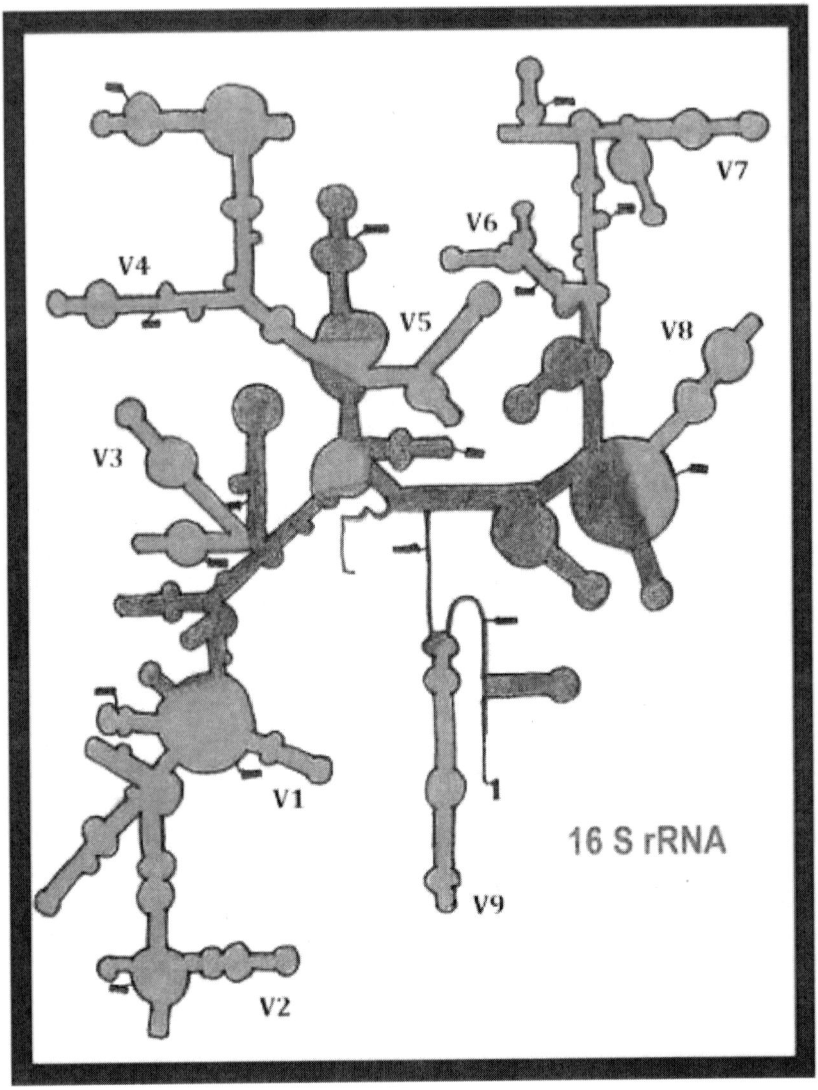

Illustration by Lizeth Perez

Figure 2. Scheme of Bacterial 16S ribosomal RNA that shows the variable secuences (V1 to V9). The variable regions area used to characterized bacteria by species level, and the constant region is used to correlated the genus.

Molecular methods of characterization based on the amplification of fragments belonging to the 16S ribosomal RNA gene through automated techniques constitute a rapid, trustworthy and simple method of molecular genotyped bacterial and fungoid strains. The aptitude to identify microorganisms at species level and at the same time to establish a comparative analysis of the different analyzed strains constitutes a time saving way to identify the food pollutant potential and therefore to eradicate the pollutant focus or to facilitate the recognition of the producing strains of some bioactive metabolite capable of inhibiting the growth of other bacterial strains or carcinogenic cells.

The 16 S ribosomal gene (16S rRNA) is constituted by a region preserved through evolution, the mutations in this gene can usually be tolerated, since these mutations would only affect ribosomal RNA, nevertheless, the number of mutations are not completely well-known, the regions that are affected by them are met like "hot commercials" which present a considerable number of mutations, these areas are not the same in all species. The 16S rRNA gene mutations can affect the susceptibility to antimicrobial agents which can be an indicator to distinguish the phenotypic resistance to these agents. Nevertheless these characteristics do not affect the gene use for taxonomical identification at the genus and species level. 16S rRNA possesses a length of 1, 550 bp and it is composed by variable regions and conserved regions, with enough interspecific polymorphisms to provide a valid statistical characterization. The primers that are usually designed for the amplification of this gene, are based on the complementary chain of the conserved regions in the beginning of the gene at about 540 bp or at the end of the sequence around 1,550 bp and the sequence of the variable region is used for taxonomic comparison intentions, making 1500bp the minimum length that should be used to compare DNA sequences. The 16S rRNA gene sequence has been determined for a big number of strains; these sequences are included in the biggest database of nucleotides known as GenBank. This database contains more than 20 million sequences of which more than 90, 000 correspond to the 16S rRNA gene.. In general, the comparison of the 16S rRNA gene sequences allows the differentiation between organisms at genus level in most bacteria phyla, also classifies the strains at multiple levels, including species and sub species (Clarridge III, 2004).

13. EXTRACTION OF BIOACTIVE COMPOUNDS FROM BACTERIA ASSOCIATED WITH MARINE ALGAE

To do a search of bioactive compounds from marine algae the following protocol is proposed:

a. Isolation of the bacterial strains from the seaweed surface

After being collected, the seaweed is placed in an Erlenmeyer flask and is rinsed with distilled water; a small sample from the flask is taken with a sterile swab and is inoculated in a general media that allows the growth of most of the bacteria present in the seaweed surface. Then the media with inoculate is incubated for periods of 24 to 48 hours at 25 °C, until the developing colonies start to emerge. Later the bacteria will be purified up to the third generation to assure the integrity of pure colonies and finally it is important to take one of the colonies of every purified strain and cryopreserved it in 15 % glycerol at -70 °C.

b. Macroscopic morphology and Gram Stain

The pure colonies are examined macroscopically evaluating their characteristics such as size, form, elevation, margin, color, type of surface, thickness, consistency, smell and pigments production. Consecutively microscopic classification of the bacterial strains, such as the Gram stain, is necessary (Gram, 1884). The Gram stain is a technique of bacterial characterization based on the chemical composition of the cellular wall of the bacteria. The Gram positive bacteria present a cytoplasmic membrane, have a thick peptidoglycan layer, contain teicoics acids and lipoteicoics that serve as chelating agents and certain type of adhesions; the bacteria representative of this group are *Firmicutes*and *Actinobacteria*, which includes many well-known genus like *Bacillus*, *Listeria*, *Staphylococcus*, *Streptococcus*, *Enterococcus*, and *Clostridium*.

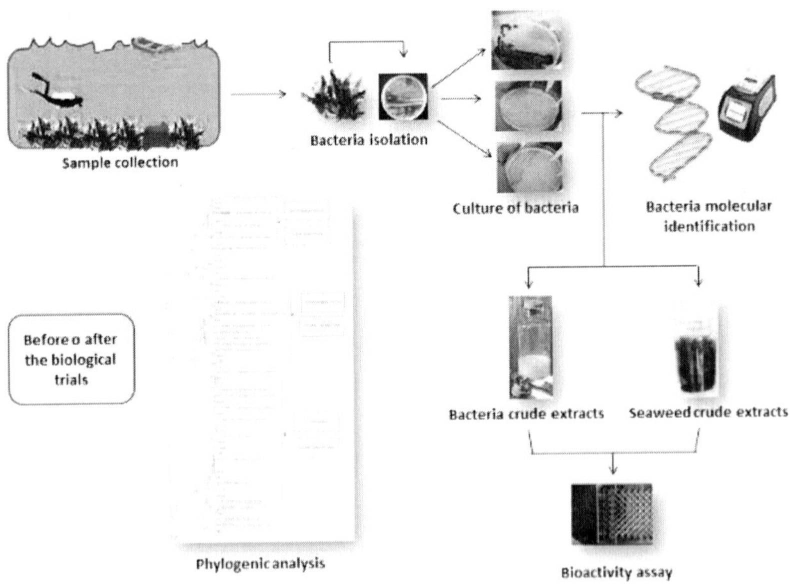

Figure 3. Proposed methodology for the search of new bioactive compounds in bacteria associated with the surface of marine algae.

On the other hand, the Gram negative bacteria contain a thin cellular wall of peptidoglycan and an external membrane that covers their cellular wall. The external membrane contains diverse proteins, like purines or channels protein that allow the path of certain substances. Also they present a structure of lipopolysaccharides (LPS). The bacteria that predominate in this group are Proteobacteria, including to Escherichia coli, Salmonella and other enteric bacteria like Pseudomonas, Moraxella, Helicobacter, Stenotrophomonas, Bdellovibrio, acetic acid bacteria, Legionnaire's disease and the proteobacteria alpha like Wolbachia among others (Madigan et al., 2005).

Previous studies done with bacterioplacton demonstrated that most of the marine bacteria are Gram negative; but in recent studies with marine sediments evidence has shown that most of the bacteria that conform the marine sediments seem to be Gram positive (Gontang et al., 2007).

In studies made to the surface of the marine alga Monostroma undulatum (Gallardo et al., 2004) Gram negative bacteria belonging to the genus: Vibrio (20 %), inactive E. coli (18 %), Flavobacteria (11 %), Flexibacter (9 %), Moraxella (9 %), Pseudomona (9 %), Aeromonas (2 %), Acinetobacter (2 %), Cotophaga (2 %), Photobacteria (2 %) and Alteromonas (2 %); predominated and only one Gram positive was found, Staphylococcus.

a. Phylogenetic analysis

Since bacterial identification was mentioned previously and bacterial characterization with molecular techniques is crucial for the achievement of phylogenetic studies that allow to have an account of the cultivable bacterial species that are present in a similar community, there are several investigators who agree with the idea, that bacteria with closely related DNA sequences produce very similar compounds. If this is true, just by knowing the bacterial ecology of a certain area it will be possible to predict the types of compounds that could be isolated from the bacteria present in that particular area.

The DNA sequences can be analyzed using the BLAST database (Basic Local Alignment Search Tool) that is a GeneBank database integral function (Altschul et al., 1999). To align the existing sequences between themselves it is possible to use the Clustal X (Staley & Ta, 1985) and Bioedit programs (Hall & Brown, 2001) for manual alignments. For the phylogenetic tree construction it is possible to use the following indications: Bootstrap test of phylogeny (1000 repetitions), p-distance joining neighbor, using the MEGA4 program (Tamura et al., 2007) using segment sequences of up to 1500 bp.

b. Biological assays and mean lethal dose DL 50

A bioassay can be defined as any test that involves living organisms. With them, it is possible to evaluate the effects of any substances or material in terms of the biological answer they produce. The main target in this type of analysis is to evaluate the level of stimulus that is necessary to obtain a response in a group of individuals of a population. The level of stimulus that causes response in 50 % of the individuals under study is an important parameter of characterization denoted like average lethal dose (DL_{50}). The amount of time during which the stimulus is exhibited, must be specified, for example, 24 hours DL_{50}, this in order to compare and to estimate the relative potency of the stimulus. For the DL_{50}determination of the first step is securing the % of survival cell for every analyte and every target, the mortalities is corrected by Abbott´s formula (Abbott, 1925).

$$M = \frac{me - mb}{1 - mb} \tag{1}$$

Where:

M = Mortality.

me = optical density in the extract.

mb = optical density in the target.

With the mortalities corrected, the obtained information is introduced in the software “BioStat 2008” (http://www.analystsoft.com) using Probit analysis to obtain the DL_{50}values (STATPLUS, 2008).

14. CONCLUSION

Natural products are a very important resource for the elaboration of medicines. Although a big number of plants, microbes and marine resources have been evaluated in the search of new bioactive compounds, it turns out to be insufficient and it is necessary and important to continue with the search of new secondary metabolites, especially those that are endophytes microorganisms of seaweed. The bad use given to antibiotics has resulted in the development of bacteria strains that are resistant to many of the known drugs. This situation has lead to a forced search for new antibiotic compounds, being the seabed a propitious site for exploration and future drug development. Also, the treatment with chemotherapy for the diverse causes of different types of cancer that at present today, appears effective, so the investigation becomes necessary in the chemistry of the natural products. The methods of bacterial culture and identification have become very promising especially, those done through molecular techniques, by which is possible to identify a strain up to species and sometimes at subspecies level. The diverse relationships that exist between microorganisms and their guests provoke that bacterial compounds can eventually be used as a source of new drugs for human well-being.

Future work in Drug Discovery

The strategies for drug discovery has been evolving constantly, today researchers do not conform with the finding of new and potent metabolites, now and for future days it has become important to do phylogenetic studies, structure elucidation of chemical compounds, bioinformatics approaches, genomics, proteomics, reverse pharmacology and so on., One fundamental field that has to be developed is the improvement of more efficient culture media, because we need to culture all the strains of bacteria to be able to evaluate and separate its compounds, in the meanwhile, we can identify the genes of cultivable and non-cultivable bacteria by molecular techniques to compare and try to demonstrate that the strains of bacteria with very similar DNA sequences have equally similar metabolites and culture requirements, if this is true, before we start screening for drug discovery purposes, researchers must do phylogenetic studies of bacterial population of a certain determinate area and decide which strains cultivate and which not, these strategies will make the drug discovery process less expensive and faster.

Methodological improvements studies based on the characterization of the extracellular polymeric substance produced by marine microorganisms and a better understanding of host-microbe interactions, should be us to provide further insight into the adaptive strategies against microbial pathogens and establish the extent to which secondary metabolites regulate microbial interactions.

The new soft ionization methods: Matrix-Assisted Laser Desorption Ionization (MALDI) and Electrospray Ionization (EI) are the recent approach used in a variety of new and innovative Mass Spectrometric (MS) applications. With them, is easier to analyze surfaces, they are tolerant to impurities and do not require extensive sample preparations. A sensitive and precise Mass Spectrometric approach like Desorption Electrospray Ionization (DESI) should be used to measure the physical location and quantities of natural products on biological tissue surfaces, cells or even complex mixed-species assemblages. These MS imaging techniques known as "molecular eyes" are very precise and represent the last technological advance used to locate natural products in biological tissues (Esquenazi et al., 2009) allowing the study of the interface between the confluence of natural products chemistry, biology and ecology.

Bioinformatics is the part of molecular biology that involves working with biological data, typically using computers, with the goal of enabling and accelerating biological research. Bioinformatics comprises a wide range of activities: data capture, automated recording of experimental results; data storage and access, using a multitude of databases and query tools; data analysis; and visualization of raw data and analytical results (Pollock & Safer, 2001).

Today, many recently developed or discovered drugs with antibacterial and anticancer activity fail in clinical trials because of inefficiency for the anticipated indication or unexpected toxicity (Kola & Landis, 2004). Apparently, it remains hard to establish a clear link between antagonism or organism of a specific target and its influence in human illness and its target associated toxicity.

A significant cause for these high attrition rates is the often misjudged complexity of protein function in higher order organisms, in which, abundant protein-protein interactions, feedback loops and redundancies play a role. The collection of recognized pathways that can be found in public databases and commercial tools do not effectively address these issues because they are mainly a reflection of experimental data that are obtained from isolated cell lines and tissues. They address typically, the signaling events that lead to binding of transcription factors to the DNA, but do not detail the pleiotropic effects that arise downstream from the induced transcriptional program, which are most important in provoking the systems response to the signaling events and may determine, the capacity and toxicity of a drug (Pollock & Safer, 2001).

Most comparative genomics tools are intended at studying conservation of single genes or gene families, whereas computationally tools address orthologous biology, i.e. conservation of the entire pathways in which the target is involved, are unusual. This truly obstructs the output and success of translational investigation from pre-clinical to clinical studies (Pollock & Safer, 2001).

The developing of bioinformatics tools that addresses the above problems will allow for quicker and better experiments aimed at evaluating multiple targets and drugs for further clinical development. This will be a first step to reduce the high attrition rates associated with drug development (Pollock & Safer, 2001).

Clinical events or phenomena not reported previously following the administration of a known or new drug can offer valuable perceptions for drug development. Natural products have provided many such unexpected bedside interpretations. Researches in genomics, proteomics and metabolomics have stimulated the discovery of many new molecules, which are yet to be tracked for their drug-like activities. A new discipline called Reverse Pharmacology (RP) has been designed to decrease costs, time and toxicity.

The scope of reverse pharmacology is to understand the mechanisms of action at multiple levels of biology and to optimize safety, efficacy and acceptability of the leads in natural products based on relevant science in this approach, as the candidate travels a reverse path from 'clinics to laboratory' rather than classical "laboratory to clinics". Actual humans are used as the ultimate model and in-depth investigation of the effects of drugs and the nature of disease progression is becoming ever more feasible because of advances in clinical biomarkers and systems biology. This articulates both structure of the system and components to play indispensable role forming symbiotic state of the whole system (Patwardhan et al., 2008).

15. ACKNOWLEDGEMENTS

The authors thank A. Prieto-Davo and P.R Jensen (CMBB,U.C.S.D.) for their collaboration, A. Licea for his help in carrying out the bioassays (CICESE),M. Ritchie for facilitating the bacterial pathogens used, R. Aguilar (†) for assistance in the seaweed identification, A. Moreno and L. Pérez for photography and Illustration, respectively and A.M. Iñiguez-Martínez for reviewing the manuscript.

REFERENCES

1. W. S. Abbott, 1925 A method for computing the effectiveness of an insecticide. Journal of Economic Entomology.18 265 7
2. S. F. Altschul, W. Gish, W. Miller, E. W. Myers, D. J. Lipman, 1990 Basic local alignment search tool. Journal of Molecular Biology. 215 403 10
3. R. J. Anderson, M. S. Wolfe, D. J. Faulkner, 1974 Autotoxic antibiotic production by a marine Chromobacterium. Marine Biology. 27 4 281 285
4. R. Avendaño-Herrera, M. Lody, C. E. Riquelme, 2005 Producción de substancias inhibitorias entre bacterias de biopelículas en substratos marinos. Revista Biología Marina y Oceanografía. 40 (2)
5. J. Berdy, 2005 Bioactive microbial metabolites. A personal view. Journal of Antibiotics. 45 581 26 , and 43: 57-90

6. L. G. Bermúdez-Humarán, N. G. Cortes-Pérez, F. Lefevre, V. Guimarães, S. Rabot, J. M. Alcocer-Gonzalez, J. J. Gratadoux, C. Rodriguez-Padilla, R. S. Tamez-Guerra, G. Corthier, A. Gruss, P. Langella, 2005 A Novel Mucosal Vaccine Based on Live Lactococci Expressing E7 Antigen and IL-12 Induces Systemic and Mucosal Immune Responses and Protects Mice against Human Papillomavirus Type 16-Induced Tumors. The Journal of Immunology. 175 7297 7302

7. J. W. Blunt, B. R. Copp, M. H. G. Munro, P. T. Northcote, M. R. Prinsep, 2006 Marine natural products. Natural Products Report. 23 26 78

8. J. W. Blunt, B. R. Copp, M. H. G. Munro, P. T. Northcote, M. R. Prinsep, 2005 Marine natural products. Natural Products Report. 22 15 61

9. P. R. Burkholder, R. M. Pfister, F. H. Leitz, 1966 Production of a Pyrrole Antibiotic by a marine bacteria. Applied Microbiology. 14 649 653

10. J. E. Clarridge, 2004 Impact of 16S rRNA Gene Sequence Analysis for Identification of Bacteria on Clinical Microbiology and Infectious Diseases. Clinical Microbiology Reviews. 17 (4). 840 862

11. G. M. Cragg, D. J. Newman, 1999 Discovery & development of antineoplastic agents from natural sources. Cancer Investigation. 17 153 163

12. P. De Rijk, Y. Van de Peer, I. Van den Broeck, R. De Wachter, 1995 Evolution according to large ribosomal subunit RNA. Journal of Molecular Evolution. 41 366 375

13. S. Egan, T. Thomas, S. Kjelleberg, 2008 Unlocking the diversity and biotechnological potential of marine surface associated microbial communities. Current Opinion in Microbiology. 11 219 225

14. T. H. Eickbush, D. G. Eickbush, 2007 Finely orchestrated movements: evolution of the ribosomal RNA genes. Genetics. 175 4777 485

15. A. Escalante-lozada, G. Gosset-Lagarda, A. Martínez-Jiménez, F. Bolívar-Zapata, 2004 Diversidad bacteriana del suelo: Métodos de estudio no dependientes de cultivo microbiano e implicaciones biotecnológicas. Departamento de Ingeniería Celular y Biocatálisis. Instituto de Biotecnología. UNAM. Agrociencia. 38 583 592

16. E. Esquenazi, P. C. Dorrestein, W. H. Gerwick, 2009 Probing marine natural product defenses with DESI-imaging mass spectrometry. Proceedings of the National Academy of Sciences. 6 7269 7270

17. D. J. Faulkner, 2002 Marine natural products. Natural Products Reports. 19 1 48

18. A. Gallardo, S. Risso, M. Fajardo, B. Estevao, 2004 Characterization of microbial population present in the edible seaweed, Monostroma undulatum, Wittrock. Departamento de Bioquímica, Facultad de Ciencias Naturales, Universidad Nacional de Patagonia San Juan Bosco, Comodoro Rivadavia, Chubut, Argentina. Archivos Latinoamericanos de Nutrición. 54 3 337 45

19. E. A. Gontang, W. Fenical, P. R. Jensen, 2007 Phylogenetic diversity of gram-positive bacteria cultured from marine sediments. Applied and environmental microbiology. 73 3273 82

20. C. Gram, 1884 The differential staining of Schizomycetes in tissue sections and in dried preparations. Fortschitte der medicine. 2 185 189

21. T. A. Hall, J. W. Brown, 2001 The ribonuclease P family. North Carolina State University, Department of Microbiology. Methods Enzymology. 341 56 77

22. H. He, 2001 Lomaiviticins A and B, potent antitumor antibiotics from Micromonospora lomaivitiensis. Journal of the American Chemical Society. 123 5362 5363

23. D. E. Hunt, V. Klepac-Ceraj, S. G. Acinas, C. Gautier, S. Bertilsson, 2006 Evaluation of 23S rRNA PCR primers for use in phylogenetic studies of bacterial diversity. Applied Enviromental Microbiology. 72 2221 2225

24. C. Isnard-Bagnis, B. Moulin, V. Launay-Vacher, H. Izzedine, I. Tostivint, G. Deray, 2005 Anticancer drug-induced nephrotoxicity. Nephrology Therapy. 1 101 114

25. S. Jasti, M. E. Sieracki, N. Poulton, M. W. Giewat, J. N. Rooney-Varga, 2005 Phylogenetic diversity and specificity of bacteria closely associated with Alexandrium spp. and other phytoplankton. Applied Environmental Microbiology. 71 7 3483 3494

26. G. D. John Davis, A. H. R. Vasanthi, 2011 Seaweed metabolite database (SWMD): A database of natural compounds from marine algae. Bioinformation. 5(8). www.bioinformation.net

27. I. Joint, M. Mühling, J. Querellou, 2010 Culturing marine bacteria: an essential prerequisite for biodiscovery. Microbial Biotechnology. 3 5 564 575

28. M. Kandhasamy, K. D. Arunachalam, 2008 Evaluation of in vitro antibacterial property of seaweeds of southeast coast of India. African Journal of Biotechnology. 7 12 1958 1961

29. I. Kola, J. Landis, 2004 Can the pharmaceutical industry reduce attrition rates? Nature Reviews Drug Discovery. 3 711 715

30. G. Kovacs, J. Burghardt, S. Pradella, P. Schumann, E. Stackebrandt, K. Marialigeti, 1999 Kocuria palustris sp. nov. and Kocuriarhizophila sp. nov.; isolated from the rhizoplane of the narrow-leaved cattail (Typhaangustifolia). International journal of systematic bacteriology. 49 167 173

31. M. Madigan, J. Martinko, J. Parker, 2005 Brock Biology of Microorganisms, Decimoprimeraedición, Prentice Hall. Southern Illinois University Carbondale. 1 102 167

32. C. Magallanes, C. Córdova, R. Orozco, 2003 Antibacterial activity of ethanolic extracts of marine algae from central coast of Peru. Revista peruana de biologia. 10 2 125 132

33. K. K. Mahmoud, S. F. Koval, 2010 Characterization of type IV pili in the life cycle of the predator bacteria Bdellovibrio. Microbiology. 156:1040

34. S. Manilal, S. Sujith, G. SeghalKiran, J. Selvin, C. Shakir, R. Gandhimathi, M. V. NatarajaPanikkar, 2009 Biopotentials of seaweeds collected from southwest coast of India. Journal of Marine Science and Technology. 17 1 67 73

35. C. Matz, J. S. Webb, P. J. Schupp, S. Y. Phang, A. Penesyan, S. Egan, P. Steinberg, S. Kjelleberg, 2008 Marine Biofilm Bacteria Evade Eukaryotic Predation by Targeted Chemical Defense. School of Biological, Earth and Environmental Sciences and Centre for Marine Bio-Innovation, University of New South Wales, Sydney, Australia. PLoSONE. 3(7)

36. D. McDougald, S. Rice, D. Weichart, S. Kjelleberg, 1998 Nonculturability: adaptation or debilitation. FEMS Microbiology Ecology. 25 1 9

37. D. Mebs, 2000 Toxicity in animals- Trends in evolution? Toxicon. Elsevier Science, Ireland 39 87 96

38. R. E. Muir, M. W. Tan, 2008 Virulence of Leucobacterchromiireducens subsp. solipictus to Caenorhabditiselegans: Characterization of a Novel Host-Pathogen Interaction. Applied Environmental Microbiology. 74 13 4185 4198

39. Y. Okami, 1986 Marine microorganisms as a source of bioactive agents. MicrobialEcology. 12 65 78

40. Organización Mundial de la Salud (OMS). 2011 Centro de prensa. Nota descriptiva 194.http://www.who.int/mediacentre/factsheets/fs194/es/index.html

41. B. Patwardhan, A. D. B. Vaidya, M. Chorghade, S. P. Joshi, 2008 Reverse Pharmacology and Systems Approaches for Drug Discovery and Development. Current Bioactive Compounds. 4 000 000

42. A. Pei, C. W. Nossa, P. Chokshi, M. J. Blaser, L. Yang, 2009 Diversity of 23S rRNA Genes within Individual Prokaryotic Genomes. PLoS ONE 4. (5): e5437.

43. A. Penesyan, S. Kjelleberg, S. Egan, 2010 Development of novel drugs from marine surface associated microorganisms, Marine Drugs. 8 438 459

44. A. E. Pérez-Matos, W. Rosado, N. S. Govind, 2007 Bacterial diversity associated with the Caribbean Tunicate Ecteinascidia turbinate. Antonie Van Leeuwenhoek. 92 155 164

45. B. Pfleger, D. Sherman, T. Nusca, J. Scaglione, Y. Lee, 2008 Petrobactin Biosynthesis: A Target for Antibiotics and a Platform for Producing Specialty Chemicals. Chemical and Biological Engineering, University of Wisconsin Madison, Madison, WI. Life Sciences Institute, University of Michigan, Ann Arbor

46. A. Prieto-Davó, W. Fenical, P. R. Jensen, 2008 Comparative actinomycete diversity in marine sediments. Aquatic Microbial Ecology. 52 1 11

47. S. Pollock, H. M. Safer, 2001 Bioinformatics in the Drug Discovery Process. Annual Reports in Medicinal Chemistry

48. S. Qin, K. Xing, J. Jiang, L. Xu, W. Li, 2010 Biodiversity, bioactive natural products and biotechnological potential of plant-associated endophytic actinobacteria. Applied Microbiology and Biotechnology. 89 3 457 473

49. G. Rheinheimer, 1992 Aquatic microbiology. 4th ed. John Wiley & Sons. West Sussex. United Kingdom

50. N. Salvador, A. Gómez-Garreta, L. Lavelli, L. Ribera, 2007 Antimicrobial activity of Iberian macroalgae. Science Marine. 71 101 113

51. H. G. Schlegel, H. W. Jannasch, 2006 Prokaryotes and Their Habitats. Prokaryotes. Chapter 1.6. 1 137 184

52. J. Staley, A. K. Ta, 1985 Measurement of in situ activities of non photosynthetic microorganisms in aquatic and terrestrial habitats. Annual Reviews in Microbiology. 39 321 46

53. STATPLUS. 2008 Probit analysis. Biostat 2008. http://www.analystsoft.com

54. C. V. Sunjaiy-Shankar, A. H. Jeba-Malar, S. M. J. Punitha, 2010 Antimicrobial activity of marine bacteria associated with Polychaetes. Bioresearch Bulletin. 1 24 28

55. K. Tamura, J. Dudley, M. Nei, S. Kumar, 2007 MEGA4: Molecular Evolutionary Genetics Analysis (MEGA) software version 4.0. Molecular Biology and Evolution

56. J. Teas, 2007 Seaweed and Soy: Companion Foods in Asian Cuisine and Their Effects on Thyroid Function in American Women. Journal Medicinal Food. 10 90 100

57. L. J. Villarreal-Gómez, I. E. Soria-Mercado, G. Guerra-Rivas, N. E. Ayala-Sánchez, 2010 Antibacterial and anticancer activity of seaweeds and bacteria associated with their surface. Revista de Biología Marina y Oceanografía. 45 2 267 275

58. N. S. Webster, D. Bourne, 2007 Bacterial community structure associated with the Antarctic soft coral, Alcyoniumantarcticum. FEMS Microbiology Ecology. 59 81 94

59. C. R. Woese, O. Kandler, M. L. Wheelis, 1990 Towards a natural system of organisms: proposal for the domains Archaea, Bacteria, and Eucarya. Proceedings of the National Academy of Sciences of the United States of America. 87 4576 4579

60. H. L. Zhang, H. M. Hua, Y. H. Pei, X. S. Yao, 2004 Anticancer activity and mechanism of Scutellaria barbata extract on human lung cancer cell line A549. Chemistry Pharmacology Bulletin. 52: 1029

61. W. Zhuang, J. Tay, A. Maszenan, L. Krumholz, S. Tay, 2003 Importance of Gram-positive naphthalene-degrading bacteria in oil-contaminated tropical marine sediments. Lett Applied Microbiology. 36 4 251 7

Chapter 4

The Halogenated Metabolism of Brown Algae (Phaeophyta), Its Biological Importance and Its Environmental Significance

Stéphane La Barre [1,2,*], Philippe Potin [1,2], Catherine Leblanc [1,2] and Ludovic Delage [1,2]

[1]*Université Pierre et Marie Curie-Paris 6, UMR 7139 Végétaux marins et Biomolécules, Station Biologique F-29682, Roscoff, France*

[2]*CNRS, UMR 7139 Végétaux marins et Biomolécules, Station Biologique F-29682, Roscoff, France*

ABSTRACT

Brown algae represent a major component of littoral and sublittoral zones in temperate and subtropical ecosystems. An essential adaptive feature of this independent eukaryotic lineage is the ability to couple oxidative reactions resulting from exposure to sunlight and air with the halogenations of various substrates, thereby addressing various biotic and abiotic stresses *i.e.*, defense against predators, tissue repair, holdfast adhesion, and protection against reactive species generated by oxidative processes. Whereas marine organisms mainly make use of bromine to increase the biological activity of secondary metabolites, some orders of brown algae such as Laminariales have also developed a striking capability to accumulate and to use iodine in physiological adaptations to stress. We review selected aspects of the halogenated metabolism of macrophytic brown algae in the light of the most recent results, which point toward novel functions for iodide accumulation in kelps and the importance of bromination in cell wall modifications and adhesion properties of brown algal propagules. The importance of halogen speciation processes ranges from microbiology to biogeochemistry, through enzymology, cellular biology and ecotoxicology.

Keywords: halogen speciation; brown algae; defense metabolites; haloperoxidases; biogeochemistry

1. INTRODUCTION

Most organisms seem to have the ability to produce organohalogens, and the reported chemodiversity of this class of compounds (3,800 in 2003) has jumped 20-fold in the last 30 years [1]. Marine halocarbon producers encompass an extensive phyletic range, and sessile life forms (algae and invertebrates) use a rich repertoire of diffusible and mucus-bound molecules, many of which are halogenated, for communication in the largest sense. Biogenic halogen chemistry is thought to have arisen in prokaryotes in response to the emergence of photosynthesis, the oxygen enrichment of the atmosphere by cyanobacteria in archean times (some three billion years ago), and in response to the cellular generation of toxic reactive oxygen species (ROS) originating from one (*i.e.*, $O_2^{\bullet -}$ or $HO_2^{\bullet}$) and two-electron reduction of O_2 (*i.e.*, H_2O_2). The call for efficient reducing biochemistries involved chlorine, bromine and iodine available in seawater, and the development of corresponding enzymatic machineries with haloperoxidases. Oxidative H_2O_2 detoxication strategies, e.g., catalases, offer an alternative to ROS reduction, but there is no mention of their co-occurrence in the Cambrian precursors of extant cyanobacteria [2]. Therefore, it is likely that the halogen chemistry of marine algae reflects an episode of their polyphyletic evolutionary history. On one hand, the latter has involved a primary endosymbiosis (the engulfing of a prokaryotic cyanobacterium by a heterotrophic host cell), which lead to the emergence of the Plantae, the green lineage (green algae and land plants) and its sister group the red algae. On the other hand, chromophytic algae evolved by an additional process termed secondary endosymbiosis [3] which includes the endosymbiotic uptake of a eukaryotic alga, presumably an ancestor of modern red algae. Brown algae belong to the Stramenopile lineage, with marine representatives including the unicellular diatoms. While phylogenomic studies have recently validated the various lineages, the evolutionary relationships between the lineages remain partly unresolved [4]. Surprinsingly, less than 1% of the secondary metabolites from brown algae contain bromine or chlorine compared with 7% of green algal compounds and 90% of those reported for red algae [5]. Regarding halogen chemistry, iodination is more frequent and chlorination is less frequent in brown algae metabolites than in the red and green lineages.

In this review, we describe the specificity of the evolution of the halogen metabolism in brown algae, pointing towards the emergence of strict specificity for the oxidation of iodide in the most evolved orders of Phaeophyceae, such as the Laminariales, and, consequently, the emergence of novel physiological adaptations with their ecological and atmospheric significance.

2. HALOGENATED METABOLITES OF BROWN ALGAE

More than 1,140 metabolites have been reported in the Phaeophyceae in 2007 [6], out of about 3,000 from the three macroalgal lineages and of a total of about 15,000 marine molecules [7]. However, in contrast to red algae, (i) the number of novel structures in brown algae decreases every year [8], (ii) surprisingly few brown algal metabolites are halogenated, yet as end products or as potential intermediates, they are involved in a wide range of primary and secondary functions, some of which are not completely established and (iii) no specific pharmacological use has been found for brown algal halogenated metabolites. We will consider the various classes of halogenated metabolites found in brown algae with considerations of their biosynthetic origin where applicable (Table 1).

2.1. Halogenated alkanes

Iodide (I^-) and bromide (Br^-) are actively taken up from seawater and (i) may directly undergo halogenation into monosubstituted halomethanes, or (ii) are oxidized respectively as HOI and HOBr by extracellular vanadium-dependent haloperoxidases (V-HPOs) which use photosynthetic hydrogen peroxide on a routine basis, and peroxide generated by oxidative burst under stress conditions, as discussed further. In the first instance, the biosynthesis of methyl bromide and methyl iodide involves the transferase - mediated nucleophilic attack of corresponding halides at the electrophilic CH_3^+S site of S-Adenosyl Methionine (SAM; Figure 1), but is clearly limited to monohalogenation [9,10], *i.e.*, the production of CH_3I and CH_3Br (Figure 2 (a). In the second case, methylation can produce di- and polysubstituted halomethanes, including a variety of hetero-substituted forms (e.g., $CHBr_2I$; Figure 2 (b)) as in *Cystoseira barbata* [11]. Electrophilic reaction of I^+ and especially Br^+ with acceptors (centers of high electron density in e.g., enols, phenolics and phloroglucinol derivatives) can be rationalized on the basis of rearrangement of the double-bond. Hence a plausible mechanism is the successive bromination of the enols of C_2 or C_3 etc. units containing C=O groups followed by the loss of C_1 (CH_2O from CH_3CHO and CH_3CHO from $CH_3.CO.CH_3$ with concomitant formation of e.g., CH_2Br_2 and $CHBr_3$ [10–12].

Whatever their origin (*i.e.*, by cationoid or anionoid halogenation), volatile halogenated organic compounds (VHOCs) globally predominate in brown kelp effluxes and ensure a fast disposal of the ROS detoxification products (HOI and HOBr) while conceivably regulating apoplastic iodine and bromine reserves (see below). Furthermore, excess HOI and HOBr resulting from vanadium-dependant bromoperoxidase (V-BrPO) upregulation under oxidative stress is thought to complement on site destruction of microbial infection by ROS, and prevent microbial biofilm formation [13] or modulate its architecture (La Barre, unpubl. results), while VHOCs would help discourage reinfection.

Table 1. Halogenated compounds from brown macrophytic algae reported in the literature. MIT and DIT = mono- and di-iodotyrosine; PG = phloroglucinol; PL = phlorethol; FC = fucol; FP= Fucophlorethol; FH = fuhalol; EK = eckol.

Species (Order)	Halogenated metabolite	Reference
Laminariales (La)	MIT, DIT	no specific reference
Laminaria digitata	volatile alkanes (Cl, Br, I)	Nightingale *et al.* (1995) [12]
Laminaria ochroleuca	monochlorotriPL C	Glombitza *et al.* (1977) [31]
Laminaria ochroleuca	monochlorotriphenol	Glombitza *et al.* (1977) (31]
Egregia menziesii	egregiachlorides A, B and C	Todd *et al.* (1993) [41]
Eisenia bicyclis	eiseniachlorides A, B and C	Kousaka *et al.* (2003) [42]
Eisenia bicyclis	eiseniaiodides A, B	Kousaka *et al.* (2003) [42]
Eisenia arborea	PG (I), EK (I)	Glombitza & Gerstberger (1985) [25]
Fucales (Fu)		
Cystoseira barbata	halogenated alkanes	Milkova *et al.* (1997) [11]
Cystophora congesta	bromotriPL A2	Koch & Gregson, (1984) (28]
Cystophora refiexa	mono, di, tri, tetraPL (Cl, Br, both), FP (Cl)	Sailer & Glombitza (1999)a [29]
Ascophyllum nodosum	iodinated meroterpene	Arizumi *et al.* (1994) (46]
Carpophyllum angustifolium	diFC (Cl), PG (Cl), diPL (I), biFH (Cl)	Glombitza & Schmidt (1999) [32]
Dictyotales (Di)		
Padina tetrastromatica	Cl and Br sesquiterpenes	Parameswaran *et al.* (1994) [45]
Colpomenia sinuosa	colpol (1,4 diphenylbutene 2)	Green *et al.* (1993) [34]
Ectocarpales (Ec)		
Analipus japonicus	tri, tetra and pentaFC	Glombitza & Zieprath (1989) [33]

Note: letters A, B, C refer to identified egregiachloride structures as shown in Figure 6 and to identified eiseniachloride and eiseniaiodide structures as shown in Figure 7.

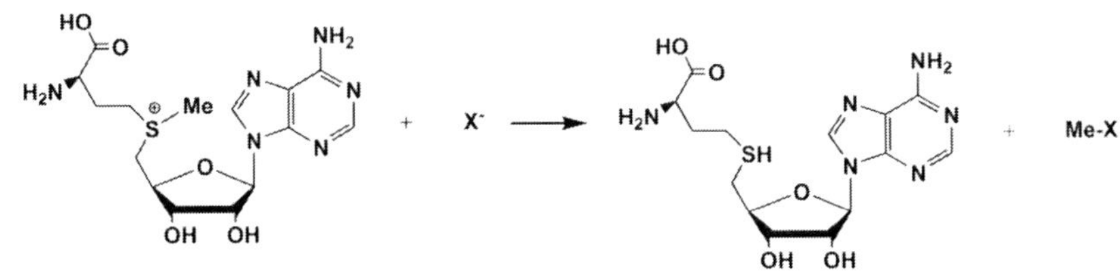

Figure 1. Methyltransferases mediate the transfer of a methyl group (Me) from SAM to a halide (X: halide ion). After [14].

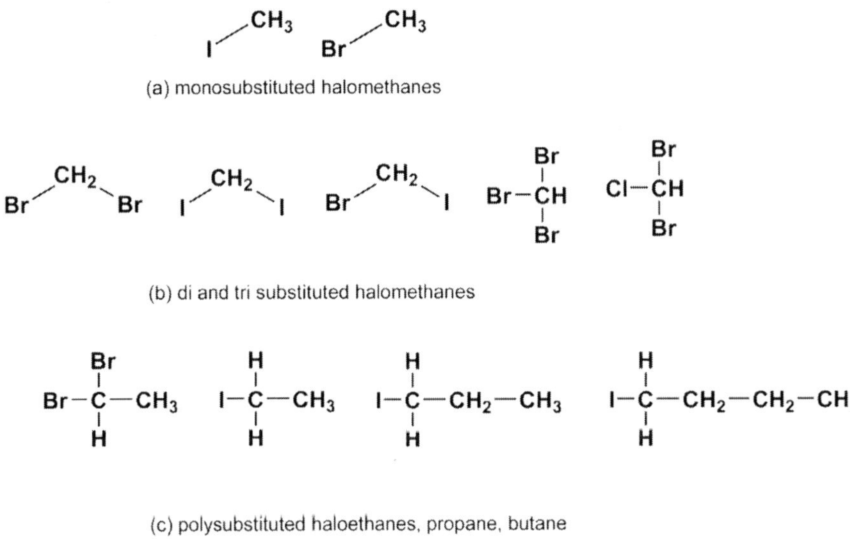

Figure 2. The most common halogenated alkanes found in effluxes from brown algae. (a) monosubstituted haloalkanes generated by action of SAM transferase; (b) and (c) polysubstituted alkanes supposedly generated as secondary products of V-BrPO action on enols. (see text).

2.2. Tyrosine-bound halogens

Non-volatile iodine is mainly concentrated from seawater in the peripheral tissues of brown algae [15]. In Laminariales, several speciation studies have concluded that up to 90% of total iodine is mainly stored in a labile inorganic form identified as iodide [16–19], while its organic forms in *Laminaria* are dominated by hormone-like tyrosine derivatives, *i.e.*, monoiodotyrosine or MIT (10–15 ppm), diiodotyrosine or DIT (20–25 ppm), shown in Figure 3. The ubiquity of iodinated tyrosines (e.g., MIT, DIT) across extant eukaryotic phyla has shown their general function as endocrine molecules involved in cell-cell communication (plants) as well as time-coordinated and dose-dependent developmental changes, as reviewed by [20]. Trophic transfers of thyroxin (TH) and thyroid hormone precursors from primary producers (possibly detected in phytoplankton upon immunological assays) to consumers are essential to the metamorphosis of larvae of marine invertebrates [21] and gene regulation and signal transcription in vertebrates. Contrary to most organohalogenates of phaeophyte origin, tyrosin halogenations into MIT and DIT is believed to occur spontaneously, *i.e.*, they are not enzyme mediated [22]. The facile halogenation of MIT and DIT and the emphasis on the signaling role of these ubiquitous metabolites in eukaryotic physiology [20] makes them possible candidates as hormone-like substances, along with known elicitors (alginate hydrolysates) of kelps [23].

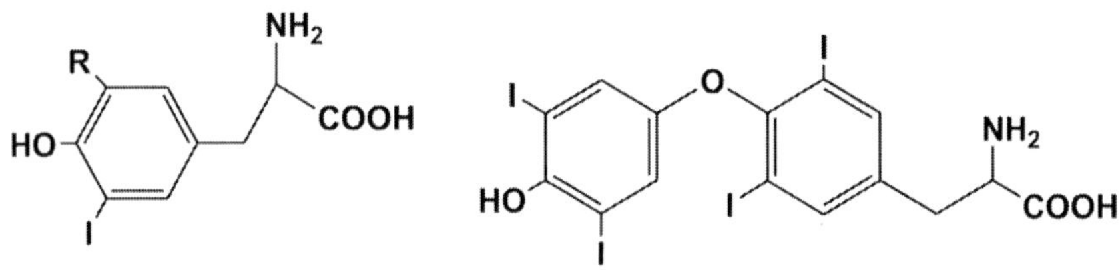

Monoiodotyrosine (R = H)
Diiodotyrosine (R = I)

Thyroxin

Figure 3. Mono- and diiodotyrosine are found in Laminariales, precursors to thyroxin (found as a thyroid hormone in some invertebrates and in higher animals).

2.3. Halogenated phenolics

Phloroglucinol and derived products are essentially plant products. Singh and Bharate [24] conveniently separates them into phloroglucinols (mono-, di-, tri-, tetra- and oligomeric) and phlorotannins. According to this classification, only a few phloroglucinols have been isolated from macrophytic algae, whereas phlorotannins are exclusively found in brown algae and are regarded as the functional equivalents of terrestrial tannins. Halogenated monomeric phenolics are also occasionally found in brown algae, as well as in a few red algae.

2.3.1. Halogenated phloroglucinols and phenols

Iodophloroglucinol and bromophloroglucinol have been identified in the Laminariale *Eisenia arborea* [25]. Interestingly, Shibata *et al.* [26] have found that the Laminariales *Eisenia bicyclis* and *Ecklonia kurome* release monomeric bromophenols (2,4-dibromophenol, 2,4,6-tribromophenol and dibromo-iodophenol) in the surrounding medium (Figure 4), and retains oligomers and polymers in their tissues. Bromophenols are found in the peripheral tissues of a number of Australian brown algae [27] and are known to be much more efficient deterrents against grazing predators than phlorotannins, yet no study to date has correlated predation pressure with production and release of monomeric bromophenols in the water column.

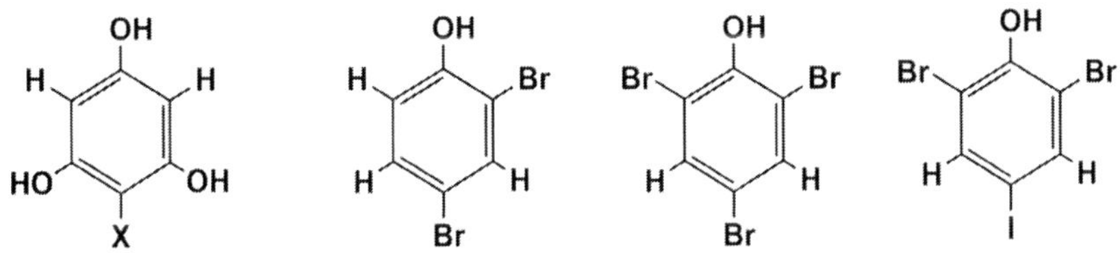

Figure 4. Halogenated phenolic monomers found in brown algae.

2.3.2. Halogenated phlorotannins

According to linkage type, phlorotannins can be classified into four subclasses, *i.e.*, phlorotannins with an ether linkage (fuhalols and phlorethols), with a phenyl linkage (fucols), with an ether and a phenyl linkage (fucophlorethols), and with a dibenzodioxin linkage (eckols and carmalols), most of which have halogenated representatives in brown algae. The Fucales have been so far the best source of halogenated phlorotannins. For example, Koch and Gregson [28] have identified bromotriphlorethol in *Cystophora congesta*, and later Sailer and Glombitza [29] have isolated and characterized no less than 17 halogenated (brominated, chlorinated and iodinated) phlorotannins along with 30 non-halogenated forms [30] from the Sargassacea *Cystophora retroflexa*. One of these compounds, monochlorotriphlorethol was also found in the Laminariale*Laminaria ochroleuca* by Glombitza *et al.* [31]. The Sargassacea *Carpophyllum angustifolium*, in addition to chlorophloroglucinol, contains iododiphlorethol, chlorobifuhalol and chlorodifucol [32]. Monosubstituted eckols have been found in the Laminariale *Eisenia arborea*, along with halogenated phloroglucinols [25]. Ectocarpales have been little investigated, but chlorinated biaryl phloroglucinol derivatives (fucols) were found in *Analipus japonicus* [33]. Colpol, a non-typical phenolic derivative was isolated by Green *et al.* [34] in the Red Sea from a cosmopolitan Scytosiphonale, *Colpomenia sinuosa*. This brominated compound has a biphenyl butene structure, with strong cytotoxic activities. These various structures are shown in Figure 5 (a), (b), (c) and (d).

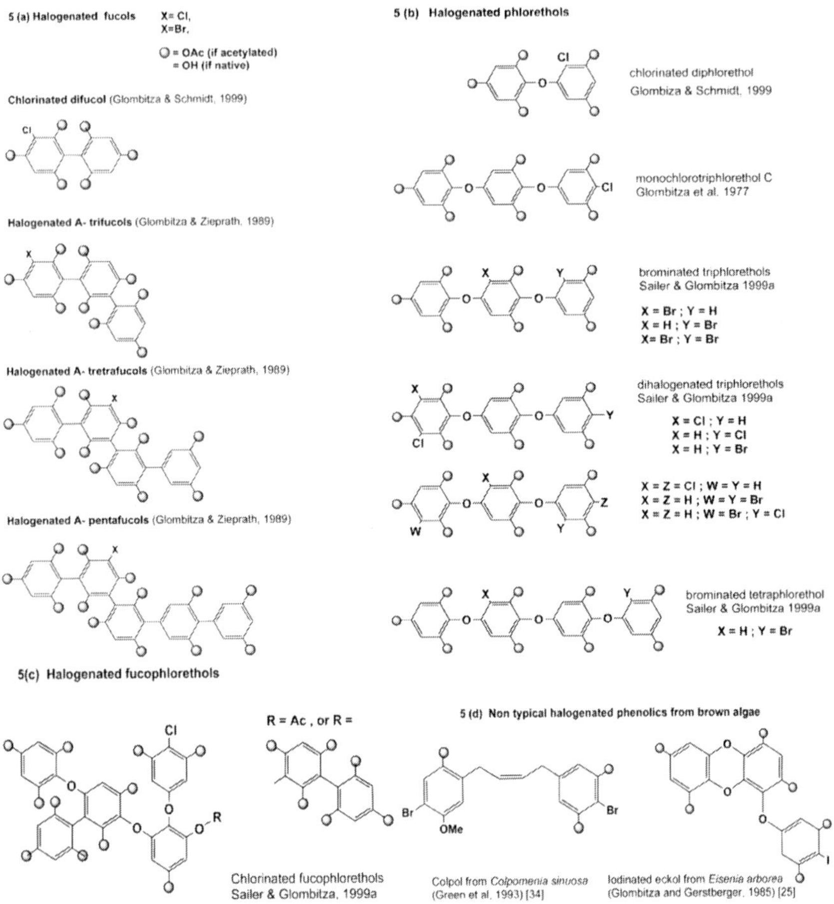

Figure 5. Halogenated phenolics from brown algae. (a)-Halogenated fucols found in the Laminariale *Analipus japonicus* (after [33]) and in the Sargassacea *Carpophyllum angustifolium* (after [32]). Spheres represent acetylation performed for spectroscopic analysis, or hydroxylation for native molecule. (b)-Halogenated phlorethols found in the Sargassacea *Cystophora reflexa* (after [29] (see also [32], and in *Laminaria ochroleuca*(after [31]). (c)-Halogenated fucophlorethols found in the Sargassacea *Cystophora reflexa* (after [29]). (d)-Non-typical halogenated phenolics from brown algae (after [34] and [25]).

2.3.3. Biosynthesis of halogenated phlorotannins

The biosynthesis of phenolics such as phloroglucinol with hydroxylations at the *meta* position are derived from the acetate-malonate pathway [35], in a process which may involve a polyketide synthase-type enzyme complex [36]. Chemically, condensation initiates intermolecular ring closure to yield hexacyclic ring systems (unstable triketide) which undergo tautomerization into the more stable aromatic form, phloroglucinol. Yet the exact biosynthesis pathway of phlorotannins is not known [37]. The involvement of apoplastic vanadium-dependent haloperoxidases, in the presence of halide ions and hydrogen peroxide has been demonstrated for *in vitro* cross-linking of phlorotannins [38,39], but the presence of halogenated species during the oxidation process is still speculative and is awaiting confirmation by kinetic studies and mass spectral analysis. Sulfated low molecular weight polyphenols are found in a wide range of brown algae [40], but mixed (sulfated and halogenated) substitutions have never been reported so far.

2.4. Halogenated fatty acids

In brown algae, the overall composition in saturated and unsaturated fatty acids is equivalent to that found in red algae, with a high proportion of C18 and C20 polyunsaturated forms (PUFA). Three chlorinated oxylipins were isolated from the Laminariale *Egregia menziesii* (Alariaceae) by Todd *et al.* [41], two originating from the C18 PUFA stearidonic acid (egregiachloride A and B, Figure 6a) and one from the C20 PUFA eicosapentaenoic acid (egregiachloride C, Figure 6b).

Kousaka *et al.* [42] isolated six halogenated (eiseniachlorides) or iodinated (eiseniaiodides) species among a whole series of C18 oxylipins from another Alariaceae, *Eisenia bicyclis*, also biosynthesized from a stearidonic acid precursor. Along with eiseniachloride A and B and eiseniaiodide A and B, two cyclization variants (Figure 7), were determined by extensive 2-D NMR analysis. Interestingly, the halogenation (*via* C13 HPOTE resulting from LOX *i.e.*, lipoxygenase oxidation) occurs inside the cell and does not include brominated forms. Finally, a C20 form (*via* addition of an ethylene group) was determined as eiseniachloride C. Anti bacterial assays on *Bacillus subtilis* and on *Staphylococcus aureus* did not shown any improvement of the activities of any of the halogenated forms over the non-halogenated ones [42]. Ecklonialactones A and B are potential feeding repellents against predating abalone seashell, but no mention is made of this ecological role for their halogenated forms [42].

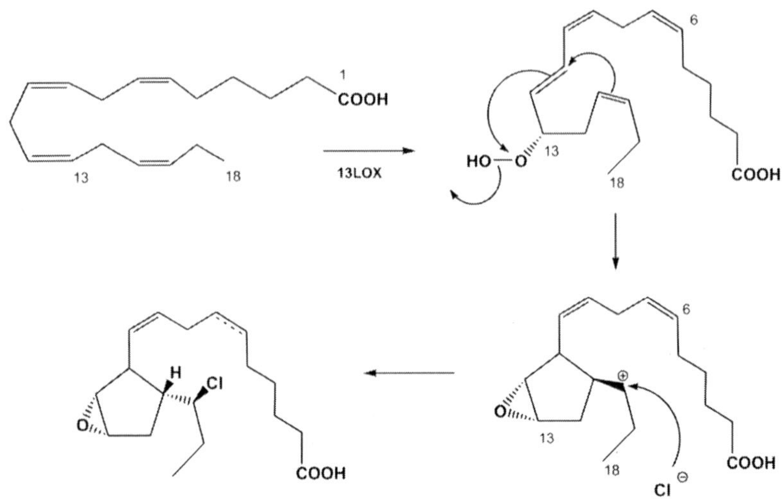

(a) Egregiachloride A (Δ6,9)
Egregiachloride B (Δ9)

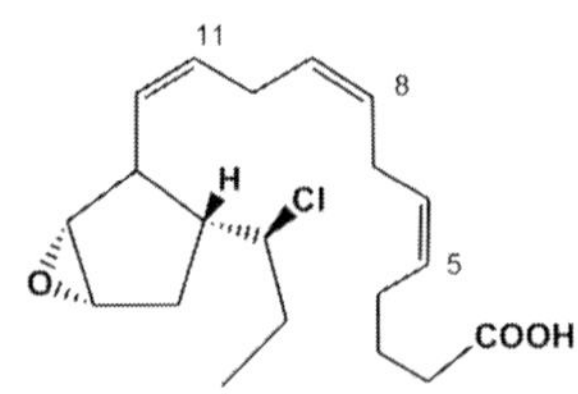

(b) Egregiachloride C (Δ5,8,11)

Figure 6. Halogenated eicosanoids (C18 oxylipins derived from stearidonic acid), isolated from the Laminariale *Egregia menziesii* [41]. (a) Egregiachloride A and B from stearidonic acic catalysis by 13LOX, cyclopentyl cyclization and subsequent carbocation attack at C16 by chlorine anion. (b) Egregiachloride C, similarly synthesized from eicosapentaenoic acid.

Similar to plants, in the brown alga *Saccharina (formerly Laminaria) angustata*, the LOX-derived fatty acid hydroperoxides can be further cleaved to form C-6 (derived from C18 PUFA) and C-9 aldehydes (derived from C20 PUFA) none of which have been reported under halogenated forms (see review [43]). Although chlorosulpholipids have been reported in a number of freshwater algae, there is no evidence that they occur in marine algae [44].

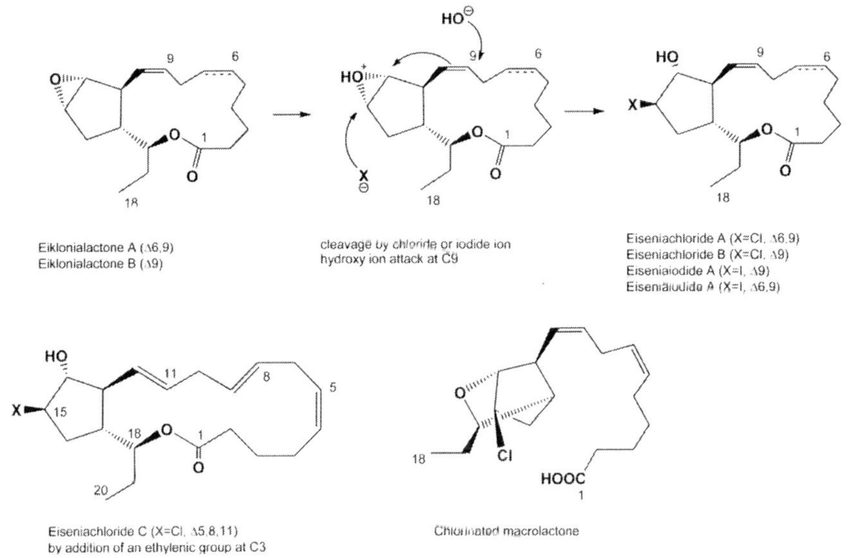

Figure 7. Halogenated eicosanoids (C18 oxylipins derived from stearidonic acid), isolated from the Laminariale *Eisenia bicyclis* [42].

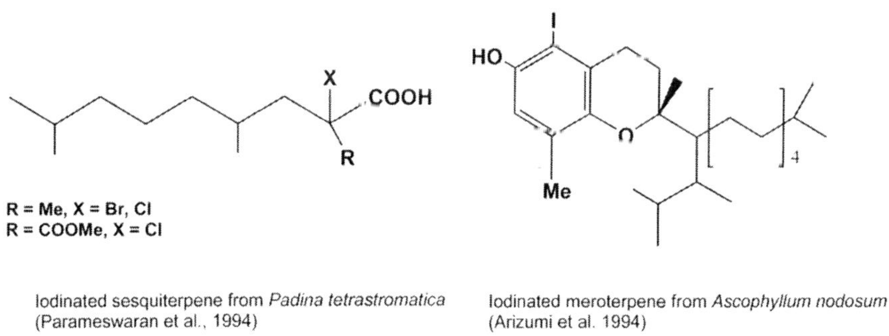

Figure 8. Halogenated linear nor-sesquiterpenes isolated from *Padina tetrastromatica*[45], and iodinated meroterpene isolated from *Ascophyllum nodosum* [46].

2.5. Halogenated terpenes

The only phaeophycean halogenated nor-sesquiterpenes were isolated from *Padina tetrastromatica* [45], possibly oxidation forms of perhydrolinalool. An atypical iodinated meroterpene (terpene with an aromatic moiety) has been characterized in*Ascophyllum nodosum* by Arizumi *et al.* [46] This is in sharp contrast to red algae, in which secondary metabolites structures are abundant (over 1,200 structures in 2005), with highly diverse halogenated terpenes (over 800 chlorinated and/or brominated forms many of which have attracted the interest of pharmacologists [47]), and which probably reflect a capacity to diversify their defense strategies which is not encountered in brown algae.

2.6. Halogenated polysaccharides

If sulfatation of carbohydrates is a common feature in brown algae that confers them with specific physical and eco-physiological properties [48], there has never been any report of halogenated polysaccharides, in contrast to polyphenols in which either substitution (sulfates or halogen) can be found.

3. THE ENZYMOLOGY OF HALOGENATION IN BROWN ALGAE

Nature's strategies for incorporating halogens into organic molecules are multiple [49] and the discovery of new enzymes for halogenation has increased tremendously during the last decade [14] revealing new metalloenzymes, flavoenzymes, *S*-adenosyl-l-methionine (SAM)-dependent enzymes and others that catalyse halide oxidation using dioxygen, hydrogen peroxide and hydroperoxides, or that promote nucleophilic halide addition reactions [50]. In brown algae, it is now widely accepted that halogenation involves vanadium-dependent haloperoxidases (V-HPOs). Together with the heme-dependent haloperoxidases, V-HPOs utilize hydrogen peroxide to convert a halide ion (X^-) to hypohalite (OX^-) intermediate that is chemically equivalent to an electrophilic "X+". They are named according to the most electronegative halide that they can oxidize, *i.e.*, chloroperoxidases (V-CPOs) can catalyze the oxidation of chloride as well as of bromide and iodide, bromoperoxidases (V-BrPOs) react with bromide and iodide, whereas iodoperoxidases (V-IPOs) are specific of iodide.

Vanadium-dependent haloperoxidases from marine sources are reviewed in this special issue [51], and a recent mini-review by Winter and Moore [52] provides an interesting phylogenetic tree of the different classes and sources of chloro- and bromoperoxidases found in nature. The first V-HPO was discovered in the fucoid brown alga *Ascophyllum nodosum*[53]. This enzyme has been extensively characterized as a bromoperoxidase at a biochemical and structural level [54,55]. As of today [14] and despite extensive researches on different V-BrPOs and V-ClPOs, the complete catalytic cycle is still uncertain and the origin of halide selectivity remains one of yet unanswered question [50,56]. Up to now, V-BrPO activities have been detected in both red and brown macroalgae, whereas V-ClPO are restricted to terrestrial fungi and to bacteria [52]. In microalgae, halogenation of organic compounds is known to involve halide methyl transferases [57] and no V-HPO has been yet identified on genomic data obtained from diatoms [58]. From algal genomic resources, several putative V-HPO homologues and dehalogenase enzymes have been identified in the red alga *Chondrus crispus* [59]. The first known V-IPO was identified and cloned in *Laminaria digitata* by [60] and phylogenetic analyses have shown that all brown algal V-HPOs present a monophyletic origin with a common ancestor with V-HPOs from red algae. However, it seems that in *L. digitata*the independent evolution of the two haloperoxidase gene families led to a novel biochemical function specialized in iodine oxidation [60]. Both V-HPO gene families seem to operate in a coordinate manner. Specific *vIPO* genes (coding for V-IPO enzymes) are upregulated following an oxidative burst to rapidly restore iodine loss, while some V-BrPO coding genes are specifically activated and likely to be involved in oxygen detoxification [61]. Recent proteomic studies on *Saccharina*(formerly *Laminaria*) *japonica* have revealed that V-BrPO are strongly upregulated during the summer months, in response to elimination of active oxygen species and protection of algal tissues from oxygen injury, as well as discouraging epiphytism which may seasonally hamper proper growth [62].

In brown algae, V-HPOs and halides are likely to play a central role in oxidative detoxication, cell wall strengthening, and chemical defense in a context of cellular defense, as well as in substrate adhesion in young sporophytes. These various functions of V-HPOs crystallize large basic and applied interests, (see reviews in [50,51]). In Figure 9, the various biological functions of V-HPO are highlighted and contrasted in the various thallus parts in which they prevail, *i.e.*, bioadhesion at the holdfast region, defense against epiphytism, predation and biofouling being optimally expressed at the peri-meristematic region of the blade.

4. THE FUNCTION OF BROMINATION IN BROWN ALGAL ADHESION

A model of oxidative cross-linking of secreted phenolics mediated *via* the catalysis of a vanadium bromoperoxidase was proposed about twenty years ago, based on some indirect evidences such as V-BrPO immunolocalization in adherent eggs and spores of fucoid brown algae [63,64]. Indeed, this poorly grounded hypothesis [65] was challenged later when sophisticated techniques were used to investigate cross-linking processes in brown algae.

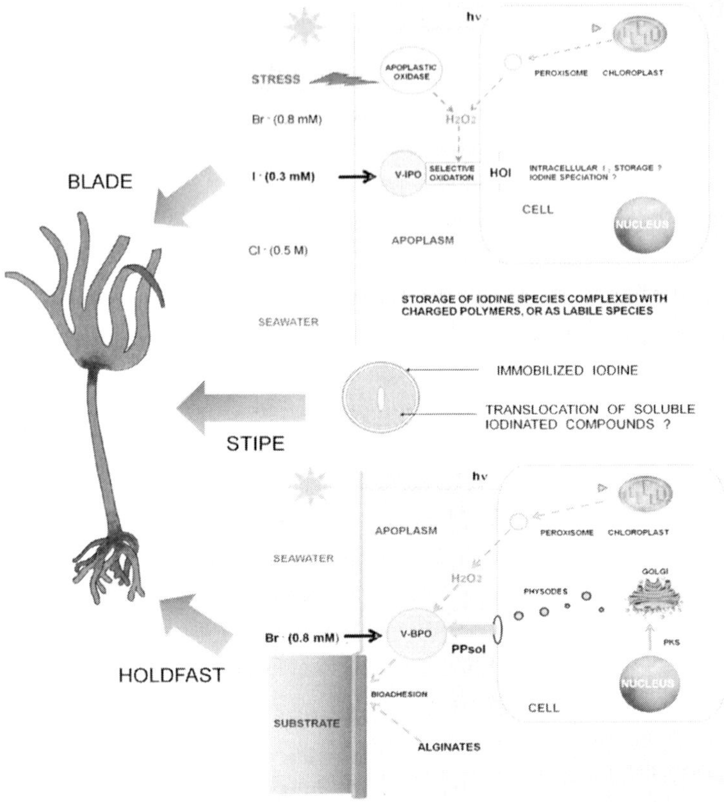

Figure 9. Halogen chemistry in *Laminaria digitata*.The different roles of V-HPO enzymes in brown kelp biology are conveniently contrasted in this diagram of a young whole thallus. In growing tissues of the blade (top), active uptake of iodine prevails as V-IPOs are upregulated to replenish iodine stocks to quench excess hydrogen peroxide (among other functions; see text). Iodine imaging revealed extracellular stocks associated with charged polymers for rapid bioavailability, rather than only intracellular I_2stocks *via* HOI trans-membrane intake as hitherto believed. In the stipe (middle), mechanical resilience is maintained by outer cuticle hardening coinciding with the highest concentration of immobilized iodine. Metabolite translocation occurs in the softer inner matrix as well as signal molecules of suspected systemy. In the holdfast (bottom), soluble phlorotannins (PP) generated in the Golgi apparatus are contained in cytoplasmic physodes, which burst out in the apoplastic space. Bioadhesion is mediated by V-BrPOs, which cross-link the released PP in the presence of hydrogen peroxide and halide ions. The adhesive is thought to result from macromolecular scaffolds between the oxidized polymers and cell wall alginates.

The cross-linking of brown algal phlorotannins catalyzed by the V-BrPO from *A. nodosum* was measured using the quartz crystal microbalance with dissipation monitoring (QCM-D) method [38]. Phlorotannins adsorbed to a quartz crystal sensor were shown to change their mechanical properties upon the addition of V-BrPO, KBr and H_2O_2. The decreased dissipation upon addition of the cross-linking agents was interpreted as intramolecular cross-links formed between different phloroglucinol units in the phlorotannins [38]. Additionnal measurements using surface plasmon resonance (SPR) and UV/Vis spectroscopy verified the results achieved with QCM-D that all components *i.e.*, V-BrPO, KBr and H_2O_2 were necessary in order to achieve intramolecular *in vitro* oxidative cross-linking of the polymers. Based on the occurrence of halogenated phlorotannins in brown algae, while in low abundance [66], the involvement of a V-BrPO in the catalysis of phenolic cross-linking is our favourite hypothesis. Hardening with alginate and/or calcium is essential for high cohesive strength as shown in shear-lap tests that measured the adhesion strength of this assemblage [67]. All formulations were capable of adhering to a variety of surfaces, however the adhesion properties were influenced by the halide used [39]. QCM-D results showed that the kinetics of the oxidation was faster with iodide than with bromide. Small angle X-ray scattering (SAXS), light scattering and cryo-Transmission Electron Microscopy (TEM) experiments [67] revealed that oxidized polyphenols self-assemble into chain-like objects, irrespective of the oxidation conditions [39]. Yet, slight differences in the aggregate size were detected. Moreover, oxidation with iodide generates stiffer networks, suggesting that the interaction between the alginate and the polyphenol could be the cause of the reduced adhesion [67]. When coupled with results showing that V-BrPO brings about curing of adhesive extracts more than other catalysts, these data implicate V-BrPO to be the key reagent in controlling the cross-linking of phenolic polymers for the assembly of brown algal adhesives. These conclusions were confirmed by independent studies investigating the interaction between polyphenolics from the brown alga *Padina gymnospora* and alginate from *Fucus vesiculosus* using size exclusion chromatography (SEC) and optical tweezers microscopy [68]. It revealed the formation of a high-molecular-weight complex only when V-BrPO was added, indicating that the enzyme is essential for the binding process, along with a decrease in alginate viscosity. However, the covalent binding of uronic acid residues with some aromatic rings suggested by Salgado *et al.* [68] are not yet demonstrated in brown algae and SAXS and cryo-TEM measurements disfavoured this hypothesis (for a detailed discussion see Potin & Leblanc [69]). In this context, oxidized bromine or iodine in brown algae participates in a number of reactions with organic substrates, in which the resulting metabolites are involved in primary (oxygen detoxication, tissue repair, bioadhesion) and secondary (surface antibacterials) roles.

5. THE ROLE OF IODINE IN BROWN ALGAE

5.1. The emergence of specificity for iodine oxidation in brown algae

The element iodine has been discovered in the ashes of brown algal kelps in the beginning of the 19th century. The kelp*Laminaria digitata* presents an average iodine content of 1.0% of dry weight, representing a ca. 30,000-fold accumulation of this element from seawater [70]. In this brown alga, micro-chemical imaging of iodine distribution reveals an unexpected sub-cellular distribution in the cell walls of peripheral cells [15], with the predominance of iodide species [71]. Although *L. digitata* represents one of the most studied models, the biochemical pathways leading to this very efficient iodide trapping and the mechanism responsible for its release into the surroundings are still speculative. Specific oxidation processes are essential in both the mechanisms of iodine uptake and release. In *L. digitata*, iodine is thought to be taken up by a mechanism based on the haloperoxidase-mediated oxidation of iodide, a mechanism which requires a constitutive apoplastic level of hydrogen peroxide of circa 50 μM [70] and which could involve an apoplastic V-IPO [60,72]. Recent studies [15,69] have shown that iodide is mainly chelated by apoplastic macromolecules. Such a storage mechanism should provide an abundant and accessible source of reduced iodine, which can be easily remobilized for potential anti-oxidative activities and chemical defense. This unique setup has never been described among all living systems. However, in the presence of exogenously-added 2 mM H_2O_2, a net efflux of iodide was observed [70]. Yet there is no clear answer as to why Laminariales have developed (or retained?) such an important and extensive metabolic dependence to iodine, as compared to most halogen-using marine life forms [71].

5.2. The function of the iodine metabolism

The molecular mass of iodine (126.90 U) is the highest by far of all elements used in biological systems, including metals. The prevalence of iodine chemistry in very early life forms has recently led to interesting speculations as its cornerstone role as a catalyst and inorganic antioxidant [20] without which the emergence of multicellularity would never have taken place. Indeed, iodine is regarded as an additional biomarker towards the presence of life in extraterrestrial environments. Early prokaryotes (LUCA) had to carry out the conversion of toxic environmental iodate into iodine which could be readily incorporated in the cytoplasm and perform a number of essential catalytic functions, e.g., by coupling with essential organic molecules. The reducing (electron loosing) capacity of halides being proportional to the atomic size of the halogen, the oxidation products of active oxygenated species (AOS) and iodide occur almost readily as compared to bromine or chlorine. Iodine production by iodoperoxidases in several phaeophyte taxa, e.g., several Laminariales, represent a very efficient way of quenching excess hydrogen peroxide and reactive oxygenated radicals, following oxidative burst, or simply accumulating in plastids from regular photosynthesis [71]. An equivalent functional (primary) role is assigned to highly nucleophilic phlorotannins which are produced in a number of shore Fucales, following seasonal patterns in western Brittany (France), especially during summer with longer exposures to sunlight, and at mid-tide levels [73]. Interestingly, it was shown that the average iodine contents were lowest in summer months (0.25–0.60% dry weight) and highest in late autumn and in winter (in the range 0.75–1.20% dry weight) in the kelp *Laminaria digitata* [74]. Taken together, these data may help understand how the two classes of compounds interplay as ROS quenchers. However, in *L. digitata*, soluble phlorotannins are very low [73] and therefore iodide is likely to play a major role as an antioxidant [71]. Further studies are required in other species of Laminariales and of Fucales in order to understand the respective roles and the possible alternation between phlorotannins and iodide. Within-thallus translocation has long been documented in red and various brown algae, the sieve elements in both lineages lacking the vascularized phloem structure of higher plants [75]. In Laminariales, translocation of carbon labeled photosynthates from older parts of the frond towards the meristematic region and to the holdfast haptera has been demonstrated [76]. Mannitol, malate, citrate, polar amino acids and proteins are non-selectively translocated *via* the sieve tube of *Macrocystis pyrifera*, as well as inorganic cations (K^+, Na^+, Mg^{2+} and Ca^{2+}) and anions among which chloride and bromide [77]. Iodide was later found to translocate in a source-to-sink manner, compatible with known distribution of this element in Laminariales [78]. As of now, organic halides have not been identified as translocates, yet there are strong suspicions that regulation of V-HPO genes operates within the context of a systemic response [61]. Systemy would operate either externally (detection in the water column of an eliciting signal generated in a stressed region of the thallus by a naïve region of the same individual, followed by a defense response), or internally *via* translocation. It could involve halogenated compounds (VHOC) or oxygenated species (aldehydes) which are produced as defense compounds in plantlets of *L. digitata* which are metabolically challenged [79,80] and thus are possible pheromone-like candidates, along with known elicitors (alginate hydrolysates) of this particular kelp.

5.3. Environmental consequences of the iodine metabolism

Iodine species are present in the marine boundary layer (MBL) due to the release of I_2 and of photo-labile iodocarbons from macro- and micro-algae (Figure 10). Whilst the primary source of inorganic chlorine and bromine species in the remote ocean is likely to be their release from the significant seasalt halide reservoir in atmospheric aerosol, the direct emission of halocarbons [81,82] from intertidal macroalgal species [79], from phytoplankton [83] and from biogenic marine aggregates [84] has been well established and contributes significantly to the coastal atmospheric burden of Reactive Halogen Species (RHS) [81,82]. Indeed shallow coastal areas where kelp beds of *Laminaria digitata* correspond to hotspots of biogenic halocarbon emission have been recently investigated with particular attention to iodine speciation. In particular, CH_2I_2 is the dominant organic iodine species released from kelps [81,82] and has it been suggested as one of the initiators of the iodine nanometric particles that function as cloud-forming nuclei [85]. The most widely-observed coastal inorganic RHS, iodine monoxide (IO), has also consistently been shown to exhibit a tidal signature, but only during daytime, consistent with photochemical formation of IO. In addition to the tidal halogen cycling, studies at Mace Head in Western Ireland revealed the rapid appearance of high concentrations of ultrafine aerosol particles at daytime low tide [86,87]. Should even a small fraction of the particles grow sufficiently large that they would act as Cloud Condensation Nuclei (CCN) at supersaturations corresponding to updraughts in typical marine stratocumulus clouds, such particle formation may significantly impact on local and regional radiative forcing and climate.

During the 2006 coastal campaign of the Reactive Halogens in the Marine Boundary Layer (RHaMBLe) project in Roscoff in Western France [88], it was clearly demonstrated that iodine-mediated coastal particle formation occurs, driven by daytime low tide emission of molecular iodine (I_2), by macroalgal species fully or partially exposed by the receding waterline. Ultrafine particle concentrations strongly correlate with the rapidly recycled reactive iodine species, IO, produced at high concentrations following photolysis of I_2. The heterogeneous macroalgal I_2 sources lead to variable relative concentrations of iodine species observed by path-integrated [89] and *in situ* measurement techniques [90]. As shown at Roscoff, rockweed (the fucoid alga *A.nodosum*) beds may also emit more constantly than kelps because there are exposed to air more frequently (even during small tides) and for longer periods of time [91,92]. However, it was also observed at Cape Grim in Australia, that the contribution to particle formation of the fucoid alga *Durvillaea potatorum* is very limited because this alga does not

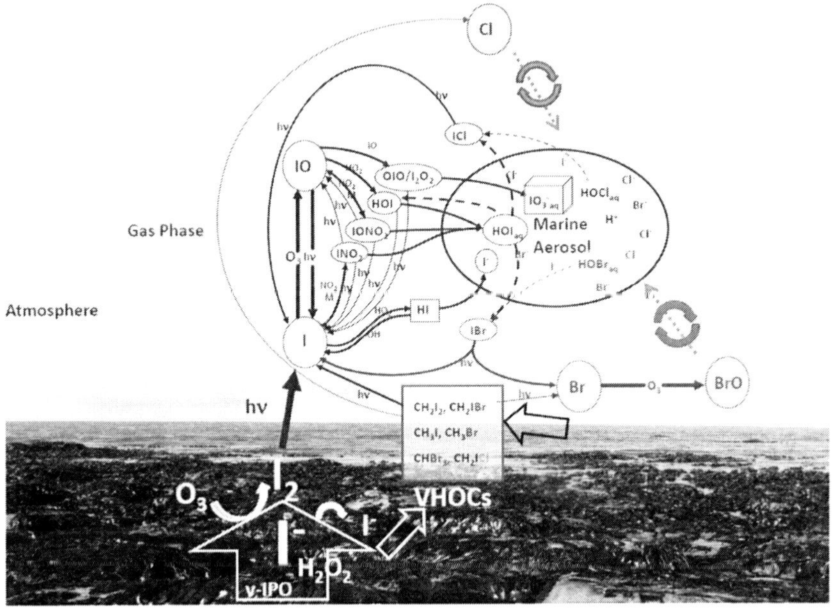

Figure 10. Iodine biogeochemistry at the Marine Boundary Layer.Schematic view of the link between kelp iodine species emissions and tropospheric iodine photooxidation, based upon current algal physiology, seaweed iodine speciation [71] and atmospheric chemistry [96] knowledge. The photograph features a kelp bed during a spring low tide in the vicinity of Roscoff. The large white arrow represents the contribution of kelps such as *Laminaria digitata* to the release of molecular iodine (I_2) directly from its apoplastic and peripheral storage in the form of reduced iodide (I^-). This oxidation is either catalyzed by endogenous specific vanadium iodoperoxidases (V-IPOs) using photosynthesis or stress- generated hydrogen peroxide (H_2O_2), or exogenously by the strong oxidant O_3, when algae are exposed to air at low tide. These oxidative processes also lead to production of volatile halogenated organic compounds (VHOCs) by kelps (thin white arrow), although an estimated 300-fold lower than I_2 fluxes [88]. Phytoplankton mainly contribute to I cycling through VHOC emission (black arrow above the sea). In the troposphere, atomic iodine (I) released by photolysis from I_2 and photolabile VHOCs, reacts with available O_3 to yield IO, rapidly establishing a photostationary state and consuming O_3 whenever IO reacts either with itself (yielding OIO), HO_2 (yielding HOI) or NO_2(yielding $IONO_2$): rather than being re-photolysed to release I atoms. HOI and $IONO_2$may be taken up by aerosol particles, releasing the dihalogen species IBr, ICl or I_2 via aqueous reaction with available Br^-, Cl^- or I^-, respectively, in the presence of sufficient acidity (H^+). Iodine cycling is also linked to Br and Cl cycling, which speciate through similar chemical reactions in the gas phase leading to similar exchanges with marine aerosols.

release I_2 [93]. These discrepancies have been tentatively explained by different capabilities of accumulation and emission between these two orders of large brown algae [92]. The evolution of new biochemical adaptations using more specific V-HPO has probably contributed to a better capacity to oxidize iodine and to use halides in kelps. In Laminariales (see section 2), iodoperoxidases activities that are specific for iodide, have been localized at least partly extracellularly in the apoplasm [60,94] and may explain the very high amount of iodide accumulated in their cell walls and higher efficiency of kelps for iodine oxidation, even in the absence of strong external oxidants, such as ozone. *Ascophyllum nodosum* was shown to possess two distinct isoforms of V-BrPO, one of them being located very superficially at the thallus surface [95] which is likely conferring a better capacity to oxidize iodide leading to high I_2 emissions. Interestingly, this agree with the modeling of I_2 emissions in the Roscoff area during the RHaMBLe project [92], which showed that the occurrence of rockweed in the mid-littoral zone of sheltered habitats complements efficiently the presence of large stands of Laminariales.

6. NEW APPROACHES, NEW ANSWERS?

Marine halogenated natural products have important biological functions as signalling molecules and defense compounds for the producing organisms. If their therapeutic potential has attracted the attention of pharmacochemists worldwide since the early seventies [97], there is a now a strong interest in exploring the enzymes involved in their biosynthesis, in particular the vanadium-dependent haloperoxidases. Some V-HPOs have the ability to halogenate a range of organic compounds in a region- and stereospecific manner as evidenced in at least two orders of Rhodophyta [98] and by the wealth of bioactive chlorinated/brominated organic molecules found in this lineage [47]. In the Phaeophyta, the primary function of haloperoxidases is to prevent the accumulation of toxic oxygenated species (the vanadium-containing catalytic site uses two molecules of hydrogen peroxide).

Ascophyllum nodosum

V-BrPOs still operate at 70 °C, in up to 60% organic solvents, they resist detergents, and maintain constant activity throughout the catalytic cycle (vanadium remains at VV oxidation state). This structural and functional resilience makes them all the more attractive as potential biocatalysts [52]. In addition, this particular enzyme is capable in vitro of carrying out sulfoxidation reactions enantioselectively on methyl phenyl substrate [99]. As biocatalysts of underwater "soft" or flexible adhesives, V-HPOs offer a very interesting alternative to "hard" or cementing biopolymers used by barnacles and many rock-dwelling molluscs. Bacterial haloperoxidases have been revealed by recent genomic studies. The chemistry of prokaryotic haloperoxidases may show new biological functions and thus greatly extend the potential of these enzymes as biocatalysts operating on novel and suitably selected organic substrates. In this area of research with potential impacts in the biosynthesis of marine natural products, it is very likely that structural biology and biotechnology will lead to important breakthroughs toward environment-friendly chemistry. To this end, methods such as exon shuffling for the directed evolution of bacterial and possibly algal enzymes will be employed.

REFERENCES

1. Gribble, G. The diversity of naturally produced organohalogens. Chemosphere 2003, 52, 289–297.

2. Bernroitner, M; Zamocky, M; Furtmüller, PG; Peschek, GA; Obinger, C. Occurrence, phylogeny, structure, and function of catalases and peroxidases in cyanobacteria. J Exp Bot 2009, 60, 423–440.

3. Palmer, JD. The symbiotic birth and spread of plastids: how many times and whodunit. J Phycol 2003, 39, 4–11.

4. Phillips, N; Calhoun, S; Moustafa, A; Bhattacharia, D; Braun, EL. Genomic insights into evolutionary relationships among heterokont lineages emphasizing the Phaeophyceae. J Phycol 2008, 44, 15–18.

5. Harper, MK; Bugni, TS; Copp, BR; James, RD; Lindsay, BS; Richardson, AD; Schnabel, PC; Tasdemir, D; VanWagoner, RM; Verbitzki, SM; Ireland, CM. McClintock, JB, Baker, BJ, Eds.; Introduction to the chemical ecology of marine natural products. In Marine Chemical Ecology; CRC: Boca Raton, FL, USA, 2001; pp. 3–71.

6. MarinLit database, Department of Chemistry, University of Canterbury. http://www.chem.canterbury.ac.nz/marinlit/marinlit.shtml (accessed January 2010).

7. Maschek, JA; Baker, BJ. Amsler, CD, Ed.; The chemistry of algal secondary metabolism. In Algal Chemical Ecology; Springer-Verlag Berlin: Heidelberg, Germany, 2008; pp. 1–24.

8. Blunt, JW; Copp, BR; Hu, WP; Munro, MHG; Northcote, PT; Prinsep, MR. Marine natural products. Nat Prod Rep 2009,26, 170–244.

9. Amachi, S; Kamagata, Y; Kanagawa, T; Muramatsu, Y. Bacteria mediate methylation of iodine in marine and terrestrial environments. Appl Environ Microbiol 2006, 67, 2718–2722.

10. Neilson, AH. Neilson, AH, Ed.; Biological effects and biosynthesis of brominated metabolites. In The Handbook of Environmental Chemistry, 1st ed; Springer: Berlin, Germany, 2003; Volume 3, pp. 75–204.

11. Milkova, T; Talev, G; Christov, R; Dimitrikova-Konaklieva, S; Popov, S. Sterols and volatiles in Cystoseira barbata andCystoseira crinita from the Black Sea. Phytochemistry 1997, 45, 93–95.

12. Nightingale, PD; Malin, G; Liss, PS. Production of chloroform and other low-molecular-weight halocarbons by some species of macroalgae. Limnol Oceanogr 1995, 40, 680–689.

13. Borchardt, SA; Allain, EJ; Michels, JJ; Stearns, GW; Kelly, RF; McCoy, WF. Reaction of acylated homoserine lactone bacterial signaling molecules with oxidized halogen antimicrobials. Appl Environ Microbiol 2001, 67, 3174–3179.

14. Wagner, C; El Omari, M; König, GM. Biohalogenation: nature's way to synthesize halogenated metabolites. J Nat Prod2009, 72, 540–553.

15. Verhaeghe, EF; Fraysse, A; Guerquin-Kern, JL; Wu, TD; Devès, G; Mioskowski, C; Leblanc, C; Ortega, R; Ambroise, Y; Potin, P. Microchemical imaging of iodine distribution in the brown alga Laminaria digitata suggests a new mechanism for its accumulation. J Biol Inorg Chem 2008, 13, 257–269.

16. Tong, W; Chaikoff, IL. Metabolism of 131I by the marine alga Nereocystis luetkeana. J Biol Chem 1955, 215, 473–484.

17. Roche, J; Yagi, Y. Sur la fixation de l'iode radioactif par les algues et sur les constituants iodés des Laminaires. C R Soc Biol Paris 1952, 146, 642–645.

18. Hou, X; Chai, C; Qian, Q; Yan, X; Fan, X. Determination of chemical species of iodine in some seaweeds (I). Sci Total Environ 1997, 204, 215–221.

19. Shah, M; Wuilloud, RG; Kannamkumaratha, SS; Caruso, JA. Iodine speciation studies in commercially available seaweed by coupling different chromatographic techniques with UV and ICP-MS detection. J Anal At Spectrom 2005,20, 176–182.

20. Crockford, SJ. Evolutionary roots of iodine and thyroid hormones in cell cell signaling. Integr Comp Biol 2009, 49, 155–166.

21. Heyland, A; Moroz, LL. Cross-kingdom hormonal signaling: an insight from thyroid hormone functions in marine larvae. J Exp Biol 2005, 208, 4355–4361.

22. Morrison, M; Schonbaum, GR. Snell, EE, Ed.; Peroxide-catalysed halogenations. In Annual Review of Biochemistry; Annual Reviews Inc: Palo Alto, CA, USA, 1976; Volume 45, pp. 861–888.

23. Küpper, FC; Müller, D; Peters, A; Kloareg, B; Potin, P. Oligoalginate recognition and oxidative burst play a key role in natural and induced resistance of the sporophytes of Laminariales. J Chem Ecol 2002, 28, 2037–2061.

24. Singh, IP; Bharate, SB. Phloroglucinol compounds of natural origin. Nat Prod Rep 2006, 23, 558–591.

25. Glombitza, K-W; Gerstberger, G. Phlorotannins with dibenzodioxin structural elements from the brown alga Eisenia arborea. Phytochemistry 1985, 24, 543–551.

26. Shibata, T; Hama, Y; Miyasaki, T; Ito, M; Nakamura, T. Extracellular secretion of phenolic substances from living brown algae. J Appl Phycol 2006, 18, 787–794.

27. Whitfield, FB; Helidoniotis, F; Shaw, KJ; Svoronos, D. Distribution of bromophenols in species of marine algae from Eastern Australia. J Agric Food Chem 1999, 47, 2367–2373.

28. Koch, ML; Gregson, RP. Brominated phlorethols and non-halogenated phlorotannins from the brown alga Cystophora congesta. Phytochemistry 1984, 13, 2633–2637.

29. Sailer, B; Glombitza, K-W. Halogenated phlorethols and fucophlorethols from the brown alga Cystophora retroflexa.Nat. Toxins 1999a, 7, 57–62.

30. Sailer, B; Glombitza, K-W. Phlorethols and fucophlorethols from the brown alga Cystophora retroflexa. Phytochemistry1999b, 50, 869–881.

31. Glombitza, K-W; Koch, M; Eckhardt, G. Chlorierte phlorethole aus Laminaria ochroleuca. Phytochemistry 1977, 16, 796–798.

32. Glombitza, K-W; Schmidt, A. Nonhalogenated and halogenated phlorotannins from the brown alga Carpophyllum angustifolium. J Nat Prod 1999, 62, 1238–1240.

33. Glombitza, K-W; Zieprath, G. Phlorotannins of the brown alga Analipus japonicus. Planta Med 1989, 55(2), 171–175.

34. Green, D; Kashman, Y; Miroz, A. Colpol, a new cytotoxic C6-C4-C6 metabolite from the alga Colpomenia sinuosa. J Nat Prod 1993, 56, 1201–1202.

35. Waterman, PG; Mole, S. Analysis of phenolic plant metabolites; Blackwell Scientific Publications: Oxford, UK, 1994.

36. Arnold, TM; Targett, N. To grow and defend: lack of tradeoffs for brown algal phlototannins. Oikos 2003, 102, 406–408.

37. Amsler, CD; Fairhead, VA. Defensive and sensory chemical ecology of brown algae. Adv Bot Res 2006, 43, 1–73.

38. Berglin, M; Delage, L; Potin, P; Vilter, H; Elwing, H. Enzymatic cross-linking of a phenolic polymer extracted from the marine alga Fucus serratus. Biomacromolecules 2004, 5, 2376–2383.

39. Bitton, R; Berglin, M; Elwing, H; Colin, C; Delage, L; Potin, P; Bianco-Peled, H. The influence of halide-mediated oxidation on algae-born adhesives. Macromol Biosci 2007, 7, 1280–1289.

40. Ragan, MA; Jensen, A. Widespread distribution of sulfated polyphenols in brown algae. Phytochemistry 1979, 18, 261–262.

41. Todd, JS; Proteau, PJ; Gerwick, WH. Egregiachlorides A-C: new chlorinated oxylipins from the brown marine algaEgregia menziesii. Tetrahedron Lett 1993, 34, 7689–7692.

42. Kousaka, K; Ogi, N; Akazawa, Y; Fujieda, M; Yamamoto, Y; Takada, Y; Kimura, J. Novel oxylipin metabolites from the brown alga Eisenia bicyclis. J Nat Prod 2003, 66, 1318–1323.

43. Andreou, A; Brodhun, F; Feussner, I. Biosynthesis of oxylipins in non-mammals. Prog Lipid Res 2009, 48, 148–170.

44. Mercer, EI; Davies, CL. Description of chlorosulfolipids in algae. Phytochemistry 1979, 18, 457–462.

45. Parameswaran, PS; Bhat, KL; Das, B; Kamat, SY; Harnos, S. Halogenated terpenoids from the brown alga Padina tetrastromatica (Hauck). Indian J Chem Sect B 1994, 33, 1006–1008.

46. Arizumi, H; Hata, K; Shimizu, N. Isolation and determination of structure of antioxidant chromanol derivative fromAscophyllum nodosum. Jpn Kokkai Tokyo Koho 1994, 122, 160312.

47. Kladi, M; Vagias, C; Roussis, V. Volatile halogenated metabolites from marine red algae. Phytochem Rev 2004, 3, 337–366.

48. Kloareg, B; Quatrano, RS. Structure of the cell walls of marine algae and ecophysiological functions of the matrix polysaccharides. Oceanogr Mar Biol Ann Rev 1988, 26, 259–315.

49. Vaillancourt, FH; Yeh, E; Vosburg, DA; Garneau-Tsodikova, S; Walsh, CT. Nature's Inventory of Halogenation Catalysts: Oxidative Strategies Predominate. Chem Rev 2006, 106, 3364–3378.

50. Butler, A; Sandy, M. Mechanistic considerations of halogenating enzymes. Nature 2009, 460, 848–854.

51. Natalio, F; Humanes, M; Wever, R. Vanadium Haloperoxidases Versatile enzymes with multiple applications. Mar Drugs 2010. submitted.

52. Winter, JM; Moore, BS. Exploring the chemistry and biology of vanadium-dependant haloperoxidases. J Biol Chem2009, 284, 18577–18580.

53. Vilter, H. Peroxidases from Phaeophyceae: a vanadium (V)-dependent peroxidase from Ascophyllum nodosum.Phytochemistry 1984, 23, 1387–1390.

54. Weyand, MH; Hecht, HJ; Kiess, M; Liaud, MF; Vilter, H; Schomburg, D. X-ray structure determination of a vanadium-dependant haloperoxidase from Ascophyllum nodosum at 2.0 A resolution. J Biol Mol 1999, 293, 595–611.

55. Feiters, MC; Küpper, FC; Meyer-Klaucke, W. X-ray absorption spectroscopic studies on model compounds for biological iodine and bromine. J Synchrotron Radiat 2005, 12, 85–93.

56. Leblanc, C; Colin, C; Cosse, A; Delage, L; La Barre, S; Morin, P; Fiévet, B; Voiseux, C; Ambroise, Y; Verhaeghe, E; et al. Iodine transfers in the coastal marine environment: the key role of brown algae and of their vanadium-dependent haloperoxidases. Biochimie 2006, 88, 1773–1785.

57. Moore, RM; Groszko, W; Niven, SJ. Ocean-atmosphere exchange of methyl chloride: Results from NW Atlantic and Pacific Ocean studies. J Geophys Res 1996, 101, 28529–28538.

58. Bowler, C; Allen, AE; Badger, JH; Grimwood, J; Jabbari, K; Kuo, A; Maheswari, U; Martens, C; Maumus, F; Otillar, RP;et al. The Phaeodactylum genome reveals the evolutionary history of diatom genomes. Nature 2008, 456, 239–244.

59. Collén, J; Roeder, V; Rousvoal, S; Collin, O; Kloareg, B; Boyen, C. An expressed sequence tag analysis of thallus and regenerating protoplasts of Chondrus crispus (Gigartinales, Rhodophyceae). J Phycol 2006, 42, 104–112.

60. Colin, C; Leblanc, C; Michel, G; Wagner, E; Leize-Wagner, E; van Dorsselaer, A; Potin, P. Vanadium-dependent iodoperoxidases in Laminaria digitata, a novel biochemical function diverging from brown algal bromoperoxidases. J Biol Inorg Chem 2005, 10, 156–166.

61. Cosse, A; Potin, P; Leblanc, C. Patterns of gene expression induced by oligoguluronates reveal conserved and environment-specific molecular defense responses in the brown alga Laminaria digitata. New Phytol 2009, 182, 239–250.

62. Yotsukura, N; Nagai, K; Kimura, H; Morimoto, K. Seasonal changes in proteomic profiles of Japanese kelp Saccharina japonica (Laminariales, Phaeophyceae). J Appl Phycol 2010. [CrossRef]

63. Vreeland, V; Laetsch, WM. Adair, WS, Mecham, RP, Eds.; A gelling carbohydrate in algal cell wall formation. InOrganization and Assembly of Plant and Animal Extracellular Matrix; Academic Press: San Diego, CA, USA, 1990; pp. 137–171.

64. Vreeland, V; Epstein, L. Linskins, HF, Jackson, JF, Eds.; Analysis of plant-substratum adhesives. In Plant Cell Wall Analysis: Modern Methods of Plant Analysis; Springer-Verlag: Berlin, Germany, 1996; Volume 17, pp. 95–116.

65. Vreeland, V; Waite, JH; Epstein, L. Polyphenols and oxydases in substratum adhesion by marine algae and mussels. J Phycol 1998, 34, 1–8.

66. Ragan, MA; Glombitza, K-W. Phlorotannins, brown algal polyphenols. Progr Phycol Res 1986, 4, 129–241.

67. Bitton, R; Ben-Yehuda, M; Davidovich, M; Balazs, Y; Potin, P; Delage, L; Colin, C; Bianco-Peled, H. Structure of Algal-Born Phenolic Polymeric Adhesives. Macromol Biosci 2006, 7, 1280–1289.

68. Salgado, LT; Cinelli, LP; Viana, NB; Tomazetto de Carvalho, R; Mourão, P; Teixeira, VL; Farina, M; Amado Filho, GM. Vanadium bromoperoxidase catalyzes the formation of high-molecular-weight complexes between brown algal phenolic substances and alginates. J Phycol 2009, 45, 193–202.

69. Potin, P; Leblanc, C. Smith, AM, Callow, JA, Eds.; Phenolic-based adhesives of marine brown algae. In Biological Adhesives; Springer: Berlin, Germany, 2006; Volume Chapter 6, pp. 105–119.

70. Küpper, FC; Schweigert, N; Ar Gall, E; Legendre, J-M; Vilter, H; Kloareg, B. Iodine uptake in Laminariales involves extracellular, haloperoxidase-mediated oxidation of iodide. Planta 1998, 207, 163–167.

71. Kupper, FC; Carpenter, L; McFiggans, GB; Palmer, CJ, Waite, TJ; Boneberg, EM; Woitsch, S; Weiller, M; Abela, R; Grolimund, D; et al. Iodide accumulation provides kelp with an inorganic antioxidant impacting atmospheric chemistry. Proc Natl Acad Sci USA 2008, 105, 6954–6958.

72. Colin, C; Leblanc, C; Wagner, E; Delage, L; Leize-Wagner, E; van Dorsselaer, A; Kloareg, B; Potin, P. The brown algal kelp Laminaria digitata features distinct bromoperoxidase and iodoperoxidase activities. J Biol Chem 2003, 278, 23545–23552.

73. Connan, S; Delisle, F; Deslandes, E; Ar Gall, E. Intra-thallus phlorotannin content and antioxidant activity in Phaeophyceae of temperate waters. Bot Mar 2006, 49, 39–46.

74. Ar Gall, E; Küpper, FC; Kloareg, B. A survey of iodine contents in Laminaria digitata. Bot Mar 2004, 47, 30–37.

75. Lobban, CS; Harrison, PJ. Lobban, CS, Harrison, PJ, Eds.; Light and photosynthesis. In Seaweed Ecology and Physiology, 1st ed; Cambridge University Press: Cambridge, UK, 1994; pp. 151–153.

76. Lobban, C. Translocation of 14C in Macrocystis pyrifera (Giant Kelp). Plant Physiol 1978, 61, 585–589.

77. Manley, SL. Composition of sieve-tube sap from Macrocystis pyrifera (Phaeophyta) with emphasis on the inorganic constituents. J Phycol 1993, 19, 118–121.

78. Amat, MA; Srivastava, LM. Translocation of iodine in Laminaria saccharina (Phaeophyta). J Phycol 1985, 21, 330–333.

79. Palmer, CJ; Anders, TL; Carpenter, LJ; Küpper, FC; McFiggans, G. Iodine and halocarbon response of Laminaria digitata to oxidative stress and links to atmospheric new particle production. Environ Chem 2005, 2, 282–290.

80. Goulitquer, S; Ritter, A; Thomas, F; Ferec, C; Salaun, JP; Potin, P. Release of volatile aldehydes by the brown algal kelpLaminaria digitata in response to both biotic and abiotic stress. ChemBioChem 2009, 6, 977–982.

81. Carpenter, LJ; Sturges, WT; Liss, PS; Penkett, SA; Alicke, B; Hebestreit, K; Platt, U. Short lived alkyl-iodides and bromides at Mace Head: Links to macroalgal emission and halogen oxide formation. J Geophys Res 1999, 104, 1679.

82. Carpenter, LJ; Malin, G; Liss, PS; Küpper, FC. Novel biogenic iodine-containing trihalomethanes and other short-lived halocarbons in the coastal East Atlantic. Global Biogeochem Cycles 2000, 14, 1191–1204.

83. Hughes, C; Malin, G; Nightingale, PD; Liss, PS. The effect of light stress on the release of volatile iodocarbons by three species of marine microalgae. Limnol Oceanogr 2006, 51, 2849–2854.

84. Hughes, C; Malin, G; Turley, C; Keely, B; Nightingale, P; Liss, P. The production of volatile iodocarbons by biogenic marine aggregates. Limnol Oceanog 2008, 53, 867–872.

85. McFiggans, G; Coe, H; Burgess, R; Allan, J; Cubison, MR; Alfarra, MR; Saunders, R; Saiz-Lopez, A; Plane, JMC; Wevill, D; et al. Direct evidence for coastal iodine particles from Laminaria macroalgae - linkage to emissions of molecular iodine. Atm Chem Phys 2004, 4, 701–713.

86. O'Dowd, C; McFiggans, G; Creasey, DJ; Pirjola, L; Hoell, C; Smith, MH; Allan, BJ; Plane, JMC; Heard, DE; Lee, JD; et al. On the photochemical production of new particles in the coastal boundary layer. Geophys Res Lett 1999, 26, 1707–1710.

87. O'Dowd, CD; Jimenez, JL; Bahreini, R; Flagan, R; Seinfeld, JH; Hämeri, K; Pirjola, L; Kulmala, M; Jennings, SG; Hoffman, T. Marine aerosol formation from biogenic iodine emissions. Nature 2002, 417, 632–636.

88. Lee, JD; McFiggans, G; Allan, JD; Baker, AR; Ball, SM; Benton, AK; Carpenter, LJ; Commane, R; Finley, BD; Evans, M;et al. Iodine-mediated coastal particle formation: an overview of the Reactive

Halogens in the Marine Boundary Layer (RHaMBLe) Roscoff coastal study. Atmos Chem Phys Discuss 2009, 9, 26421–26489.

89. Mahajan, AS; Oetjen, H; Saiz-Lopez, A; Lee, JD; McFiggans, G; Plane, JMC. Reactive iodine species in a semi-polluted environment. Geophys Res Lett 2009, 36, L16803. [CrossRef]

90. Whalley, LK; Furneaux, KL; Gravestock, T; Atkinson, HM; Bale, CSE; Ingham, T; Bloss, WJ; Heard, DE. Detection of iodine monoxide radicals In the Marine Boundary Layer using laser induced fluorescence spectroscopy. J Atmos Chem2007, 58, 19–39.

91. Ball, SM; Hollingsworth, AM; Humbles, J; Leblanc, C; Potin, P; Langridge, JM; LeCrane, JP; McFiggans, G. Spectroscopic studies of molecular iodine emitted into the gas phase by seaweed. Atmos Chem Phys Discuss 2009, 9, 26329–26376.

92. Leigh, RJ; Ball, SM; Whitehead, J; Leblanc, C; Shillings, AJL; Mahajan, AS; Oetjen, H; Dorsey, JR; Gallagher, M; Jones, RL; et al. Measurements and modelling of molecular iodine emissions, transport and photodestruction in the coastal region around Roscoff. Atmos Chem Phys Discuss 2009, 9, 21165–21198.

93. Cainey, IM; Keywood, M; Bigg, EK; Grose, MR; Gillett, RW; Meyer, M. Flux chamber study of particle formation fromDurvillaea potatorum. Environ Chem 2007, 4, 151–154.

94. Almeida, M; Filipe, S; Humanes, M; Maia, MF; Melo, R; Severino, N; da Silva, JAL; Fraùsto da Silva, JJR; Wever, R. Vanadium haloperoxidases from brown algae of the Laminariaceae family. Phytochemistry 2001, 57, 633–642.

95. Krenn, BE; Tromp, MG; Wever, R. The brown alga Ascophyllum nodosum contains two different vanadium bromoperoxidases. J Biol Chem 1989, 264, 19287–92.

96. Carpenter, LJ. Iodine in the Marine Boundary Layer. Chem Rev 2003, 103, 4953–4962.

97. Kornprobst, J-M. Kornprobst, J-M, Ed.; Les ressources documentaires. In Substances Naturelles d'Origine Marine, 1st ed; Lavoisier Tech & Doc: Paris, France, 2005; Volume 1, pp. 89–101.

98. Carter-Franklin, J; Butler, A. Vanadium bromoperoxidase-catalyzed biosynthesis of halogenated marine natural products. J Am Chem Soc 2004, 126, 15060–15066.

99. Ten Brink, HB; Schoemaker, HE; Wever, R. Sulfoxidation mechanism of vanadium bromoperoxidase from Ascophyllum nodosum-evidence for direct oxygen transfer catalysis. Eur J Biochem 2001, 268, 132–138.

Chapter 5

The Skeletal Amino Acid Composition of the Marine Demosponge *Aplysina cavernicola*

Susanne Ueberlein [1], Susanne Machill [1], Hendrik Niemann [2], Peter Proksch [2] and Eike Brunner [1,*]

[1] *Bioanalytical Chemistry, TU Dresden, Dresden 01062, Germany*

[2] *Institute of Pharmaceutical Biology and Biotechnology, Heinrich Heine University Düsseldorf, Universitaetsstrasse 1, Geb. 26.23, Düsseldorf 40225, Germany*

ABSTRACT

It has been discovered during the past few years that demosponges of the order Verongida such as *Aplysina cavernicola* exhibit chitin-based skeletons. Verongida sponges are well known to produce bioactive brominated tyrosine derivatives. We could recently demonstrate that brominated compounds do not exclusively occur in the cellular matrix but also in the skeletons of the marine sponges *Aplysina cavernicola* and *Ianthella basta*. Our measurements imply that these yet unknown compounds are strongly, possibly covalently bound to the sponge skeletons. In the present work, we determined the skeletal amino acid composition of the demosponge *A. cavernicola* especially with respect to the presence of halogenated amino acids. The investigations of the skeletons before and after MeOH extraction confirmed that only a small amount of the brominated skeleton-bound compounds dissolves in MeOH. The main part of the brominated compounds is strongly attached to the skeletons but can be extracted for example by using $Ba(OH)_2$. Various halogenated tyrosine derivatives were identified by GC-MS and LC-MS in these $Ba(OH)_2$ extracts of the skeletons.

Keywords: demosponges; skeletons; amino acid composition; halogenated amino acids; GC-MS; LC-MS

1. INTRODUCTION

Sponges (*Porifera*) belong to the oldest *Metazoans* and are the simplest animals on earth [1,2]. Although they do not possess morphological defense strategies, these sessile filter feeders successfully withstand the attacks of predators, as well as overgrowth by fouling organisms or bacterial infections. This evolutionary success is mainly due to an effective chemical defense based on deterrent, cytotoxic and/or antibiotically active compounds [3,4,5,6].

Sponges possess a skeleton which consists of a composite of natural biomaterials containing organic constituents and/or inorganic compounds. One function of these skeletons is mechanical support, that means the prevention of the collapse of the sponge body [7,8]. Furthermore, the skeletons seem to play a role in the protection against predators. For example, Hill*et al.* showed that the sponge *Anthosigmella varians* increases the spicule concentration during the attack of predators [9,10].

Based on the skeletal composition, the phylum *Porifera* is divided into three classes: Calcareous sponges (*Calcarea*), glass sponges (*Hexactinellida*), and demosponges (*Demospongia*) [11]. Demosponges form the largest class and possess a skeleton made of a composite material with different organic compounds like proteins [12] and polysaccharides [13,14]. They can also contain siliceous spicules [11,15]. The skeletons of three taxonomic orders of demosponges (Dendroceratida, Dictyoceratida, Verongida) are characterized by the lack of siliceous spicules. Instead, their skeletons contain spongin, a collagenous protein [16].

Until now, the chemical composition of spongin has not been exactly defined. Gross *et al.* isolated two morphologically distinct forms of spongin described as "spongin A" and "spongin B" [17]. Spongin fibers are more resistant than collagen fibers against enzymatic digestion [18]. Today, spongin is characterized as a halogenated protein [16]. Ehrlich *et al.*demonstrated recently that the polysaccharide chitin is an integral part of the skeleton of different demosponges of the order Verongida [13,14,19]. So far, chitin could be found in the skeletons of the genus *Aplysina* [13,19], in the skeletons of*Verongula gigantea* [19], *Ianthella basta* [14], and the freshwater demosponge *Spongilla lacustris* [20]. Moreover, chitin could be isolated from a million year old fossil of the basal demosponge *Vauxia gracilenta* [21].

It is unknown yet how the organic components such as proteins (spongin) are connected with the chitin in sponge skeletons [16]. However, there is a variety of examples in nature showing that proteins are strongly bound to chitin. For example, Hackman suggested that proteins are covalently bound to chitin in different insects and crustacea [22]. Blackwell*et al.* developed a model for the three-dimensional structure of an insect chitin-protein complex with chitin fibrils surrounded by layers of proteins [23].

Furthermore, Verongida sponges such as *A. cavernicola* are well-known for the biosynthesis of brominated tyrosine derivatives—characteristic bioactive natural products [24,25]. Up to now it has remained unclear whether these compounds are exclusively present in the cellular matrix or whether they may also be incorporated into the chitin-based skeletons. Earlier investigations showed that aerothionin, a typical brominated tyrosine-derivative, is present in the spherulous cells of the marine sponge *Aplysina fistularis* [26]. Another earlier report demonstrated that the brominated compounds are localized also in the skeletal fibers of the demosponge *Aplysina aerophoba* [27]. We recently demonstrated that brominated compounds occur not exclusively in the cellular matrix but also in the skeletons of the marine sponges *A. cavernicola* and *I. basta*. The bromine content of the skeletons of these sponges was measured by quantitative potentiometric titration. A MeOH treatment only resulted in the removal of rather insignificant amounts of bromine. It was therefore concluded that these yet unknown brominated compounds are strongly, possibly covalently bound to the chitin-based sponge skeletons [28]. The structure and composition of these compounds is yet unknown. One possibility could be a covalent incorporation of halogenated amino acids into the skeletons.

Until now the pure skeletal amino acid composition of the chitin-containing Verongida sponges has been completely unknown since only the amino acid compositions of the commercial unbleached sponge *Hippospongia equina* and of the bath sponge *Spongia officinalis obliqua* which both belong to the order Dictyoceratida have been investigated [29,30]. The analyses of these sponges indicated that not only proteinogenic amino acids but also halogenated tyrosines occur in these sponges. Iodated tyrosines were found in *Hippospongia equina* [29], while iodated as well as brominated tyrosines could be detected in *Spongia officinalis obliqua* [30].

In contrast to these previous studies, the goal of the present study was to examine the pure skeletal amino acid composition of the Verongida sponge *A. cavernicola*, especially with respect to halogenated compounds. We therefore isolated the sponge skeletons as described previously [28]. Furthermore, we developed a method to analyze the amino acid composition of the skeletons. In order to evaluate the influence of the established MeOH extraction upon the skeletal amino acid composition, the sponge skeletons were studied before and after MeOH extraction. MeOH is widely used for the extraction of bioactive natural products like aerothionin [31]. In addition, the MeOH extract was analyzed in order to identify possible MeOH-extractable soluble components.

2. RESULTS AND DISCUSSION

2.1. Examination of the Skeletons by SEM

The morphology of the isolated sponge skeletons before and after MeOH treatment was studied by scanning electron microscopy (SEM) (Figure 1). The SEM image of the isolated skeletons before MeOH treatment shows a skeletal fiber network system with network fibers composed of concentric multilayers. The core channel of these fibers is filled with a porous material, a pith. The SEM images of the skeletons after MeOH extraction show the same network of fibers with concentric multilayered channels. However, the porous core material is removed by the MeOH treatment showing that this material is only loosely attached to the inner layer surface. This MeOH-soluble pith material represents only 1.4% of the total mass of the isolated sponge skeleton.

Moreover, subsequent energy dispersive X-ray spectroscopy (EDX) measurements show that bromine, chlorine, and iodine are present in the skeletons before as well as after MeOH extraction (see supporting information Figures S1 and S2). This is in line with our aforementioned hypothesis that halogenated compounds are tightly attached/covalently bound to the sponge skeletons.

2.2. Amino Acid Extraction, Selection of the Derivatization Agent and the Internal Standard for GC-MS

Alkaline extraction of pure chitin scaffolds from marine sponges using NaOH as previously described by Ehrlich *et al.*[19] leads to a degradation and removal of all other skeleton-associated or incorporated biomolecules such as brominated tyrosine-derivatives or proteins like spongin—but leaves the chitin undissolved. The proteins are hydrolyzed, e.g., disintegrated into their amino acids by this treatment. These extracts, however, contain a huge amount of NaOH which interferes with the further analytical procedure. In order to circumvent this problem, a saturated $Ba(OH)_2$ solution was used as extracting and hydrolyzing agent. Subsequently it was investigated whether the $Ba(OH)_2$ treatment had the same effect as the NaOH treatment. ATR-

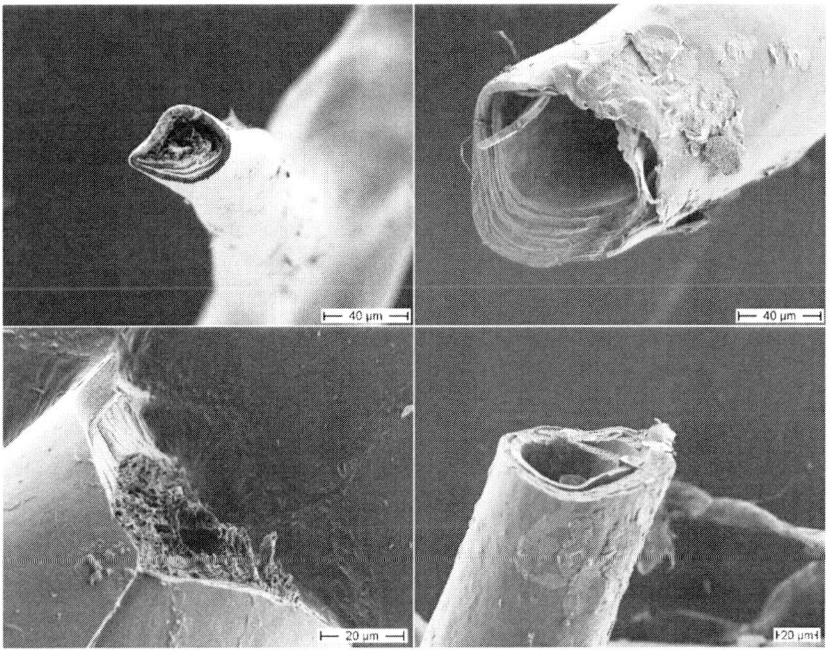

Figure 1. Scanning electron microscopy (SEM) images of the skeletons of *A. cavernicola*before MeOH extraction (left) and after MeOH extraction (right), scale bars: 40 µm (top), 20 µm (bottom).

FTIR measurements (Figure 2) and microscopic studies (Figure 3) show that the $Ba(OH)_2$ as well as the NaOH extraction lead to the removal of all other organic material (cf. [28]) apart from the pure chitin scaffolds. The remaining chitin represents 8.0% ± 1.4% of the mass of the isolated sponge skeleton. In contrast to NaOH, however, the $Ba(OH)_2$ extract can be easily neutralized by adding H_2SO_4. The resulting $BaSO_4$ forms a precipitate which is separated by centrifugation whereas the extracted amino acids and other soluble compounds remain in the supernatant. After freeze drying, these extracted compounds can be identified by gas chromatography-mass spectrometry (GC-MS). The latter technique requires a preceding derivatization of the compounds.

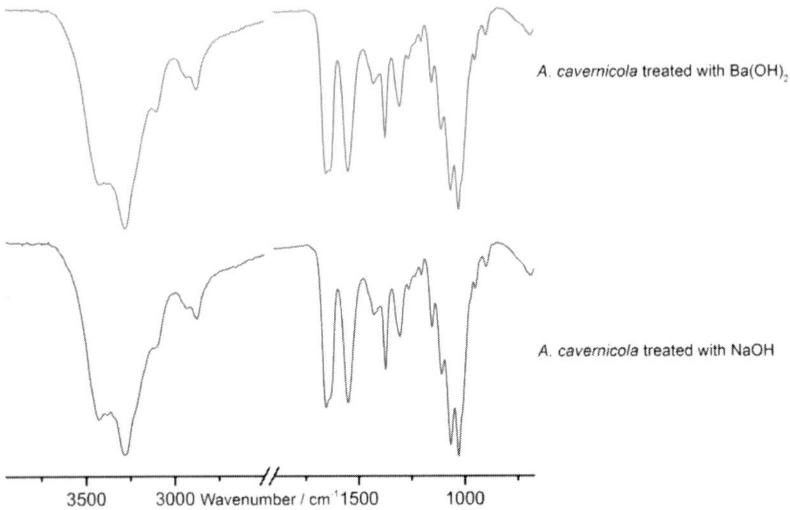

Figure 2. Attenuated total reflectance infrared (ATR-IR) spectra of the purified chitin-scaffolds of *A. cavernicola* after $Ba(OH)_2$ and NaOH treatment.

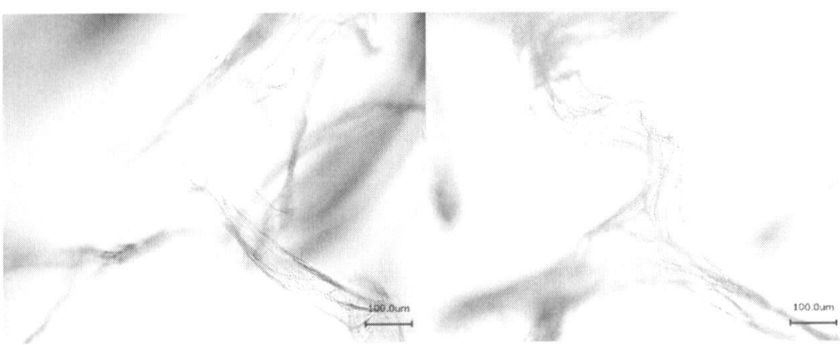

Figure 3. Light microscopic images of the purified chitin-scaffolds of *A. cavernicola*after $Ba(OH)_2$ (left) and NaOH treatment (right); scale bars: 100 μm.

For this purpose, the derivatization agent *N*-*tert*-butyldimethylsilyl-*N*-methyltrifluoroacetamide (MTBSTFA) containing 1% *tert*-butyldimethylchlorosilane (TBDMSCl) was selected since *tert*-butyldimethylsilyl (TBDMS) derivatives of amino acids are more stable than the traditional trimethylsilyl (TMS) derivatives [32]. The amino acids were identified based on their mass spectra and—If available—By comparison with standards. Therefore, the relative retention times of the amino acids found in the extract were compared with the pure reference compounds (standards). The compound 5-Bromotryptophan was selected as an internal standard due to its similarity with the halogenated compounds found in the skeletons, *i.e.*, the brominated aromatic ring system. This internal standard shows two GC-signals due to different degrees of derivatization (first peak: two TBDMS groups; second peak: three TBDMS groups).

2.3. GC-MS Analysis of the Skeletal Amino Acid Composition

2.3.1. Skeletal Amino Acid Composition before MeOH Extraction

The isolated skeletons [28] of the demosponge *A. cavernicola* were treated with a saturated $Ba(OH)_2$ solution and derivatized using MTBSTFA as described in Section 2.2 and in the Experimental Section. The GC-MS measurements of the isolated *A. cavernicola* sponge skeletons show the presence of various amino acids (see Table 1 and Figure 4).

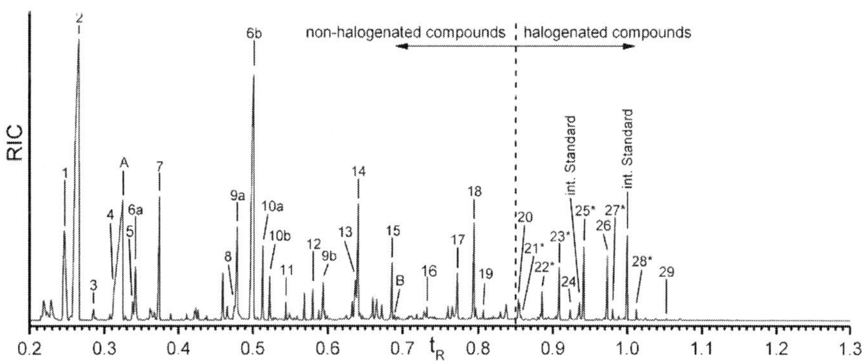

Figure 4. Gas chromatogram of the $Ba(OH)_2$ extract of the isolated *A. cavernicola* sponge skeletons before MeOH treatment. The relative retention time is related to the second peak of the internal standard. Components with * could not be verified with pure standards due to the lack of availability of these reference compounds.

Table 1. Amino acids detected in the $Ba(OH)_2$ extract of isolated *A. cavernicola* sponge skeletons before MeOH treatment. Components with * could not be verified with pure standards due to the lack of availability of these reference compounds.

Peak	*tert*-Butyldimethylsilyl (TBDMS)-Derivative	Proteinogenic	Halogenated
1	Alanine	X	
2	Glycine	X	
3	α-Aminobutyric Acid (AABA)		
4	Valine	X	
A	Urea		
5	Leucine	X	
6a	Serine (2 TBDMS)	X	
7	Proline	X	
8	Oxoproline		
9a	Hydroxyproline (2 TBDMS)		
6b	Serine (3 TBDMS)	X	
10a	Threonine (3 TBDMS)	X	
10b	Threonine (3 TBDMS)	X	
11	Phenylalanine	X	
12	Aspartic Acid	X	
9b	Hydroxyproline (3 TBDMS)		
13	Glutamic Acid	X	
14	Ornithine		
15	Lysine	X	
B	Aerothionin or its derivatives		
16	Arginine	X	
17	Histidine	X	
18	Tyrosine	X	
19	Tryptophan	X	
20	3-Monochlorotyrosine		X
21*	Monobromohistidine		X
22*	Monobromotyrosine		X
23*	Dichlorotyrosine		X
24	3-Monoiodotyrosine		X
25*	Monobromo-monochlorotyrosine		X
26	3,5-Dibromotyrosine		X
27*	Monochloro-monoiodotyrosine		X
28*	Monobromo-monoiodotyrosine		X
29	3,5-Diiodotyrosine		X

Nineteen different non-halogenated amino acids elute below a relative retention time of t_R = 0.85. Fifteen of them are proteinogenic amino acids. Several amino acids give rise to multiple peaks. Serine (peaks 6a, 6b) and hydroxyproline (peaks 9a, 9b) exhibit two signals due to different degrees of derivatization. Threonine (peaks 10a, 10b) yields two peaks for the same TBDMS derivative in the extracts as well as in the standard. Due to the existence of two stereocenters, threonine (peaks 10a, 10b) exhibits two different diastereomers [33] which can be separated by gas chromatography.

The largest peaks in the chromatogram are due to glycine (peak 2) and serine (peaks 6a, 6b). Moreover, proline (peak 7), threonine (peaks 10a, 10b), and tyrosine (peak 18) occur in larger quantities, while aspartic acid (peak 12), glutamic acid (peak 13), lysine (peak 15), and histidine (peak 17) occur in smaller amounts only. Leucine (peak 5), phenylalanine (peak 11), arginine (peak 16), and tryptophan (peak 19) exhibit the smallest concentrations. The amount of valine (peak 4) cannot be determined exactly due to the overlap with the urea peak. Nevertheless, an evaluation of specific ion tracks belonging to valine is possible and indicates a low concentration. Furthermore, the non-proteinogenic amino acids α-aminobutyric acid (peak 3), oxoproline (peak 8), hydroxyproline (peaks 10a, 10b), and ornithine (peak 14) can be identified. Measurements of the arginine standard treated with $Ba(OH)_2$ under the same conditions as the skeletons reveal that one part of arginine is cracked into urea (peak A) and ornithine by the alkaline treatment. This leads to the assumption that the detected amount of urea in the $Ba(OH)_2$ extracts of the sponge skeletons may arise from the $Ba(OH)_2$ treatment of arginine. However, the comparison of the arginine/ornithine and arginine/urea ratios in the standard and the sample of the skeletons (see Table 2) reveal that the relative amounts of ornithine and urea related to arginine are larger in the $Ba(OH)_2$ extract of the sponge skeletons than in the standard. This leads to the assumption that urea and ornithine are indeed present in the sponge skeletons and are not just artefacts of the $Ba(OH)_2$ treatment.

Table 2. Comparison of the arginine/ornithine and arginine/urea ratios calculated for the standard and the skeleton sample before MeOH treatment.

Sample	Arginine/Ornithine Proportion	Arginine/Urea Proportion
Standard: arginine after Ba(OH)2	1:2.6	1:1.1
Ba(OH)2 extract of sponge skeletons before MeOH	1:8.8	1:9.1

Ten halogenated amino acids elute at relative retention times larger than 0.85. Interestingly, nine of them are tyrosine derivatives. Monohalogenated (e.g., monobromotyrosine (peak 22*)), dihalogenated (e.g., dichlorotyrosine (peak 23*)) as well as mixed halogenated (e.g., monobromo-monoiodotyrosine (peak 28*)) tyrosine occur. Only one halogenated derivative of another amino acid is identified, a monobrominated histidine (peak 21*). Dichlorotyrosine (peak 23*), monobromo-monochlorotyrosine (peak 25*), and 3,5-dibromotyrosine (peak 26) represent the most abundant halogenated amino acids. Monobromotyrosine (peak 22*) also occurs at relatively high concentration. The other halogenated amino acids occur only in small amounts.

Due to the lack of pure standard compounds, most of the halogenated amino acids were identified by their electon impact (EI) mass spectra. Figure 5 shows the EI mass spectra of the TBDMS derivatives of tyrosine and various halogenated tyrosines. The theoretical molecular weights of the expected compounds were calculated and compared with the experimentally observed fragmentation patterns in the mass spectra. Usually, the molecular ion peak is very weak or missing. The same is true for the (M-15) peak caused by the loss of a methyl group. Nevertheless, the spectra provide characteristic fragments. In particular, the (M-57) peak due to the loss of a *tert*-butyl group of the TBDMS group is intense in all spectra and can be used to determine the molecular weight of the respective compound. Furthermore, the peaks due to the loss of a *tert*-butyl group and a CO group (M-85) as well as of a CO-O-TBDMS group (M-159) are characteristic and intense. The base peak at *m/z* 302 is due to the [TBDMS-NH-CH-CO-O-TBDMS]$^+$-ion representing the backbone of each amino acid.

Brominated and chlorinated compounds could be easily identified by the characteristic isotope patterns due to the presence of two abundant isotopes. Bromine naturally occurs as ^{79}Br and ^{81}Br with relative abundances of approximately 1:1. Chlorine occurs as ^{35}Cl and ^{37}Cl with relative abundances of approximately 3:1. This results in characteristic isotope peaks with a mass difference of two mass units [34].

Measurements of a mixture of the standards tyrosine, 3-monoiodotyrosine, 3,5-diiodotyrosine and 3,5-dibromotyrosine treated with $Ba(OH)_2$ following the protocol as for the sponge skeletons reveal that the $Ba(OH)_2$ treatment has no influence on the structure of the halogenated tyrosines. The GC-MS data show that the $Ba(OH)_2$ treatment did not cause any chemical transformation of the amino acids. It can, therefore, be assumed that all detected tyrosine derivatives occur in the native sponge skeletons.

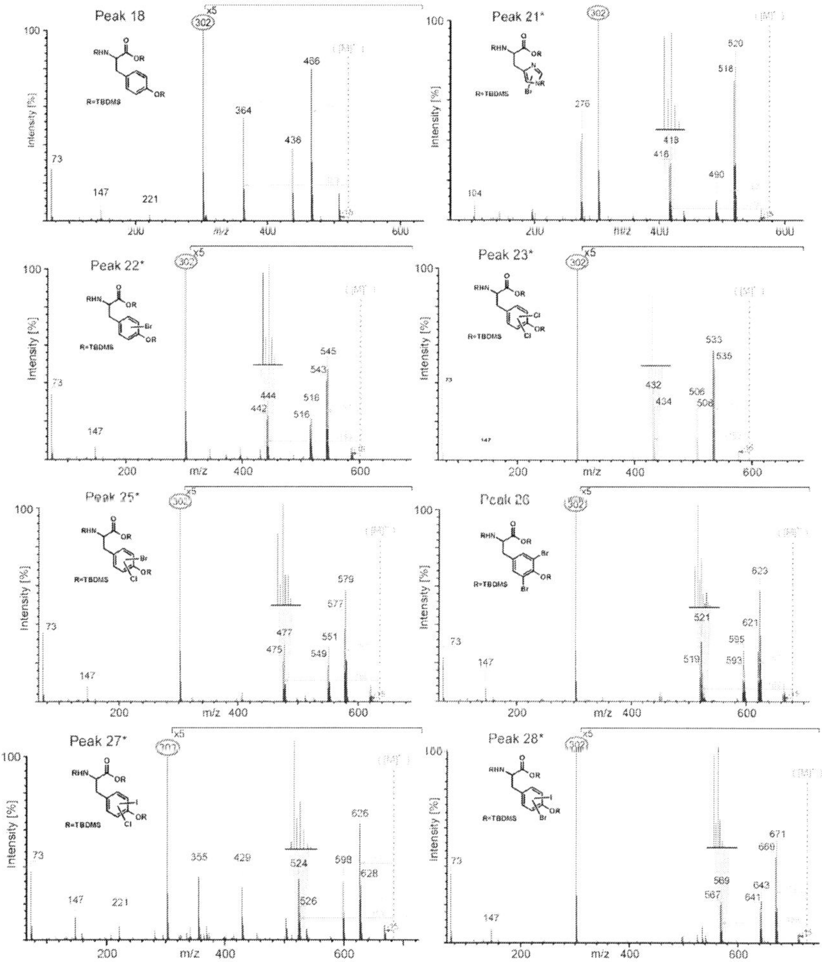

Figure 5. Electron impact (EI)-MS data of TBDMS-derivatives of tyrosine (peak 18), monobromohistidine (peak 21*), monobromotyrosine (peak 22*), dichlorotyrosine (peak 23*), monobromo-monochlorotyrosine (peak 25*), 3,5-dibromotyrosine (peak 26), monochloro-monoiodotyrosine (peak 27*) and monobromo-monoiodotyrosine (peak 28*).

The comparison of the observed amino acid composition of *A. cavernicola* with the known amino acid compositions of different sponges shows a general agreement—but also some characteristic differences. The results of these investigations are summarized in Table 3. The extraction of the amino acids from *Hippospongia equina* [29] and the bath sponge *Spongia officinalis obliqua* [30] was also based on an alkaline solution of $Ba(OH)_2$, *i.e.*, the data are well comparable. The observed differences in the amino acid compositions may be related to the fact that both, *H. equina* and the bath sponge, belong to the order Dictyoceratida. In contrast, *A. cavernicola* belongs to the order Verongida.

Table 3. Comparison of the found amino acids with the known amino acid composition of spongin from the literature.

Amino Acids (AAs)	Present Work	AAs in *Hippospongia equina* [29]	AAs in Spongia *Officinalis obliqua* [30]
α-Aminobutyric Acid (AABA)	X		X
γ-Aminobutyric Acid (GABA)		X	
Alanine	X	X	X
Arginine	X	X	
Aspartic Acid	X	X	X
Cystine		X	
Glutamic Acid	X	X	X
Glycine	X	X	X
Histidine	X	X	
Hydroxyproline	X	X	X
Leucine	X	X	X
Lysine	X	X	X
Methionine			X
Ornithine	X	X	
Oxoproline	X		
Phenylalanine	X	X	
Proline	X	X	X
Serine	X	X	
Threonine	X	X	
Tryptophan	X	X	X
Tyrosine	X	X	X
Valine	X	X	X
Monobromohistidine	X		
Monobromotyrosine	X		
3-Monochlorotyrosine	X		
3-Monoiodotyrosine	X		X
Monochloro-monoiodotyrosine	X		
Monobromo-monochlorotyrosine	X		
Monobromo-monoiodotyrosine	X		
Dichlorotyrosine	X		
3,5-Dibromotyrosine	X		X
3,5-Diiodotyrosine	X	X	X

The most striking difference between the amino acid composition of the *A. cavernicola* skeleton and the amino acid compositions described in the literature is the presence of various halogenated amino acids in the *A. cavernicola* sponge skeletons. In particular, the halogenated amino acids monobromotyrosine (peak 22*), monobromo-monochlorotyrosine (peak 25*), 3-monochlorotyrosine (peak 20), dichlorotyrosine (peak 23*), monochloro-monoiodotyrosine (peak 27*), and monobromohistidine (peak 21*) do not occur in *H. equina* and *S. officinalis obliqua*. However, the naturally occurring amino acid monobromo-monochlorotyrosine could already be isolated from the gastropod mollusk *Buccinum undatum* [35]. In addition, the occurrence of AABA (peak 3) or GABA seems to depend on the taxonomy of the investigated sponges. Alanine (peak 1), aspartic acid (peak 12), glutamic acid (peak 13), glycine (peak 2), leucine (peak 5), lysine (peak 15), proline (peak 7), tryptophan (peak 19), tyrosine (peak 18), valine (peak 4) as well as the halogenated amino acid diiodotyrosine (peak 29) are found in both *A. cavernicola* skeletons and the dictyoceratid sponges *H. equina* and *S. officinalis obliqua*. The identified amino acids α-aminobutyric acid (peak 3), hydroxyproline (peaks 9a, 9b), oxoproline (peak 8), and ornithine (peak 14) were also detected previously in *H. equina* and *S. officinalis obliqua*. Both α-aminobutyric acid and hydroxyproline are present in the bath sponge *Spongia officinalis obliqua* [35]. Ornithine and oxoproline were found in *Aplysina aerophoba* [36].

Furthermore, the $Ba(OH)_2$ extract of the skeletons was examined with respect to the presence of aerothionin—one major bromotyrosine derivative found in the MeOH extracts of *A. cavernicola* skeletons [28]. Therefore, a standard of aerothionin was derivatized and measured by GC-MS. This measurement shows that aerothionin causes different GC peaks due to the decomposition into smaller fragments during GC injection. In comparison, only the degradation product at t_R = 0.69 (Peak B in Figure 4) can be found in the $Ba(OH)_2$ extract of the skeletons. The retention time, as well as the fragmentation pattern of peak B, are consistent with those of the aerothionin standard. The mass spectrum of this fragment of the standard is shown in the Supplementary Information (Figure S3). Based on the very small intensity of the peak and the lack of the other peaks observed in the standard it can be assumed that aerothionin only occurs in trace amounts. Since other aerothionin derivatives like homoaerothionin, 11-oxoaerothionin, or isofistularin-3 could cause the same fragment occurring at t_R = 0.69 due to their similar structure, it is not clear whether this peak represents aerothionin only. Its derivatives may also be present as minority components.

2.3.2. Skeletal Amino Acid Composition after MeOH Extraction

The relative amount of each amino acid after MeOH treatment was compared to the amount present before MeOH treatment.

Therefore, all intensities (peak heights) were normalized to the sample weight and the total intensity of both peaks of the internal standard. The comparison of the intensities of each amino acid before and after MeOH treatment enables the estimation of the decrease due to the MeOH extraction. The results are summarized in Table 4.

The comparison of the GC-MS data of the skeletons after MeOH extraction (Figure 6) with the GC-MS data of the skeletons before MeOH treatment reveals some differences. All amino acids found in the $Ba(OH)_2$ extract of the skeletons before MeOH extraction are present. However, their relative amounts have changed. That means, MeOH selectively reduces the amount of several amino acids. Interestingly, the largest decreases are observed for the proteinogenic amino acids. This leads to the assumption that either free amino acids or small proteins/peptides which are not tightly bound to the skeletons are removed by the MeOH extraction.

In particular, the amount of threonine (peaks 10a, 10b) decreases very strongly. The amounts of AABA (peak 3), valine (peak 4), leucine (peak 5), phenylalanine (peak 11), aspartic acid (peak 12), and histidine (peak 17) also reduced considerably. For serine (peaks 6a, 6b), the decrease is different for the two TBDMS derivatives. The derivative with two TBDMS groups (incomplete derivatization) shows almost no decrease whereas the derivative with three TBDMS groups exhibits a medium decrease. This means, the total serine amount is slightly reduced. The same phenomenon is observed for hydroxyproline (peaks 9a, 9b). The amount of the derivative with three TBDMS groups strongly decreases whereas the amount of the derivative with two TBDMS groups (incomplete derivatization) only shows a medium decrease.

Table 4. Changes of the detected amounts of amino acids after MeOH extraction in comparison with the amounts before MeOH extraction. An average experimental error of approximately 15% is estimated (see Supplementary Information, Table S1).

TBDMS-Derivative	Decrease [1]
Alanine	+
Glycine	++
α-Aminobutyric Acid (AABA)	+++
Valine	+++
Leucine	+++
Serine (2 TBDMS)	−
Proline	++
Oxoproline	+
Hydroxyproline (2 TBDMS)	++
Serine (3 TBDMS)	++
Threonine (3 TBDMS)	++++
Threonine (3 TBDMS)	++++
Phenylalanine	+++
Aspartic Acid	+++
Hydroxyproline (3 TBDMS)	+++
Glutamic Acid	−
Ornithine	++
Lysine	++
Arginine	++
Histidine	+++
Tyrosine	+
Tryptophan	+
3-Monochlorotyrosine	−
Monobromohistidine	++
Monobromotyrosine	+
Dichlorotyrosine	−
3-Monoiodotyrosine	−
Monobromo-Monochlorotyrosine	−
3,5-Dibromotyrosine	−
Monochloro-Monoiodotyrosine	−
Monobromo-Monoiodotyrosine	−
3,5-Diiodotyrosine	−

[1] ++++ very strong decrease (residual content of 0%–25%); +++ strong decrease (residual content of 26%–50%); ++ medium decrease (residual content of 51%–75%); + weak decrease (residual content of more than 75%); − no decrease (residual 100% ± 15%).

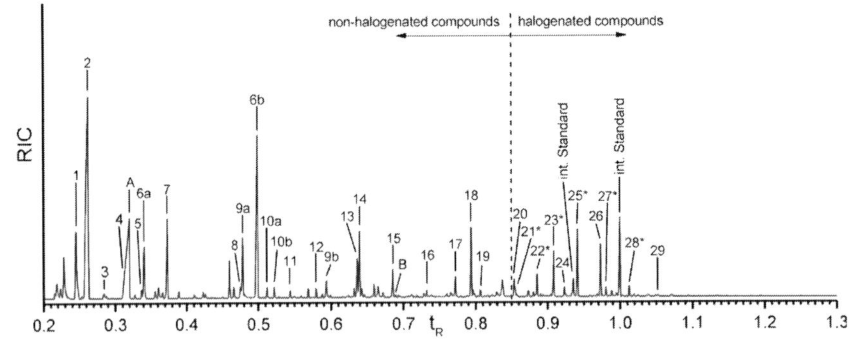

Figure 6. Gas chromatogram of the amino acids in the isolated *A. cavernicola* sponge skeletons after MeOH treatment. Retention time is the relative retention time based on the second peak of the internal standard. Components with * could not be verified with standards. Numbering of the peaks is as in Table 1.

In contrast, the halogenated amino acids do not show a pronounced reduction, except for monobromohistidine (peak 21*). This observation leads to the conclusion that the halogenated tyrosines are strongly bound to the skeletons and confirms our hypothesis that halogenated molecules are tightly attached/covalently bound to the sponge skeleton.

Remarkably, traces of aerothionin or its derivatives can also be found in the skeletons after MeOH treatment. The identification was carried out as for the skeletons before MeOH treatment. This means, traces of such compounds are also incorporated into the skeletons of *A. cavernicola*. Also in this case, the retention time and the fragmentation pattern of peak B are consistent with those of the aerothionin standard.

2.3.3. Analysis of the MeOH Extract

In the MeOH extracts, different non-halogenated amino acids could be detected by GC-MS. The detected amino acids were: alanine, glycine, valine, leucine, proline, serine, tyrosine, and 3,5-diiodotyrosine. Interestingly, threonine which was effectively removed by MeOH extraction is not detected in the MeOH extract. That means, a significant amount of the extracted molecules must be present in the form of peptides or smaller proteins—which will not be detected by the applied analytical method. Furthermore, aerothionin or its derivatives can be found in the MeOH extract, which confirms our previous results [28]. The identification was carried out as in the skeletons before MeOH treatment. The retention time and the fragmentation pattern of the found aerothionin fragment are consistent with those of the aerothionin standard. The mass spectrum of the found Aerothionin fragment is shown in the Supplementary Information (Figure S4).

2.4. LC-MS Analysis of the Skeletal Amino Acid Composition

2.4.1. Skeletal Amino Acid Composition before MeOH Extraction

In addition to the GC-MS measurements, an on-line LC-ESI-MS analysis was performed with the skeleton extract resulting from the $Ba(OH)_2$ treatment. The focus of these measurements was placed on the verification of the presence of halogenated tyrosines. Since most of the other amino acids elute within the injection peak, they could not be determined via LC-MS. Apart from aliphatic hydroxyproline, ornithine, and arginine, the pseudo-molecular ions ($[M + H]^+$) of aromatic tryptophan, phenylalanine, and tyrosine were detected (data not shown). For tyrosine, different halogenated derivatives were identified within the (+)-ion trace as shown in Figure 7. For monobromo-, 3,5-dibromo-, 3-monoiodo-, and 3,5-diiodotyrosine the identity of the skeleton constituents was established via retention time and mass spectra comparison with native standards as demonstrated in Figure 8. In addition, the corresponding $[M + H]^+$-ions of mono- and dichloro-, as well as the mixed halogenated monobromo-monochloro-, monobromo-monoiodo- and monochloro-monoiodotyrosine were detected (spectra see Supplementary Information Figure S5).

2.4.2. Skeletal Amino Acid Composition after MeOH Extraction

In analogy to 2.4.1, the $Ba(OH)_2$ extracts of the skeletons after MeOH treatment were also analyzed by LC-MS. The halogenated tyrosines found before MeOH treatment remained present after extraction with the organic solvent (spectra see Supplementary Information Figure S6). Moreover, the MeOH extract of the *A. cavernicola* skeleton was also analyzed via LC-MS. A specific search for the pseudo-molecular ions of all the halogenated amino acids found in the $Ba(OH)_2$ extracts was performed. None of the halogenated tyrosines identified in the $Ba(OH)_2$ extracts were detectable in the MeOH extract. These observations confirm the aforementioned results of GC-MS (Subsections 2.3.1 and 2.3.2) which demonstrated that the halogenated tyrosines are strongly attached or incorporated into the skeletons.

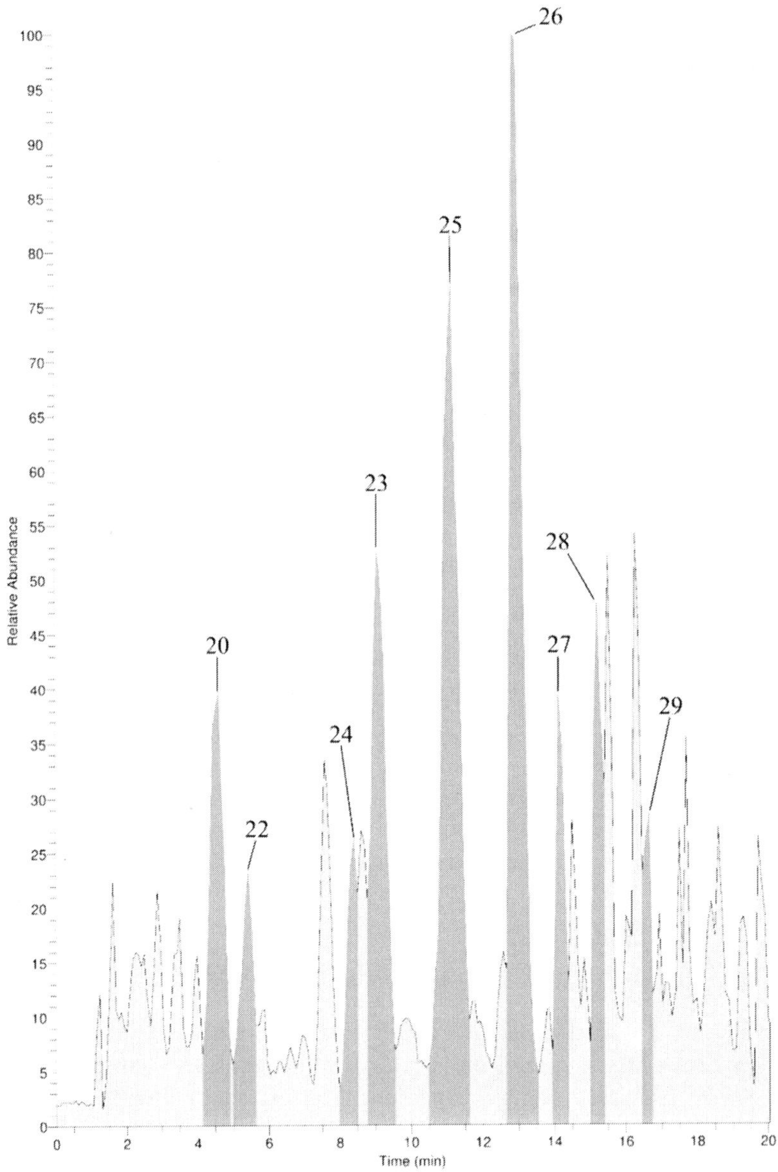

Figure 7. (+)-Ion trace of LC-MS analysis of the $Ba(OH)_2$-extract prior MeOH extraction. Dark grey peaks correspond to halogenated tyrosines. Numbering refers toTable 1.

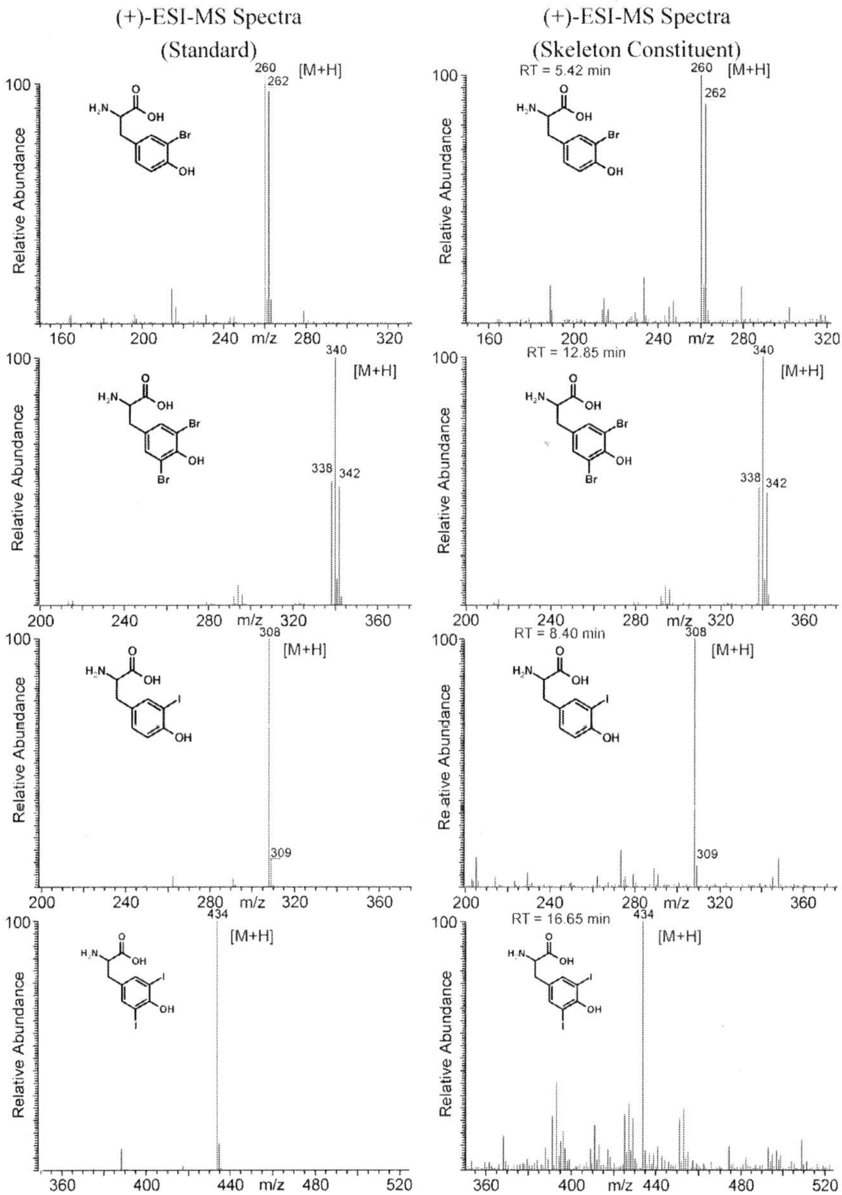

Figure 8. Structures and corresponding LC-ESI-MS spectra of brominated and iodinated tyrosine derivatives obtained from native standards and skeleton constituents of *A. cavernicola.*

3. EXPERIMENTAL SECTIONS

3.1. Sponge Samples

The *A. cavernicola* samples were collected in the Mediterranean Sea by the Hydra-Institute at Elba, Italy [37] and purchased from the Hydra Institut für Meereswissenschaften AG (Munich, Germany). After underwater collection the sponge samples were shock frozen. The samples were transported and stored on dry ice.

3.2. Extraction of the Skeletons

3.2.1. Isolation of the Skeleton

A. cavernicola skeletons were isolated from the sponge samples following the protocol described previously [28]. Approximately 10 g of the wet sponge were soaked in 40 mL of TE100 (10 mM Tris-HCl, 100 mM EDTA, pH 8). After two weeks, the remaining skeletons were washed in distilled water for 24 h under continuous shaking. The washing procedure was repeated six times.

3.2.2. MeOH Extraction of the Skeletons

The MeOH extraction of the purified skeletons was performed with methanol and acetonitrile as described previously [28]. The isolated skeletons were transferred into 200 mL methanol and sonicated for 1 min. After 24 h, the solvent was renewed and the samples were stirred for a further 24 h. Afterwards one extraction cycle was performed in 200 mL acetonitrile. The extracted skeletons were freeze-dried. The extracts were combined and dried under a gentle stream of nitrogen.

3.2.3. $Ba(OH)_2$ Extraction

Thirty mg of each dried isolated skeleton before and after MeOH extraction was treated with 15 mL of saturated $Ba(OH)_2$solution containing 0.5 mg 5-bromotryptophan as internal standard at 37 °C for 6 days. Subsequently, the insoluble residue (chitin-fibers) was removed and the $Ba(OH)_2$ solution was neutralized with H_2SO_4 and centrifuged. The supernatant was removed and freeze dried.

3.3. Derivatization

3.3.1. Preparation of Standard Solutions

For the standard solutions, 12 mg of each amino acid was dissolved in a mixture of 5 mL H_2O and 1 mL 2.5 M HCl. The solutions were stored in a refrigerator until analysis. As an internal standard, a solution containing 5-bromotryptophan was prepared following the same procedure.

3.3.2. TBDMS-Derivatization of the Standard Solutions

Ten µL of the standard solution of the halogenated amino acids (alternatively 5 µL of the solution of the other amino acids) and 10 µL of the internal standard were mixed and dried under a gentle stream of nitrogen. The residue was soaked in 20 µL 2.5 M HCl and dried again. Subsequently, the residue was soaked twice in 40 µL EtOH and dried under nitrogen. 50 µL acetonitrile and 50 µL *N*-*tert*-butyldimethylsilyl-*N*-methylfluoroacetamide (MTBSTFA) with 1% *tert*-butyldimethylchlorosilane (TBDMSCl) were added to the dry residue. The mixture was sonicated for 30 s and then heated at 70 °C for 30 min. One µL of the resulting solution was injected into the GC-MS.

3.3.3. TBDMS-Derivatization of the Sponge Samples

One mg of the dried $Ba(OH)_2$ extract containing the internal standard was soaked in 20 µL 2.5 M HCl and dried under a gentle stream of nitrogen. Subsequently, the residue was soaked twice in 40 µL EtOH and dried under nitrogen. Fifty µL acetonitrile and 50 µL MTBSTFA were added to the dry residue. The mixture was sonicated for 30 s and then heated to 70 °C for 30 min. One µL of the resulting solution was injected into the GC-MS.

3.4. GC-MS Measurements

Analyses were carried out on a Varian 3400 gas chromatograph (Varian, Palo Alto, CA, USA) directly coupled to a Finnigan MAT 95 mass spectrometer (Finnigan/Thermo Fisher Scientific Inc., Waltham, MA, USA). The GC separations were performed on a SPB®-5 capillary GC column (Sigma-Aldrich, St. Louis, MO, USA). The flow of helium as carrier gas was 1 mL/min. The injector temperature was 300 °C. Split/Splitless injection was used (splitless time 1 min). The column temperature was programmed as followed: isothermal 115 °C for 3 min, then heating up to 300 °C at rate of 4K/min, then isothermal 300 °C for 30 min.

The ion source temperature was 250 °C and the transfer line temperature was 300 °C. The mass spectra were recorded with a scan cycle time of 1.284 s in the electron impact (EI) ionization mode at 70 eV, *m/z* range 70–850. The chromatograms were recorded after 3 min solvent delay. The retention time t_R was normalized to the second peak of the internal standard 5-bromotryptophan. The intensity was normalized to the weighted sample and the total intensity of both peaks of the internal standard.

3.5. Liquid Chromatography-Mass Spectrometry

3.5.1. Preparation of Standard Solutions

Amino acids were dissolved in MeOH/H_2O (10/1) to yield a sample concentration of 1 mg/mL.

3.5.2. Preparation of Sponge Extract Samples

Dried extracts resulting either from the $Ba(OH)_2$ treatment or the MeOH extraction of the *A. cavernicola* skeleton were dissolved in MeOH/H_2O (10/1) to yield a sample concentration of 1 mg/mL.

3.5.3. Measurement Conditions

All LC-MS analyses were performed on a Thermoquest Finnigan LCQDeca (Thermo Fisher Scientific Inc., Waltham, MA, USA) connected to an Agilent 1100 Series LC (Agilent, Santa Clara, CA, USA) with a Knauer Eurospher 100-3 C18, 100 × 2 mm column (Knauer, Berlin, Germany). As eluents 0.1% formic acid (Eluent A) and MeOH (Eluent B) were utilized and a gradient as shown in Table 5 was applied for all measurements. Electrospray ionization (ESI) mode was chosen for all analyzed samples.

3.6. FTIR Spectroscopy

IR spectra were recorded using a Bruker FTIR spectrometer IFS 88 (Bruker, Karlsruhe, Germany). The samples were deposited on SPECAC Golden-Gate-ATR equipment (LOT-Oriel, Darmstadt, Germany). The spectra were measured in the range from 4000 to 650 cm^{-1} with a spectral resolution of 0.5 cm^{-1}. Each spectrum was recorded by the accumulation of 1000 scans. Subsequently, an ATR intensity correction was carried out. The spectra were baseline corrected and normalized to the most intensive band at about 1625 cm^{-1}.

Table 5. Eluent system utilized for LC-MS analyses.

t [min]	Eluent A [%]	Eluent B [%]
0	90	10
2	90	10
35	0	100
50	0	100
51	90	10
60	90	10

3.7. Scanning Electron Microscopy (SEM) and Energy Dispersive X-ray Spectroscopy (EDX)

Some dried pieces of the skeletons were applied on a sample holder and coated with carbon. The SEM images were then recorded on a ZEISS DSM 982 GEMINI field emission scanning electron microscope (ZEISS, Oberkochen, Germany). Furthermore, EDX spectra were recorded. The spectra were measured with an acceleration voltage of 15 keV. The live time was 60 s.

3.8. Light Microscopy

Small pieces of the purified chitin-scaffolds after $Ba(OH)_2$ or NaOH were put on a sample holder. Microscopic studies were carried out on a Keyence BZ-8000K microscope (Keyence, Osaka, Japan). The images were acquired at 10-fold magnification.

4. CONCLUSIONS

The isolated skeletons of the marine demosponge *A. cavernicola* before and after the conventional MeOH extraction were analyzed with respect to the presence of halogenated amino acids. For this purpose, a $Ba(OH)_2$-based extraction method was applied which effectively removes all organic material from the remaining pure chitin. The $Ba(OH)_2$ extracts of the sponge skeletons of *A. cavernicola* were studied by GC-MS and LC-MS. These investigations revealed that the skeletons contain 10 halogenated amino acids. Nine of these 10 amino acids are halogenated tyrosines. These halogenated tyrosines are strongly attached to the skeletons since the conventional MeOH extraction method does not significantly reduce the amount of halogenated tyrosines in the skeletons. Furthermore, 19 different non-halogenated amino acids were identified. Among them are 15 proteinogenic amino acids. Glycine and serine exhibit the largest concentrations, while leucine, phenylalanine, arginine, and tryptophan are less abundant. In addition, trace amounts of aerothionin and/or its derivatives are present.

To summarize, it should be emphasized that the identified halogenated tyrosines are integral parts of the chitin-based skeletons of *A. cavernicola*. It is tempting to speculate that these compounds are covalently bound to the skeletons. In contrast, the amount of non-halogenated organic material is reduced during MeOH treatment. Investigations of the MeOH extracts suggest that these removed molecules are not only free amino acids but also peptides or small proteins.

ACKNOWLEDGMENTS

The authors gratefully acknowledge financial support from the Deutsche Forschungsgemeinschaft (grant No. Br 1278/17-1, PE 348/27-1, PR 229/15-1).

AUTHOR CONTRIBUTIONS

SU and SM designed the GC-MS experiments. SU performed the isolation of the sponge skeletons and the GC-MS experiments. SU and SM analyzed data resulting from GC-MS experiments. SU performed the FTIR experiments. PP and HN conceived and designed the LC-MS experiments. HN performed the LC-MS experiments. HN and PP analyzed data resulting from LC-MS experiments. EB supervised the scientific work. SU, SM, HN, PP and EB wrote this manuscript.

CONFLICTS OF INTEREST

The authors declare no conflict of interest.

REFERENCES

1. Müller, W.E.G. Origin of metazoa: Sponges as living fossils. Naturwissenschaften 1998, 85, 11–25.

2. Li, C.-W.; Chen, J.-Y.; Hua, T.-E. Precambrian sponges with cellular structures. Science 1998, 279, 879–882.

3. Proksch, P.; Putz, A.; Ortlepp, S.; Kjer, J.; Bayer, M. Bioactive natural products from marine sponges and fungal endophytes. Phytochem. Rev. 2010, 9, 475–489.

4. Thoms, C.; Wolff, M.; Padmakumar, K.; Ebel, R.; Proksch, P. Chemical defense of Mediterranean sponges Aplysina cavernicola and Aplysina aerophoba. Z. Naturforsch. C 2004, 59, 113–122.

5. Thoms, C.; Ebel, R.; Proksch, P. Activated chemical defense in Aplysina. sponges revisited. J. Chem. Ecol. 2006, 32, 97–123.

6. Paul, V.J.; Ritson-Williams, R.; Sharp, K. Marine chemical ecology in benthic environments. Nat. Prod. Rep. 2011, 28, 345–387.

7. Hickman, C.P.; Roberts, L.S.; Larson, A.; l'Anson, H.; Eisenhour, D.J. Zoologie, 13th ed.; Pearson Studium Verlag: München, Germany, 2008; pp. 375–387.

8. Harris, V.A. Sessile Animals of the Sea Shore; Chapman and Hall: London, UK, 1990; pp. 280–282.

9. Hill, M.S.; Hill, A.L. Morphological Plasticity in the Tropical Sponge Anthosigmella. varians: Responses to Predators and Wave Energy. Biol. Bull. 2002, 202, 86–95.

10. Hill, M.S.; Lopez, N.A.; Young, K.A. Anti-predator defenses in western North Atlantic sponges with evidence of enhanced defense through interactions between spicules and chemicals. Mar. Ecol. Prog. Ser. 2005, 291, 93–102.

11. Wehner, R.; Gehring, W.J. Zoologie; Georg Thieme Verlag: Stuttgart, Germany, 2007; pp. 698–699.

12. Bergquist, P.R.; Cook, S.D.C. Order Verongida Bergquist, 1978. In Systema Porifera: A Guide to the Classification of Sponges; Hooper, J.N.A., van Soest, R.W.M., Eds.; Kluwer Academic/Plenum Publishers: New York, NY, USA, 2002; Volume I, pp. 1081–1096.

13. Ehrlich, H.; Maldonado, M.; Spindler, K.-D.; Eckert, C.; Hanke, T.; Born, R.; Goebel, C.; Simon, P.; Heinemann, S.; Worch, H. First evidence of chitin as a component of the skeletal fibers of marine sponges. Part I. Verongidae (Demospongia: Porifera). J. Exp. Zool. B Mol. Dev. Evol. 2007, 308, 347–356.

14. Brunner, E.; Ehrlich, H.; Schupp, P.; Hedrich, R.; Hunoldt, S.; Kammer, M.; Machill, S.; Paasch, S.; Bazhenov, V.V.; Kurek, D.V.; et al. Chitin-Based scaffolds are an integral part of the skeleton of the marine demosponge Ianthella basta.J. Struct. Biol. 2009, 168, 539–547.

15. Uriz, M.-J.; Turon, X.; Becerro, M.A.; Agell, G. Siliceous spicules and skeleton frameworks in sponges: Origin, diversity, ultrastructural patterns, and biological functions. Microsc. Res. Tech. 2003, 62, 279–299.

16. Ehrlich, H. Biological Materials of Marine Origin; Biologically-Inspired Systems (Book 1); Springer Verlag: Dordrecht, The Netherlands, 2010; pp. 245–256.

17. Gross, J.; Sokal, Z.; Rougvie, M. Structural and chemical studies on the connective tissue of marine sponges. J. Histochem. Cytochem. 1956, 4, 227–246.

18. Junqua, S.; Robert, L.; Garrone, R.; Pavans de Ceccatty, M.; Vacelet, J. Biochemical and morphological studies on the collagens of Horny Sponges. Ircinia filaments compared to spongines. Connect. Tiss. Res. 1974, 2, 193–203.

19. Ehrlich, H.; Ilan, M.; Maldonado, M.; Muricy, G.; Bavestrello, G.; Kljajic, Z.; Carballo, J.L.; Shiaparelli, S.; Ereskovsky, A.V.; Schupp, P.; et al. Three-Dimensional chitin-based scaffolds from Verongida sponges (Demospongiae: Porifera). Part I. Isolation and identification of chitin. Int. J. Biol. Macromol. 2010, 47, 132–140.

20. Ehrlich, H.; Kaluzhnaya, O.V.; Brunner, E.; Tsurkan, M.V.; Ereskovsky, A.; Ilan, M.; Tabachnick, K.R.; Bazhenov, V.V.; Paasch, S.; Kammer, M.; et al. Identification and first insights into the structure and biosynthesis of chitin from the freshwater sponge Spongilla lacustris. J. Struct. Biol. 2013, 183, 474–483.

21. Ehrlich, H.; Keith Rigby, J.; Botting, J.P.; Tsurkan, M.V.; Werner, C.; Schwille, P.; Petrášek, Z.; Pisera, A.; Simon, P.; Sivkov, V.N.; et al. Discovery of 505-million-year old chitin in the basal demosponge Vauxia gracilenta. Sci. Rep. 2013,3, 3497.

22. Hackman, R.H. Studies on chitin IV. The occurrence of complexes in which chitin and protein are covalently linked.Aust. J. Biol. Sci. 1960, 13, 568–577.

23. Blackwell, J.; Weih, M.A. Structure of chitin-protein complexes: Ovipositor of the ichneumon fly Megarhyssa. J. Mol. Biol. 1980, 137, 49–60.

24. Teeyapant, R.; Woerdenbag, H.; Kreis, P.; Hacker, J.; Wray, V.; Witte, L.; Proksch, P. Antibiotic and cytotoxic activity of brominated compounds from the marine sponge Verongia aerophoba. Z. Naturforsch. C 1993, 48, 939–945.

25. Faulkner, D.J. Marine pharmacology. Antonie Van Leeuwenhoek 2000, 77, 135–145.

26. Thomson, J.E.; Barrow, K.D.; Faulkner, D.J. Localization of two brominated metabolites, aerothionin and homoaerothionin, in spherulous cells of the marine sponge Aplysina. fistularis (=Verongia thiona). Acta Zool. 1981, 64, 199–210.

27. Turon, X.; Becerro, M.A.; Uriz, M.J. Distribution of brominated compounds within the sponge Aplysina. aerophoba: Coupling X-ray microanalysis with cryofixation techniques. Cell Tissue Res. 2000, 301, 311–322.

28. Kunze, K.; Niemann, H.; Ueberlein, S.; Schulze, R.; Ehrlich, H.; Brunner, E.; Proksch, P.; van Pée, K.-H. Brominated Skeletal Components of the Marine Demosponges, Aplysina cavernicola and Ianthella basta: Analytical and Biochemical Investigations. Mar. Drugs 2013, 11, 1271–1287.

29. Saper, J.; White, W.E. Amino-acid Composition of Sclero-protein of the Sponge Hippospongia equina. Nature 1958, 181, 285–286.

30. Low, E.M. Halogenated amino acids of the bath sponge. J. Mar. Res. 1951, 10, 239–245.

31. Ebada, S.S.; Edrada, R.A.; Lin, W.; Proksch, P. Methods of isolation, purification and structural elucidation of bioactive secondary metabolites from marine invertebrates. Nat. Protoc. 2008, 3, 1820–1831.

32. Sobolevsky, T.G.; Revelsky, A.I.; Miller, B.; Oriedo, V.; Chernetsova1, E.S.; Revelsky, I.A. Comparison of silylation and esterification/acylation procedures in GC-MS analysis of amino acids. J. Sep. Sci. 2003, 26, 1474–1478.

33. North, M. Principles and Applications of Stereochemistry; CRC Press: Cheltenham, UK, 1998; pp. 75–77.

34. Reichenbächer, M.; Popp, J. Strukturanalytik Organischer Und Anorganischer Verbindungen—Ein Übungsbuch; Teubner Verlag: Wiesbaden, Germany, 2007.

35. Hunt, S.; Breuer, S.W. Isolation of a new naturally occuring halogenated amino acid: Monochloromonobromotyrosine. Biochim. Biophys. Acta 1971, 252, 401–404.

36. Čmelik, S. Über einen Farbstoff von Protein-Natur aus dem Schwamme Aplysina aerophoba Nardo. Hoppe-Seyler's Z. Physiol. Chem. 1952, 289, 218–220.

37. Institut für angewandte Hydrobiologie; HYDRA AG; HYDRA Institut für Meereswissenschaften AG; HYDRA Büro für Gewässerökologie Mürle & Ortlepp GbR; HYDRA Wiesloch—Dipl-Biol. Andreas Becker. Available online: http://www.hydra-institute.com (accessed on 17 March 2013).

Chapter 6

Halogenated Compounds from Marine Algae

Maria Teresa Cabrita [1,*], Carlos Vale [1] and Amélia Pilar Rauter [2]

[1]IPIMAR, Av. de Brasília, 1449-006 Lisboa, Portugal

[2]Centro de Química e Bioquímica/Departamento de Química e Bioquímica da Faculdade de Ciências da Universidade de Lisboa, Ed C8, Piso 5, Campo Grande, 1749-016 Lisboa, Portugal

ABSTRACT

Marine algae produce a cocktail of halogenated metabolites with potential commercial value. Structures exhibited by these compounds go from acyclic entities with a linear chain to complex polycyclic molecules. Their medical and pharmaceutical application has been investigated for a few decades, however other properties, such as antifouling, are not to be discarded. Many compounds were discovered in the last years, although the need for new drugs keeps this field open as many algal species are poorly screened. The ecological role of marine algal halogenated metabolites has somehow been overlooked. This new research field will provide valuable and novel insight into the marine ecosystem dynamics as well as a new approach to comprehending biodiversity. Furthermore, understanding interactions between halogenated compound production by algae and the environment, including anthropogenic or global climate changes, is a challenging target for the coming years. Research of halogenated metabolites has been more focused on macroalgae than on phytoplankton. However, phytoplankton could be a very promising material since it is the base of the marine food chain with quick adaptation to environmental changes, which undoubtedly has consequences on secondary metabolism. This paper reviews recent progress on this field and presents trends on the role of marine algae as producers of halogenated compounds.

Keywords: marine algae; halogenated compounds; biotechnological applications; ecological role

1. INTRODUCTION

Marine algae produce a wide variety of remarkable natural compounds, usually referred to as secondary metabolites because they are not involved in the basic machinery of life [1]. Although these molecules often contribute to only a very small fraction of the organism total biomass [2], the contribution of these compounds to survival may sometimes be comparable to metabolites resulting from the primary metabolism [3]. In that sense, the use of the term "secondary metabolite" seems less appropriate since these compounds also contribute to growth, reproduction and defense and thus play a primary role for the organism integrity.

Many of these secondary metabolites are halogenated, reflecting the availability of chloride and bromide ions in seawater. Interestingly, bromide is more frequently used by algae for organohalogen production, although chlorine occurs in higher concentrations than bromine in seawater. Marine halogenated compounds comprise a varied assembly of compounds, ranging from peptides, polyketides, indoles, terpenes, acetogenins and phenols to volatile halogenated hydrocarbons [4]. The prevalence of halogens is not similar in marine algae: chlorine and bromine appear to be the main halogens used to increase biological activity of secondary metabolites, whereas iodine and fluorine remain quite unusual within the chemical structures [5]. However, some orders of brown algae such as Laminariales accumulate and use iodine for halogenation processes. For example, the kelp *Laminaria digitata* accumulates iodine to more than 30,000-times the concentration found in seawater, representing an average content of 1% of dry weight [6]. In fact, iodination is more frequent in brown algae than in red and green algae metabolites [6]. As a result, only less than 1% of secondary metabolites from of brown algae contain bromine or chlorine in contrast with as much as 90 and 7% of red and green algal compounds, respectively [7].

Halogenation often provides these compounds with interesting key features and marine algae hold diverse and unique biosynthetic pathways for the production of halogenated metabolites. The halogenated sesterterpenes, neomangicols A–C, isolated from the marine fungus *Fusarium* [8], offer a striking example of the halogenation effect. Neomangicol A and B display *in vitro* cytotoxic effect toward the HCT-116 human colon tumor cell line, while their nonhalogenated analog neomangicol C was shown to be inactive [8].

Biological properties of halogenated compounds have been researched for the past decades, with results showing antibacterial, antifungal, antiviral, anti-inflammatory, antiproliferative, antifouling, antifeedant, cytotoxic, ichthyotoxic, and insecticidal activity [9]. Research major focal points indubitably have been the discovery and characterization of new halogenated compounds, along with a remarkable effort toward the evaluation of their possible biomedical and biotechnological applications. Also, chemical profiles have been used to differentiate cryptic species but the chemotaxonomic value of natural halogenated compounds has been questioned due to geographical and seasonal variations in the chemical composition of algal species [10]. The ecological role of marine halogenated metabolites, alongside with other natural compounds, has been disregarded, although a few halogenated metabolites have been shown to have important and critical roles on the community structure of marine ecosystems in previous years [11–17]. In fact, most of the publications on marine ecological issues rarely include a chemical approach of compounds responsible for the ecological interactions found. Excellent reviews on marine natural compounds have been recently published [9,18,19], with no particular emphasis on halogenated metabolites. These showed a variety of structure types that were isolated from a wide range of marine organisms, including microorganisms and phytoplankton, macroalgae, sponges, cnidarians, bryozoans, molluscs, tunicates, echinoderms and true mangrove plants. During 2009, new naturally occurring algal halogenated compounds were found, most of them with little or no reported biological activity. Reports on the ecological role of algal natural compounds, presenting both chemical and ecological approaches were still few. The present paper focuses on halogenated compounds only, and is restricted to micro and macroalgae as natural sources. It attempts to provide an overview of new marine halogenated compounds reported in 2009 and to examine progress and present trends on the role of marine algae as producers of halogenated compounds.

2. MACROALGAE

Interest in the actual marine natural compounds responsible for such a wide range of properties is far more recent and new compounds are still being discovered and isolated, chemical structures elucidated and properties being sorted out, with the aim of finding new molecular entities with industrial application. From time to time, a new compound emerges as particularly promising in a specific area and additional testing starts to allow further pharmacological evaluation.

Many compounds have been found in marine macroalgae in recent years, mainly in red and brown algae, and fewer in green algae [9]. Among all marine macroalgae, red algae are the main producers of halogenated compounds. *Laurencia*(family Rhodomalaceae, order Ceramiales, class Rhodophyceae, phylum Rhodophyta) is considered one of the most prolific genera [20,21], being mainly found in tropical, subtropical, and temperate coastal waters. It has been intensively screened over the last fifty years, although a variety of new halogenated molecules are still being reported. Characteristically, the halogenation degree found in compounds from *Laurencia* is relatively high [19]. Diterpenes sesquiterpenes, triterpenes, and C15-acetogenins are the main secondary compounds of this genus [22,23] with which antimicrobial [24], antifeedant [25], antihelmintic [26,27] and cytotoxic [28,29] properties are generally associated.

Five new chlorinated compounds, C15 acetogenin en-ynes (**1–5**), were obtained from *Laurencia glandulifera* collected from the island of Crete (Figure 1). Four of them were evaluated for their cytotoxicity toward HT-29 (colorectal adenocarcinoma), MCF-7 (mammary adenocarcinoma), PC-3 (prostate adenocarcinoma), HeLa (cervical adenocarcinoma), and A431 (epidermoid carcinoma) human tumor cell lines, but no significant activity was found [30]. The characteristic terminal *cis*ene-yne moiety is also present in C15 eight-membered cyclic ethers previously isolated from *L. glandulifera* collected on the Crete Island, which exhibited antistaphylococcal activity with minimum inhibitory concentrations (MICs) in the range of 8–256 mg/mL [31].

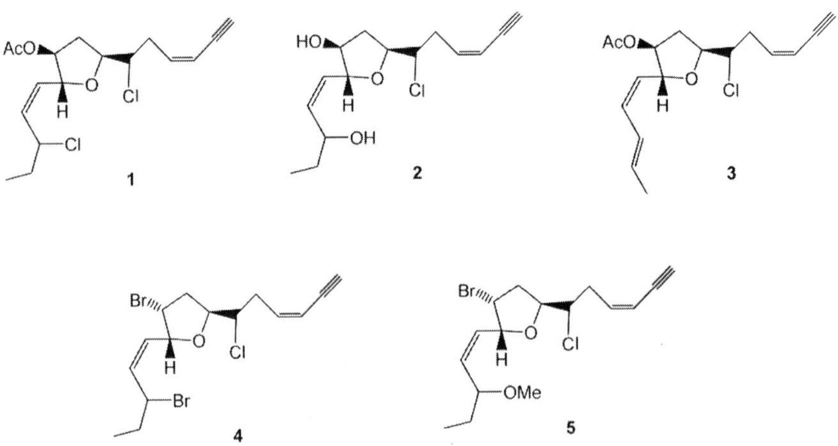

Figure 1. Structures of compounds **1–5** isolated from *Laurencia glandulifera*.

Elatol (**6**)(Figure 2), a halogenated sesquiterpene alcohol, commonly found in many species of *Laurencia*, and known for its potent antibacterial activity, was isolated for the first time in *Laurencia microcladia*, collected in the Southern Brazilian coast [32]. Previous analysis of anti-herbivory proprieties of metabolites from *Laurencia* species (including elatol) have been conducted but no investigation had been reported for *Laurencia microcladia*. Elatol anti-herbivory properties were investigated using the black sea urchin *Echinometra lucunter*, but it was found that this species can tolerate elatol, at least in the concentrations tested [32]. However, this compound was able to deter feeding of *Thalassia* by reef fishes with a reduced loss of *Thalassia* by 60% and was shown to be a very efficient deterrent against the sea urchin *Diadema antillarum*, reducing grazing by 86% [11]. However, anti-herbivory proprieties could not be detected by testing the compound on the black sea urchin *Echinometra lucunter*.

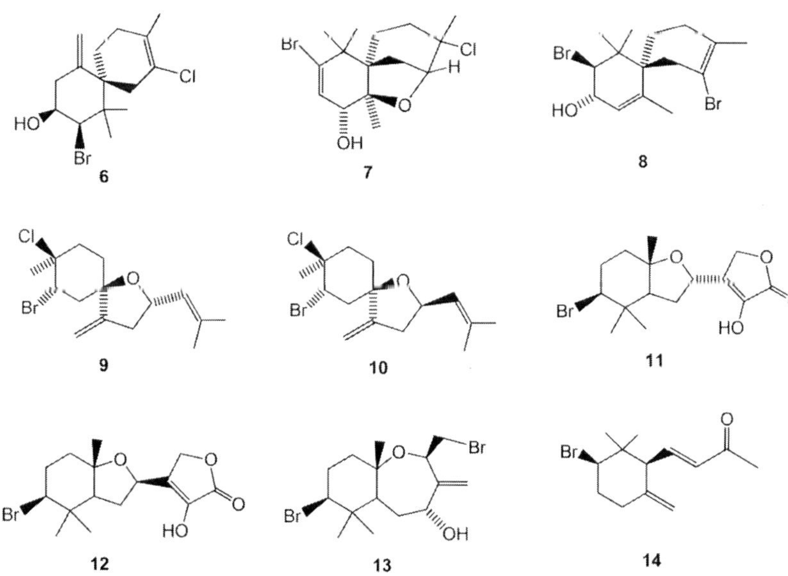

Figure 2. Structures of halogenated compounds **6–14** isolated from *Laurencia saitoi*.

Laurencia saitoi, with exceptionally few reported halogenated compounds [25] in the past, was found to produce four novel halogenated sesquiterpenes: 10-bromo-3-chloro-2,7-epoxychamigr-9-en- 8-ol (**7**), 2,10-dibromochamigra-2,7-dien-9-ol (**8**), (9*S*)-2-bromo-3-chloro-6,9-epoxybisabola-7(14),10-diene (**9**), and (9*R*)-2-bromo-3-chloro-6,9-

epoxybisabola-7(14),10-diene (**10**)[33](Figure 2). In addition, other brominated compounds were already reported for different macroalgal species, namely aplysistatin, a well known antileukemic agent [34,35], 5-acetoxypalisadin B, palisadin A, palisadin B belonging to a series of antimicrobial compounds, and 2,3,5,6-tetrabromoindole [36]. Cytotoxicity of the isolated compounds was evaluated by the MTT method, all the tested compounds being found inactive [36]. New brominated sesquiterpenes and a norsesquiterpene were also reported from the same species [37], namely 2-hydroxyluzofuranone (**11**), 2-hydroxyluzofuranone B (**12**), 4-hydroxypalisadin C (**13**), and 2-bromo-γ-ionone (**14**)(Figure 2).

Other red algal genera have also been screened and interesting findings were recently reported. From the chemical-rich genus *Plocamium*, a South African red algae *Plocamium cornutum* yielded five halogenated monoterpenes (**15–19**) from which two are new (compounds **18–19**)(Figure 3). The antiplasmodial activity against the chloroquine sensitive strain of the most frequent and deadly human malaria parasite *Plasmodium falciparum* was tested. Although the compounds were significantly less active than standard chloroquine, compounds **16** and **17** containing 7-dichloromethyl moiety were the most active ones (IC_{50} = 16 and 17 μM, respectively), followed by compound **15** (IC_{50} = 27 Mm), which contains an aldehyde functional group at this position, while the new compounds were essentially inactive [38].

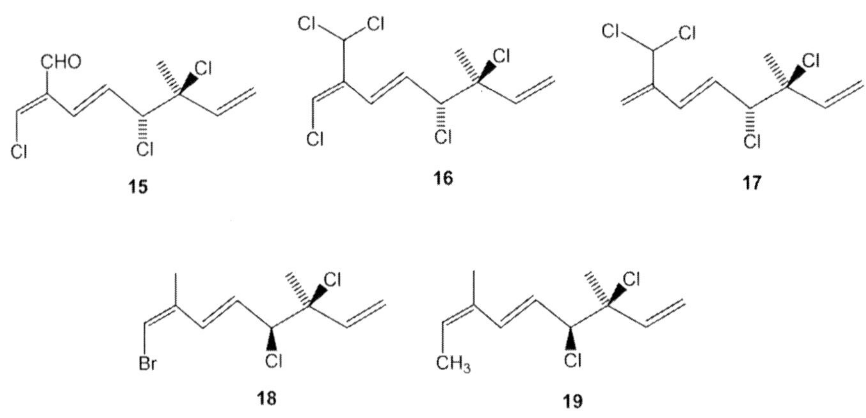

Figure 3. Structures of monoterpenes **15–19** isolated from *Plocamium cornutum*.

Another red algal species, the Fijian *Callophycus serratus*, was found to produce eight bromophycolides J–Q (**20–27**)(Figure 4), which exhibited IC_{50} values against *Plasmodium falciparum* in the low micromolar range (44 for compound **22**, 0.5 for **23**, 1.4 for **24**, **25** and **27**)[39]. Antimalarian activity appeared to be associated with the presence of a macrolide motif in the chemical structure of these molecules. Antibacterial assays were performed using methicillin-resistant *Staphylococcus aureus*and vancoymcin-resistant *Enterococcus faecium* as test pathogens. The macrolides were also evaluated against a panel of 12 tumor cell lines including breast, colon, lung, prostate, and ovarian cancer cells. Of the eight tested compounds, bromophycolides **26** and **27** exhibited the most potent antibacterial activity against *S. aureus* and *E. faecium,* suggesting that conformational rigidity and/or hydrophobicity conferred by the tetrahydropyran system contributes to antibacterial activity. While all tested bromophycolides exhibited moderate antineoplastic activity, only **24** displayed some cell line selectivity, with an IC_{50} of 1.5 μM against the breast tumor cell line. Interestingly, while **24** demonstrated cancer cell line selectivity, its regioisomer **23** was quite active against all cancer cell lines tested (IC_{50}'s 2.1–7.2 μM). Bromophycolide **27** was the most potent *C. serratus* natural product evaluated but showed little cell line selectivity.

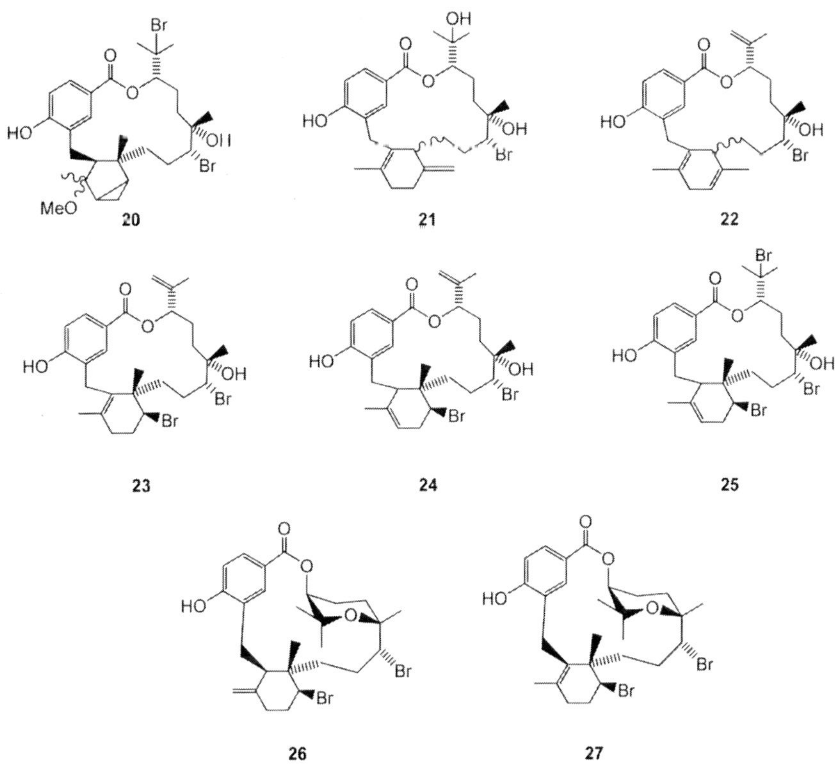

Figure 4. Structures of bromophycolides **20–27** from *Callophycus serratus*.

Halogenated metabolites from brown algae, reported as unusual for this algal group [40], have been found to be mainly terpenes. However, some new molecules were reported for brown algae in 2009. A new halogenated meroditerpenoid, fallachromenoic acid (**28**)(Figure 5), was isolated from the southern Australian brown algae *Sargassum fallax*, and displayed antitumor activities against a P388 Murine Leukaemia cell line [41]. Although there were no previous reports of halogenated compounds in the *Stypopodium* genus, Areche *et al.* [40] found an unusual 40-chlorostypotriol triacetate (**29**)(Figure 5) in *Stypopodium flabelliforme*, from which biological properties are still unknown. Another brown algal species,*Dictyopteris divaricata*, was found to produce two new brominated selinane sesquiterpenes, 1-bromoselin-4(14),11-diene (**30**) and 9-bromoselin-4(14),11-diene (**31**)[42](Figure 5).

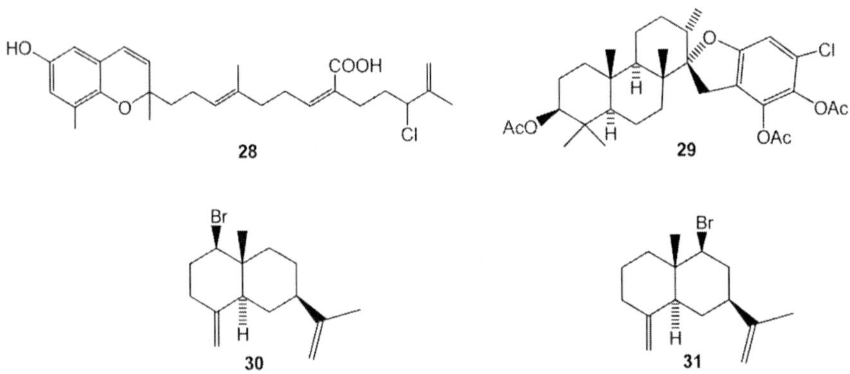

Figure 5. Structures of compounds **28–31** isolated from brown algae.

No reports associated with green algae were found in the selected bibliography from 2009.

3. CYANOBACTERIA

Marine phytoplankton has been much less investigated than macroalgae although marine microorganisms are, in general, increasingly considered successful sources of natural products. Earlier reviews and reports on marine natural products including phytoplankton refer mainly to cyanobacteria and dinoflagellates [9,18,43,44] as sources of natural compounds.

Selected examples of recently discovered halogenated molecules produced by marine phytoplankton, from 2009 literature, exhibited the same trend.

Among phytoplankton major groups, cyanobacteria have come forward as one of the most promising groups of microorganisms for the isolation of interesting new natural halogenated compounds [45,46]. A wide range of compounds with different properties is produced by these blue-green algae [44]. For example, many of these compounds were found to be anticancer agents or powerful neurotoxins performing either as blockers or activators of the eukaryotic voltage-gated sodium (Nav) channels [44].

Cyanobacterial toxins have received increased research effort in recent years [47–49] because these molecules are among the most found hazardous substances in surface waters and occurrence of harmful cyanobacterial bloom events is rising worldwide [50].

The cyanobacteria *Lyngbya majuscula*, from an Eastern Caribbean collection, was found to produce two new halogenated fatty acid amides, grenadamides B and C (**32–33**), and two new depsipeptides, itralamides A and B (**34–35**)[51](Figure 6). The first two compounds displayed marginal activity against the beet armyworm (*Spodoptera exigua*).

From the same genus, a new brominated compound, lyngbyastatin 10 (**36**)(Figure 7), closely related to lyngbyastatins, was found in *Lyngbya semiplena*, collected in Tumon Bay (Guam, Pacific ocean), inhibiting porcine pancreatic elastase [52]. Another cyanobacteria, *Fischerella ambigua*, obtained from a culture, produces five newly found antibacterial chlorinated molecules, ambiguine K–O isonitriles (**37–41**)[53](Figure 7). Ambiguine K and M isonitriles showed the most potent activity against *Mycobacterium tuberculosis*, the causal agent of most cases of tuberculosis. Ambiguine A isonitrile was the most active one against *Bacillus anthracis*, the bacterium that causes anthrax. A new brominated indole alkaloid, named as bromoanaindolone, (IUPAC name: 6-bromo-3-hydroxy-3-methyl-indol-2-one)(**42**)(Figure 7), yielded by the cyanobacteria*Anabaena constricta* [54], showed antibacterial activity against the Gram-positive species *Bacillus cereus*, the bacterium that causes foodborne disease commonly known as food poisoning. Bromoanaindolone also displayed anticyanobacterial activity against the filamentous species *Arthrospira laxissima* and *Nostoc carneum*, and also against the unicellular species*Chroococcus minutus*, *Synechocystis aquatilis* and *Synechococcus* sp., which indicates the allelopathic potential of this compound.

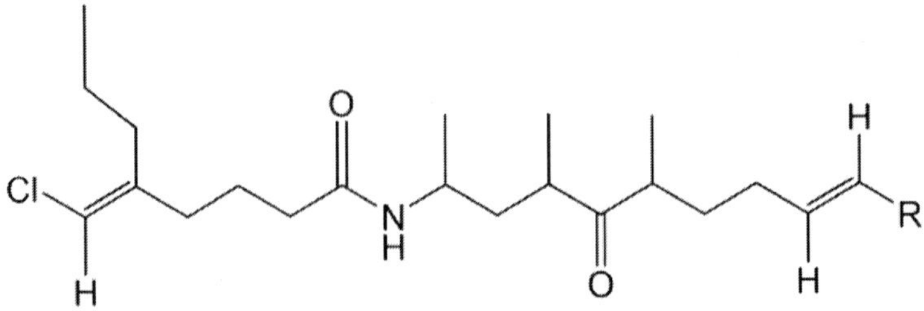

32 R = H Grenadamide B
33 R = Cl Grenadamide C

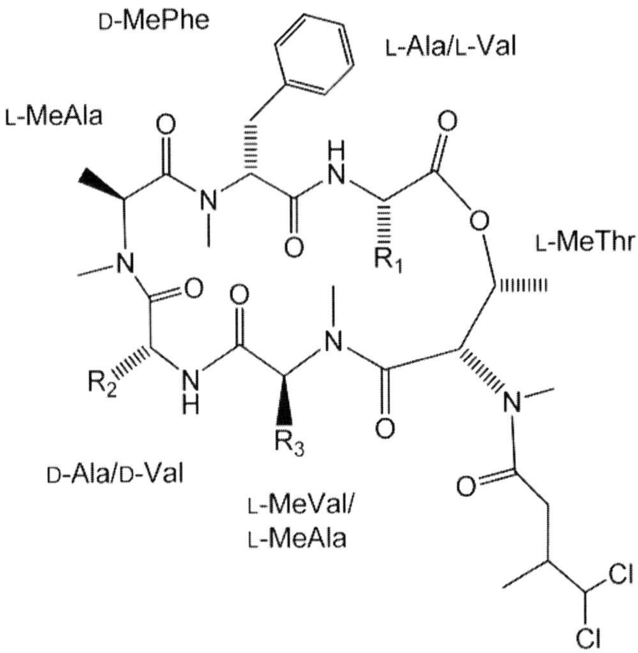

34 $R_1 = R_2 = CH_3$, $R_3 = CH(CH_3)_2$ Itralamide A
35 $R_1 = R_2 = CH(CH_3)_2$, $R_3 = CH_3$ Itralamide B

Figure 6. Structures of compounds **32–35** isolated from the cyanobacteria *Lyngbya majuscula*.

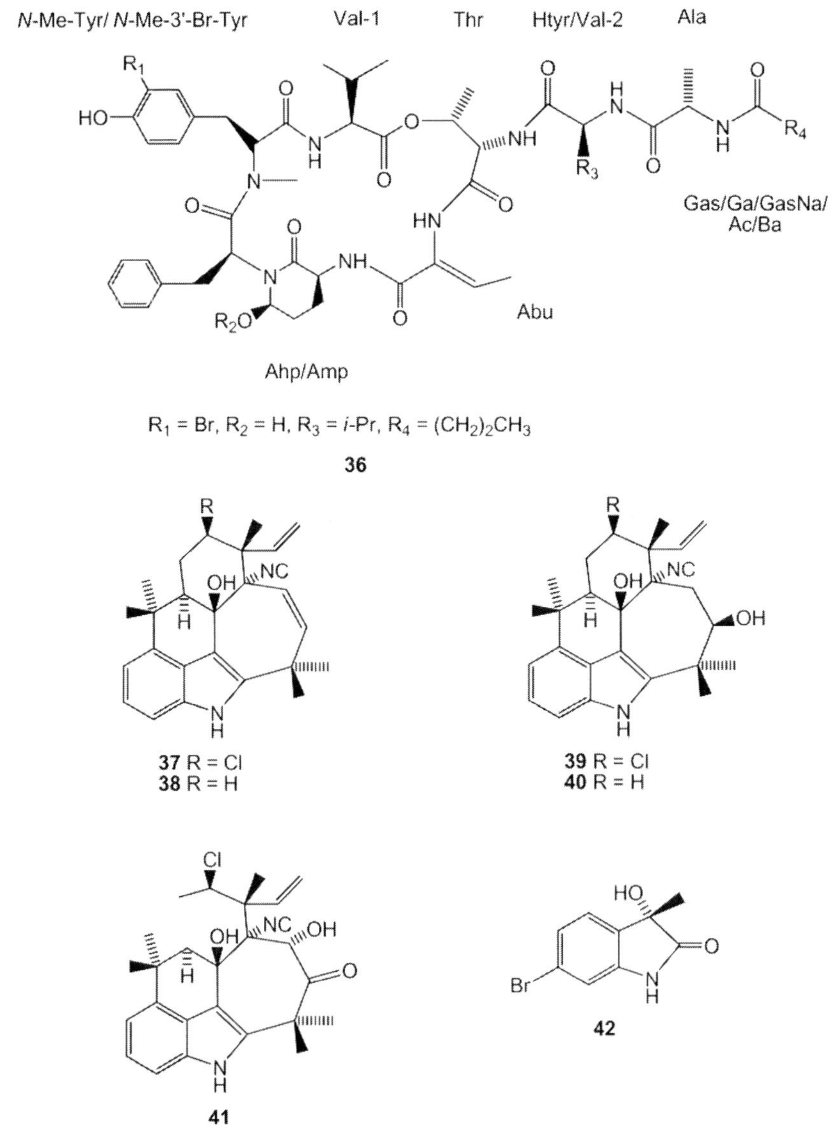

Figure 7. Structures of compounds **36–42** isolated from cyanobacteria.

4. LIMITATIONS AND POSSIBLE SOLUTIONS TO DETECTION OF BIOACTIVITY

The fact that some of the newly found halogenated compounds show minor or no activity at all against a specific target does not exclude the possibility of other hidden unidentified active biological effects. Additionally, the supposedly absence of bioresponse may be related to limitations in the analytical chemistry methods employed. Bioassay-guided fractionation is the iterative approach traditionally applied to disclose bioactive natural compounds [55,56]. Difficulties in perception of bioactivity may be linked to compound instability, caused by fractionation and isolation from the natural cellular environment or simply because compounds may act synergistically or more than one compound may be associated to a specific property. This is particularly true for macroalgae and microalgae which are complex compound matrices [57]. Metabolite-oriented approaches, namely metabolite profiling and metabolomics, may supplement bioassay-guided fractionation [58]. These two approaches are focused on the chemical properties of the metabolome, which includes the complete set of metabolites of an organism (metabolomics), or of a limited group of pre-defined metabolites (metabolite profiling)[59]. In the latter approach, pre-defined metabolites are selected either according to the class they belong to (organic phosphates, carbohydrates, *etc.*) or to an associated specific pathway. Both metabolite profiling and metabolomics allow all compounds to be simultaneously measured, so that detection of unstable compounds is facilitated and synergistic effects detected [59]. Also, the influence of a particular condition on the organism physiology can be revealed through qualitative and quantitative differences in the metabolic profiles obtained [60,61]. This could be a valuable tool for the assessment of effects of environmental changes on the community structure and organism physiology. However, useful metabolomics may be used for a more thorough and complete detection of metabolites, limitations subsist when applied to chemical ecology, due to the difficulty in establishing a link between one or more specific metabolites and an ecological role [58].

Other techniques have been applied for the study of halogenated compounds in marine algae. Desorption electrospray ionization mass spectrometry (DESI-MS) and some applications, such as imaging, have very recently started to be used for natural products detection on intact algal tissue surfaces [62,63]. DESI-MS is an ambient ionization technique coupled with mass spectrometry, allowing probing the surface of solids, liquids, frozen solutions, and adsorbed gases [64]. In ambient DESI-MS, samples are kept under atmospheric pressure in open air, with minimum or no preparation at all [64]. Tissue surfaces are subject to a focused spray of charged particles of a polar solvent, which leads to the release of intact gaseous ions from surfaces into the mass spectrometer [65]. Low detection limits and high analysis speed are achieved, and innate chemical information is preserved to a maximum [64]. DESI-MS has been shown to be a sensitive and effective approach to detect algal diterpene-benzoate macrolide natural products, namely bromophycolides, directly on the surface and interior of a marine red alga, *Callophycus serratus* [62]. Reactive DESI approaches were investigated to improve ionization efficiency and detection limits. Different polar solvent compositions, tested directly on the algal surfaces, were demonstrated to enhance sensitivity for discovery of various bromophycolides, which would have otherwise been undetected. Imaging, one of DESI-MS possible applications, has been shown to provide an exceptional capability to map secondary metabolites to distinct algal surface sites [63]. Bromophycolides were shown to be non homogenously distributed across surfaces but instead associated with distinct patches, again in the red algae *Callophycus serratus*. DESI-MS imaging appears to be a powerful tool for the investigation of the function of surface-associated natural products in ecological interactions, as spatially-resolved measurements with lateral resolutions in the hundreds of micrometers are made possible. These studies [62,63] illustrate the potential of DESI-MS and its applications, such as imaging, in understanding chemically-mediated biological processes in macroalgae.

5. ECOLOGICAL ROLE

Micro and macroalgal survival and success in the marine environment reflect to a great extent the many strategies these organisms have had to employ throughout their evolutionary history to adapt to a hostile and high resource-demanding milieu. Extreme competition for space, light and nutrients has shaped the organisms' physiology, resulting in a complex array of biologically active metabolites characteristic of each species. Many of these secondary metabolites have been shown to support the defense mechanisms developed by marine algae [66–69]. Secondary metabolites are now suggested to be responsible for marine biodiversity on the genetic, species, and ecosystem levels [70,71].

Chemical ecology, which tackles the role of natural compounds in the interactions between organisms and also between organisms and their environment, has already a few decades of investigation dedicated to marine systems [46]. Historically, interest in natural products from marine algae was initially driven to meet pressing biomedical requirements for new drugs against fungal [72], parasitic [73], bacterial [74], and viral [75] diseases, which were either used in their natural form or as templates for synthesis and further chemical structure modification [46]. For this purpose, macroalgae from tropical areas were heavily screened and many new halogenated compounds were found in the last decade [18]. Apart from potent and original therapeutic agents for infectious diseases and cancer, among many other disorders, natural products isolated from marine algae were also found to clearly control interactions between organisms [11–13], and therefore influence population structure, communities organization, and ecosystem function [14–17]. Biodiversity in marine systems may be a result of chemical diversity [68]. Presently, specific ecological aspects such as chemical sensing of the environment by algae, intraspecific signaling, allelopathy, predator-prey and host-parasite interactions, and bioaccumulation and transfer of toxins within food webs have been addressed on recent research on the ecology of natural compounds from marine algae. Excellent reviews and essays on marine chemical ecology covering years prior to 2009 have been published (see [3,17,68,76–78]), however, with no particular focus on halogenated compounds. Interactions between algae and herbivorous invertebrates or describing allelopathic effects have received most of the attention. These ecological interactions continue to be predominantly documented from an ecological perspective [79,80]; the chemical identification of compounds responsible for the found ecological relationships was overlooked during 2009. A multidisciplinary approach including organic chemistry, biology, and ecology components is required for the in depth elucidation of the ecological relationships in the near future. So far, the ecological and the chemical approaches rarely coincide in the same study; the cellular and molecular bases for these interactions remain disregarded. In fact, to the best of our knowledge, an ecological study on marine macroalgae, including elucidation of chemical structure of molecules responsible for ecological interactions, was found during 2009. A direct fine-scale evaluation of bromophycolides and callophycoic acids was conducted on red macroalga *Callophycus serratus* surfaces in order to evaluate whether these natural compounds had a role in surface-mediated defense against pathogenic microbes [63]. These novel compounds had been reported for the first time in *C. serratus* [39], represent the largest group of algal antifungal compounds described to date, and were shown to inhibit growth of *Lindra thalassiae*, a marine pathogenic fungus [63]. DESI-MS imaging revealed bromophycolides among heterogeneous patches on algal surfaces and within internal algal tissues. The bromophycolide concentrations found on these surface patches were sufficient suppress growth of *L. thalassia*, indicating that probably these compounds are kept internally and released at sparsely distributed surface sites. The above cited study [63] provides the first direct evidence for localization of chemical signals with spatial resolution <200 μm on biological surfaces in concentrations sufficient for targeted antimicrobial defense, highlighting the potential of DESI-MS imaging for the understanding of small-scale ecological interactions.

6. PRESENT TRENDS

A lot still remains to be done concerning research on the role of marine natural halogenated compounds: (i) isolation and characterization of new halogenated compounds (ii) screening untested micro and macroalgal species (iii) improving assessment in the detection of bioactivities, fully exploring potential of metabolite-oriented approaches, (iv) testing biomedical and ecological relevance of novel and known chemical natural compounds, (v) ensuring reliable taxonomic identification of investigated species, (vi) biogeographical assessing of micro- and macroalgae with relevant compounds, and (vii) developing appropriate strategies for data management.

From a purely ecological point of view, success toward the in-depth understanding of marine ecological interactions is very much dependent on a multidisciplinary approach, relying on adequate bioactivity detection methodologies. Chemical metabolite-oriented approaches may prove to be reliable tools helping to elucidate compound's biological properties, which may not be detectable in any other way. Ecological studies may just benefit from an interactive and close combination of chemical methodologies with ecological experiments.

ACKNOWLEDGEMENTS

This study was funded by "Fundação para a Ciência e Tecnologia" grant SFRH/BPD/50348/2009 to M.T. Cabrita.

REFERENCES

1. Cimino, G; Ghiselin, MT. McClintock, JB, Baker, BJ, Eds.; Marine natural products chemistry as an evolutionary narrative. In Marine Chemical Ecology; CRC Press: Boca Raton, FL, USA, 2001; pp. 115–154.

2. Cannell, RJP. Cannell, RPJ, Ed.; How to approach the isolation of a natural product. In Natural Products Isolation, Methods in Biotechnology; Humana Press: Totowa, NJ, USA, 1998; Volume 4, pp. 1–51.

3. Ianora, A; Boersma, M; Casotti, R; Fontana, A; Harder, J; Hoffmann, F; Pavia, H; Potin, P; Poulet, SA; Toth, G. New trends in marine chemical ecology. Estuaries Coasts 2006, 29, 531–551.

4. Butler, A; Sandy, M. Mechanistic considerations of halogenating enzymes. Nature 2009, 460, 848–854.

5. Neumann, CS; Fujimori, DG; Walsh, CT. Halogenation strategies in natural product biosynthesis. Chem. Biol 2008, 15, 99–109.

6. Küpper, FC; Schweigert, N; Ar Gall, E; Legendre, J-M; Vilter, H; Kloareg, B. Iodine uptake in Laminariales involves extracellular, haloperoxidase-mediated oxidation of iodide. Planta 1998, 207, 163–167.

7. Harper, MK; Bugni, TS; Copp, BR; James, RD; Lindsay, BS; Richardson, AD; Schnabel, PC; Tasdemir, D; Van Wagoner, RM; Verbitzki, SM; Ireland, CM. McClintock, JB, Baker, BJ, Eds.; Introduction to the chemical ecology of marine natural products. In Marine Chemical Ecology; CRC: Boca Raton, FL, USA, 2001; pp. 3–71.

8. Renner, MK; Jensen, PR; Fenical, W. Neomangicols: structures and absolute stereochemistries of unprecedented halogenated sesterterpenes from a marine fungus of the genus Fusarium. J. Org. Chem 1998, 63, 8346–8354.

9. Blunt, JW; Copp, BR; Hu, WP; Munro, MHG; Northcote, PT; Prinsep, MR. Marine natural products. Nat. Prod. Rep2009, 26, 170–244.

10. Fenical, W; Norris, JN. Chemotaxonomy in marine algae: chemical separation of some Laurencia species (Rhodophyta) from the Gulf of California). J. Phycol 1975, 11, 104–108.

11. Hay, ME; Fenical, W; Gustafson, K. Chemical defense against diverse coral-reef herbivores. Ecology 1987, 68, 1581–1591.

12. Vairappan, CS. Potent antibacterial activity of halogenated metabolites from Malaysian red algae, Laurencia majuscula(Rhodomelaceae, Ceramiales). Biomol. Eng 2003, 20, 255–259.

13. Vairappan, CS; Ang, MY; Ong, CY; Phang, SM. Biologically active polybrominated indoles in the red alga Laurencia similis from the coastal waters of Sabah (Rhodomelaceae, Ceramiales). Malaysian J. Sci 2004, 23, 119–126.

14. Paul, NA; de Nys, R; Steinberg, PD. Seaweed–herbivore interactions at a small scale: direct tests of feeding deterrence by filamentous algae. Mar. Ecol. Prog. Ser 2006, 323, 1–9.

15. Harlin, MM; Rice, EL. Allelochemistry in marine macroalgae. Crit. Rev. Plant Sci 1987, 3, 237–249.

16. Bolser, RC; Hay, ME. Are tropical plants better defended? Palatability and defenses of temperate vs. tropical seaweeds. Ecology 1996, 77, 2269–2286.

17. Hay, ME. Marine chemical ecology: Chemical signals and cues structure marine populations, communities, and ecosystems. Annu. Rev. Mar. Sci 2009, 1, 193–212.

18. Blunt, JW; Copp, BR; Hu, W-P; Munro, MHG; Northcote, PT; Prinsep, MR. Marine natural products. Nat. Prod. Rep2007, 24, 31–86.

19. Hill, RA. Marine natural products. Annu. Rep. Prog. Chem., Sect. B: Org. Chem 2007, 103, 125–139.

20. Faulkner, DJ. Marine natural products. Nat. Prod. Rep 2001, 18, 1–49.

21. Wright, AD; Goclik, E; König, GM. Three new sesquiterpenes from the red alga Laurencia perforate. J. Nat. Prod 2003,66, 435–437.

22. Erickson, KL. Scheuer, PJ, Ed.; Constituents of Laurencia. In Marine Natural Products: Chemical and Biological Perspectives; Academic Press: New York, NY, USA, 1983; Volume 5, pp. 131–257.

23. Faulkner, DJ. Marine natural products. Nat. Prod. Rep 1995, 12, 223–269.

24. König, GM; Wright, AD. Laurencia rigida: Chemical investigations of its antifouling dichloromethane extract. J. Nat. Prod 1997, 60, 967–970.

25. Kurata, K; Taniguchi, K; Agatsuma, Y; Suzuki, M. Diterpenoid feeding-deterrents from Laurencia saitoi. Phytochemistry1998, 47, 363–369.

26. Davyt, D; Fernandez, R; Suescun, L; Mombrú, AW; Saldaña, J; Domínguez, L; Coll, J; Fujii, MT; Do Manta, E. New sesquiterpene derivatives from the red alga Laurencia scoparia. Isolation, structure determination, and anthelmintic activity. J. Nat. Prod 2001, 64, 1552–1555.

27. Topcu, G; Aydogmus, Z; Imre, S; Gören, AC; Pezzuto, JM; Clement, JA; Kingston, DGI. Brominated sesquiterpenes from the red alga Laurencia obtusa. J. Nat. Prod 2003, 66, 1505–1508.

28. Juagdan, EG; Kalidindi, R; Scheuer, P. Two new chamigranes from an hawaiian red alga, Laurencia cartilaginea.Tetrahedron 1997, 53, 521–528.

29. Sun, J; Shi, D; Ma, M; Li, S; Wang, S; Han, L; Yang, Y; Fan, X; Shi, J; He, L. Sesquiterpenes from the red alga Laurencia tristicha. J. Nat. Prod 2005, 68, 915–919.

30. Kladi, M; Vagias, C; Papazafiri, P; Brogi, S; Tafi, A; Roussis, V. Tetrahydrofuran acetogenins from Laurencia glandulifera. J. Nat. Prod 2009, 72, 190–193.

31. Kladi, M; Vagias, C; Stavri, M; Rahman, M; Gibbons, S; Roussis, V. C15 acetogenins with antistaphylococcal activity from the red alga Laurencia glandulifera. Phytochem. Lett 2008, 1, 31–36.

32. Lhullier, C; Donnangelo, A; Caro, M; Palermo, JA; Horta, PA; Falkenberg, M; Schenkel, EP. Isolation of elatol fromLaurencia microcladia and its palatability to the sea urchin Echinometra lucunter. Biochem. Syst. Ecol 2009, 37, 254–259.

33. Ji, N-Y; Li, X-M; Li, K; Wang, B-G. Halogenated sesquiterpenes from the marine red alga Laurencia saitoi(Rhodomelaceae). Helv. Chim. Acta 2009, 92, 1873–1879.

34. Pettit, GR; Herald, CL; Allen, MS; Von Dreele, RB; Vanell, LD; Kao, JPY; Blake, W. The isolation and structure of aplysistatin. J. Am. Chem. Soc 1977, 99, 262–263.

35. Pandey, PK. Endangered medicinal species of the Indian Ocean: radical need for conservation. Chem. Biodivers 2009, 6, 990–1001.

36. Su, H; Yuan, Z; Li, J; Guo, S; Han, L; Zhu, X; Shi, D. Studies on chemical constituents of Laurencia saitoi. Zhongguo Zhong Yao Za Zhi 2009, 34, 871–874.

37. Su, H; Yuan, Z-H; Li, J; Guo, S-J; Deng, L-P; Han, L-J; Zhu, X-B; Shi, D-Y. Sesquiterpenes from the marine red algaLaurencia saitoi. Helv. Chim. Acta 2009, 92, 1291–1297.

38. Afolayan, AF; Mann, MGA; Lategan, CA; Smith, PJ; Bolton, JJ; Denzil, R; Beukes, DR. Antiplasmodial halogenated monoterpenes from the marine red alga Plocamium cornutum. Phytochemistry 2009, 70, 597–600.

39. Lane, AL; Stout, EP; Lin, A-S; Prudhomme, J; Le Roch, K; Fairchild, CR; Franzblau, SG; Hay, ME; Aalbersberg, W; Kubanek, J. Antimalarial bromophycolides J-Q from the fijian red alga Callophycus serratus. J. Org. Chem 2009, 74, 2736–2742.

40. Areche, C; San-Martín, A; Rovirosa, J; Soto-Delgado, J; Contreras, R. An unusual halogenated merediterpenoid fromStypopodium flabelliforme: Studies by NMR spectroscopic and computational methods. Phytochemistry 2009, 70, 1315–1320.

41. Reddy, P; Urban, S. Meroditerpenoids from the southern Australian marine brown alga Sargassum fallax.Phytochemistry 2009, 70, 250–255.

42. Ji, N-Y; Wen, W; Li, X-M; Xue, Q-Z; Xiao, H-L; Wang, B-G. Brominated selinane sesquiterpenes from the Marine Brown Alga Dictyopteris divaricata. Mar. Drugs 2009, 7, 355–360.

43. Cardozo, KHM; Guaratini, T; Barros, MP; Falcão, VR; Tonon, AP; Lopes, NP; Campos, S; Torres, MA; Anderson, O; Souza, AO; Colepicolo, P; Pinto, E. Metabolites from algae with economical impact. Comp. Biochem. Physiol. C: Toxicol. Pharmacol 2007, 146, 60–78.

44. Tan, LT. Bioactive natural products from marine cyanobacteria for drug discovery. Phytochemistry 2007, 68, 954–979.

45. Borowitzka, MA. Microalgae as sources of pharmaceuticals and other biologically active compounds. J. Appl. Phycol1995, 7, 3–15.

46. Burja, AM; Banaigs, B; Abou-Mansour, E; Burgess, JG; Wright, PC. Marine cyanobacteria-a prolific source of natural products. Tetrahedron 2001, 57, 9347–9377.

47. Kwan, JC; Rocca, JR; Abboud, KA; Paul, VJ; Luesch, H. Total structure determination of grassypeptolide, a new marine cyanobacterial cytotoxin. Org. Lett 2008, 10, 789–792.

48. Luesch, H; Yoshida, WY; Moore, RE; Paul, VJ; Corbett, TH. Total structure determination of apratoxin A, a potent novel cytotoxin from the marine cyanobacterium Lyngbya majuscula. J. Am. Chem. Soc 2001, 123, 5418–5423.

49. Taori, K; Paul, VJ; Luesch, H. Structure and activity of largazole, a potent antiproliferative agent from the Floridian marine cyanobacterium Symploca sp. J. Am. Chem. Soc 2008, 130, 1806–1807.

50. Paerl, HW; Huisman, J. Climate change: a catalyst for global expansion of harmful cyanobacterial blooms. Environ. Microbiol. Rep 2009, 1, 27–37.

51. Jiménez, JI; Vansach, T; Yoshida, WY; Sakamoto, B; Pörzgen, P; Horgen, FD. Halogenated fatty acid amides and cyclic depsipeptides from an eastern caribbean collection of the cyanobacterium Lyngbya majuscule. J. Nat. Prod 2009, 72, 1573–1578.

52. Kwan, JC; Taori, K; Paul, VJ; Luesch, H. Lyngbyastatins 8–10, elastase inhibitors with cyclic depsipeptide scaffolds isolated from the marine cyanobacterium Lyngbya semiplena. Mar. Drugs 2009, 7, 528–538.

53. Mo, S; Krunic, A; Chlipala, G; Orjala, J. Antimicrobial ambiguine isonitriles from the cyanobacterium Fischerella ambigua. J. Nat. Prod 2009, 72, 894–899.

54. Volk, R-B; Girreser, U; Al-Refai, M; Laatsch, H. Bromoanaindolone, a novel antimicrobial exometabolite from the cyanobacterium Anabaena constricta. Nat. Prod. Res 2009, 23, 607–612.

55. Hayes, KF; Millar, JG. Methods in Chemical Ecology: Bioassay Methods; Kluwer Academic: Norwell, MA, USA, 1998.

56. Millar, JG; Hayes, KF. Methods in Chemical Ecology: Chemical Methods; Kluwer Academic: Norwell, MA, USA, 1998.

57. Plaza, M; Santoyo, S; Jaime, L; García-Blairsy Reina, G; Herrero, M; Señoráns, FJ; Ibáñez, E. Screening for bioactive compounds from algae. J. Pharm. Biomed. Anal 2010, 51, 450–455.

58. Prince, EK; Pohnert, G. Searching for signals in the noise: metabolomics in chemical ecology. Anal. Bioanal. Chem 2010,396, 193–197.

59. Fiehn, O. Combining genomics, metabolome analysis, and biochemical modeling to understand metabolic networks.Compar. Funct. Genom 2001, 2, 155–168.

60. Bundy, JG; Davey, MP; Viant, MR. Environmental metabolomics: a critical review and future perspectives.Metabolomics 2009, 5, 3–21.

61. Barofsky, A; Vidoudez, C; Pohnert, G. Metabolic profiling reveals growth stage variability in diatom exudates. Limnol. Oceanogr. Meth 2009, 7, 382–390.

62. Nyadong, L; Hohenstein, EG; Galhena, AS; Lane, AL; Kubanek, J; Sherrill, CD; Fernandez, FM. Reactive desorption electrospray ionization mass spectrometry (DESI-MS) of natural products of a marine alga. Anal. Bioanal. Chem 2009,394, 245–254.

63. Lane, AL; Nyadong, L; Galhena, AS; Shearerb, TL; Stout, EP; Parry, RM; Kwasnik, M; Wang, MD; Hay, ME; Fernandez, FM; Kubanek, J. Desorption electrospray ionization mass spectrometry reveals surface-mediated antifungal chemical defense of a tropical seaweed. Proc. Natl. Acad. Sci. USA 2009, 106, 7314–7319.

64. Wiseman, JM; Laughlin, BC. Desorption electrospray ionization (DESI) mass spectrometry: a brief introduction and overview. Curr. Sep. Drug Dev 2007, 22, 11–14.

65. Cooks, RG; Ouyang, Z; Takats, Z; Wiseman, JM. Ambient mass spectrometry. Science 2006, 311, 1566–1570.

66. Lobban, CS; Harrison, PJ. Seaweed Ecology and Physiology; Cambridge University Press: New York, NY, USA, 1994.

67. Amsler, CD; Iken, K; McClintock, JB; Baker, BJ. Defenses of polar macroalgae against herbivores and biofoulers. Bot. Mar 2009, 52, 535–545.

68. Hay, ME; Fenical, W. Chemical ecology and marine biodiversity: insights and products from the sea. Oceanography1996, 9, 10–19.

69. Lane, AL; Nyadong, L; Galhena, AS; Shearer, TL; Stout, EP; Parry, RM; Kwasnik, M; Wang, MD; Hay, ME; Fernandez, FM; Kubanek, J. Desorption electrospray ionization mass spectrometry reveals surface-mediated antifungal chemical defense of a tropical seaweed. Proc. Natl. Acad. Sci. USA 2009, 106, 7314–7319.

70. Norse, EA. Global Marine Biological Diversity: A Strategy for Building Decision into Decision Making; Island Press: Washington DC, USA, 1993.

71. Paul, VJ; Arthur, KE; Ritson-Williams, R; Ross, C; Sharp, K. Chemical defenses: from compounds to communities. Biol. Bull 2007, 213, 226–251.

72. Nagai, H; Murata, M; Torigoe, K; Satake, M; Yasumoto, T. Gambieric acids: new potent antifungal substances with unprecedented polyether structures from a marine dinoflagellate Gambierdiscus toxicus. J. Org. Chem 1992, 57, 5448–5453.

73. Capon, RJ; Barrow, RA; Rochfort, S; Jobling, M; Skene, C. Marine nematodes: tetrahydrofurans from a Southern Australian brown alga Notheia anomala. Tetrahedron 1998, 54, 2227–2242.

74. Etahiri, S; Bultel-Ponce, V; Caux, C; Guyot, M. New bromoditerpenes from the red alga Sphaerococcus coronopifolius. J. Nat. Prod 2001, 64, 1024–1027.

75. Sakemi, S; Higa, T; Jefford, CW; Bernardinelli, G. Venustatriol, a new anti-viral triterpenes tetracyclic ether fromLaurencia venusta. Tetrahedron Lett 1986, 27, 4287–4290.

76. Pohnert, G; Steinke, M; Tollrian, R. Chemical cues, defense metabolites and the shaping of pelagic interspecific interactions. Trends Ecol. Evol 2007, 22, 198–204.

77. Amsler, CD. Amsler, CD, Ed.; Algal sensory chemical ecology. In Algal Chemical Ecology; Springer: Berlin, Heidelberg, Germany, 2008; pp. 297–309.

78. Poulson, KL; Sieg, RD; Kubanek, J. Chemical ecology of the marine plankton. Nat. Prod. Rep 2009, 26, 729–745.

79. Prince, EK; Myers, TL; Naar, J; Kubanek, J. Competing phytoplankton undermines allelopathy of a bloom-forming dinoflagellate. Proc. R. Soc. B 2008, 275, 2733–2741.

80. Tameishi, M; Yamasaki, Y; Nagasoe, S; Shimasaki, Y; Oshima, Y; Honjo, T. Allelopathic effects of the dinophyteProrocentrum minimum on the growth of the bacillariophyte Skeletonema costatum. Harmful Algae 2009, 8, 421–429.

Chapter 7

Bioactivities from Marine Algae of the Genus *Gracilaria*

Cynthia Layse F. de Almeida, Heloina de S. Falcão, Gedson R. de M. Lima, Camila de A. Montenegro, Narlize S. Lira,Petrônio F. de Athayde-Filho, Luis C. Rodrigues, Maria de Fátima V. de Souza, José M. Barbosa-Filho, and Leônia M. Batista*

Department of Pharmaceutical Sciences, Laboratory of Pharmaceutical Technology, Federal University of Paraiba, João Pessoa, PB 58051-900, Brazil

ABSTRACT

Seaweeds are an important source of bioactive metabolites for the pharmaceutical industry in drug development. Many of these compounds are used to treat diseases like cancer, acquired immune-deficiency syndrome (AIDS), inflammation, pain, arthritis, as well as viral, bacterial, and fungal infections. This paper offers a survey of the literature foralgae extracts with biological activity, and identifies avenues for future research. Nineteen species of this genus that were tested for antibacterial, antiviral, antifungal, antihypertensive, cytotoxic, spermicidal, embriotoxic, and anti-inflammatory activities are cited from the 121 references consulted.

Keywords: *Gracilaria*; macroalgae; seaweed; biological activity; natural product; review

1. INTRODUCTION

The ocean environment contains over 80% of world's plant and animal species [1] and with more than 150,000 seaweeds found in the intertidal zones and tropical waters of the oceans, it is a primary source of natural products [2].

Seaweeds are floating and submerged plants of shallow marine meadows. They have salt tolerance because the osmolarity of cytoplasm is adjusted to match the osmolarity of the seawater so that desiccation does not occur. They lack true stems, roots and leaves; however, they possess a blade that is leaf like, a stipe that is stem like, and a holdfast that resembles roots like terrestrial plants. Seaweeds contain photosynthetic pigments and use sunlight to produce food and oxygen from carbon dioxide, and the water [3].

Marine macroalgae are important ecologically and commercially to many regions of the world, especially in Asian countries such as China, Japan and Korea [4]. They are a valuable food resource which contains low calories, and they are rich in vitamins, minerals, proteins, polysaccharides, steroids and dietary fibers [5–7]. Since as early as 3000 BC, they were also considered important as traditional remedies [4]. The Japanese and Chinese use brown algae in the treatment of hyperthyroidism and other glandular disorders [8–11]. The unsaturated lipids afford protection against cardiovascular pathogens [12].

Seaweeds have been one of the richest and most promising sources of bioactive primary and secondary metabolites [13] and their discovery has significantly expanded in the past three decades [4,14,15]. The algae synthetize a variety of compounds such as carotenoids, terpenoids, xanthophylls, chlorophyll, vitamins, saturated and polyunsaturated fatty acids, amino acids, acetogenins, antioxidants such as polyphenols, alkaloids, halogenated compounds and polysaccharides such as agar, carrageenan, proteoglycans, alginate, laminaran, rhamnan sulfate, galactosyl glycerol and fucoidan [16–25].

These compounds probably have diverse simultaneous functions for the seaweeds and can act as allelopathic, antimicrobial, antifouling, and herbivore deterrents, or as ultraviolet-screening agents [26]. They are also used by the pharmaceutical industry in drug development to treat diseases like cancer, acquired immune-deficiency syndrome (AIDS), inflammation, pain, arthritis, infection for virus, bacteria and fungus [27]. Currently, algae represent about 9% of biomedical compounds obtained from the sea [28].

Compounds with cytostatic, antiviral, antihelmintic, antifungal and antibacterial activities have been detected in green, brown and red algae [29,30]. The algae produce pure forms of the fatty acids found in human milk that appear to be building blocks for mental and visual development [31] and have been extensively screened for syntheses of new drugs [32,33].

During the 1970s, Ryther and collaborators evaluated numerous species of red, green and brown macroalgae for their potential growth rates and dry weight yields [34]. They demonstrated that the genus *Gracilaria* was the most attractive candidate because of its ability to achieve high yields and while producing commercially valuable extracts [35].

Gracilaria Greville genus (Gracilariales, Rhodophyta) is a macroalgae group with more than 300 species of which 160 have been accepted taxonomically. These are usually red, green or greenish brown with a three-phase cycle and can be found in tropical and subtropical seas [36,37].

The *Gracilaria* species are important for the industrial and biotechnological uses because they have phycocolloids, the main source of agar α-(1,4)-3,6-anhydro-L-galactose and β-(1,3)-D-galactose with little esterification in cell wall [2,38]. Among the carbohydrates, agar and other polysaccharides are present in *G. confervoides* [39], *G. dura* [40], *G. chilensi* and *G. secundata* [41,42].

These algae also produce important bioactive metabolites like the primary compound with antibiotic activity acrylic acid [43], and the eicosanoids which are derivatives C_{20} polyunsaturated fatty acid (PUFA) metabolism through oxidative pathways that originate mainly from arachidonic acid and eicosapentaenoic acids, the precursors of prostaglandins (PGs) [44,45]. Species such as *G. asiatica* and *G. lichenoids* contain PGE_2 [46,47]. PGF_2 and 15-keto-PGE_2 were respectively isolated from *G. lichenoids* and *G. asiatica* [45];*G. verrucosa* contains PGA_2 that appears to be responsible for a gastrointestinal disorder, known as "ogonori" poisoning in Japan [48]

Lipids are abundant in this genus being mainly prostaglandins [49], steroids, such as cholesterol and clinoasterol are present in *G. crassa* and *G. coronopifolia* respectively [50–52], as well as *G. longa*[48,53–57] and *G. dura*. Other steroids such as 3-beta-hydroxy-poriferast-5-en-7-one, 3-beta-7-alpha-diol-poriferast-5-ene and 5-alpha-poriferast-9(11)-en-3-beta-ol are isolated from *G. dura* [50]; cholestane-3-β-5-diol,5-α:24(S)-ethyl [52], poriferastene 8 [50], poriferast-5-ene-3-β-7-β-diol [51] and poriferast-5-ene-3-β-7-α-diol [51] were identified in *G. coronopifolia; G. longa* also has a variety of compounds like alpha linolenic acid, gamma linolenic acid [58], glycolipids [59], 5-dehydro avenasterol, fucosterol, myristic acid, desmosterol and 5-alpha-24(S)-ethyl-cholestane-3-beta-6-beta-diol [60]. Phytochemical studies with extracts from fresh thallus of *G. andersoniana* showed the following isolates: oleic acid, linoleic acid, cholesterol, prostaglandin A_2, prostaglandin E_2, leukotriene B_4 and phytol [61–63].

Studies with *G. asiatica* reported the diterpenes cis and trans-phytol [63]. A variety of lactones are present in*Gracilaria* from the Pacific Ocean, such as aplysiatoxin isolated from *G. confervoides* [64,65], polycavernoside B, polycavernoside B_2, and polycavernoside A_2 and A_3 isolated from *G. crassa* [49,66]. Other constituents are also containedin this genus such as proteins r-phycoerythrin from *G. salicornia* [67] and *G. longa* [68], gigartinine from *G. chilensis* [69] and proteoglycan from *G. longa* [70].

The possibility of finding new molecules from natural products is immeasurable. For this reason the plants and their derivatives are major sources of all drugs, affecting about 30% of pharmaceutical market [71]. According to Newman *et al.* (2003), between the years 1981 and 2002, 877 new molecules were introduced into the market, with 49% of substances isolated from natural sources followed by semi-synthetic derivatives or synthesized molecules taking the structures of natural origin as models [29].

The search for new effective medicines remains a challenge for scientists. Therefore around the world, many researchers have focused on natural sources for new molecules with algae among the targets of these studies. So in this study we reviewed the literature related to bioactivities for *Gracilaria* algae.

2. RESULTS AND DISCUSSION

In this review, among the 160 species of *Gracilaria* already identified taxonomically, only 19 of them had their extracts and fractions chemically tested for toxicity, cytotoxic, spermicidal, antiimplantation, antibacterial, antiviral, antifungal, antiprotozoa, antihypertensive, antioxidant, anti-inflammatory, analgesic, and spasmolytic effects in gastrointestinal tract (Table 1).

Table 1. Bioactivities of marine algae of the *Gracilaria* genus.

Botanical Name	Part used	Type of extract	Bioassays models, organism, dose or route of administration	Result
Studies of toxicity				
Gracilaria bursa-pastoris (S.G.Gmelin) P.C.Silva	FzDTh	H_2O Ext.	Cytotoxic activity-cell culture-10.0 µg/mL	Inactive [72]
	FTh	95% EtOH Ext. or $CHCl_3$ Ext.	Cytotoxic activity-cell culture-10.0 µg/mL	Inactive [72]
Gracilaria chorda (Holmes)	FsO	H_2O Ext.	Toxicity assessment-mouse-1.2 mg/animal-i.p.	Active [48]
Gracilaria coronopifolia (J. Agardh)	FTh	Plant	Toxic effect-human adult-oral	Active [65]
Gracilaria corticata (J.Agardh) J.Agardh	Th	50% EtOH-H_2O Ext.	Toxicity assessment-mouse-DL50 1000 mg/kg-ip	Active [73]
Gracilaria domingensis (Kutzing) Sonder ex Dickie	DO	90% EtOH Ext	Cytotoxity-*Artemia salina* L.-200 µg/mL	Active [74]
Gracilaria edulis (S.G Gmelin) P.C Silva	DTh	Plant	Toxicity effect (death)-human adult-oral	Active [49]
	SDTh	90% EtOH Ext	Toxicity assessment-mouse-DL50 0.825 mg/kg-i.p.	Active [75]
Gracilaria foliifera (Forsskål) Borgesen	DEP	(1:1) EtOH-H_2O Ext	Cytotoxic activity-cell culture-dose: dry weight of plant	Active [76]
Gracilaria textorii (Surıngar) De Toni	FzDO	MeOH Ext	Cytotoxic activity-cell culture (CA 9 KB)	Inactive [77]
	FsTh	Hexane Ext.	Cytotoxic activity-culture cell (LEUK P 388)-ED 50 > 100 µg/mL	Equivocal [78]
		CCl_4 Ext.	Cytotoxic activity-culture cell (LEUK P 388)-ED 50 22.2 µg/mL	Equivocal [78]
		$CHCl_3$ Ext.	Cytotoxic activity-culture cell (LEUK P 388)-ED 50 32.2 µg/mL	Inactive [78]

Gracilaria verrucosa (Hudson) Papenfuss	DO	H_2O Ext	Toxicity assessment-mouse-1.2 mg/animal-i.p.	Active [48]
	FzDO	MeOH Ext	Cytotoxic activity-cell culture (CA 9 KB)	Inactive [77]
	FO	30% EtOH Ext	Cytotoxic activity-cell culture (CA 9 KB)-10.0 µg/mL	Inactive [79]
		(1:1) $CHCl_3$-MeOH Ext.	Cytotoxic activity-cell culture (CA 9 KB)-1.0 µg/mL	Equivocal [79]
	FTh	H_2O Ext. and 95% EtOH Ext	Cytotoxic activity-cell culture (LEUK P 388-P 3)-10.0 µg/mL	Inactive [72]
Effects on the nervous system				
Gracilaria corticata J.Agardh	SDTh	90% EtOH Ext	Autonomic effects-dog-50 mg/kg-iv	Inactive [75]
			CNS effects-mouse	Inactive [75]
			Analgesic activity-mouse	Inactive [75]
			Anticonvulsant activity-mouse	Inactive [75]
Gracilaria edulis (S.G.Gmelin) P.C.Silva	SDTh	90% EtOH Ext.	Autonomic effects-dog-50 mg/kg-iv	Inactive [75]
			CNS effects-mouse	Inactive [75]
			Analgesic activity-mouse	Inactive [75]
			Anticonvulsant activity-mouse	Inactive [75]
Gracilaria verrucosa (Hudson) Papenfuss	SDTh	90% EtOH Ext.	CNS effects-mouse	Inactive [75]
Contraception activity				
Gracilaria corticata J.Agardh	DTh	(1:1) MeOH-CH_2Cl_2 Ext.	Embryotoxic effect-pregnant rat-1.0 mg/kg-intragastric	Inactive [80]
	SDTh	90% EtOH Ext.	Antiimplantation effect-pregnant rat-100.0 mg/kg	Inactive [75]
			Spermicidal effect-rat-2.0 %	Inactive [75]

Table 1. *Cont.*

Botanical Name	Part used	Type of extract	Bioassays models, organism, dose or route of administration	Result
Gracilaria edulis (S.G.Gmelin) P.C.Silva	SDTh	90% EtOH Ext.	Antiimplantation effect-pregnant rat-100.0 mg/kg	Inactive [75]
			Spermicidal effect-rat-2.0%	Inactive [75]
Gracilaria verrucosa (Hudson) Papenfuss	SDTh	90% EtOH Ext.	Spermicidal effect-rat-2.0%	Inactive [75]
Anti-inflammatory activity				
Gracilaria textorii (Suringar) De Toni	EP	H_2O Ext.	Platelet aggregation inhibition (adenosine diphosphate; arachidonic acid or collagen stimulation)-100.0 µg/mL	Inactive [81]
			Venotonic activity (platelet aggregating factor stimulation)-100.0 µg/mL	Inactive [81]
Gracilaria verrucosa (Hudson) Papenfuss	DTh	Polysaccharide fraction	Immunostimulant activity-mouse-4.0 mg/animal-i.p.	Active [82]
			Phagocytosis stimulation-mouse-4.0 mg/animal-i.p.	Active [82]
	SDTh	90% EtOH Ext.	Antiinflammatory activity rat intragastric	Inactive [75]
Antioxidant activity				
Gracilaria verrucosa (Hudson) Papenfuss	Plant	MeOH Ext.	Radical scavenging effect (DPPH radicals)-IC50 480.0 µg	Active [83]
	DTh	Polysaccharide fraction	Oxygen radical formation induction-mouse-4.0 mg/animal-i.p.	Active [82]
Gastrointestinal effects				
Gracilaria chorda (Holmes)	FsO	H_2O Ext.	Mouse-0.5 mg/animal-gastric intubation and dose 0.5 mg/loop-i.p.	Active [48]
Gracilaria verrucosa (Hudson) Papenfuss	DO	H_2O Ext.	Mouse-0.5 mg/animal-gastric intubation	Active [48]
Cardiovascular effects				
Gracilaria corticata (J.Agardh) J.Agardh	SDTh	90% EtOH Ext.	Cardiovascular effects-dog-50 mg/kg-iv	Inactive [75]
Gracilaria edulis (S.G.Gmelin) P.C.Silva	SDTh	90% EtOH Ext.	Cardiovascular effects-dog-50 mg/kg-iv	Inactive [75]
			Diuretic activity-rat-intragastric	Active [75]
Gracilaria lichenoides (Greville)	EP	H_2O Ext.	Antihypertensive activity-rat-iv	Active [84]
	FsTh	H_2O Ext.	Antihypertensive activity-rat-iv	Active [85]
Gracilaria verrucosa (Hudson) Papenfuss	SDTh	90%EtOH Ext.	Cardiovascular effects-dog-50 mg/kg-iv	Inactive [75]
Hypoglycemic activity				
Gracilaria corticata J.Agardh	SDTh	90% EtOH Ext.	Rat-250 mg/kg – intragastric	Inactive [75]
Gracilaria edulis (S.G.Gmelin) P.C.Silva	SDTh	90% EtOH Ext.	Rat-250.0 mg/kg – intragastric	Inactive [75]
Anti-enzymes activity				
Gracilaria arcuata (Zanardini)	DTh	MeOH Ext.	Tyrosinase inhibition-0.33 mg/mL	Inactive [86]
Gracilaria corticata (J.Agardh) J.Agardh	DO	PET Ether Ext.; $CHCl_3$ Ext. or MeOH Ext.	Penicillinase inhibition-1.0 µg/units	Inactive [87]
Gracilaria textorii (Suringar) De Toni	EP	H_2O Ext.	Aldose reductase inhibition-10.0 µg/mL	Inactive [81]
	FzDO	MeOH Ext.	Cyclic AMP phosphodiesterase inhibition	Inactive [77]
Gracilaria verrucosa (Hudson) Papenfuss	FzDO	EtOAc Ext.	Lipase inhibition	Equivocal [88]
		MeOH Ext.	Cyclic AMP phosphodiesterase inhibition	Inactive [77]

Respiratory effects				
Gracilaria corticata (J.Agardh) J.Agardh	SDTh	90% EtOH Ext.	Respiratory depressant-dog-50 mg/kg-iv	Inactive [75]
Gracilaria edulis (S.G Gmelin) P.C Silva	SDTh	90% EtOH Ext.	Respiratory depressant-dog-50 mg/kg-iv	Inactive [75]
Gracilaria verrucosa (Hudson) Papenfuss	SDTh	90% EtOH Ext.	Respiratory depressant-dog-50.0 mg/kg-iv	Inactive [75]
Spasmolytic activity				
Gracilaria corticata (J.Agardh) J.Agardh	SDTh	90% EtOH Ext.	Spasmolytic activity-guinea pig	Inactive [75]
Gracilaria edulis (S.G Gmelin) P.C.Silva	SDTh	90% EtOH Ext.	Negative chronotropic effect-dog-50.0 mg/kg-iv	Inactive [75]
Antibacterial activity				
Gracilaria cervicornis (Turner) J.Agardh	DEP	95% EtOH Ext.	Agar plate-*Staphylococcus aureus*-5.0 mg/mL	Active [89]
			Agar plate-*Proteus vulgaris; Escherichia coli; Aspergillus fumigates; Candida albicans; Pseudomonas aeruginosa; Streptococcus pyogenes*-50.0 mg/mL	Inactive [89]
Gracilaria corticata (J.Agardh) J.Agardh	DO	PET Ether Ext.; $CHCl_3$ Ext. or MeOH Ext.	Agar plate-*Staphylococcus aureus; Escherichia coli*-MIC >200 µg/mL	Inactive [90]
	FsO	MeOH Ext.	Agar plate-*Escherichia coli; Salmonella paratyphi A; Salmonella paratyphi B; Shigella sonnei*	Inactive [91]
			Agar plate-*Bacillus subtilis; Staphylococcus aureus; Bacillus megaterium; Streptococcus viridans*	Active [91]
	SDTh	90% EtOH Ext.	Agar plate-*Klebsiella pneumonia; Pseudomonas aeruginosa; Staphylococcus aureus; Escherichia coli; Streptococcus faecalis*	Inactive [75]

Table 1. *Cont.*

Botanical Name	Part used	Type of extract	Bioassays models, organism, dose or route of administration	Result
Gracilaria debilis (Forsskål) Borgesen	DO	95% EtOH Ext.	Agar plate-*Escherichia coli; Staphylococcus aureus*	Active [92]
			Agar plate-Mycobacterium smegmatis	Inactive [92]
Gracilaria domingensis (Kützing) Sonder ex Dickie	DO	95% EtOH Ext.	Agar plate-*Escherichia coli; Staphylococcus aureus*	Active [92]
		Acetone Ext. or Ether Ext.	Agar plate-*Escherichia coli; Staphylococcus aureus*	Inactive [92]
		95% EtOH Ext. or Acetone Ext.	Agar plate-*Mycobacterium smegmatis*	Active [92]
Gracilaria edulis (S.G.Gmelin) P.C Silva	SDTh	90% EtOH Ext.	Agar plate-*Escherichia coli; Streptococcus faecalis; Staphyiococcus aureus; Pseudomonas aeruginosa; Klebsiella pneumoniae*	Inactive [75]
Graciiaria pygmea (Borgesen)	FsO	MeOH Ext.	Agar plate-*Bacillus subtilis; Staphylococcus aureus; Escherichia coli; Salmonella paratyphi A; Streptococcus viridans; Shigella sonnei; Salmonella paratyphi B*	Inactive [91]
			Agar plate-*Bacillus megaterium*	Active [91]
Gracilaria sjoestedii (Kylin)	DO	95% EtOH Ext.	Agar plate-*Escherichia coli; Staphylococcus aureus*	Active [92]
			Agar plate-Mycobacterium smegmatis	Inactive [92]
Gracilaria tikvahiae McLachlan	DEP	$CHCl_3$ Ext. or EtOH Ext.	Agar plate -*Staphylococcus aureus*	Active [93]
			Agar plate-*Streptococcus faecalis; Pseudomonas aeruginosa*	Inactive [93]
Gracilaria verrucosa (Hudson) Papenfuss	FTh	**	Agar plate-*Vibrio marinofulvis; Micrococcus infimus; Pseudomonas atlantica*-40.0 µg/µL	Inactive [94]
	Th	70% EtOH Ext.	Antiphage activity-agar plate-Bacteriophage T 1; Bacteriophage T 2; Bacteriophage T 4. Bacteriophage T 7; Bacteriophage MS 2; Bacteriophage PHI-CHI 174-0.50 µg/mL	Inactive [95]

Antifungal activity				
Gracilaria corticata (J.Agardh) J.Agardh	FsO	MeOH Ext.	Agar plate-*Aspergillus niger; Fusarium solani; Alternaria solani; Penicillium funiculosum*	Inactive [91]
	SDTh	90% EtOH Ext.	Agar plate-*Sporotrichum schenckii; Cryptococcus neoformans; Candida albicans; Trichophyton mentagrophytes; Aspergillus fumigates*	Inactive [75]
Gracilaria debilis (Forsskål) Borgesen	DO	95% EtOH Ext.	Agar plate-*Candida albicans*	Active [92]
			Agar plate-*Neurospora crassa*	Inactive [92]
Gracilaria domingensis (Kutzing) Sonder ex Dickie	DO	95% EtOH Ext. and Acetone Ext.	Agar plate-*Candida albicans; Neurospora crassa*	Active [92]
		Ether Ext.	Agar plate-*Candida albicans*	Inactive [92]
Gracilaria edulis (S.G.Gmelin) P.C.Silva	SDTh	90% EtOH Ext.	Agar plate-*Sporotrichum schenckii; Candida albicans; Cryptococcus neoformans; Trichophyton mentagrophytes; Aspergillus fumigates*	Inactive [75]
Gracilaria pygmea (Borgesen)	FsO	MeOH Ext.	Agar plate-*Aspergillus niger; Fusarium solani; Alternaria solani; Penicillium funiculosum*	Inactive [91]
Gracilaria sjoestedii (Kylin)	DO	95% EtOH Ext.	Agar plate-*Candida albicans*	Active [92]
			Agar plate-*Neurospora crassa*	Inactive [92]
Gracilaria tikvahiae McLachlan	DEP	$CHCl_3$ Ext. and EtOH Ext.	Agar plate-*Candida albicans*	Active [93]
Antiviral activity				
Gracilaria bursa-pastoris (S.G.Gmelin) P.C.Silva	FzDTh	**	Cell culture-*Herpes simplex* 1 and HIV Virus	Inactive [96]
Gracilaria corticata (J.Agardh) J.Agardh	Th	50% EtOH-H_2O Ext.	Cell culture-*Semlicki-forest* Virus-0.05 mg/mL	Equivocal [73]
			Cell culture-*Ranikhet* and *Vaccinia* Virus-0.05 mg/mL	Inactive [73]
	SDTh	90% EtOH Ext.	Cell culture-*Ranikhet* Virus	Inactive [75]
Gracilaria edulis (S.G.Gmelin) P.C.Silva	SDTh	90% EtOH Ext.	Cell culture-*Semlicki-forest* and *Ranikhet* Virus	Inactive [75]
Gracilaria pacifica (I. A. Abbott)	DO	MeOH Ext.	Cell culture-*Herpes simplex* 1 Virus-400.0 μg/mL	Inactive [97]
			Cell culture-*Virus sindbis*-200.0 μg/mL	Active [97]
Gracilaria species	FzDTh	**	Cell culture-Herpes simplex 1 and HIV Virus	Inactive [96]
Gracilaria textorii (Suringar) De Toni	FzDO	MeOH Ext.	Cell culture-*Herpes simplex* 1 Virus	Inactive [77]
	Th	H_2O Ext.	Cell culture-HIV Virus-MIC > 1000 μg/mL	Inactive [98]
	Fresh Th	MeOH Ext.	Epstein-Barr virus early antigen activation inhibition (telocidin b-4 induced Epstein-Barr virus induced activation)-4.0 μg/mL	** [99]
Gracilaria verrucosa (Hudson) Papenfuss	FzDO	MeOH Ext.	Cell culture-*Herpes simplex* 1 Virus	Inactive [77]
Antiprotozoal activity				
Gracilaria corticata (J.Agardh) J.Agardh	SDTh	90% EtOH Ext.	Agar plate-*Entamoeba histolytica; Plasmodium berghei*	Inactive [75]
Gracilaria edulis (S.G.Gmelin) P.C.Silva	SDTh	90% EtOH Ext.	Agar plate-*Entamoeba histolytica; Plasmodium berghei*	Inactive [75]
Allelophatic activity				
Gracilaria compressa (C.Agardh) Greville	DEP	95% EtOH Ext.	Agar plate-*Helianthus tuberosus*-dose: dry weight of plant	Active [76]
Gracilaria foliifera (Forsskål) Borgesen	DEP	H_2O Ext.	Agar plate-*Helianthus tuberosus*-dose: dry weight of plant	Active [76]
Gracilaria verrucosa (Hudson) Papenfuss	DEP	95% EtOH Ext.	Agar plate-*Helianthus tuberosus*-dose: dry weight of plant	Active [76]

Legend: DEP = Dried entire plant; DO = Dried organism; DTh = Dried thallus; EP = Entire plant; FO = Frozen organism; FsO = Fresh organism; FsTh = Fresh thallus; FTh = Frozen thallus; FzDO = Freeze dried organism; FzDTh = Freeze Dried thallus; SDTh = Shade dried thallus; Th = Thallus; PET Ether); ** = Not stated.

These biological studies were mainly developed in Japan and Brazil. This fact is justified by the extensive coastlines and marine biodiversity and is influenced by several factors for the development of these species, such as temperature, radiation, salinity, metal ions and other chemically fundamental components. Australia and Guam have recently become interested in the study of algae and diverse marine species. The consumption of algae has increased in European countries in recent decades with 15 to 20 species of algae being marketed in Italy, France and Greece. In western countries like Venezuela, USA and Canada, the macroalgae are industrially used as a source of hydrocolloids agar, carrageenan and alginate [100]. Carrageenan has been found to be useful in ulcer therapy and alginates are known to prolong the period of activity of certain drugs [8–11].

2.1. Studies of Toxicity

In France, extract studies with ethanol/water draw up from dried entire plant of *G. foliifera* showed toxicity in humans when treated with oral dose and cytotoxicity studies [75,76]. *G. coronopifolia* and *G. edulis* were also toxic to humans [65,49] (See Table 1). Carbohydrate, heparin [97], agar [101], manauealide A, manauealide B [64], manauealide C [102], palmitic, palmitoleic, oleic, lauric and myristic acids [103], steroids and alkaloids malyngamide [104] were found in these species (Figure 1).

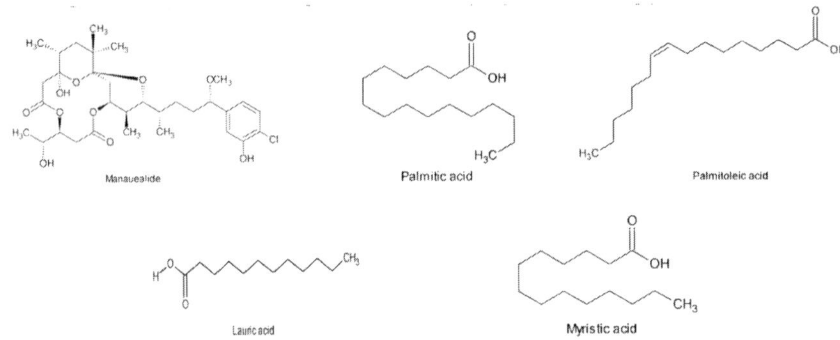

Figure 1. Structure of the compounds found in *G. foliifera, G. coronopifolia* and*G. edulis.*

There is currently a tendency to substitute the use of laboratory animals in toxicological tests with alternative methods to reduce their numbers in experiments, or refine the existing methodology in order to minimize pain and stress [105]. A rapid and effective alternative to realize primary toxicity and biological action screening of compounds is the estimation of the 50% lethal concentration (LC_{50}) through brine shrimp assay using*Artemia salina* L. [106]. A 90% ethanol extract of *G. domingensis* had LC_{50} of 200 μg/mL against *A. salina*[74].

Another method to evaluate toxicity is determining cytotoxic activity. In this context aqueous extract from dried thallus of *G. bursa-pastoris* (10.0 μg/mL), chloroform and methanol extracts from *G. textorii,* which was isolated steroid cholest-4-en-3-one [107], and ethanol extract from *G. verrucosa* were not toxic in cell culture. However, aqueous extract from *G. verrucosa* at a dose of 1.2 mg/animal showed toxicity to mice [48], according to Table 1. In this seaweed, lipids were indentified, such as PGF_{α} [84,85], glycerol, ethanolamine-phosphatidyl [58], choline-phosphatidyl [58,108], ethanol-phosphatidyl [58], floridoside [109], and carbohydrates, such as agar [110–113] (Figure 2).

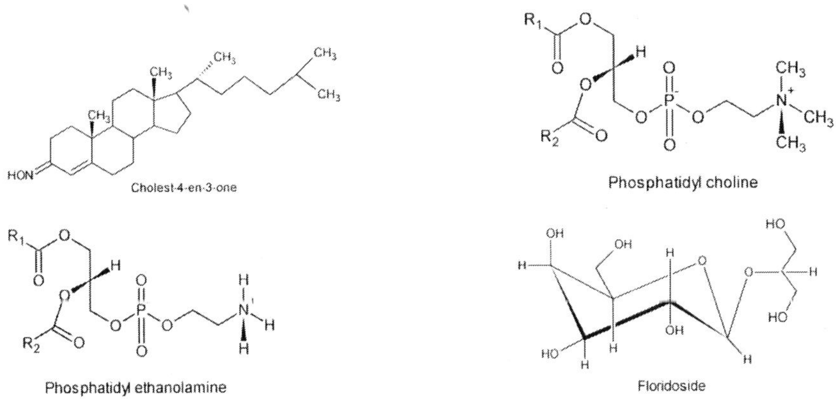

Figure 2. Structure composed of species of *Gracilaria* tested in cytotoxicity.

2.2. Effects on the Nervous System

Studies related to nervous system are important to understanding and treat complex degenerative and behavioral diseases. 90% ethanol extracts from *G. corticata, G. edulis* and *G. verrucosa* did not cause central or periphery effects for mice or dogs (50 mg/kg), and did not show analgesic or anticonvulsant activities for mice [75] (Table 1).

2.3. Contraception Activity

The researchers have also investigated new molecules with anticonceptive action; the post-coital contraceptive action of marine seaweeds was also evaluated in animals. Methanol: methylene chloride (1:1) extract from *G. corticata* was orally administered at 500 or 1000 mg/kg/day to female rats from day 1 to day 7 of their pregnancies. Higher doses produced significant post-coital contraceptive activity due to enhanced pre-implantation without any marked side effects. These findings indicate that red marine algae are a potential source for post-coital contraceptive drugs [80].

90% Ethanol extracts from *G. edulis* (100 mg/kg) and *G. corticata* were inactivated before the antiimplantation effect when they tested in pregnant rats [75,80]. Ethanol extracts from shade dried thallus of*G. edulis* and *G. verrucosa* were inactive in spermicidal bioassays [75]. Extracts from *G. edulis* showed 100% inhibition of sperm motility and this effect was related to disruption of the plasma membrane by spermicidal compounds [3] (Table 1).

2.4. Anti-Inflammatory and Antioxidant Activities

The anti-inflammatory activity of seaweeds has been studied. Polysaccharide fractions from *G. verrucosa* at a dose of 4.0 mg/animal were orally and intraperitoneally administered to mice and showed immunopotentiating activity stimulating phagocytosis [82]. Methanol extract and polysaccharide fractions from *G. verrucosa* were also antioxidant [82,83]. Aqueous extract from *G. textorii* at a dose of 100 µg/mL did not inhibit platelet aggregation induced by adenosine diphosphate, arachidonic acid or collagen [81]. *G. verrucosa, G. asiatica, G. lichenoides* and others species contain PGE_2 [47,85], that have physiological effects including hyperthermia, hypotension, smooth muscle dilatation, hyperalgesia and gastric secretion inhibition [114,115] (Table 1).

2.5. Gastrointestinal Effects

Aqueous extract from dried *G. verrucosa* algae or fresh *G. chorda* algae at a dose of 0.5 mg/animal controlled gastrointestinal disorders in mice [48] (Table 1), resulting from zeaxanthin and antheraxanthin [116], carotenoids, pyrimidine 2-amino-4-carboxy, non-alkaloid nitrogen heterocycle [90], steroids, 5-alpha-poriferastane, 3-beta-6-alpha-diol poriferastane, 5-alpha-3-beta-6-beta-diol [51] and gigatinine [85] (Figure 3).

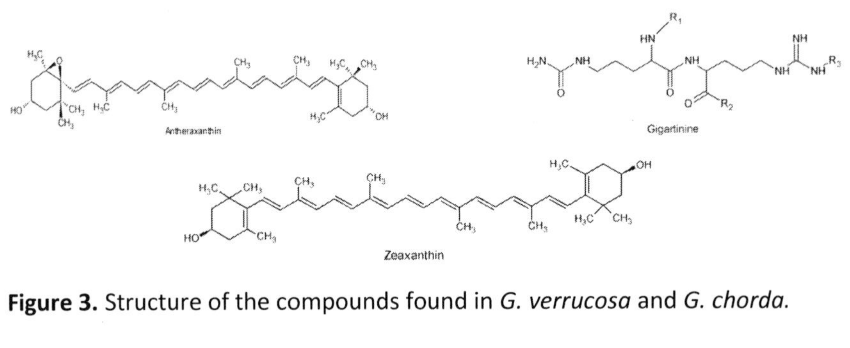

Figure 3. Structure of the compounds found in *G. verrucosa* and *G. chorda*.

2.6. Cardiovascular Effects

90% Ethanol extracts from *G. corticata, G. edulis* and *G. verrucosa* showed no cardiovascular effects in dogs (50 mg/kg) [75]. 90 % ethanol extract from *G. edulis* showed diuretic activity [75]. Aqueous extract from *G. lichenoides* was administered intravenously in rats and it was antihypertensive [84]. Tyrosinase inhibition was not induced by methanol extract from *G. arcuata* [86] and aqueous extract from *G. textorii*, 10 μg/mL, was negligable on aldose reductase [83] (Table 1).

2.7. Antibiotic Activity

Extracts or ingredients from various algae have shown antibacterial activity *in vitro* against gram-positive and gram-negative bacteria [117]. The agar disc diffusion method for antibacterial susceptibility was used for evaluation and 6 mm discs were impregnated with 20 μL of the extracts and placed in inoculated Muller Hinton agar. Antibacterial activity from chloroform extract of *G. edulis* (Gmelin) Silva was tested against bacterial strains of *Vibrio cholera, Staphylococcus aureus, Shigella dysenteriae, Shigella bodii, Salmonella paratyphi, Pseudomonas aeruginosa* and *Klebsiella pneumonia* (Table 1). We observed higher activity for*G. edulis* extract than *S. aureus* extract [12]. Yet it was inactive for *Sporotrichum schenckii, Candida albicans* and *Cryptococcus neoformans* [75]. In the present investigation, the chemical compounds isolated from the species were steroids (carotenoids, β-cryptoxanthin and β-carotene) [118] and carbohydrates [84,85,119] (Figure 4).

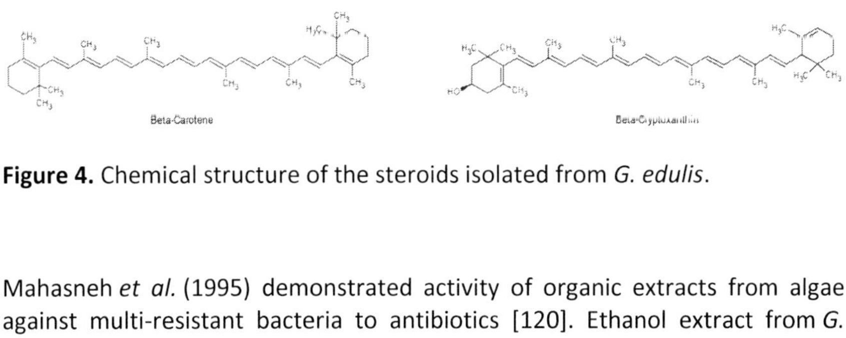

Figure 4. Chemical structure of the steroids isolated from *G. edulis*.

Mahasneh *et al.* (1995) demonstrated activity of organic extracts from algae against multi-resistant bacteria to antibiotics [120]. Ethanol extract from *G. debilis* showed antibacterial activity against *S. aureus* but was inactive against *Mycobacterium smegmatis* [92].

95% ethanol extract from whole dried *G. cervicornis* algae was active against *S. aureus* at a concentration of 5.0 mg/mL [89]. Methanol extract from fresh *G. corticata* was active against *Bacillus subtilis*, *Bacillus megaterium, S. aureus* and *Streptococcus viridians* [91].

G. corticata and *G. pygmea* did not inhibit the growth of *Aspergillus niger, Fusarium solani, Alternaria solani,* or *Penicillium funiculosum* [91]. Petroleum ether, chloroform and methanol extracts from this seaweed at a concentration of 1.0 μg/units proved to be inactive on the inhibition of penicillinase enzyme

[87]. From this specie, stearic lipids and capric acids were isolated [121] (Figure 5).

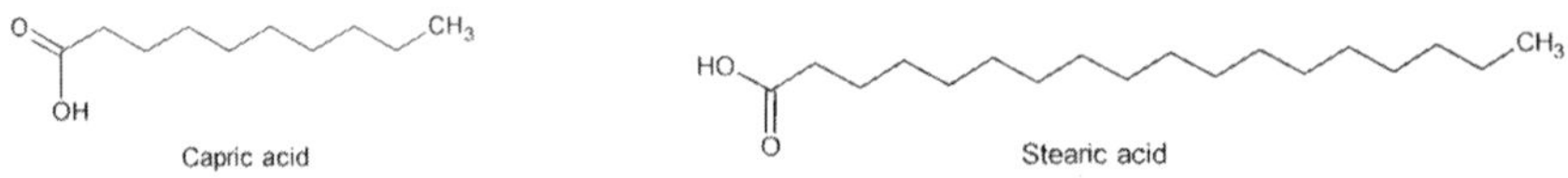

Figure 5. Structure of compounds found in species of *Gracilaria* with antifungal activity.

Ethanol extracts from *G. domigensis* and *G. sjoestedii* showed antibacterial activity against *E. coli* and *S. aureus*. Ethanol extracts from *G. debilis, G. domingensis* and *G. sjoestedii* were active against *Candida albicans* shown by agar plate method [92]; Chloroform, ether and methanol extracts from *G. tikvahiae* were inactive [93]. The growth of *Neurospora crassa* was not inhibited by extracts from *G. sjoestedii* and *G. debilisi*; ethanol extract from *G. domigensis* was active against *Mycobacterium smegmatis* and *Neurospora crassa* [92]. *G. domigensis* has as chemical constituents, polysaccharide CT-1 [122], palmitic acid and steroids (stigmasterol, sitosterol, campesterol, cholest-7-en-3-β-ol and brassicasterol) [52] (Figure 6).

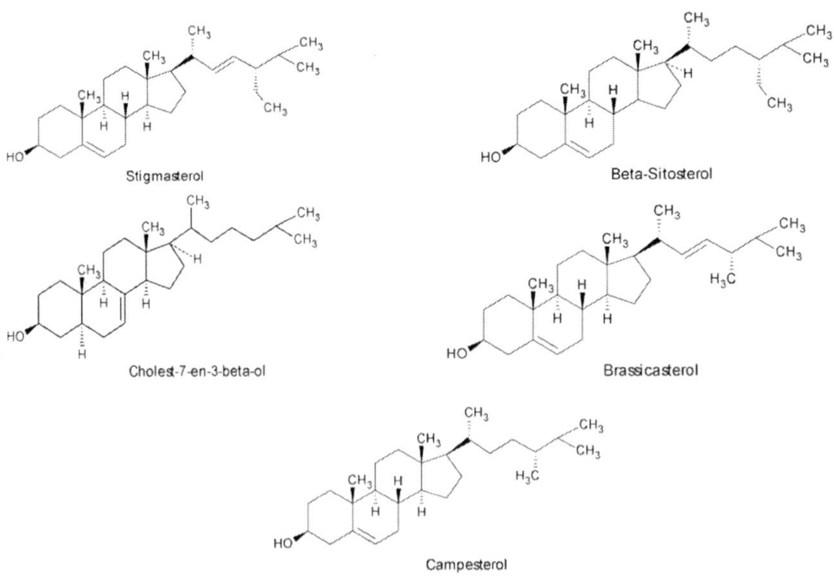

Figure 6. Structure of the steroids isolated from *G. domingensis*.

Some studies highlighting antiparasitic activity of seaweeds also were verified. 90 % ethanol extract from *G. corticata* and *G. edulis* were tested against *Entamoeba histolytica* and *Plasmodium berghei* and were not active [75].

2.8. Antivirial Activity

Extracts from *G. bursa-pastoris* and *Gracilaria* sp were inactive against the *Herpes simplex* 1 virus (HSV) and the human immunodeficiency virus (HIV) when evaluated in cell cultures [96]. Granin BP and citrullinyl-arginine proteins were isolated from these extracts [123,124]. Methanol extract from dried *G. pacifica* at a concentration of 200.0 µg/mL was active against *Sindbis* virus, but was not effective against *H. simplex* 1 when tested at a concentration of 400 µg/mL. Extracts and compounds obtained from *Gracilaria*sp with anti-HIV activity are also active against other retroviruses such as HSV. However, the pharmacodynamic mechanisms of the antiretroviral activity are still unknown because bioactive compounds from seaweed poorly investigated [9] (Table 1) (Figure 7).

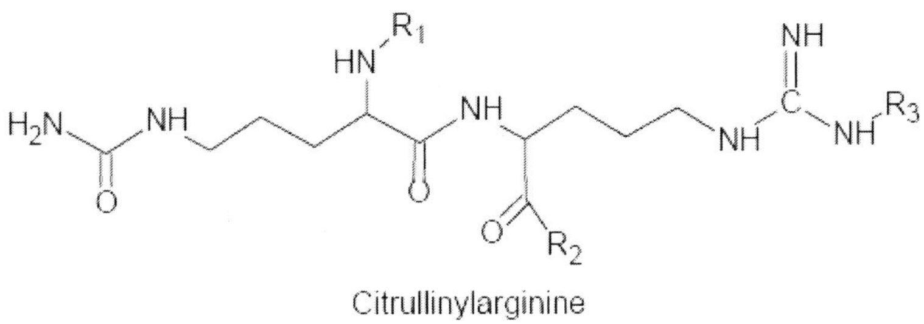

Figure 7. Structure of a compound found in *Gracilaria* sp and *G. bursa-pastoris*.

3. MATERIAL AND METHODS

In this article, some reports about bioactivity of *Gracilaria* algae were reviewed in the specialized literature published up to January 2011. The search was carried out using data banks such as; Biological Abstracts, AlgaeBase, SciFinder Scholar, Pubmed and NAPRALERT (acronym for Natural Products ALERT-University of Illinois in Chicago, USA).

4. CONCLUSIONS

Algae are abundant in the oceans and represent a rich source of as yet unknown secondary metabolites. In this review, we found only a few studies with complete chemical profiles and pharmacological potential of the *Gracilaria* species. Most studies raised concerns about antimicrobial activity against *Staphylococcus, Streptococcus, Candida* and *Herpes* genus. Others referenced the cytotoxicity bioassays in which these algae species were not active, but they produce various types of prostaglandins and others substances that can be toxic to humans such as gastrointestinal disorders and lethality caused by *G. verrucosa* and *G. edulis*, respectively. To research new drugs it is necessary to evaluate other bioassay models to preserve the safety, efficacy and quality of the end products. In Brazil, there is a great need for toxicological, pharmacological, preclinical and clinical studies, as recommended by the RDC 48/2004.

Finally, we conclude that algae of the *Gracilaria* genus are a potential source for synthesis of new natural medicines. It is important to taxonomically classify and standardize extractions, while identifying the active compounds to attenuate possible environmental interference that could undermine the pharmacochemical profile, and thus generate different pharmacologic effects. In addition, it is important to sensitize corporate researchers and financial agencies to support this cause.

ACKNOWLEDGMENTS

The authors thank CNPq/CAPES/PRONEX-FAPESQ-PB-Brazil for financial support.

REFERENCES

1. Jha RK, Zi-rong X. Biomedical compounds from marine organisms. Mar. Drugs. 2004;2:123–146.

2. Falcão VR. PhD Thesis. Institute of Chemical, University of São Paulo; São Paulo, Brazil: 2006. Aspectos moleculares de nitrato redutase da macroalga marinha Gracilaria tenuistipitata (Rhodophyta): Seqüenciamento do gene e estudo da expressão do RNA mensageiro; pp. 1–187.

3. Babuselvam M, Ravikumar S. Screening of Male Anti-Fertility Compounds from Marine Seaweed Macro Algae. Division of Marine

Microbiology and Medicine, Manonmaniam Sundaranar University; Rajakkamangalam, India: 1993. [accessed on 14 May 2011]. pp. 1–14. Available online:http://www.scisoc.or.th/stt/32/sec_h/paper/stt32_H_H0001.pdf.

4. Smit AJ. Medicinal and pharmaceutical uses of seaweed natural products: A review. J. Appl. Phycol.2004;16:245–262.

5. Ito K, Hori K. Seaweed: Chemical composition and potential uses. Food Rev. Int. 1989;5:101–1144.

6. Darcy-Vrillon B. Nutritional aspects of the developing use of marine macroalgae for the human food industry. Int. J. Food Sci. Nutr. 1993;44:523–535.

7. Lahaye M. Marine algae as a source of dietary fibers: Determination of soluble and insoluble dietary fiber contents in some 'sea vegetable' J. Sci. Food Agric. 1993;54:523–535.

8. Elena M, Francisco Y, Erickson KL. Mailiohydrin, a cytotoxic chamigrene dibromohydrin from a Phillippine Laurencia species. J. Nat. Prod. 2001;64:790–791.

9. Kim JB, Hudson AM, Huang K, Bannistes A, Jin TJ, Choi GHN, Towers YK, Wreede RE. Biological activity of seaweed extracts from British, Colombia, Canada and Korea. I. Antiviral activity. Can. J. Bot.1997;75:1656–1660.

10. Okai Y, Highasi OK, Ishizaka S, Yamashita U. Enhancing effect of polysaccharides from a edible brown algae, Hijikia furiform (Hijki) on release of tumour necrosis factor alpha from macrophages of endotoxin non responder C3H/HCl mice. Nutr. Cancer. 1997;27:381–386.

11. Premila JC, Raviraja NS, Sridhar KR. Antimicrobial activity of some marine algae of south-west coast of India. Indian J. Mar. Sci. 1996;26:201–205.

12. Vallinayagam K, Arumugan R, Ragupathi Raja Kannan RRR, Thirumaram G, Anantharaman P. Antibacterial activity of some selected seaweeds from Pudumadam coastal regions. Glob. J. Pharmacol.2009;3:50–52.

13. Faulkner DJ. Marine natural products. Nat. Prod. Rep. 2002;19:1–48.

14. Cardozo KHM, Guaratini T, Barros MP, Falcão VR, Tonon AP, Lopes NP, Campos S, Torres MA, Souza AO, Colepicolo P, et al. Metabolites from algae with economical impact. Comp. Biochem. Physiol. C: Comp. Pharmacol. 2006;146:60–78.

15. O'Sullivan L, Murphy B, McLoughlin P, Duggan P, Lawlor PG, Hughes H, Gardiner GE. Prebiotics from marine macroalgae for human and animal health application. Mar. Drugs. 2010;8:2038–2064.[PMC free article]

16. Paniagua-Michel J, Capa-Robles W, Olmos-Soto J, Gutierrez-Millan LE. The carotenogenesis pathway via the isoprenoid-beta-carotene interference approach in a new strain of Dunaliella salina isolated from Baja California Mexico. Mar. Drugs. 2009;7:45–56. [PMC free article]

17. Cen-Pacheco F, Nordstrom L, Souto ML, Martin MN, Fernandez JJ, Daranas AH. Studies on polyethers produced by red algae. Mar. Drugs. 2010;8:1178–1188. [PMC free article]

18. Klisch M, Hader DP. Mycosporine-like amino acids and marine toxins—The common and the different.Mar. Drugs. 2008;6:147–163. [PMC free article]

19. Pallela R, Na-Young Y, Kim SK. Anti-photoaging and photoprotective compounds derived from marine organisms. Mar. Drugs. 2010;8:1189–1202. [PMC free article]

20. D'Ayala GG, Malinconico M, Laurienzo P. Marine derived polysaccharides for biomedical applications: Chemical modification approaches. Molecules. 2008;13:2069–2106.

21. Kellmann R, Stuken A, Orr RJS, Svendsen HM, Jakobsen KS. Biosynthesis and molecular genetics of polyketides in marine Dinoflagellates. Mar. Drugs. 2010;8:1011–1048. [PMC free article]

22. Souza ET, Lira DP, Queiroz AC, Silva DJC, Aquino AB, Mella EAC, Lorenzo VP, Miranda GEC, Araújo-Júnior JX, Chaves MCO, et al. The antinociceptive and anti-inflammatory activities of caulerpin, a bisindole alkaloid isolated from seaweeds of the genus Caulerpa. Mar. Drugs. 2009;7:689–704.[PMC free article]

23. Guven KC, Percot A, Sezik E. Alkaloids in marine algae. Mar. Drugs. 2010;8:269–284.[PMC free article]

24. Cabrita MT, Vale C, Rauter AP. Halogenated compounds from marine algae. Mar. Drugs. 2010;8:2301–2317. [PMC free article]

25. La Barre S, Potin P, Leblanc C, Delage L. The halogenated metabolism of brown algae (Phaeophyta), its biological importance and its environmental significance. Mar. Drugs. 2010;8:988–1010. [PMC free article]

26. Ianora A, Boersma M, Casotti R, Fontana A, Harder J, Hoffmann F, Pavia H, Potin P, Poulet SA, Toth G. New trends in marine chemical ecology. Estuaries Coasts. 2006;29:531–551.

27. Deig EF, Ehresmann DW, Hatch MT, Riedlinger DJ. Inhibition of herpesvirus replication by marine algae extracts. Antimicrob. Agents Chemother. 1974;6:524–525. [PMC free article]

28. Jha RK, Zi-rong X. Biomedical compounds from marine organisms. Mar Drugs. 2004;2:123–146.

29. Newman DJ, Cragg GM, Snader KM. Natural products as sources of new drugs over the period 1981–2002. J. Nat. Prod. 2003;66:1022–1037.

30. Lindequest U, Schweder T. Marine biotechnology. In: Rehm HJ, Reed G, editors. Biotechnology. Vol. 10. Wliey-VHC; Weinheim, Germany: 2001. pp. 441–484.

31. Linsert P. Revolution in infant formula brewing in Herman's calves. DNA algae. Genet. Eng. Biotechnol. Monit. 1994;1:45–46.

32. Khotimchenko SV, Vaskovsky VE, Titlyanavo TV. Fatty acids of marine algae from the 12 substances from marine algae Puerto Rico. Antimicrob. Agents Chemother. 1963;161:68–72.

33. Ryther JH, Goldman JC, Gifford CE. Physical models of integrated waste recycling marine polyculture systems. Aquaculture. 1975;5:163–177.

34. Capo TR, Jaramillo JC, Boyd AE, Lapointe BE, Serafy JE. Sustained high yields of Gracilaria(Rodophyta) grown in intensive large-scale culture. J. Appl. Phycol. 1999;11:143–147.

35. Guiry MD. AlgaeBase. Martin Ryan Institute, National University of Ireland; Galway, Ireland: 1996–2011. [accessed on 14 May 2011]. Available online: http://www.algaebase.org.

36. Skriptsova AV, Titlyanova TV, Titlyanov EA. Red algae of the genus Gracilaria in south of the Russian far east. Russ. J. Mar. Biol. 2001;27:S38–S52.

37. Kain JM, Destombe C. A review of the life history, reproduction and phenology of Gracilaria. J. Appl. Phycol. 1995;7:69–281.

38. Misawa M. Production of natural substances by plant cell cultures described in japanese patents. In: Barz W, Reinhard E, Zenk MH, editors. Plant Tissue Culture Its Bio-Technol. Springer-Verlag; Berlin, Germany: 1977. pp. 17–26.

39. Murano E, Toffanin R, Paoletti S, Rizzo R. Pyruvate-rich agarose from the red alga Gracilaria dura.Planta Med. 1992;58:A588–A589.

40. Hemmingson JA, Furneaux RX, Murray-brown VH. Biosynthesis of agar polysaccharides in Gracilaria chilensis bird. Carbohydr. Res. 1996;287:101–115.

41. Brasch DJ, Chuah CT, Melton LD. Marine algal polysaccharides, Part 2. The agar-type polysaccharide from the red alga Gracilaria secundata. Carbohydr. Res. 1983;115:191–198.

42. Glombitza KW. In: Marine Algae in Pharmaceutical Science. Hoppe HA, Levring T, editors. Vol. 1. Walter de Gruyter; New York, NY, USA: 1979. pp. 303–342.

43. Glickman M. Utilisation of seaweed hydrocolloids in the food industry. Hydrobiology.1987;151/152:31–47.

44. Imbs AB, Vologodskaya AV, Nevshupova NV, Khotimchenko SV, Titlyanoy EA. Response of prostaglandin content in the red alga Gracilaria verrucosa to season and solar irradiance. Phytochemistry.2001;58:1067–1072.

45. Chapman VJ, Chapman DJ. Seaweeds and Their Uses. Springer-Verlag; Berlin, Germany: 1980.

46. Sajiki J. Effect of acetic acid treatment on the concentrations of arachidonic acid and prostaglandin E2 in the red algae, Gracilaria asiatica and G. rhodocaudata. Fish Sci. 1997;63:128–131.

47. Fusetani N, Hashimoto K. Prostaglandin E2: A candidate for causative agent of “Ogonori” poisoning.Bull. Jpn. Soc. Sci. Fish. 1984;50:465–469.

48. Yotsu-yamashita M, Haddock RL, Yasumoto T. Polycavernoside A: A novel glycosidic macrolide from the red alga Polycavernosa tsudai (Gracilaria edulis) J. Am. Chem. Soc. 1993;115:1147–1148.

49. Das B, Srinivas KVNS. Minor C29-steroids from the marine red alga, Gracilaria edulis. Phytochemistry.1992;31:2427–2429.

50. Das B, Srinivas KVNS. Dihydroxysterols from the marine red alga, Gracilaria edulis. Phytochemistry.1992;31:4731–4373.

51. Combres A, Bianchini JP, Gaydou EM. Fatty acid and sterol composition of red algae of the Indian ocean. Oceanol. Acta. 1986;9:339–342.

52. Toffanin R, Murano E, Modricky C, Kvam BJ, Paoletti S, Rizzo R, Pollesello P. Free and acylated cholesterol in the red alga Gracilaria longa: detection and quantification by 1H- and 13C-NMR on lipid extracts. Planta Med. 1992;58:A589–A590.

53. Castedo L, Quintela JM, Vilalta R. Sterols from red and brown algae from the Galician coast. An. Quim. Ser. C. 1985;8:113–115.

54. Vilalta R, Quintela JM, Riguera R, Castedo L. Natural marine products from algae and cnidaria of the Galician estuaries. Cuad. Area Cienc. Mar. 1984;2:617–625.

55. Henriquez P, Trucco R, Silva M, Sammes PG. Cholesterol in Iridaea laminarioides and Gracilaria verrucosa. Phytochemistry. 1972;11:1171.

56. Prostaglandin E-2. Patent-Japan Kokai Tokkyo Koho. 1982;59:73–565.

57. Araki S, Sakurai T, Oohusa T, Kayama M. Component fatty acid of lipid from Gracilaria verrucosa.Bull. Jpn. Soc. Sci. Fish. 1986;52:1871–1874.

58. Son BW. Glycolipids from Gracilaria verrucosa. Phytochemistry. 1990;29:307–309.

59. Das B, Srinivas KVNS. Two new sterols from the marine red alga Gracilaria edulis. Planta Med.1993;59:572–573.

60. Sajiki J, Hakimi H. Identification of eicosanoids in the red algae, Gracilaria asiatica, using high-performance liquid chromatography and electrospray ionization mass spectrometry. J. Chromatogr.1998;795:227–237.

61. Ravi BN, Faulkner DJ. Acyclic diterpenes from the marine sponge Didiscus sp. J. Org. Chem.1979;44:968–970.

62. Sims JJ, Pettus JA., Jr Isolation of free cis and trans-phytol from the red alga Gracilaria andersoniana.Phytochemistry. 1976;15:1076–1077.

63. Nagai H, Yasumoto T, Hokama Y. Manauealides, some of the causative agents of a red alga Gracilaria coronopifolia poisoning in Hawaii. J. Nat. Prod. 1997;60:925–928.

64. Nagai H, Yasumoto T, Hokama Y. Aplysiatoxin and debromoaplysiatoxin as the causative agents of a red alga Gracilaria coronopifolia poisoning in Hawaii. Toxicon. 1996;34:753–761.

65. Yotsu-yamashita M, Seki T, Paul VJ, Naoki H, Yasumoto T. Four new analogs of polycavernoside A.Tetrahedron Lett. 1995;36:5563–5566.

66. D'agnolo E, Rizzo R, Paoletti S, Murano E. R-phycoerythrin from the red alga Gracilaria longa.Phytochemistry. 1994;35:693–696.

67. Talarico L, Kosovel V. Properties and ultrastructures of r-phycoerythrin from Gracilaria verrucosa.Photosynthetica. 1978;12:369–374.

68. Wilcox SJ, Bloor SJ, Hemmingson JA, Furneaux RH, Nelson WA. The presence of gigartinine in a New Zealand Gracilaria species. J. Appl. Phycol. 2001;13:409–413.

69. Kanoh H, Kitamura T, Kaboyashi Y. A sulfated proteoglycan from the red alga Gracilaria verrucosa is a hemagglutinin. Comp. Biochem. Physiol. B. 1992;102:445–449.

70. Kirkpatrick P. Antibacterial drugs. Stitching together naturally. Nat. Rev. Drug Discovery. 2002;1:748–748.

71. Kosovel V, Avanzini A, Scarcia V, Furlani A. Algae as possible sources of antitumoural agents: Preliminary evaluation of the "in vitro" cytostatic activity of crude extracts. Pharmacol. Res. Commun.1988;20:27–31.

72. Kamat SY, Wahidulla S, D'Souza L, Naik CG, Ambiye V, Bhakuni DS, Goel AK, Garg HS, Srimal RC. Bioactivity of marine organisms. VI. Antiviral evaluation of marine algal extracts from the Indian Coast.Bot. Mar. 1992;35:161–164.

73. Lhullier C, Horta PA, Falkenberg M. Avaliação de extratos de macroalgas bênticas do litoral catarinense utilizando o teste de letalidade para Artemia salina. Rev. Bras. Farmacogn. 2006;16:158–163.

74. Bhakuni DS, Dhawan BN, Garg HS, Goel AK, Mehrotra BN, Srimal RC, Srivastava MN. Bioactivity of marine organisms: Part VI-Screening of some marine flora from Indian coasts. Indian J. Exp. Biol.1992;30:512–517.

75. Chenieux JC, Verbist JF, Biard JF, Clement E, Le Boterff J, Maupas P, Lecocq M. Seaweeds of French atlantic coast with antimitotic activity. Planta Med. 1980;40:152–162.

76. Arisawa M, Hayashi K, Nikaido T, Koike K, Fujita D, Nunomura N, Tanaka M, Sasaki T. Screening of some marine organism extracts for camp phosphodiesterase inhibition, cytotoxicity, and antiviral activity against HSV-1. Int. J. Pharmacogn. 1997;35:6–11.

77. Numata A, Kanbara S, Takahashi C, Fujiki R, Yoneda M, Fujita E, Nabeshima Y. Cytotoxic activity of marine algae and a cytotoxic principle of the brown alga Sargassum tortile. Chem. Pharm. Bull.1991;39:2129–2131.

78. Avanzini A, Kosovel V, Scarcia V, Furlani A, Ravalico L. Green, red and brown algae from North Adriatic sea as source of possible cytotoxic products. Fitoterapia. 1987;58:391–394.

79. Ratnasooriya WD, Premakumara GAS, Tillekeratne LMV. Post-coital contraceptive activity of crude extracts of Sri Lankan marine red algae. Contraception. 1994;50:291–299.

80. Okada Y, Miyauch N, Suzuki K, Kobayashi T, Tsutsui C, Mayuzumi K, Okuyama T. Search for naturally occurring substances for prevention against the complications of diabetes; inhibitory effect on aldose reductase and platelet aggregation. Nat. Med. 1994;48:324–329.

81. Yoshizawa Y, Tsunehiro J, Nomura K, Itoh M, Fukui F, Ametani A, Kaminogawa S. In vivomacrophage-stimulation activity of the enzyme-degraded water-soluble polysaccharide fraction from a marine alga (Gracilaria verrucosa) Biosci. Biotechnol. Biochem. 1996;60:1667–1671.

82. Choi JS, Lee JH, Park HJ, Kim HG, Young HS, Mun SI. Screening for antioxidant activity of plants and marine algae and its active principles from Prunus davidiana. Korean J. Pharmacogn. 1993;24:299–303.

83. Funayama S, Hikino H. Hypotensive principles from plants. Heterocycles. 1981;15:1239–1256.

84. Gregson RP, Marwood JF, Quinn RJ. The occurrence of prostaglandins PGE2 and PGF2α in a plant-the red alga Gracilaria lichenoides. Tetrahedron Lett. 1979;20:4505–4506.

85. Choi BW, Lee BH, Kang KJ, Lee ES, Lee NH. Screening of the tyrosinase inhibitors from marine algae and medicinal plants. Korean J. Pharmacogn. 1998;29:237–242.

86. Sridhar P, Lakshmi VV, Polasa H, Reddy VS, Rao CHP, Srimannarayana G. Biological activity of some marine algal extracts. Indian J. Mar. Sci. 1984;13:90–91.

87. Bitou N, Inomiya M, Tsujita T, Okuda H. Screenning of lipase inhibitors from marine algae. Lipids.1999;34:441–445.

88. Perez RM, Avila JG, Perez S, Martinez A, Martinez G. Antimicrobial activity of some American algae.J. Ethnopharmacol. 1990;29:111–116.

89. Salleh A, Wati Haron N, Mahmud N, Mohammad J. Distribution of pyrimidine derivatives in algae.Biochem. Syst. Ecol. 1994;22:860.

90. Usmanghani K, Shameel M, Sualeh M, Khan KH, Mahmood ZA. Antibacterial and antifungal activities of marine algae from Karachi seashore of Pakistan. Fitoterapia. 1984;55:73–77.

91. Albuquerque MR, Campos-Takaki, Koening ML. Detection of antimicrobial activity in marine seaweeds. Rev. Inst. Antibiot. Univ. Fed Pernambuco Recife. 1983;21:127–138.

92. Oranday MA, Verde MSJ, Martínez-Lozano NH, Waksman J. Active fractions from four species of marine algae. Phyton. 2004;73:165–170.

93. Lustigman B, Lee LH, Thees N, Masucci J. Production of antibacterial substances by macroalgae of the New York/New Jersey coast, USA. Bull. Environ. Contam. Toxicol. 1992;49:743–749.

94. Couladis M, Vagias C, Roussis V, Verykokidou E, Skaltsa H. Antiphage properties of some Greek algae extracts. Phytomedicine. 1998;5:479–483.

95. Hayashi K, Hamada J, Hayashi T. A screening strategy for selection of anti-HSV-1 and anti- HIV extracts from algae. Phytother. Res. 1996;10:233–237.

96. Kamat SY, Wahidulla S, D'Souza L, Naik CG, Ambiye V, Bhakuni DS, Goel AK, Garg HS, Srimal RC. Bioactivity of marine organisms. VI. Antiviral evaluation of marine algal extracts from the Indian Coast.Bot. Mar. 1992;35:161–164.

97. Nakamura H, Ohnuki N, Sadamasu K, Sekine H, Tanaka J, Okada Y, Okuyama T. Anti-human immunodeficiency virus (HIV) activities of aqueous extracts from marine algae. Nat. Med. 1994;48:173–179.

98. Ohigashi H, Sakai Y, Yamaguchi K, Umezaki I, Koshimizu K. Possible anti-tumor promoting properties of marine algae and in vivo activity of

wakame seaweed extract. Biosci. Biotechnol. Biochem. 1992;56:994–995.

99. Hsu B-Y, Tsao C-Y, Chiou T-K, Hwang D-F. Factors affeecting PGE2 production in seaweedGracilaria tenuistipitata. J. Food Drug Anal. 2008;16:59–65.

100. Laserna EC, Veroy RL, Luistro AH, Cajipe GJB. Extracts from some red and brown seaweeds of the Philippines. In: Levring T, editor. Tenth International Seaweed Symposium. Walter de Gruyter & Co; Berlin, Germany: 1980. pp. 443–448.

101. Nagai H, Kan Y, Fujita T, Sakamoto B, Kokama Y. Manauealide C and anhydrodebromoaplysiatoxin, toxic constituents of the hawaiian red alga, Gracilaria coronopifolia. Biosci. Biotechnol. Biochem.1998;62:1011–1013.

102. Parekh KS, Parekh HH, Rao PS. Fatty acid content of some Indian marine algae. Indian J. Mar. Sci.1984;13:45–46.

103. Kan Y, Fujita T, Nagai H, Sakamoto B, Hokama Y. Malyngamides M and N from the hawaiian red alga Gracilaria coronopifolia. J. Nat. Prod. 1998;61:152–155.

104. Parra AL, Yhebra RS, Sardiñas IG, Buela LI. Comparative study of the assay of Artemia salina L. and the estimate of the medium lethal dose (LD50 value) in mice, to determine oral acute toxicity of plant extracts. Phytomedicine. 2001;8:395–400.

105. Meyer BN, Ferrigni NR, Putnam JE, Jacobsen LB, Nichols DE, McLaughlin JL. Brine shrimp: A convenient general bioassay for active plant constituints. Planta Med. 1982;45:31–34.

106. Kanazawa A, Yoshioka M. Occurrence of Cholest-4-en-3-one in the Red Alga. Gracilaria textorii Proceedings of the Seventh International Seaweed Symposium; Sapporo, Japan. 1–12 August 1971; New York, NY, USA: Wiley; 1972. pp. 502–505.

107. Kunzler K, Eichenberger W. Betaine lipids and zwitterionic phospholipids in plants and fungi.Phytochemistry. 1997;46:883–892.

108. Roh YS, Son W, Im KS, Choi HD. Structure of floridoside, a glycerol glycoside from the marine red alga Gracilaria verrucosa. Korean J. Pharmacogn. 1994;25:117–120.

109. Laserna EC, Veroy RL, Luistro AH, Cajipe GJB. Extracts from some red and brown seaweeds of the Philippines. In: Levring T, editor. Tenth

International Seaweed Symposium. Walter de Gruyter & Co; Berlin, Germany: 1980. pp. 443–448.

110. Matsuhashi T. Effects of the freezing and drying method and the mechanical dehydration method by pressure on gel properties of dried agar. Reito. 1974;49:756–760.

111. Shi SY, Zhang YX, Liu WQ, Li z. Seasonal variation in yield, physical properties and chemical composition of agar from Gracilaria verrucosa. Oceanol. Limnol. Sin. 1983;14:272–278.

112. Friedlander M, Lipkin Y, Yaphe W. Composition of agars from Gracilaria verrucosa and Pterocladia capillacea. Bot. Mar. 1981;24:595–598.

113. Minghetti L, Levi G. Microglia as effector cells in brain damage and repair: Focus on prostanoids and nitric oxide. Prog. Neurobiol. 1998;54:99–125.

114. Nishihara I, Minami T, Uda R, Ito S, Hyodo M, Hayaishi O. Effect of NMDA receptor antagonists on prostaglandin E2-induced hyperalgesia in conscious mice. Brain Res. 1995;677:138–144.

115. Aihara MS, Yamamoto H. Occurrence of antheraxanthin in two Rhodophyceae Acanthophora spiciferaand Gracilaria lichenoides. Phytochemistry. 1968;7:497–499.

116. Tuney I, Çadirci BH, Unal D, Sukatar A. Antimicrobial activities of the extracts of marine algae from the coast of Urla. Turk. J. Biol. 2006;30:171–175.

117. Aihara MS, Yamamoto H. Occurrence of antheraxanthin in two Rhodophyceae Acanthophora spiciferaand Gracilaria lichenoides. Phytochemistry. 1968;7:497–499.

118. Panossian AG. Search of prostaglandins and related compounds in plants: A review of the occurrence of prostaglandins and prostaglandin-like compounds in plants. prostaglandins. 1987;33:363–381.

119. Mahasneh I, Jamal M, Kashashneh M, Zibdeh M. Antibiotic-activity of marine-algae against multi-antibiotic resistant-bacteria. Microbios. 1995;83:23–26.

120. Parekh KS, Parekh HH, Rao PS. Fatty acid content of some Indian marine algae. Indian J. Mar. Sci.1984;13:45–46.

121. Fernandez LE, Valiente OG, Mainardi V, Bello JL, Velez H, Rosado A. Isolation and characterization of an antitumor active agar-type polysaccharide of Gracilaria dominguensis. Carbohydr. Res. 1989;190:77–83.

122. Okamoto R, Hori K, Miyazawa K, Ito K. Isolation and charcterization of a new hemagglutinin from the red alga Gracilaria bursa-pastoris. Experientia. 1990;46:975–977.

123. Laycock MV, Craigie JS. The occurrence and seasonal variation of gigartinine and l-citrullinyl-l-arginine in Chondrus crispus stackh. Can. J. Biochem. 1977;55:27–30.

Chapter 8

Halogenated Indole Alkaloids from Marine Invertebrates

Patrícia Mendonça Pauletti, Lucas Silva Cintra, Caio Guedes Braguine, Ademar Alves da Silva Filho, Márcio Luís Andrade e Silva, Wilson Roberto Cunha and Ana Helena Januário *

Núcleo de Pesquisas em Ciências Exatas e Tecnológicas, Universidade de Franca. Av. Dr. Armando Salles de Oliveira, 201, CEP 14404-600, Franca, São Paulo, Brazil

ABSTRACT

This review discusses the isolation, structural elucidation, and biological activities of halogenated indole alkaloids obtained from marine invertebrates. Meridianins and related compounds (variolins, psammopemmins, and aplicyanins), as well as aplysinopsins and leptoclinidamines, are focused on. A compilation of the ^{13}C-NMR spectral data of these selected natural indole alkaloids is also provided.

Keywords: marine invertebrates; halogenated indole alkaloids; structure elucidation; bioactivity; ^{13}C-NMR spectral data

1. INTRODUCTION

Marine organisms are among the most promising sources of bioactive molecules [1–3]. Unlike terrestrial organisms, marine organisms often produce halogenated secondary metabolites, particularly alkaloids [4]. The majority of halogenated metabolites contain bromine and they are especially abundant in the marine environment, whereas chlorinated compounds are preferably synthesized by terrestrial organisms. In contrast to brominated and chlorinated metabolites, iodinated and fluorinated compounds are quite rare [5,6].

Marine life produces most of the 4,000 known natural organohalogens. Almost all of the 2,100 natural organobromine compounds are found in marine organisms. Although there is much less bromide than chloride in the oceans (bromine 65 mg/L; chlorine 19,000 mg/L), marine organisms can oxidize bromide more easily for incorporation into organic compounds. Nevertheless, a large number of marine metabolites contain both bromine and chlorine [7,8].

Ecological pressures within the marine ecosystem, including significant competition for space, deterrence of predation, and a high level of symbiosis between different species, are partially responsible for the unique secondary metabolism of marine life that give rise to the chemical components of these actions and interactions [9,10].

The presence of halogen substituents in many natural products profoundly influences their biological activity [6]. Examples of such biologically active compounds are the antibiotics vancomycin, chloramphenicol aureomycin, and salinosporamide A; a proteasome inhibitor currently under clinical trials for multiple myeoloma treatment; and the antimicrobial rebeccamycin [6,8].

Among halogenated alkaloids, bromoalkaloids are the most widely distributed group of natural compounds. This group is predominantly found in marine eukaryotes, is significantly rarer in prokaryotic microorganisms, and is practically absent from terrestrial plants and animals [4]. Iodoalkaloids compose a rare group of natural compounds that has been isolated from marine organisms [4].

The first iodinated indoles found in a natural source, either marine or terrestrial, were the plakohypaphorines A–C (**1–3**,Figure 1) isolated from the Caribbean sponge *Plakortis simplex* [8,11].

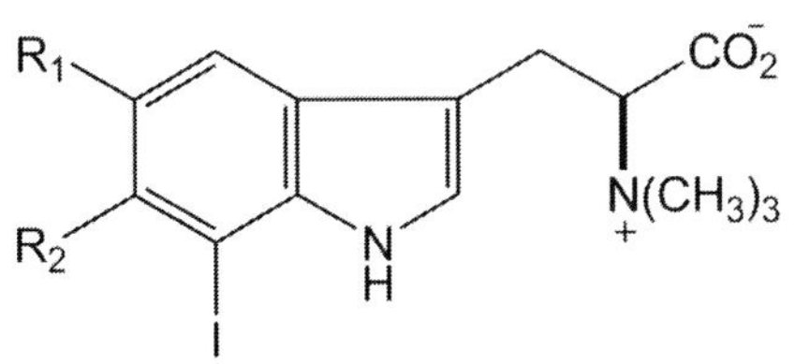

	R_1	R_2
(1) Plakohypaphorine A	H	H
(2) Plakohypaphorine B	H	I
(3) Plakohypaphorine C	I	H

Figure 1. Structures of plakohypaphorines A, B, and C (**1–3**).

A huge diversity of indole alkaloids are frequently found in marine invertebrates and they have been considered lead compounds for the discovery of new drugs in medicinal chemistry [9,12]. The biological activity of marine indole alkaloids is clearly a product of the unique functionality and elements involved in the biosynthesis of marine natural products. For instance, bromination of many natural products has the potential to increase biological activity significantly [9].

In this report we have focused on the halogenated indole alkaloids from marine invertebrates, particularly meridianins; their related compounds variolins, psammopemmins, and aplicyanins as well as the aplysinopsins and leptoclinidamines. Also summarized are the methods of structure determination, observed biological activities and a compilation of ^{13}C-NMR spectral data is provided.

1.1. Biohalogenation

The halogenation of natural products is a frequent modification of secondary metabolism that allows for optimization of the bioactivity of small molecules, providing evolutionary advantage [6].

Many biohalogenation enzymes have been isolated and characterized. Chloroperoxidase, bromoperoxidase, iodoperoxidase, and the enzymes involved in the biosynthesis of fluoroacetic acid (fluoroacetaldehyde dehydrogenase and 5′-fluorodeoxyadenosine synthase) are some examples [8].

Halogenating enzymes have been discovered in a broad range of organisms and they can be grouped into two main classes: (i) highly substrate-specific halogenases requiring dioxygen for enzymatic activity and (ii) less specific haloperoxidases (HPO) utilizing hydrogen peroxide. In dioxygen-dependent halogenases, either flavin ($FADH_2$-dependent halogenases) or R-ketoglutarate (non-heme FeII/R-ketoglutarate/O_2- dependent halogenases) are found to function as co-substrates. Furthermore, methyltransferases are involved in the formation of the carbon halogen bonds of CH_3Cl, CH_3Br, and CH_3I, and other enzymes requiring *S*-adenosyl-L-methionine as catalyst have been identified to be involved in fluorination and chlorination [13].

In the recent years, the understanding of biohalogenation processes has been extended extraordinarily. The cloning and sequencing of biosynthetic gene clusters have revealed new mechanisms leading to halogen incorporation and stimulated detailed mechanistic studies of these enzymes [6,8]. New groups of halogenating enzymes have been discovered and investigated at both biochemical and genetic levels. Each group of these enzymes performs halogenation reactions on chemically distinct substructures using a specific reaction mechanism. For instance, some $FADH_2$-dependent halogenases are directly involved in the halogenation of aromatic compounds, recognizing tryptophan or indole moieties, while other groups of $FADH_2$-dependent halogenases participate in the halogenation of aliphatic compounds [13].

1.2. Meridianins

Meridianins are marine alkaloids which were first isolated from the Ascidian *Aplidium meridianum* [14]. Structurally, the meridianins comprise a brominated and/or hydroxylated indole nucleus substituted at C-3 by a 2-aminopyrimidine. Seven meridianins A–G (**4–10**) have been discovered so far. Bromine substitution occurs on position 5 for meridianin C (**6**), on position 6 for B (**5**) and D (**7**), on position 7 for E (**8**), and on positions 5 and 6 for F (**9**) (Figure 2).

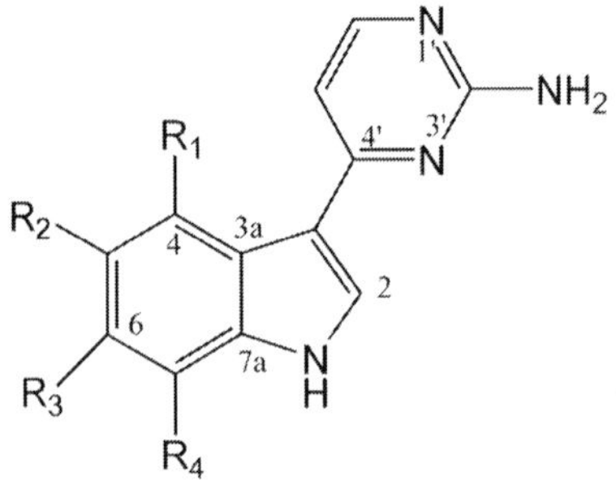

	R_1	R_2	R_3	R_4
(**4**) Meridianin A	OH	H	H	H
(**5**) Meridianin B	OH	H	Br	H
(**6**) Meridianin C	H	Br	H	H
(**7**) Meridianin D	H	H	Br	H
(**8**) Meridianin E	OH	H	H	Br
(**9**) Meridianin F	H	Br	Br	H
(**10**) Meridianin G	H	H	H	H

Figure 2. Structures of meridianins **4–10**.

Meridianins have been described as potent inhibitors of various protein kinases (Table 1) and they display antitumor activity. Meridianins B (**5**) and E (**8**) are the most potent and, for this reason meridianin E was selected for further selectivity studies on 25 highly purified kinases [15]. Essentially, all physiological processes and most human diseases involve protein phosphorylation. Phosphorylation of proteins on serine, threonine, and tyrosine residues by the 518 protein kinases encoded in the human genome constitutes one of the major mechanisms used by cells to regulate their metabolism and functions. The recent appreciation of the implication of abnormal protein phosphorylation in many human diseases has sparked considerable interest in the search for pharmacological inhibitors of kinases [16–18].

Table 1. Effects of meridianins A–G (**4–10**) on the activity of protein kinases (IC_{50} in μM).

Protein kinase	Meridianins						
	A	B	C	D	E	F	G
CDK1/cyclin B	2.50	1.50	3.00	13.00	0.18	20.00	150.00
CDK5/p25	3.00	1.00	6.00	5.50	0.15	20.00	140.00
PKA	11.00	0.21	0.70	1.00	0.09	3.20	120.00
PKG	200.0	1.00	0.40	0.80	0.60	0.60	400.00
GSK-3β	1.30	0.50	2.00	2.50	2.50	2.00	350.00
CK1	nt [1]	1.00	30.00	100.00	0.40	nt [1]	nt [1]

[1] nt: not tested.

Protein phosphorylation regulates most aspects of cell life, whereas abnormal phosphorylation is a cause or consequence of diseases. For instance, among the 518 human kinases cyclin-dependent kinases (CDK) have attracted considerable interest given their involvement in many essential physiological pathways and numerous abnormalities in multiple human diseases, especially cancer and neurodegenerative diseases such as Alzheimer's and Parkison's diseases [16,18,19].

Investigations of structure-activity relationships of meridianins have revealed that the substitution at C-5 and the methylation of the indole nitrogen are important for either kinase inhibitory activity or *in vitro* antiproliferative activities. Related to CDK1 and CDK5, the bromine substitution on position 7 and the hydroxyl on position 4 provide the best inhibitory activity. A single bromine substitution on position 5 or 6 of the indole ring results in considerable improvement in potency. On the other hand, two bromide substitutions slightly reduce the inhibitory potency [20,21].

Meridianins B, C, D, and E (**5–8**) display cytotoxicity toward LMM3 (murine mammalian adenocarcinoma cell line) with IC_{50} values of 11.4 μM, 9.3 μM, 33.9 μM, and 11.1 μM, respectively [14]. Certainly, meridianins constitute a new scaffold exhibiting micromolar inhibition of protein kinases from which more potent and selective inhibitors can be designed [15].

Meridianins are closely related to the variolins, a class of marine alkaloids from the Antarctic sponge *Kirkpatrickia varialosa* [22,23].

1.3. Variolins

In 1994, the Blunt, Munro and Faulkner laboratories reported the isolation and structural elucidation of the variolins from the rare Antarctic sponge *Kirkpatrickia varialosa* [22,23]. Variolins are the first examples of either terrestrial or marine natural products with a pyrido[3′,2′:4,5]pyrrolo[1,2-c]pyrimidine system. This rare pyridopyrrolopyrimidine skeleton has made the variolins an interesting class of alkaloids from both structural and biogenetic viewpoints. Variolins can also be considered as guanidine-based alkaloids in which the guanidine moiety is found in the guise of a 2-aminopyrimidine ring [24–26].

The isolated compounds included variolin A (**11**), variolin B (**12**), *N*(3′)-methyl tetrahydrovariolin B (**13**), and variolin D (**14**), the latter of which was reported to be an artifact of the extraction process produced by aerial oxidation of the variolins (Figure 3). This type of compounds exhibit a potent cytotoxic activity against P388 murine leukemia cell line, also being effective against Herpes simplex type I. Variolin B (**12**) is the most active of this family of natural products [26].

There has been considerable interest in the synthesis of variolins due to the novelty of their structures, not to mention their biological properties and low natural occurrence [25]. To date, four total syntheses of variolin B have been reported in the literature [21,27–33], and the preparation of the synthetic deoxyvariolin B (**15**) has also been described [34,35]. The synthesis of new derivatives of variolin B with different substituents at positions C-5 and C-7 has also been reported [26].

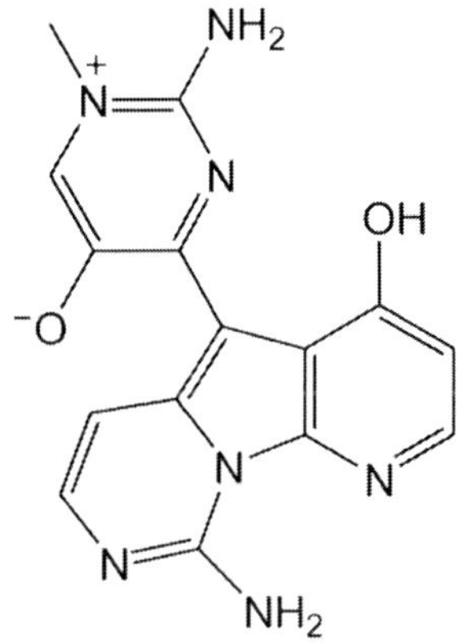

(**11**) Variolin A

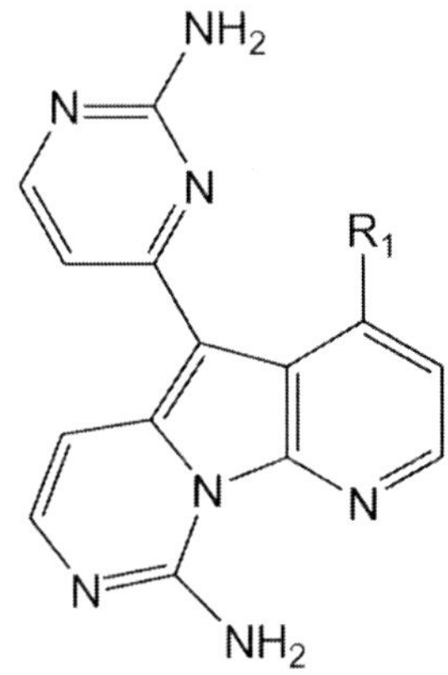

	R_1
(**12**) Variolin B	OH
(**15**) Deoxyvariolin B	H

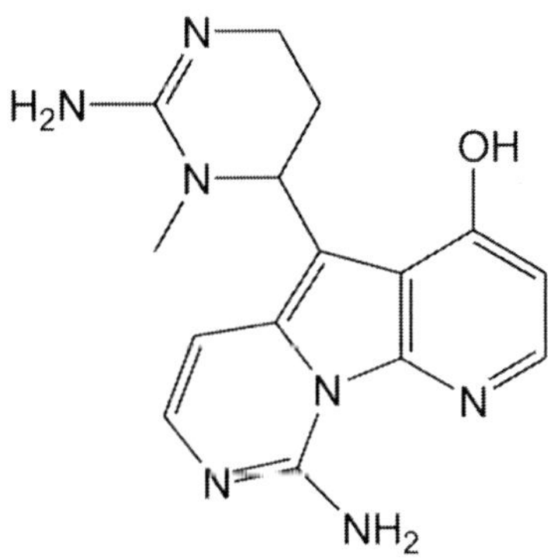

(**13**) *N*(3')-methyltetrahydrovariolin B

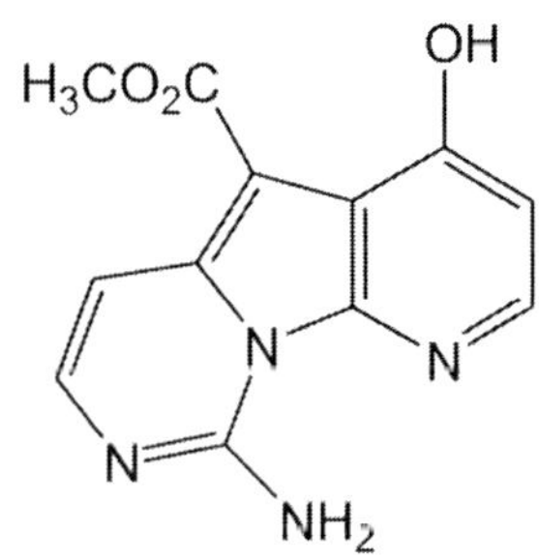

(**14**) Variolin D

Figure 3. Structures of variolins **11–15**.

Although the natural variolins isolated are not halogenated, this type of skeleton along with the structure of meridianins have been an inspiration for the synthesis of the hybrid meriolins 1–14 (**16–29**, Figure 4), including the halogenated meriolins 10 (**25**) and 11 (**26**) [18].

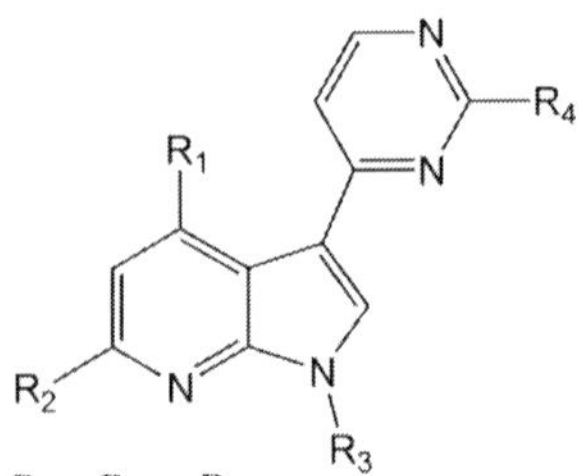

	R_1	R_2	R_3	R_4
(**16**) Meriolin 1	H	H	H	NH_2
(**17**) Meriolin 2	OH	H	H	NH_2
(**18**) Meriolin 3	OMe	H	H	NH_2
(**19**) Meriolin 4	OEt	H	H	NH_2
(**20**) Meriolin 5	OPr	H	H	NH_2
(**21**) Meriolin 6	OiPr	H	H	NH_2
(**22**) Meriolin 7	$O(CH_2)_2OMe$	H	H	NH_2
(**23**) Meriolin 8	OH	H	Me	NH_2
(**24**) Meriolin 9	OMe	H	Me	NH_2
(**25**) Meriolin 10	Cl	H	H	NH_2
(**26**) Meriolin 11	H	Br	H	NH_2
(**27**) Meriolin 12	OMe	H	H	SMe
(**28**) Meriolin 13	OH	H	H	H
(**29**) Meriolin 14	OMe	H	H	H

Figure 4. Structures of meriolins **16–29**.

1.4. Meriolins

Variolins with a pyridopyrrolopyrimidine system and meridianins possessing a pyrimidyl-substituted indole skeleton bear some structural similarities. Through a combination of the common features of these natural products, a new class of 7-azaindole-containing analogues (**16–29**) known as meriolins has been designed by Meijer and co-workers [21].

Meriolins [3-(pyrimidin-4-yl)-7-azaindoles], a chemical hybrid of the variolins and meridianins, display potent inhibitory activity toward CDKs (especially CDK2 and CDK9). This class of compounds also exhibit better antiproliferative and proapoptotic properties in cell cultures compared with their "inspirational parent" molecules [18,19].

The resemblance between the chemical structures of the two natural products meridianins and variolin B has inspired the synthesis of a hybrid structure referred to as meriolins, which display better antiproliferative and proapoptotic properties in human tumor cell cultures than their parent molecules. A selectivity study performed on 32 kinases has shown that, compared with variolin B, meriolins exhibit enhanced specificity toward CDKs, with marked potency on CDK2 and CDK9 [19].

The structures of pCDK2/cyclin A/meriolin 3, pCDK2/cyclin A/meriolin 5, and pCDK2/cyclin A/variolin B complexes have been determined by X-ray crystallography, which revealed that these inhibitors bind within the ATP binding site of the kinase, but in different orientations [18,19,21].

All synthesized meriolins 1–14, along with variolin B as a reference, were tested on seven purified protein kinases, namely CDK1/cyclin B, CDK2/cyclin A, CDK5/p25, CDK9/cyclin T, GSK-3 δ/β, CK1δ/ε, and DYRK1A (Table 2). Structure-Activity studies complemented with the crystal structure have provided some clarification on the action mechanisms of these molecules on their CDK target [18].

Table 2. Effects of variolin B (**12**) and meriolins 1(**16**), 10 (**25**), and 11 (**26**) on the activity of protein kinases (IC_{50} in μM).

Protein kinase	Variolin B	Meriolin 1	Meriolin 10	Meriolin 11
CDK1/cyclin B	0.06	0.78	0.24	2.20
CDK2/cyclin A	0.08	0.09	0.06	1.3
CDK5/p25	0.09	0.51	0.23	0.68
CDK9/cyclin T	0.026	0.026	0.05	1.00
GSK-3α/β	0.07	0.63	2.00	30.0
CK1	0.005	0.2	3.0	1.3
DYRK1A	0.08	0.13	0.13	0.3

In the case of meriolin 11 (**26**), addition of a bromide atom at C-5 leads to a drop in inhibitory activity for almost all tested protein kinases, but this effect is particularly pronounced against CDK9 and GSK-3. CDK1, CDK2, and CDK5 are less affected by the bromide addition. Moreover, addition of a chloride atom at C-4 in meriolin 10 (**25**) results in decreased potency compared to the non-halogenated meriolin 1 (**16**). Taken together, these observations suggest that meriolins constitute a new CDK inhibitory scaffold with promising antitumor activity, and they can be derived from molecules initially isolated from marine organisms [19].

1.5. Psammopemmins

Psammopemmins represent an unusual group of natural products isolated as an amine salt from an Antarctic marine sponge *Psammopemma* sp and they comprise three structurally related compounds designated psammopemmins A–C (**30–32**, Figure 5). All of the psammopemmins incorporate the 4-hydroxyindole moiety substituted at the 3-position by an unusual 2-bromopyrimidine system. Compounds containing 4-oxygenated indoles often display potent pharmacological properties. Psammopemmins B (**31**) and C (**32**) contain further bromination on the indole ring. Unfortunately, the small amounts of material isolated so far have precluded any further investigation of their biological activity. The assigned structure of the psammopemmin family likewise remains to be confirmed by total synthesis [21,36].

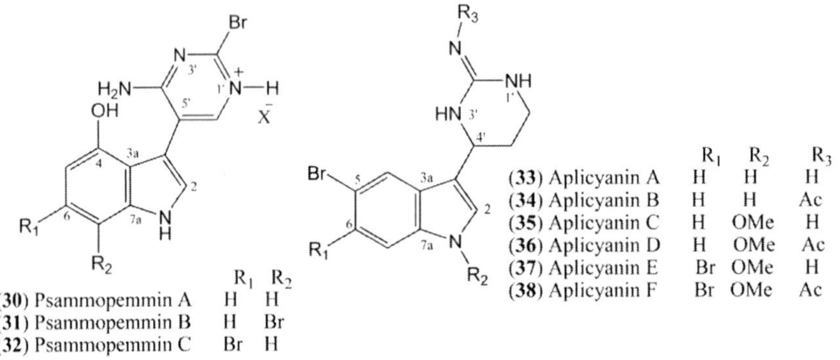

	R_1	R_2
(**30**) Psammopemmin A	H	H
(**31**) Psammopemmin B	H	Br
(**32**) Psammopemmin C	Br	H

	R_1	R_2	R_3
(**33**) Aplicyanin A	H	H	H
(**34**) Aplicyanin B	H	H	Ac
(**35**) Aplicyanin C	H	OMe	H
(**36**) Aplicyanin D	H	OMe	Ac
(**37**) Aplicyanin E	Br	OMe	H
(**38**) Aplicyanin F	Br	OMe	Ac

Figure 5. Structures of psammopemmins **30–32** and aplycianins **33–38**.

1.6. Aplicyanins

A new family of indole alkaloids was recently isolated from the Antarctic tunicate *Aplidium cyaneum* by Reyes and co-workers [37]. The aplicyanins A–F (**33–38**, Figure 5) contain a bromoindole nucleus and a 6-tetrahydropyrimidine substituent at C-3. The main structural variations present in aplicyanins include additional bromination of indole ring and the presence of *N*-methoxy group as shown in aplicyanins C–F (**35–38**). The aplicyanins share a common 3-(pyrimid-4-yl)indole structure with meridianins A–G (**4–10**), the psammopemmins A–C (**30–32**) and variolins A–D (**11–14**). The tetrahydropyrimidine system of the aplicyanins has a stereocenter at C 4′, in contrast with the planar pyrimidine ring of the meridianins [21].

Aplycianins are cytotoxic to the human tumor cell lines MDA-MB-231 (breast adenocarcinoma), A549 (lung carcinoma), and HT-29 (colorectal carcinoma). They also exhibit antimitotic activity [38]. Lastly, given the high cytotoxicity typical of bromoindole derivatives, the presence of a bromoindole moiety in some aplicyanins warrants their investigation as anticancer drugs. Recently, the first total synthesis of (±)-aplicyanins A, B, and E and 17 analogues has been reported [38].

Regarding the aplicyanin family of indole alkaloids, the six variants of aplicyanins isolated were evaluated for cytotoxicity against a panel of three human tumor cell lines, colon (HT-29), lung (A-549), and breast (MDA-MB-231). The antimitotic activity of these variants has also been assessed. Cytotoxic activity in the submicromolar range as well as antimitotic properties have been found for aplicyanin B (**34**), D (**36**), and F (**38**), with IC_{50} values in the low to sub-μM range. On the other hand, aplicyanin A (**33**) and C (**35**) proved to be inactive at the highest concentrations tested, whereas aplicyanin E (**37**) displayed weak cytotoxic properties (Table 3). These results indicate a key role for the presence of the acetyl group in the biological activity of the aplicyanin family [37].

Table 3. Cytotoxicity (GI_{50} values reported in μM) and antimitotic activity (IC_{50}, mM) of aplicyanins B (**34**), D (**36**), E (**37**), F (**38**) and (±) aplicyanin A, B, and E.

Compound	Cell lines			Antimitotic
	A-549	HT-29	MDA-MB-231	Activity
Aplicyanin B	0.66	0.39	0.42	1.19
Aplicyanin D	0.63	0.33	0.41	1.09
Aplicyanin E	8.70	7.96	7.96	nt[2]
Aplicyanin F	1.31	0.47	0.81	0.18–0.036
(±)-aplicyanin A	0.27	0.11	0.27	nt
(±)-aplicyanin B	0.51	0.33	0.98	nt
(±)-aplicyanin E	na [1]	na	10.9	nt

[1] na: not active; [2]nt: not tested.

In order to establish the structure-activity relationships of the aplicyanins, the total synthesis of (±)-aplicyanins A, B, and E, plus 17 analogues was carried out by Sísa and co-workers in 2009 [38]. The compounds were again screened for cytotoxicity against the same three human tumor cell lines used for the natural compounds. Racemic (±)-aplicyanin A exhibited activity in the submicromolar range, despite the inactivity of the corresponding natural product. Racemic (±)-aplicyanin B was as active as its corresponding natural product in all three tested cellular lines, whereas aplicyanin E maintained the activity only towards the MDA-MB-231cell line (Table 3). The decreased cytotoxicity observed for racemic aplicyanin E compared to the natural product, indicates that one enantiomer is more active than the other [38].

Table 4. Comparison of the biological activity of the main natural halogenated indole alkaloids meridianins, psammopemmins, aplicyanins, and aplysinopsins.

Compound	Biological Activity
Meridianins	
Meridianin B (**5**)	Inhibition of protein kinases: Cytotoxicity [14,15]
Meridianin C (**6**)	Inhibition of protein kinases: Cytotoxicity [14,15]
Meridianin D (**7**)	Inhibition of protein kinases: Cytotoxicity [14,15]
Meridianin E (**8**)	Inhibition of protein kinases: Cytotoxicity [14,15]
Meridianin F (**9**)	Inhibition of protein kinases [14]
Psammopemmins	
Psammopemmin B (**31**)	nt [1]
Psammopemmin C (**32**)	nt
Aplicyanins	
Aplicyanin A (**33**)	na [2]
Aplicyanin B (**34**)	Cytotoxicity and antimitotic activity [37]
Aplicyanin C (**35**)	na
Aplicyanin D (**36**)	Cytotoxicity and antimitotic activity [37]
Aplicyanin E (**37**)	Cytotoxicity [37]
Aplicyanin F (**38**)	Cytotoxicity and antimitotic activity [37]
Aplysinopsins	
6-bromo-2'-de-N-methylaplysinopsin (**40**)	Antimalarial [46]; Serotonin receptors modulator [46] Inhibitor of nitric oxide synthase (nNOS) [47]
6-bromoaplysinopsin (**41**)	Antimalarial [46]; Serotonin receptors modulator [46] Allelochemical [54]
6-bromo-4'-de-*N*-methylaplysinopsin (**42**)	nt
6-bromo-4'-demethyl-3'-*N*-methylaplysinopsin (**43**)	nt
5,6-dibromo-2'-demethylaplysinopsin (**44**)	Inhibitor of nitric oxide synthase (nNOS) [47]
6-bromo-1',8-dihydro-aplysinopsin (**46**)	Antimicrobial [48]
6-bromo-1'-hydroxy-1',8-dihydroaplysinopsin (**47**)	Antimicrobial [48]
6-bromo-1'-methoxy-1',8-dihydroxyaplysinopsin (**48**)	Antimicrobial [48]
6-bromo-1'-ethoxy-1',8-dihydroxyaplysinopsin (**49**)	Antimicrobial [48]
6-bromo-3'-deimino-3'-oxoaplysinopsin (**50**)	nt
6-bromo-3'-deimino-2',4'-bis(demethyl)-3'-Oxoaplysinopsin (**51**)	nt
Dimer of 6-bromo-2'-de-*N*-methylaplysinopsin (**52**)	Antimicrobial [54]
Tubastrindole A (**53**)	-

[1] nt: not tested. [2] na: not active.

Fourteen of the synthesized compounds also exhibited considerable cytotoxic activity, and these results suggest that the bromine at position 5 of the indole nucleus strongly favors antiproliferative activity, and the acetyl group at the imine nitrogen also acts in some compounds. These results demonstrate the potential of aplycianins structure as a scaffold for anticancer drug discovery [38].

1.7. Aplysinopsins

In 1977, Kazlauskas, Rymantas, and co-workers reported the isolation of aplysinopsin (**39**) from the dictoyoceratid sponge *Aplysinopsis* [39,40].

Aplysinopsin derivatives belong to a class of indole alkaloids and they have also been found in other dictyoceratid and astrophorid sponges as well as in dendrophylliid scleractinian corals [41]. Additionally, aplysinopsins have been described in anemone, in a symbiotic association, and in a mollusk that feeds on the coral *Tubastrea coccinea* [39].

The halogenated aplysinopsins natural derivatives (Figure 6) contain a 6-bromoindole moiety, and an iminoimidazolidinone or imidazolidinedione system, both varying in terms of the number and position of *N*-methylation. The iminoimidazolidinone portion of compounds **39–45** are shown as the exocyclic imino tautomer. Only compound **44**contains an additional bromine at the C-5 of the indole core. The aplysinopsins derivatives also differ in terms of the presence and absence of the C-8-C-1′ double bond. Thus, aplysinopsins with C-8-C-1′ double bonds, the most abundant type, can occur as two geometrical isomers (*E*/*Z*). Also, it has been observed that (*Z*)-aplysinopsins are generally less abundant than the (*E*)-isomers [41,42]. Aplysinopsins substituted at the nitrogen atom of the indole ring and dimers have also been isolated or identified, although compound **45** could be an artifact [43–45].

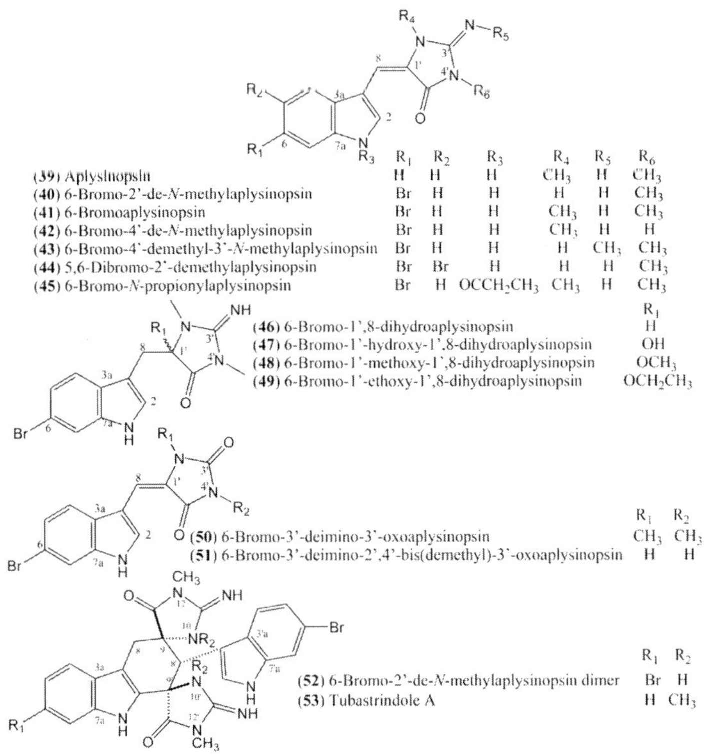

Figure 6. Structures of aplysinopsins **39–53**.

Aplysinopsins exhibit cytoxicity towards tumour cells, as well as some antimalarial and antimicrobial activities. However, properties related to neurotransmission modulation seem to be the most significant pharmacological feature of these compounds. Aplysinopsins have the potential to influence monoaminooxidase (MAO) and nitric oxide synthase (NOS) activities. They have also been found to modulate serotonin receptors [39].

Aplysinopsin-type compounds have been reported from multiple sources, with brominated aplysinopsins being described from sponges [46–49], corals [41–45], anemone, and mollusks [50,51]. Natural aplysinopsins differ in the bromination pattern of the indole ring. Almost all natural occurring aplysinopsins display halogenations at the position 6 of the indole ring. The only exception is the compound 5,6-dibromo-2′-demethylaplysinopsin (**44**), which an additional bromine atom at C-5 [39].

The compounds 6-bromo-2′-de-*N*-methylaplysinopsin (**40**) and 6-bromoaplysinopsin (**41**) isolated from the Jamaican sponge *Smenospongia aurea* displayed high-affinity [^{3}H]antagonist binding from cloned human serotonin 5-HT_{2C} receptors expressed in a mammalian cell line (K_i = 2.3 μM and K_i = 0.33 μM, respectively). Compound **41** also displayed high-affinity [^{3}H]antagonist binding from the 5-HT_{2A} receptor subtype (K_i = 2.0 μM) compared with serotonin affinity values K_i = 0.32 μM at the 5-HT_{2A} receptor and K_i = 0.13 μM at the 5-HT_{2C} receptor [46].

The structure-activity relationship data reveal a role for the R_1, R_2, and R_3 functional groups at positions 6, 2′, and 3′, respectively, in the binding to human serotonin 5-HT_2 receptors. The length of the alkyl chain at the R_3 position as well as the bromination at position R_1 seems to be important for activity. In addition, bromination at the R_1 position is also relevant for the binding affinity of aplysinopsins and for their selective binding to the 5-HT_{2C} receptor subtype, since both compounds **40** and **41** are brominated and both selectively bind the 5-HT_{2C} receptor subtype over the 5-HT_{2A} receptor subtype. Methylation at the R_2 position facilitates binding to the 5-HT_{2A} receptor subtype. A larger number of analogues will be required to confirm this proposed structure-activity relationship [46]. Pharmacological and genetic studies have revealed that these receptors influence feeding, glucose homeostasis, and the energy efficiency of physical activity, sleep, sensory processing and learning, affective functioning, and the pathophysiology of several neuropsychiatric disorders [52,53].

6-Bromo-2′-de-*N*-methylaplysinopsin (**40**) and 6-bromoaplysinopsin (**41**) have also been tested *in vitro* against a D6 clone of *Plasmodium falciparum* for their *in vitro* antimalarial activity. 6-Bromoaplysinopsin (**41**) exhibited activity at 0.34 μg/mL with selective index 14 (S.I. = [IC_{50} (Vero cells)/IC_{50} (*P. falciparum*)], while 6-bromo-2′-de-*N*-methylaplysinopsin (**40**) showed moderate activity at 1.1 μg/mL with low selectivity. Moreover, compound **40** inhibited the antimalarial target plasmepsin II enzyme with IC_{50} 53 μM (FRET) and 66 μM (FP) [46].

Additionally, 6-bromoaplysinopsin (**41**) has been reported to be involved in the symbiotic association between *Radianthus kuekentbali* (sea anemone) and *Amphiprum perideraion* (anemone fish) [50].

A number of aplysinopsin alkaloids have also been evaluated for their neuromodulatory activity in two types of nitric oxide synthase (NOS) isozymes. Nitric oxide (NO) is known to be an important second messenger having numerous functions which regulate many physiological processes; e.g., inflammation, blood pressure regulation, platelet adhesion, neurotransmission, and defense mechanisms. The biosynthesis of NO is catalyzed by nitric oxide synthase (NOS), which is classified into three isoforms: inducible NOS (iNOS), endothelial NOS (eNOS), and neuronal NOS (nNOS). Therefore, a selective inhibitor of NOS isozymes would be expected to have significant therapeutic potential as a neuromodulator [47]. 6-Bromo-2′-de-*N*-methylaplysinopsin (**40**) and the isomers 5,6-dibromo-2′-demethylaplysinopsin *Z*-**44** and *E*-**44** isolated from the sponge *Hyrtios erecta* display selective inhibitory activity against nNOS, with 100% inhibition of nNOS at 125 μg/mL [47]. Compounds *Z*-**44** and *E*-**44** showed no inhibitory activity against iNOS. In turn, aplysinopsin **40** inhibited only 7.5% of iNOS activity at a concentration of 125 μg/mL [47].

Regarding the antimicrobial potential of halogenated aplysinopsins, Koh and Sweatman [54] have reported the screening of the Australian coral *Tubastraea faulkneri* extract for antimicrobial assay against seven species of microbes (*Vibrio alginolyticus*, *V. harveyi*, *V. parahaemolyticus*, *Photobacterium damsela*, *Alteromonas rubra*, *Staphylococcus aureus*, and*Synechococcus* sp). Aplysinopsin (**39**), 6-bromoaplysinopsin (**41**), 6-bromo-2′-de-*N*-methylaplysinopsin (**40**), and its dimer **52**were the compounds isolated accounting for 72% of the activity of the *T. faulkneri* methanol extract. This study also suggested that these aplysinopsins are toxic to the larvae of other coral species that are potential competitors and could act as allelochemicals [54]. The aplysinopsins **46–49** isolated from the sponge *Thorectandra* sp were evaluated for antimicrobial activity against *Staphylococcus epidermidi*. All of the compounds were found to have either weak or moderate minimum inhibitory concentrations (MIC) ranging from 6.25 to 100 μg/mL as compared to the standard vancomycin (0.625 μg/mL) [48].

1.8. Leptoclinidamines

Three new indole alkaloids, namely leptoclinidamines A–C (**54–56**, Figure 7), have been recently isolated from the Australian ascidian *Leptoclinides durus* [55].

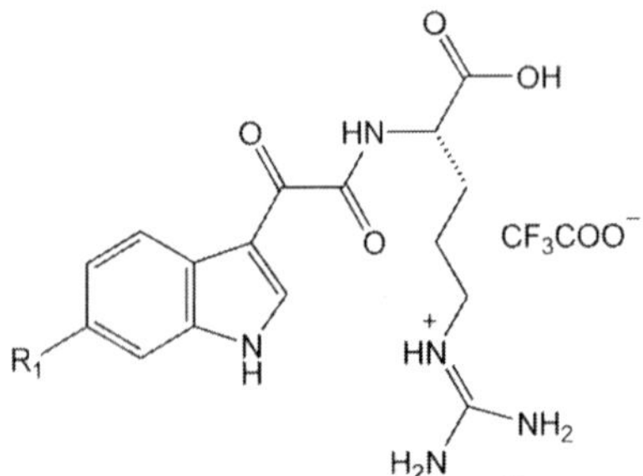

R$_1$
(**54**) Leptoclinidamine A H
(**55**) Leptoclinidamine B OH

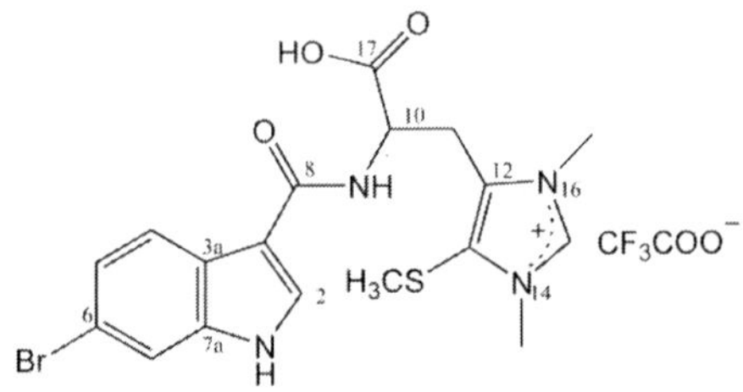

(**56**) Leptoclinidamine C

Figure 7. Structures of leptoclinidamines **54–56**.

The leptoclinidamines A (**54**) and B (**55**) both contain an indoleglyoxylic acid attached to an L-arginine residue, while leptoclinidamine C (**56**) contains the rare 1,3-dimethyl-5-(methylthio)histidine moiety attached to a 6-bromoindole-3-carboxylic acid. The structure of leptoclinidamine A was confirmed by total synthesis. The compounds were tested for bioactivity against chloroquine-sensitive and chloroquine-resistant strains of the malarial parasite *Plasmodium falciparum*, for trypanosomal activity against *Trypanosoma brucei*, and for cytotoxicity against the cancerous cell line HeLa and noncancerous HEK 293 cells, but none of the compounds were bioactive [55].

1.9. Chartelline, Chartellamide, Securamines and Securines

Chartelline A, Chartellamide A, B and C (**57–59**, Figure 8) are unusual β-lactam-imidazole alkaloids isolated from the marine bryozoans *Chartella papyracea* (Flustridae) [56,57]. In addition, other halogenated indole-imidazole alkaloids named securamines were isolated from *Securiflustra securifrons* (Pallas), another member of this family. The halogenated securamines B (**61**) and C (**62**) only differ from securamines A (**60**) and D (**63**), respectively by the presence of a bromine substituent in the benzene ring [58]. Securamines E (**64**), F (**65**) and G (**68**) were isolated from the same bryozoans *S. securifrons* (Pallas) [59]. Securine A (**66**) and B (**67**) were obtained by dissolving securamine A (**60**) and B (**61**), respectively, in DMSO-d_6 [59].

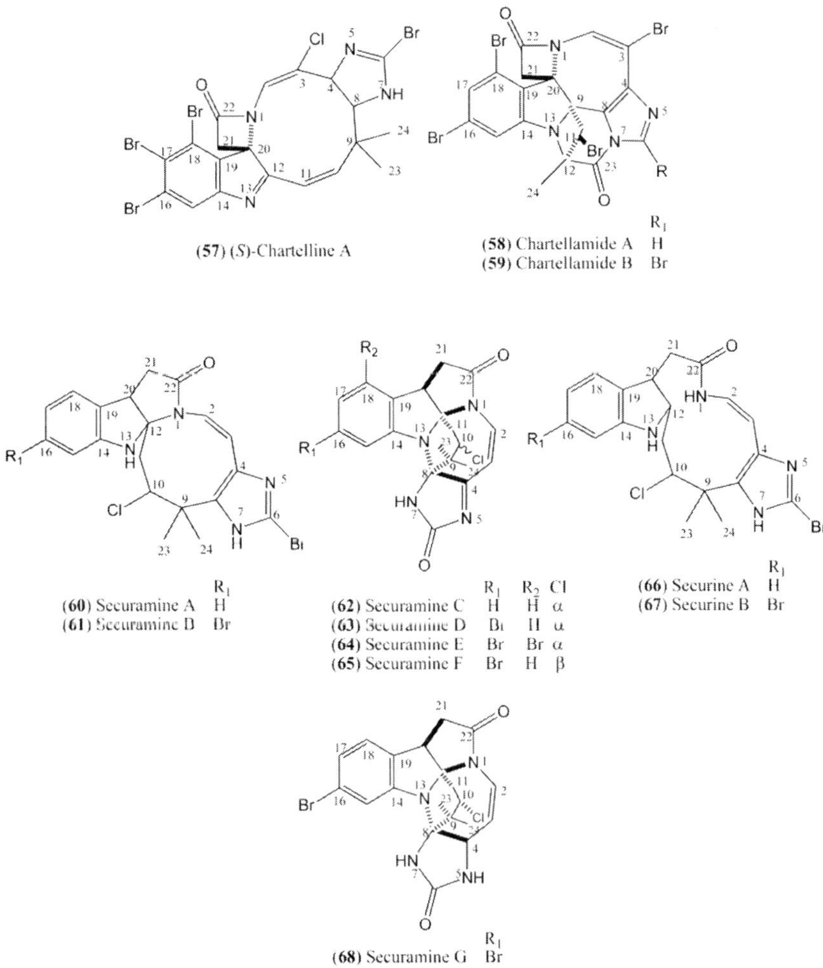

Figure 8. Structures of chartelline, chartellamide, securamines and securines **57–68**.

1.10. Structural Elucidation

This section reports a compilation of the ^{13}C chemical shifts of the halogenated marine indole alkaloids derivatives, meridianins (**5–9**), psammopemmins (**30** and **32**), aplicyanins (**33–38**), aplysinopsins (**40–41, 43–44, 46–51, 53**), and leptoclinidamines (**56**), which have in common the presence of a 3-substituted indole nucleus. Additionally, the ^{13}C data of**10** and **39** are presented for comparison of the ^{13}C chemical shifts with halogenated examples. The literature data are listed in Tables 5, 6, 7 and 8. The solvent (A = DMSO-d_6, B = CD_3OD, and C = $CDCl_3$) and references are shown in the first line of the tables.

Table 5. ^{13}C chemical shifts (δ in ppm) of meridianins, psammopemmins, and aplicyanins halogenated derivatives.

Carbon	5	6	7	8	9	10	30	32	33	34	35	36	37
Solvent	A	A	A	A	B	B	A	A	B	B	B	B	B
Ref.	14	14	14	14	60	60	25	25	37	37	37	37	37
2	129.9	129.6	129.2	129.2	131.6	129.1	128.3	128.8	125.3	125.6	123.8	124.1	124.7
3	113.7	113.3	114.8	116.1	114.9	115.4	113.7	113.6	113.6	113.8	112.0	111.2	112.3
3a	114.0	127.1	124.5	115.2	127.6	126.8	114.3	113.9	124.1	127.8	124.3	124.1	123.5
4	153.0	124.6	124.3	152.0	127.7	122.7	152.0	152.9	121.9	121.8	122.5	122.4	124.6
5	108.8	113.4	123.1	107.3	118.4	123.4	105.4	108.4	115.2	114.3	114.4	114.6	119.3
6	116.7	124.7	113.9	126.7	117.1	121.9	124.3	116.4	125.9	126.1	126.9	127.1	116.4
7	105.3	113.9	114.5	92.6	117.5	112.8	102.3	105.0	114.5	114.6	111.4	111.5	114.6
7a	139.7	135.9	138.0	136.9	138.5	138.9	139.2	139.5	137.2	137.2	132.7	132.7	133.6
2'	160.7	163.6	163.6	160.2	165.3	165.6	161.7	161.6	155.7	152.3	155.7	152.4	155.7
4'	160.8	162.3	162.3	161.8	163.9	165.6	160.7	159.7	48.1	48.2	47.6	47.7	47.4
5'	104.6	105.4	105.4	104.8	107.1	107.6	158.3	158.8	28.3	26.9	28.3	26.6	28.3
6'	157.1	157.2	157.2	159.0	156.2	157.5	104.3	104.3	38.6	38.6	38.4	38.2	38.3
CH_3CO										173.9		174.0	
CH_3CO										24.1		24.1	
OCH_3											66.8	66.7	67.0

Table 6. ^{13}C chemical shifts (δ in ppm) for halogenated aplicyanin **38** and aplysinopsins derivatives.

Carbon	38	39	40 (Z)	40 (E)	41	43 (Z)	43 (E)	44 (*Z*)	44 (*E*)	50 (E)	51 (Z)	51 (E)
Solvent	B	A	A	A	A	A	A	A	A	A	A	A
Ref.	37	62	42	42	43	42	42	47	47	41	41	41
2	125.0	127.4	129.6	129.0	127.7	129.9	129.0	130.6	132.6	129.3	127.5	130.1
3	111.5	108.4	111.9	110.7	108.7	112.0	110.8	108.3	108.2	108.7	108.7	108.9
3a	123.2	127.8	125.7	126.7	126.9	125.7	126.8	127.8	128.4	127.5	126.3	127.3
Solvent	B	A	A	A	A	A	A	A	A	A	A	A
Ref.	37	62	42	42	43	42	42	47	47	41	41	41
4	124.5	118.1	121.0	119.9	119.6	121.1	120.0	123.6	122.5	120.2	120.1	119.2
5	119.5	119.5	122.4	122.5	121.8	122.4	122.5	116.9	116.9	122.6	122.9	122.8
6	116.6	121.8	114.5	114.4	121.8	114.5	114.5	115.2	115.2	114.0	115.0	114.6
7	114.6	111.8	114.3	114.4	114.0	114.3	114.4	116.8	117.2	114.6	114.4	115.0
7a	133.6	135.7	136.7	136.5	136.2	136.5	136.5	135.8	135.8	136.5	136.6	136.5
8		102.8	106.1	113.3	101.5	106.5	113.9	108.9	115.1	107.5	101.0	106.5
1'		126.5	136.9	134.9	126.9	136.9	136.6	135.7	135.7	125.1	124.9	125.4
2'	152.3											
3'	26.8	150.8	157.7	155.0	162.1	157.1	154.7	155.9	152.7	152.8	155.4	153.4
4'	47.6											
5'	26.8	162.3	169.0	167.0	150.4	169.0	167.1	163.2	160.8	162.0	167.3	163.9
6'	38.1											
2'-NCH_3		27.0			24.4	27.8	27.8			24.3		
4'- NCH_3		24.9	25.6	25.6	26.6	25.5	25.4	26.0	26.0	26.3		
OCH_3	67.1											
CH_3CO	174.0											
CH_3CO	24.1											

Table 7. ^{13}C chemical shifts (δ in ppm) for halogenated aplysinopsins and leptoclinidamines derivatives.

Carbon	46	47	48	49	53	56	Carbon	46	47	48	49	53	56
Solvent	B	B	B	B	ni[1]	A	4'					119.7	
Ref.	48	48	48	48	44	55							
2	124.8	125.1	125.4	125.4	123.3	129.0	5'	171.8	171.9	169.7	170.0	124.8	
3	106.5	105.3	104.6	104.7	115.0	109.4	6'					117.3	
3a	125.7	125.6	125.6	125.6	126.4	124.9	7'					115.9	
4	119.3	119.3	119.4	119.0	120.1	122.9	7a'					137.4	
5	121.9	122.0	122.1	122.0	121.5	123.4	8'					44.5	
6	114.7	114.8	114.9	114.9	125.9	114.6	9'					72.3	
7	113.9	114.0	114.0	114.0	113.0	114.8	11'					159.0	
7a	137.2	137.1	137.2	137.2	139.5	137.0	13'					172.5	
8	29.4	30.1	30.1	30.4	27.6	164.1	2'-NCH_3	24.7	25.3	25.6	25.6		
9					72.3		4'- NCH_3	24.1	24.6	24.7	24.6		
10						50.0	10-NCH_3					33.1	
11					161.6	25.7	12-NCH_3					26.6	
12						136.4	13-SCH_3						18.6
13					174.0	125.9	14-NCH_3						33.5
15						138.1	16-NCH_3						34.2
17						172.2	10'-NCH_3					28.4	
1'	64.0	89.0	94.3	93.8			12'-NCH_3					26.5	
2'					125.6		OCH_3			52.3			
3'	158.1	156.6	157.2	157.0	104.4		OCH_2				61.5		
3'a					127.7		CH_3				13.7		

[1] ni: not informed

Table 8. ^{13}C chemical shifts (δ in ppm) for halogenated chartelline, chartellamides, securamines and securines derivatives.

Carbon	58	59	60	61	62	63	64	65	66	67	68
Solvent	C	C	C	C	C	C	C	C	A	A	C
Ref.	57	57	58	58	58	58	59	59	58	58	59
2	120.4	120.6	127.4	127.1	135.9	136.1	136.4	135.9	130.2	130.3	48.3
3	109.5	108.1	95.1	95.3	101.6	101.2	101.2	101.5	100.9	103.6	96.3
4	130.5	130.8	115.8	116.0	187.5	188.0	187.3	187.2	121.1	121.5	140.7
6	133.2	116.6	122.5	121.1	166.6	166.7	166.4	166.0	125.0	127.6	156.8
8	126.6	129.5	145.5	144.8	85.6	85.7	85.4	84.7	135.6	135.3	80.7
9	65.9	65.2	41.6	41.9	44.0	43.9	44.2	43.7	40.6	40.8	39.2
10	41.6	41.6	64.9	64.6	59.4	59.5	58.7	52.1	71.2	70.9	61.4
11	45.9	46.8	48.6	48.3	41.8	41.7	41.9	42.8	30.8	30.8	41.0
12	67.9	70.5	87.4	87.4	89.2	89.1	88.0	89.8	132.7	133.9	87.9
14	141.5	141.1	147.0	148.0	147.0	145.7	148.0	146.9	134.4	134.5	147.5
15	117.6	117.6	109.3	112.2	114.7	111.1	113.5	114.7	110.9	113.2	114.6
16	125.9	126.0	129.0	122.3	123.1	129.4	120.6	123.0	120.5	114.1	122.3
17	132.5	132.5	119.9	122.5	124.9	121.9	128.0	124.9	118.1	119.4	123.5
18	119.4	119.4	123.9	125.0	125.6	124.6	123.8	125.5	117.5	121.1	125.2
19	124.8	124.7	127.8	126.7	128.0	128.8	126.3	127.9	128.5	126.0	130.4
20	67.4	67.6	50.0	49.4	45.0	45.3	46.8	44.9	105.7	106.3	45.6
21	47.8	48.0	34.1	33.8	34.2	34.4	32.6	34.2	30.7	30.6	33.8
22	162.5	162.1	172.8	172.2	170.3	170.5	170.0	170.0	169.4	169.1	171.2
23	164.9	164.1	19.0	18.9	17.2	17.3	17.1	18.6	19.8	19.8	15.4
24	15.4	17.1	31.9	31.8	21.1	21.1	21.1	22.6	28.7	28.7	21.1

Inspection of the ^{13}C-NMR data of compounds **5**, **8**, **30** and **32** as compared with **10** (Table 5) reveals that introduction of a hydroxyl group in the C-4 indole moiety results in downfield signals at the α carbon. Additionally, comparison of the ^{13}C data of meridianin G (**10**), which bears only a 3-substituted indole core, with the other bromine indole derivatives shows that introduction of a bromine in the indole skeleton results in upfield signals at the α carbon.

The meridianin family skeleton can be recognized by the typical ^{1}H-NMR signals, as for example, in the case of compound **10**: a pair of doublet for the pyrimidine protons (δ 7.02 and 8.05, J = 5.5 Hz), together with a singlet for H-2, the typical pattern of a 3-substituted indole nucleus. The ^{13}C-NMR downfield signals at δ C-2′, C-4′, and CH-6′ corroborate the presence of 2-aminopyrimidine at C-3 in compounds **5–10** [60].

The basic difference between the psammopemmins and the meridianins is the presence of a 5′-substituted 4′-amino-2′-bromopyrimidine at C-3 of the indole nucleus. The distinguishing ^{1}H-NMR signals of the heterocyclic ring of the psammopemmins class can be recognized by the signals at δ 7.12 (d, J = 5.4 Hz) and 8.12 (br d, J = 5.4 Hz), attributed to the pyrimidine proton H-6′ and to NH at position 1′, as in the case of compound **30**. The ^{13}C-NMR downfield signals at δ C-2′, C-4′, and C-5′confirm the presence of 5′-substituted 4′-amino-2′-bromopyrimidine [28].

The aplicianins′ ^{13}C-NMR spectra differ from those of the meridianins and psammopemmins because of the presence of the signals due to a guanidine group at low field (C-2′) and three chemicals shifts at upfield, ascribed to C-4′ (CH), C-5′ (CH_2), and C-6′ (CH_2). Additionally, the ^{1}H-NMR coupling constants of the 6-tetrahydropyrimidine protons are important to establish the difference between aplicyanins, meridianins, and psammopemmins [37].

Aplysinopsins (**39–41**, **43–44**), with the iminoimidazolidinone substituted at the C-3 of the indole core, normally show a ^{1}H-NMR spectrum with signals due to N-methyl groups in the range of δ 3.0 to 3.5 (s, 3H), as well as a singlet characteristic of an olefinic proton in the δ 6.38–6.46 range. The ^{13}C NMR spectrum reveals the signals for two olefinic carbons C-8 (CH) and C-1′ (C), methyl, guanidine, and amide carbonyl, as well as those of the indole ring, as already mentioned [43,47,48]. Analysis of the ^{13}C data of **39**, which bears a 3-substituted indole core, and comparison with data of the other bromine indole derivatives show that the presence of bromine in the indole moiety results in upfield signals at the carbon α.

The spectra of aplysinopsins (**50–51**) differ in terms of the signals at C-8, C-3′, and C-5′, if compared with data for 3-iminoimidazolidinone, where C=NH (C-3′) is replaced by C=O (C-3′) [41].

The E or Z-configuration of the double bond at C-8 could be assigned on the basis of a ^{1}H, ^{13}C heteronuclear coupling constant. The coupling constant value obtained for the E isomer was larger than in the Z [41,42]. The geometry of the C-8-C-1′ olefin could be determined by comparison of the chemical shift of the H-2 proton and C-8 carbon. In the *Z* isomer, the δ values of C-8 and H-2 were upfield compared to the values obtained for the *E* isomer [41,42,47]. Aplysinopsin type compounds without substituents at N-2′ are predominantly of *Z* configuration, whereas the converse is true for compounds bearing a methyl group at N-2′. Although it is important to note that, *Z* and *E* aplysinopsin alkaloids undergo rapid isomerization [41,42,61].

Comparison of the ^{13}C-NMR data of **46–49** with previous aplysinopsins reveals that the C-8 and C-1′ signals are shifted upfield according to R_1 at C-1′, thereby confirming that the double bond at C-8-C-1′ is absent. Segraves and Crews considered that **48** and **49** are artifacts formed from **47** during the extraction process [48].

The ^{13}C-NMR data of compound **53** indicates the presence of two indoles and two iminoimidazolidinones. Biogenetically, this compound could be formed from an enzymatic Diels–Alder cycloaddition of two molecules of aplysinopsin, which were probably derived from tryptophan and guanidine, followed by some modifications [44].

The structure of leptoclinidamine C (**56**) has been established as a 3,6-disubstituted indole and a β-substituted alanine by 1D and 2D NMR data. The ^{13}C data indicate the presence of two *N*-methyl groups at C-14 and C-16; a third methyl group at C-13 is attributable to an S-methyl. As mentioned, the chemical shift of the quaternary carbon C-6 (δ 114.6) indicates that the bromine was substituted at this position [55].

2. CONCLUSIONS

In recent decades the number of new isolated natural compounds, many of which contain halogen, has increased significantly as a consequence of improved collection methods (scuba diving and remote submersibles for accessing deep water organisms), selective bioassays, new separation and purification techniques, and powerful identification methods such as multi-dimensional NMR spectroscopy, high-resolution mass spectrometry, and X-ray diffraction [8,3]. The assignment of carbon signals of a given isolated compound by comparison with the data of known compounds is an important tool for the discovery of novel natural compounds, when the ^{13}C-NMR data of appropriate model compounds are available. This was the case with meridianins A–E, which were deduced by 2D NMR spectroscopic methods in combination with comparison to literature data reported for the related natural products the psammopemmins. The indole alkaloids are a class of marine natural products displaying unique promising properties for the development of new drug leads, and they are a wonderful challenge to synthetic chemists. The majority of marine indole alkaloids are rather simple compounds. However, some of the indole alkaloids carry unique structural features. Bacteria and algae have yielded simple halogenated indoles, while more complicated structures have been isolated from marine sources [9]. Over the past 5 years there has clearly been an increasing interest in the isolation, determination of the biological and ecological significance, and synthesis of meridianins, aplysinopsis, and analogues, as confirmed by number of articles and reviews about these marine natural molecules [21,39,63]. Among the different classes of compounds reported here, the protein kinase inhibitors meridianins deserve prominence. Along with variolins, these compounds have inspired the design of the synthetic hybrid meriolins, which constitute a new CDK inhibitory scaffold with promising antitumor activity. On the other hand, aplycianins because of their pronounced antimitotic and cytotoxic potential, have been considered a novel model for anticancer drug discovery. Unfortunately, the biological potential of psammopemmins and the recently isolated leptolinidamines are unknown so far. Finally, aplysinopsins show specific toxicity for cancer cells; however, the most potent pharmacological activity of aplysinopsins is related to modulation of the central nervous system. An interesting fact in all these types of indole skeletons covered here is that halogenations generally occur at C-5, sometimes at C-6, or at both C-5 and C-6 of the indole ring. The bromination of many of the mentioned natural products could be associated with increased biological activity [9].

ACKNOWLEDGEMENTS

CNPq (The National Council for Scientific and Technological Development) is acknowledged for Research Productivity Fellowships granted to A.A.S.F., M.L.A.S., W.R.C. and A.H.J. C.G.B. and L.S.C. were supported by FAPESP (São Paulo Research Foundation) scholarships.

REFERENCES

1. Blunt, JW; Copp, BR; Munro, MHG; Northcote, PT; Prinsep, MR. Marine natural products. Nat Prod Rep 2005, 22, 15–61.

2. Blunt, JW; Copp, BR; Hu, W-P; Munro, MHG; Northcote, PT; Prinsep, MR. Marine natural products. Nat Prod Rep2009, 26, 170–244.

3. Bhakuni, DS; Rawat, DS. Bioactive Marine Natural Products, 1 ed; Springer: Anamaya, India, 2005; pp. 100–269.

4. Dembitsky, VM. Bromo-and iodo-containing alkaloids from marine microorganisms and sponges. Russ J Bioorg Chem2002, 28, 170–182.

5. Kling, E; Schmid, C; Unversucht, S; Wage, T; Zehner, S; van Pee, K-H. Wohlleben, W, Spellig, T, Müller-Tiemann, B, Eds.; Enzymatic incorporation of halogen atoms into natural compoundsBiocombinatorial Approaches for Drug Finding. In Ernst Schering Foundation Symposium Proceedings; Springer: Berlin Heidelberg, Germany, 2005; Volume 51, pp. 165–194.

6. Neumann, CS; Fujimori, DG; Walsh, CT. Halogenation strategies in natural product biosynthesis. Chem Biol 2008, 15, 99–109.

7. Gribble, GW. The diversity of naturally occurring organobromine compounds. Chem Soc Rev 1999, 28, 335–346.

8. Gribble, GW. Natural organohalogens: A new frontier for medicinal agents? J Chem Educ 2004, 81, 1441–1449.

9. Gul, W; Hamann, MT. Indole alkaloid marine natural products: An established source of cancer drug leads with considerable promise for the control of parasitic, neurological and other diseases. Life Sci 2005, 78, 442–453.

10. Konig, GM; Wright, AD; Sticher, O; Angerhofer, CK; Pezzuto, JM. Biological activities of selected marine natural products. Planta Med 1994, 60, 532–537.

11. Campagnuolo, C; Fattorusso, E; Taglialatela-Scafati, O. Plakohypaphorines A-C, iodine-containing alkaloids from the Caribbean SpongePlakortis simplex. Eur J Org Chem 2003, 284–287.

12. Frederich, M; Tits, M; Angenot, L. Potential antimalarial activity of indole alkaloids. Trans R Soc Trop Med Hyg 2008,102, 11–19.

13. Wagner, C; Omari, ME; König, GM. Biohalogenation: Nature's way to synthesize halogenated metabolites. J Nat Prod2009, 72, 540–553.

14. Franco, LH; Joffé, EBdeK; Puricelli, L; Tatian, M; Seldes, AM; Palermo, JA. Indole alkaloids from the Tunicate Aplidium meridianum. J Nat Prod 1998, 61, 1130–1132.

15. Gompel, M; Leost, M; Joffe, EBDK; Puricelli, L; Franco, LH; Palermoc, J; Meijera, L. Meridianins, a new family of protein kinase inhibitors isolated from the Ascidian Aplidium meridianum. Bioorg Med ChemLett 2004, 14, 1703–1707.

16. Cohen, P. Protein kinases-the major drug targets of the twenty-first century? Nat Rev Drug Discov 2002, 1, 309–315.

17. Noble, MEM; Endicott, JA; Johnson, LN. Protein Kinase inhibitors: Insights into drug design from structure. Science2004, 303, 1800–1805.

18. Echalier, A; Bettayeb, K; Ferandin, Y; Lozach, O; Clément, M; Valette, A; Liger, F; Marquet, B; Morris, JC; Endicott, JA; Joseph, B; Meijer, L. Meriolins (3-(Pyrimidin-4-yl)-7-azaindoles): Synthesis, kinase inhibitory activity, cellular effects, and structure of a CDK2/Cyclin A/Meriolin complex. J Med Chem 2008, 51, 737–751.

19. Bettayeb, K; Tirado, OM; Marionneau-Lambot, S; Ferandin, Y; Lozach, O; Morris, JC; Mateo-Lozano, S; Drueckes, P; Schächtele, C; Kubbutat, MHG; Liger, F; Marquet, B; Joseph, B; Echalier, A; Endicott, JA; Notario, V; Meijer, L. Meriolins, a new class of cell death-inducing kinase inhibitors with enhanced selectivity for cyclin-dependent kinases. Cancer Res 2007, 67, 8325–8334.

20. Gedu, RA; Debiton, E; Ferandin, Y; Meijer, L; Prudhomme, M; Anizon, F; Moreau, P. Synthesis and biological activities of aminopyrimidyl-indoles structurally related to meridianins. Bioorg Med Chem 2009, 17, 4420–4424.

21. Walker, SR; Carter, EJ; Huff, BC; Morris, JC. Variolins and related alkaloids. Chem Rev 2009, 109, 3080–3098.

22. Perry, NB; Ettouati, L; Litaudon, M; Blunt, JW; Munro, MHG; Parkin, S; Hope, H. Alkaloids from the antarctic spongeKirkpatrickia varialosa. Part 1: Variolin B, A new antitumour and antiviral compound. Tetrahedron 1994, 50, 3987–3992.

23. Trimurtulu, G; Faulkner, DJ; Perry, NB; Ettouati, L; Litaudon, M; Blunt, JW; Munro, MHG; Jameson, GB. Alkaloids from the antarctic sponge Kirkpatrickia varialosa. Part 2: Variolin A and N(3')-methyl tetrahydrovariolin B. Tetrahedron1994, 50, 3993–4000.

24. Lagoja, IM. Pyrimidine as constituent of natural biologically active compounds. Chem Biodiver 2005, 2, 1–50.

25. Urban, S; Hickford, SJH; Blunt, JW; Munro, MHG. Bioactive Marine Alkaloids. Curr Org Chem 2000, 4, 765–807.

26. Fresneda, PM; Delgado, S; Francesch, A; Manzanares, I; Cuevas, C; Molina, P. Synthesis and cytotoxic evaluation of new derivatives of the marine alkaloid Variolin B. J Med Chem 2006, 49, 1217–1221.

27. Anderson, RJ; Morris, JC. Total synthesis of variolin B. Tetrahedron Lett 2001, 42, 8697–8699.

28. Anderson, RJ; Morris, JC. Studies toward the total synthesis of the variolins: Rapid entry to the core structure.Tetrahedron Lett 2001, 42, 311–312.

29. Ahaidar, A; Fernández, D; Danelón, G; Cuevas, C; Manzanares, I; Albericio, F; Joule, JA; Álvarez, M. Total syntheses of Variolin B and Deoxyvariolin B. J Org Chem 2003, 68, 10020–10029.

30. Ahaidar, A; Fernández, D; Pérez, O; Danelón, G; Cuevas, C; Manzanares, I; Albericio, F; Joule, JA; Álvarez, M. Synthesis of variolin B. Tetrahedron Lett 2003, 44, 6191–6194.

31. Molina, P; Fresneda, PM; Delgado, S. Carbodiimide-mediated mreparation of the Tricyclic pyrido[3′,2′:4,5]pyrrolo[1,2-c]pyrimidine ring system and its application to the synthesis of the potent antitumoral marine alkaloid Variolin B and analog. J Org Chem 2003, 68, 489–499.

32. Molina, P; Fresneda, PM; Delgado, S; Bleda, JA. Synthesis of the potent antitumoral marine alkaloid Variolin B.Tetrahedron Lett 2002, 43, 1005–1007.

33. Baeza, A; Mendiola, J; Burgos, C; Alvarez-Builla, J; Vaquero, JJ. Palladium-mediated C–N, C–C, and C–O functionalization of azolopyrimidines: A new total synthesis of Variolin B. Tetrahedron Lett 2008, 49, 4073–4077.

34. Álvarez, M; Fernández, D; Joule, JA. Synthesis of deoxyvariolin B. Tetrahedron Lett 2001, 42, 315–317.

35. Anderson, RJ; Hill, JB; Morris, JC. Concise Total Syntheses of Variolin B and Deoxyvariolin B. J Org Chem 2005, 70, 6204–6212.

36. Butler, MS; Capon, RJ; Lu, CC. Psammopemmins (A-C), novel brominated 4-hydroxyindole alkaloids from an Antarctic sponge, Psammopemma sp. Aust J Chem 1992, 45, 1871–1877.

37. Reyes, F; Fernández, R; Rodríguez, A; Francesch, A; Taboada, S; Ávila, C; Cuevas, C. Aplicyanins A–F, new cytotoxic bromoindole derivatives from the marine tunicate Aplidium cyaneum. Tetrahedron 2008, 64, 5119–5123.

38. Sísa, M; Pla, D; Altuna, M; Francesch, A; Cuevas, C; Albericio, F; Álvarez, M. Total Synthesis and Antiproliferative Activity Screening of

(±)-Aplicyanins A, B and E and Related Analogues. J Med Chem 2009, 52, 6217–6223.

39. Bialonska, D; Zjawiony, JK. Aplysinopsins—Marine indole alkaloids: Chemistry, bioactivity and ecological significance. Mar Drugs 2009, 7, 166–183.

40. Mancini, I; Guella, G; Zibrowius, H; Pietra, F. On the origin of quasi-racemic aplysinopsin cycloadducts, (bis)indole alkaloids isolated from scleractinian corals of the family Dendrophylliidae. Involvement of enantiodefective Diels–Alderases or asymmetric induction in artifact processes involving adventitious catalysts? Tetrahedron 2003, 59, 8757–8762.

41. Guella, G; Mancini, I; Zibrowius, H; Pietra, F. Novel aplysinopsin-type alkaloids from scleractinian corals of the family Dendrophylliidae of the Mediterranean and the Philippines. Configurational-assignment criteria, stereospecific synthesis, and photoisomerization. Helv Chim Acta 1988, 71, 773–782.

42. Guella, G; Mancini, I; Zibrowius, H; Pietra, F. Aplysinopsin-type alkaloids from Dendrophyllia sp., a scleractinian coral of the family Dendrophylliidae of the Philippines. Facile photochemical (Z/E) photoisomerization and thermal reversal. Helv Chim Acta 1989, 72, 1444–1450.

43. Fattorusso, E; Lanzotti, V; Magno, S; Novellino, E. Tryptophan derivatives from a Mediterranean anthozoan, Astroides calycularis. J Nat Prod 1985, 48, 924–927.

44. Iwagawa, T; Miyazaki, M; Okumara, H; Nakatani, M; Doe, M; Takemura, K. Three novel bis(indole) alkaloids from a stony coral Tubastraea sp. Tetrahedron Lett 2003, 44, 2533–2535.

45. Koh, EGL; Sweatman, H. Chemical warfare among scleractinians: Bioactive natural products from Tubastraea faulkneriWells kill larvae of potential competitors. J Exp Mar Biol 2000, 251, 141–160.

46. Hu, J-F; Schetz, JA; Kelly, M; Peng, J-N; Ang, KKH; Flotow, H; Leong, CY; Ng, SB; Buss, AD; Wilkins, SP; Hamann, MT. New antiinfective and human 5-HT2 receptor binding natural and semisynthetic compounds from the Jamaican sponge Smenospongia aurea. J Nat Prod 2002, 65, 476–480.

47. Aoki, S; Ye, Y; Higuchi, K; Takashima, A; Tanaka, Y; Kitagawa, I. Novel neuronal Nitric Oxide Synthase (nNOS) selective inhibitor,

Aplysinopsin-type indole alkaloid, from marine sponge Hyrtios erecta. Chem Pharm Bull 2001, 49, 1372–1374.

48. Segraves, NL; Crews, P. Investigation of brominated tryptophan alkaloids from two Thorectidae sponges: Thorectandraand Smenospongia. J Nat Prod 2005, 68, 1484–1488.

49. Djura, P; Stierle, DB; Sullivan, B; Faulkner, DJ. Some metabolites of the marine sponges Smenospongia aurea andSmenospongia (Polyfibrospongia) echina. J Org Chem 1980, 45, 1435–1441.

50. Murata, M; Miyagawa-Kohshima, K; Nakanishi, K; Naya, Y. Characterization of compounds that induce symbiosis between sea anemone and anemone fish. Science 1986, 234, 585–587.

51. Okuda, RK; Klein, D; Kinnel, RB; Li, M; Scheuer, PJ. Marine natural products: The past twenty years and beyond. Pure Appl Chem 1982, 54, 1907–1914.

52. Landolt, H-P; Wehrle, R. Antagonism of serotonergic 5-HT2A/2C receptors: Mutual improvement of sleep, cognition and mood? Eur J Neurosci 2009, 29, 1795–1809.

53. Giorgetti, M; Tecott, LH. Contributions of 5-HT2C receptors to multiple actions of central serotonin systems. Eur J Pharmacol 2004, 488, 1–9.

54. Koha, EGL; Sweatmanb, H. Chemical warfare among scleractinians: Bioactive natural products from Tubastraea faulkneri wells kill larvae of potential competitors. J Exp Mar Biol Ecol 2000, 251, 141–160.

55. Carroll, AR; Avery, VM. Leptoclinidamines A-C, indole alkaloids from the Australian Ascidian Leptoclinides durus. J Nat Prod 2009, 72, 696–699.

56. Chevolot, L; Chevolot, A-M; Gajhede, M; Larsen, C; Anthoni, U; Christophersen, C. Chartelline A: A pentahalogenated alkaloid from the marine bryozoan Chartella papyracea. J Am Chem Soc 1985, 107, 4542–4543.

57. Anthoni, U; Bock, K; Chevolot, L; Larsen, C; Nielsen, PH; Christophersen, C. Chartellamide A and B, halogenated β-lactam indole-imidazole alkaloids from the marine bryozoan Chartella papyracea. J Org Chem 1987, 52, 5638–5639.

58. Rahbaek, L; Anthoni, U; Christophersen, C; Nielsen, PH; Petersen, BO. Marine alkaloids. 18. Securamines and Securines, halogenated indole-

imidazole alkaloids from the marine bryozoan Securiflustra securifrons. J Org Chem1996, 61, 887–889.

59. Rahbaek, L; Christophersen, C. Marine alkaloids. 19. Three new alkaloids, Securamines E-G, from the marine bryozoan Securiflustra securifrons. J Nat Prod 1997, 60, 175–177.

60. Seldes, AM; Brasco, MFR; Franco, LH; Palermo, JA. Identification of two meridianins from the crude extract of the tunicate Aplidium meridianum by tandem mass spectrometry. Nat Prod Res 2007, 21, 555–563.

61. McKay, MJ; Carroll, AR; Quinn, RJ; Hooper, JNA. 1,2-Bis(1H-indol-3-yl)ethane-1,2-dione, an indole alkaloid from the marine sponge Smenospongia sp. J Nat Prod 2002, 65, 595–597.

62. Fusetani, N; Asano, M; Matsunaga, S; Hashimoto, K. Bioactive marine metabolites—XV. Isolation of aplysinopsin from the scleractinian coral Tubastrea aurea as an inhibitor of development of fertilized sea urchin eggs. Comp Biochem Physiol 1986, 85B, 845–846.

63. Stanovnik, B; Svete, J. The synthesis of aplysinopsins, meridianines, and related compounds. Mini-Rev Org Chem 2005,2, 211–224.

Chapter 9

Anticancer Drugs from Marine Flora: An Overview

N. Sithranga Boopathy and K. Kathiresan

Center of Advanced Study in Marine Biology, Faculty of Marine Sciences, Annamalai University, Parangipettai 608 502, Tamil Nadu, India

ABSTRACT

Marine floras, such as bacteria, actinobacteria, cyanobacteria, fungi, microalgae, seaweeds, mangroves, and other halophytes are extremely important oceanic resources, constituting over 90% of the oceanic biomass. They are taxonomically diverse, largely productive, biologically active, and chemically unique offering a great scope for discovery of new anticancer drugs. The marine floras are rich in medicinally potent chemicals predominantly belonging to polyphenols and sulphated polysaccharides. The chemicals have displayed an array of pharmacological properties especially antioxidant, immunostimulatory, and antitumour activities. The phytochemicals possibly activate macrophages, induce apoptosis, and prevent oxidative damage of DNA, thereby controlling carcinogenesis. In spite of vast resources enriched with chemicals, the marine floras are largely unexplored for anticancer lead compounds. Hence, this paper reviews the works so far conducted on this aspect with a view to provide a baseline information for promoting the marine flora-based anticancer research in the present context of increasing cancer incidence, deprived of the cheaper, safer, and potent medicines to challenge the dreadful human disease.

1. INTRODUCTION

Cancer is a dreadful human disease, increasing with changing life style, nutrition, and global warming. Cancer treatments do not have potent medicine as the currently available drugs are causing side effects in some instances. In this context, the natural products derived from medicinal plants have gained significance in the treatment of cancer. According to the WHO, 80% of the world's population primarily those of developing countries rely on plant-derived medicines for the health care [1]. Natural products and their derivatives represent more than 50% of all the drugs in clinical use of the world. Higher plants contribute not less than 25% of the total. Almost 60% of drugs approved for cancer treatment are of natural origin. Fruits and vegetables are the principal sources of vitamins C, B, E, carotenoids, and fibers, and these contribute to the apparent cancer-protective effects of the foods. There is a positive correlation between the increased dietary intake of natural antioxidants and the reduced coronary heart diseases, cancer mortality, as well as longer life expectancy [2, 3]. Herbal drug formulations for the prevention and treatment of cancer appeared in the last three decades, and the interest on natural sources of potential chemotherapeutic agents is continuing.

Antioxidants play an important role in the later stages of cancer development. There is increasing evidence that oxidative processes promote carcinogenesis, although the mechanisms for this are not well understood. The antioxidants may be able to cause the regression of premalignant lesions and inhibit their development into cancer. Preliminary studies have indicated that some antioxidants, particularly β-carotene, may be of benefit in the treatment of precancerous conditions such as oral leukoplakia, possibly a precursor of oral cancer [4]. Several herbs and spices including rosemary, sage, thyme, nutmeg, turmeric, white pepper, chilli, pepper, ginger, and plenty of other medicinal plants are reportedly exhibiting antioxidant activity [5–7]. Majority of the active antioxidant compounds are flavonoids, isoflavones, flavones, anthocyanins, coumarins, lignans, catechins, and isocatechins. In addition to these, vitamins C and E, β-carotene, and α-tocopherol present in natural foods, are known to possess antioxidant potential [8–10]. Thus, potential antioxidant and anticancer properties of plant extracts or isolated products of plant origin can possibly be explored for developing the anticancer drugs [11].

From the past few decades, there has been an upsurge in the search for new plant-derived drugs. This process has facilitated to produce remarkably a diverse array of over 1,39,000 natural products, containing medicinally useful terpenoid derivatives, alkaloids, glycosides, polyphenolics, steroids, and so forth. The National Cancer Institute (NCI) of the United States of America (USA) has screened about 1,14,000 extracts from an estimated 35,000 plant samples against a number of tumor systems [12]. Of the 92 anti-cancer drugs commercially available prior to 1983 in the USA and approved world-wide between 1983 and 1994, approximately 62% can be related to natural origin [13]. Some examples include vinblastine and vincristine (Catharanthus roseus), epipodophyllotoxin, an isomer of podophyllotoxin (Podophyllum peltatum roots), paclitaxel (Taxus baccata, T. brevifolia, T. canadensis), camptothecin (Camptotheca acuminata), homoharringtonine (Cephalotaxus harringtonia var. drupacea), elliptinium (Bleekeria vitensis), flavopiridol (Dysoxylum binectariferum), and ipomeanol (Ipomoea batatas). The two plant-derived natural products, paclitaxel and camptothecin were estimated to account for nearly one-third of the global anticancer market, respectively to the tune of about $3 and $9 billion, in the year 2002 [14].

Numerous types of bioactive compounds have been isolated from plant sources. Several of them are currently in clinical trials or preclinical trials or undergoing further investigation. Although marine compounds are under-represented in current pharmacopoeia, it is anticipated that the marine environment will become an invaluable source of novel compounds in the future, as it represents 95% of the biosphere [15]. However, development of marine floral compounds as therapeutic agents is still in its embryonic stage due to lack of an analogous ethno-medical history as compared to terrestrial habitats, together with the relative technical difficulties in collecting the marine floral samples. Over the last few decades, significant efforts have been made, by both pharmaceutical companies and academic institutions, to isolate and identify new marine-derived, natural products especially from faunal species. However, the marine floras are only little unexplored and these works are reviewed here as a baseline data for promoting further research in this field.

2. UNIQUENESS OF MARINE FLORAL DRUGS

Marine floras include microflora (bacteria, actinobacteria, cyanobacteria and fungi), microalgae, macroalgae (seaweeds), and flowering plants (mangroves and other halophytes). Occupying almost 71% of globe, the ocean is rich in biodiversity, and the microflora and microalgae alone constitute more than 90% of oceanic biomass [16]. This vast marine floral resource will offer a great scope for discovery of new drugs. It is increasingly recognized that ocean contains a huge number of natural products and novel chemical entities with unique biological activities that may be useful in finding the potential drugs with greater efficacy and specificity for the treatment of human diseases [17]. It cannot be denied that with 3.5 billion years of existence on earth and experience in biosynthesis, the marine microfloras remain nature's best source of chemicals. The marine organisms produce novel chemicals to withstand extreme variations in pressure, salinity, temperature, and so forth, prevailing in their environment, and the chemicals produced are unique in diversity, structural, and functional features [18].

The efforts to extract drugs from the sea started in the late 1960s. However, the systematic investigation began in the mid-1970s. During the decade from 1977 to 1987, about 2500 new metabolites were reported from a variety of marine organisms. These studies have clearly demonstrated that the marine environment is an excellent source of novel chemicals, not found in terrestrial sources. So far, more than 10,000 compounds have been isolated from marine organisms with hundreds of new compounds are still being discovered every year. About 300 patents on bioactive marine natural products were issued between 1969 and 1999 [18]. Some marine organisms are proved to be the potent sources of drugs. These are mostly invertebrates that include sponges, soft corals, sea fans, sea hares, nudibranchs, bryozoans, and tunicates. It is now believed that microbial floras present in the invertebrates are responsible for the production of medicinal compounds. The search is mostly confined to marine faunal species, and floral species are largely ignored. Some of the compounds derived from marine organisms have antioxidant property and anticancer activities, but they are largely unexplored.

Marine floras have been used for medicinal purposes in India, China, the Near East and Europe, since ancient times. The people of China and Japan have been using seaweeds for consumption. The seaweeds especially brown seaweeds are rich in iodine and hence there is a least incidence of goiter and glandular diseases. History reveals that maritime countries have been using seaweeds as vermifuge, anesthetics and ointment as well as for the treatment of cough, wounds, gout, goiter, venereal disease, and so forth. Sterols and related compounds present in seaweeds have ability to lower blood plasma cholesterol level. Seaweed dietary fibers perform varied range of functions such as antioxidant, antimutagenic, anticoagulant, and antitumor. The seaweeds also play an important role in modification of lipid metabolism in the human body. High intake of calcium, potassium, and sodium is associated with lower mean systolic pressure and lower risk of hypertension. All seaweeds offer an extraordinary level of potassium that is very similar to our natural plasma level. Seaweed extract is interestingly similar to human blood plasma. Two Japanese surgeons have used a novel technique of mixing seaweed compounds with water to substitute whole blood in transfusion and this has been successfully tried in over 100 operations [4].

Although, the use of seaweeds in medicine is not as wide spread as once it was, the use of seaweed polymer extract in pharmacy, medicine, and biochemistry is well established. Clinical trials are also in progress to make diabetic patients free from injection by introducing insulin secreting "jelly capsule" made of seaweed-derived alginic acid [19]. The capsule renders protection to white blood cells and the patient's immune system. Seaweed gums like carrageenan (extracted from red seaweed) or algin (from brown seaweed) are rich sources of soluble fibers [4].

3. ANTICANCER AGENTS FROM MARINE FLORAS

3.1. Bacteria

Marine microorganisms are a source of new genes, and exploitation of which is likely to lead to the discovery of new drugs and targets. Secondary metabolites produced by marine bacteria have yielded pharmaceutical products such as novel anti-inflammatory agents (e.g., pseudopterosins, topsentins, scytonemin, and manoalide), anticancer agents (e.g., bryostatins, discodermolide, eleutherobin, and sarcodictyin), and antibiotics (e.g., marinone). The contribution of probiotic bacteria, such as lactobacilli and bifidobacteria, is mainly in the control of pathogenic microbes, through production of antibacterial protein namely, bacteriocin [20, 21] and anticancer substances [22]. The dietary supplements of lactobacilli are reportedly decreasing the induction of experimental colon cancer [23]. They stimulate and modulate the mucosal immune system by reducing the production of proinflammatory cytokines through actions on NFκB pathways, increasing production of anti-inflammatory cytokines such as IL-10 and host defense peptides such as β-defensin 2, enhancing IgA defenses and influencing dendritic cell maturation as well as modulation of cell proliferation and apoptosis through cell responses to short chain fatty acids [24].

Most of the marine animal phyla produce toxins and some studies show that these marine toxins may be produced by marine bacteria associated the animals [25–27]. The microbial toxins are useful in neurophysiological and neuropharmacological studies. For example, bacteria present in Noctiluca scintillans are responsible for causing red tides. The major metabolite, macrolactin-A, inhibits B16-F10 murine melanoma cancer cells, mammalian herpes simplex virus (HSV) (types I and II), and protects T lymphocytes against human immunodeficiency virus (HIV) replication [28].

Kahalalide F (KF) is a depsipeptide isolated from the mollusk Elysia rubefescens from Hawaii and the compound is believed to be synthesized by microbes associated with the animal. KF induces cytotoxicity and blocks the cell cycle in G1 phase in a p53-independent manner. In vitro, KF displays activity against solid tumors with an interesting pattern of selectivity in prostate cancer cell lines. In addition, extensive in vivo work demonstrates that the agent has activity in breast and colon cancers.

Only a few marine bacteria can be isolated under laboratory conditions and there is an urgent need to develop new culture techniques to isolate slow-growing bacteria and also to isolate the bacteria that are unique in production of novel natural products [29].

3.2. Actinomycetes

For more than 50 years, the soil-derived actinomycetes of terrestrial origin have provided a major pharmaceutical resource for the discovery of antibiotics and related bioactive compounds. However, marine actinomycetes received only very recent attention. Gutingimycin is a highly polar trioxacarcin derivative fromStreptomyces species, isolated from sediment of the Laguna de Terminos, Gulf of Mexico [30]. The sameStreptomyces species also yields trioxacarcins D–F, in addition to the known trioxacarcins A–C [30]. Among the antibiotic-producing microbes, marine actinomycetes within the family Micromonosporaceae are very promising. These microbes are found to be a potent sources of anticancer agents that target proteasome function and their industrial potential is validated by several pharmaceuticals.

Thiocoraline is a novel bioactive depsipeptide isolated from Micromonospora marina, a marine microorganism located in the Mozambique Strait that inhibits RNA synthesis. The bioactive compound is also selectively cytotoxic against lung and colon cancer cell lines as well as melanoma. Interestingly, the compound exerts preferential antiproliferative effects in colon cancer cell lines with defective p53 systems [31]. Thiocoraline represents a model of an anticancer agent acquired from marine microorganisms and illustrates how the problems of drug supply can be overcome by artificial culture.

3.3. Marine Fungi

A rich profile of biologically active metabolites is described from filamentous fungi of terrestrial origin, especially from just three genera: Penicillium, Aspergillus, and Fusarium [32]. However, the marine fungi are least studied than terrestrial counterparts and other ecological groups. Obligate marine fungi are still an unexplored resource, although, marine facultative fungi, have been studied due to their production of new metabolites which are not found in terrestrial fungi. Recently more interest has been generated on studying biologically active metabolites from higher fungi (Basidiomycetes), endophytic fungi and filamentous fungi from marine habitats, the symbiotic lichens.

In one study, the lignicolous fungus Leptosphaeria oraemaris (Pleosporaceae) yielded leptosphaerin [33, 34]. A further study of the same fungal species yielded none of the previously found metabolites, but the polyketides, leptosphaerolide, its o-dihydroquinone derivative, and leptosphaerodione [35]. This leads to a conclusion that the production of secondary metabolites might be highly dependent on the culture conditions and the origin of the strains. To produce these metabolites and to maximize the potential chemical diversity, they need to be grown in various nutrient-limited media. For example, media for Penicillium spp. that are deficient in carbon can produce penicillins, those that are phosphorus-limited can produce cephalosphorins and vancomycin, and those that are nitrogen-limited can produce carbapenems [36].

Marine-derived fungi are known to be a source of antioxidative natural products: (i) Acremonin A fromAcremonium sp. [37] and (ii) Xanthone derivative from Wardomyces anomalus [38]. Reactions of free radicals, such as super-oxide radical, hydroxyl radical, peroxyl radical and other reactive oxygen and nitrogen are associated with diseases such as atherosclerosis, dementia, and cancer. Antioxidants delay or prevent oxidative damage and thus they may be useful as therapeutics or food additives.

3.4. Micro Algae

Marine blue-green algae (Cyanobacteria) are considered to be one of the potential organisms which can be the richest sources of known and novel bioactive compounds including toxins with potential for pharmaceutical applications [39, 40]. Some of the marine cyanobacteria appear to be potential sources for large-scale production of vitamins (B complex, E) of commercial interest. Scytonemin is a protein serine/threonine kinase inhibitor [41], isolated from the cyanobacterium Stigonema sp. and this compound is a yellow-green ultraviolet sunscreen pigment, known to be present in the extracellular sheaths of different genera of aquatic and terrestrial blue-green algae. Scytonemin regulates mitotic spindle formation as well as enzyme kinases involved in cell cycle control and the compound also inhibits proliferation of human fibroblasts and endothelial cells. Thus scytonemin may provide an excellent drug as protein kinase inhibitors to have antiproliferative and anti-inflammatory activities [42].

More than 50% of the marine cyanobacteria are potentially exploitable for extracting bioactive substances which are effective in either killing the cancer cells by inducing apoptotic death, or affecting the cell signaling through activation of the members of protein kinase-c family of signaling enzymes. The cell extracts ofCalothrix isolates inhibit the growth in vitro of a chloroquine-resistant strain of the malarial parasite,Plasmodium falciparum, and of human HeLa cancer cells in a dose-dependent manner [43]. Bioassay directed fractions of the extracts have led to their isolation and structural characterization of Calothrixin A (I) and B (II), pentacyclic metabolites with an indole [3, 2 – j] phenanthridine alkaloids which exert their growth inhibitory effects at nanomolar concentrations [43]. Another compound, Curacin-A, isolated from the organic extracts of Curacao collections of Lyngbya majuscula is an exceptionally potent antiproliferative agent as it inhibits the polymerization of the tubulin and it also displays the inhibitory activity selectively on colon, renal, and breast cancer-derived cell lines [28].

Largazole is unique chemical scaffold with impressive antiproliferative activity derived from Symploca sp. [44]. The apratoxins are another class of cyanobacterial compounds that inhibit a variety of cancer cell lines at nanomolar concentrations. The parental compound, apratoxin A, isolated from a strain of Lyngbya boullonishows cytotoxicity to an adenocarcinoma [45]. The coibamide A is a compound derived from a strain ofLeptolyngbya [46], and it exhibits significant cytotoxicity against NCIH460 lung and mouse neuro-2a cells. The cytotoxicity is a common mechanism of action for many cyanobacterial compounds [47].

In recent times, the most significant discoveries are of borophycin, cryptophycin 1 & 8, and cyanovirin. Borophycin is a boron-containing metabolite, isolated from marine cyanobacterial strains of Nostoc linckia andN. spongiaeforme var. tenue [48]. The compound exhibits potent cytotoxicity against human epidermoid carcinoma (LoVo) and human colorectal adenocarcinoma (KB) cell lines [49]. Borophycin is related both to the boron containing boromycins isolated from a terrestrial strain of Streptomyces antibioticus and to the aplasmomycins isolated from a marine strain of Strepetomyces griseus (actinomycetes) [48].

Cryptophycin 1 was first isolated from Nostoc sp. ATCC 53789 by researchers at Merck and found to be a potent fungicide. As it was highly toxic, it was disregarded as a natural product lead. Subsequently, the same compound isolated from Nostoc sp. GSV 224 exhibited potent cytotoxicity against human tumor cell lines and good activity against a broad spectrum of drug sensitive and drug-resistant murine and human solid tumors [50]. Nevertheless, cryptophycin 1 again appears to be too toxic to become a clinical candidate. This leads to a detailed structure-function study which has resulted in the isolation of cryptophycin 8, a semisynthetic analogue with greater therapeutic efficiency and lower toxicity than cryptophycin 14 in vivo [51]. Although neither cryptophycin, nor any of its analogues have entered clinical trails to-date, but interest in these compounds continues.

3.5. Macro Algae (Seaweed)

Seaweeds are important sources of protein, iodine, vitamins, and minerals and hence, their metabolites have shown promising activities against cancer incidences [52]. The seaweeds also contain high amounts of polyphenols such as catechin, epicatechin, epigallocatechin gallate, and gallic acid, as reported in Halimeda sp. (Chlorophyceae) [53]. In the past three decades, many researchers have worked on the antioxidant, antitumor, and immunomodulating activities of seaweeds [54]. Edible seaweed like Palmaria palmate is shown to be effective antioxidant, capable of inhibiting cancer cell proliferation [55]. The alcoholic extract of the red algaAcanthophora spicifera exhibits tumoricidal activity on Ehrlich's ascites carcinoma cells developed in mice at a dose of 20 mg/kg, comparable to the standard drug, 5-flurouracil. This is evidenced by increase in the mean survival time, decrease in tumor volume, and viable cell count. The smear study exhibits membrane blebbing, vacuole formation, and reduction in staining intensity, which further ascertains the tumoricidal activity. The seaweeds Acanthaphora spicifera, Ulva reticulata, Gracilaria foliifera, and Padina boergesenii of the Gulf of Mannar region are reportedly exhibiting cytotoxic activity in their alcoholic extracts [56, 57].

Algae have gained special interest owing to their biological properties. There are many reports on the immunomodulating and antitumor activities of algae [54, 58–71]. An extract from the brown seaweedSargassum thunbergii has shown antitumour activity [72] and inhibition of tumour metastasis in the rat mammary adeno carcinoma cell (13762 MAT) [73]. Moreover, low-molecular weight fucoidan isolated fromAscophyllum nodosum shows an anti-proliferative effect on both normal and malignant cells, including fibroblasts (Hamster Kidney Fibroblast CCL39), sigmoid colon adenocarcinoma cells (COLO320 DM), and smooth muscle cells [74]. Fucoidans exhibit antitumour, anticancer, antimetastatic, and fibrinolytic properties in mice [73, 75]. Stylopoldione, isolated from Stypodium sp. is a potent cytotoxic metabolite, which halts mitotic spindle formation [76]. The compound Condriamide-A from Chondria sp. exhibits cytotoxicity towards human nasopharyngeal and colorectal cancer cells [77]. Caulerpenyne from Caulerpa sp. shows its bioactivity against human cell lines and to have anticancer, antitumour, and antiproliferating properties. Two compounds, meroterpenes and usneoidone, showing antitumour properties have been isolated from Cystophora sp. [78–81] Phloroglucinol and its polymers, namely, eckol (a trimer), phlorofucofuroeckol A (a pentamer), dieckol, and 8,8′-bieckol (hexamers) isolated from the brown alga Eisenia bicyclis are shown to have antioxidant activity [82,83].

The brown alga Eclonia cava has been hydrolyzed by using five different types of carbohydrases such as AMG, Celluclast, Termamyl, Ultraflo, and Viscozyme to produce enzymatic extracts and proved them to be potential natural water-soluble antioxidants with dose dependent radical scavenging activities [94]. Further studies have shown that a sulfated polysaccharide purified from the same algal species selectively and dose-dependently suppresses the proliferation of the cancer cell lines in vitro [95]. The polysaccharide is composed of fucose (82%), galactose (14%), and small amounts of xylose and mannose. Its high anticoagulant activity has also been investigated for its antiproliferative effect on murine colon carcinoma (CT-26), human leukemic monocyte lymphoma (U-937), human promyelocytic leukemia (HL-60), and mouse melanoma (B-16) cell lines. The growth inhibition rate of CT-26 cells increases consistently with the sample concentration, in which the highest activity (around 40%) is recorded at 100 µg mL^{-1} sample [95]. The apoptosis induction is confirmed by the cell cycle analysis, while pronounced sub-G1 phase arrests of 9.5% and 13.8% are also clearly observed when the cells are treated at 15 and 30 µg mL^{-1} of the sulphated polysaccharides in the U-937 cell line. The compound dose dependently enhances the DNA fragmentation on the U-937 cell line as observed after 24-h incubation. The western blot analyses conducted with several antibodies such as caspase-7, caspase-8, Bax, Bcl-xL, and PARP and ECSP have exhibited a clear effect on the caspase-7 and -8 which cleave protein substrates, including PARP, an inducer of apoptosis responsible for DNA cleavage [95].

Table 1: Some of the marine floral derivatives and their anticancer activities.

Marine flora	Chemical	Biological activity	Reference
		Microbial flora	
Microcystis aeruginosa	MicroviridinToxin BE-4, Siatoxin	Antibiotic, anticancer	[84, 85]
Streptomyces peucetius	Daunorubicin	Anticancer activities on acute myeloid leukemia and acute lymphocytic leukemia	[86]
		Algal flora	
Cyanobacteria *Nostoc linckia* and *Nostoc spongiaeforme* var. *tenue*	Borophycin	Cytotoxicity against human epidermoid carcinoma (LoVo) and human colorectal adenocarcinoma activity	[48]
Cyanobacteria	Apratoxins	Inhibit a variety of cancer cell lines	[45]
Nostoc linckia	Cyptophycin 1	Cytotoxicity against human tumor cell lines and human solid tumors	[50]
Nostoc spongiaeforme	Cryptophycin 8	Greater therapeutic efficiency and lower toxicity than cryptophycin 14 *in vivo*	[51]
Stylopodium sp.	Stypoldione	Cytotoxic	[76]
Chondria sp.	Condriamide A	Cytotoxicity	[77]
Caulerpa sp.	Caulerpenyne	Cytotoxicity, anticancer, antitumour, and antiproliferating activity	[78–80]
Cystophora sp.	Meroterpenes and Usneoidone	Antitumour	[81]
Symploca sp.	Largazole	Antiproliferative activity	[44]
Lyngbya boulloni	apratoxin A	Cytotoxicity to adenocarcinoma	[45]
Leptolyngbya sp.	coibamide A	Cytotoxicity against NCIH460 lung and mouse neuro-2a cells	[46]

Stigonema sp.	Scytonemin	Antiproliferative and anti-inflammatory activities	[41]
Acanthophora spicifera	Crude	Tumoricidal activity on Ehrlich's ascites carcinoma cells developed in mice	[56, 57]
Acanthophora spicifera	Crude	Antioxidants and inhibiting cancer cell proliferation	[56, 57]
Palmaria palmata	Phloroglucinol and its polymers, namely, eckol (a trimer), phlorofucofuroeckol A (a pentamer), dieckol, and 8,8'-bieckol (hexamers)	Antioxidant activity of the phlorotannins	[55]
Eisenia bicyclis	Phloroglucinol and its polymers, namely eckol (a trimer), phlorofucofuroeckol A (a pentamer), dieckol, and 8,8'-bieckol (hexamers)	Antioxidant activity of the phlorotannins	[82, 83]
Sargassum thunbergii	Crude	Antitumour activity, inhibition of tumour metastasis in rat mammary adeno carcinoma cell (13762 MAT)	[72, 73]
Ascophyllum nodosum	Fucoidan	Antiproliferative antitumour, anticancer, antimetastatic, and fibrinolytic	[74, 75]
Mangroves and other coastal plants			
Ceriops decandra	Lignins	Antioxidant	[87]
Ceriops decandra	Mangrove tea	Anticancer	[88]
Acanthus ilicifolius	Ribose derivatives of benzoxazoline	Anticancer	[89, 90]
Calophyllum inophyllum	Xanthone, biflavonoids, benzophenones, neoflavanoids, and coumarin derivatives	Anticancer, antitumour, and lipid peroxidation	[91, 92]
Excoecaria agallocha	Diterpenes exhibited remarkable antitumour promoting activity *in vivo* on two-stage carcinogenesis test of tumour	Antitumour activity of methanolic extract based on three assays: (i) DPPH radical scavenging, (ii) linoleic acid oxidation assay, and (iii) oxidative cell death assay	[93]

3.6. Mangroves and Other Higher Plants

Mangroves have long been used in fisher-folk medicine to treat diseases [96, 97]. Sixteen plants are the possible source of anticancer drugs, based on traditional knowledge and preliminary scientific work (Table 1). A sulphur containing alkaloid, 1,2-dithiolane (Brugine) isolated form Bruguiera sexangula displays antitumor activity against Sarcoma 180 and Lewis. Tannin from the same plant also exhibits anticancer activity against lung carcinoma. A ribose derivative of 2-Benzoxazoline isolated from Acanthus ilicifolius shows anticancer and antiviral activities [98]. Tea from the mangrove plant Ceriops decandra is shown to successfully prevent the dimethyl benz[a]anthracine-induced hamster buccal pouch carcinogenesis; consequently it enhances beneficial bacteria like lactobacilli in oral cavity of the animals [88].

4. CHEMICAL CONSTITUENTS OF MARINE FLORA

Marine floras are rich in biologically active and medicinally potent chemicals. Polyphenols and polysaccharides are the most predominant group of compounds which are applicable for antioxidant and anticancer activities. There are more than 40,000 different species of phytoplankton, 680 species of marine algae belonging to Rhodophyta, Phaeophyta, Chlorophyta commonly known as red, brown, and green seaweeds, respectively, and 71 mangrove plant species have been documented in the global marine biotope. They provide essential fatty acids, ionic trace minerals, vitamins, enzymes, bioflavonoids, amino acids, and other nutrients.

4.1. Polyphenols

Polyphenols are widely distributed in plants and they are reportedly acting as free radical scavengers, antimicrobial and anticancer agents [99, 100]. Marine plants such as seaweeds, sea grass, and mangroves also contain high amounts of polyphenols such as phenolic acids, flavonoids, anthocyanidins, lignin, tannins, catechin, epicatechin, epigallocatechin, and gallic acid [53, 101]. These polyphenolic compounds have shown many health-benefiting bioactivities, such as antioxidant, anticancer, antiviral, anti-inflammatory, and an ability to inhibit human platelet aggregation [102–104]. Some studies have shown a positive correlation between the increased dietary intake of natural antioxidants and the reduced coronary heart disease, cancer mortality, as well as longer life expectancy [2, 3]. Moreover, they are natural metal chelators with high antioxidant activity that may be successfully used to prevent a variety of toxic metal ion-induced organ dysfunctions [105]. Earlier reports suggest that polyphenols may regenerate α-tocopherol through reduction of the α-tocopheroxyl radical [106]. A close association between anticarcinogenic activity and antioxidant activity has been reported in a chemically induced mouse carcinoma system with low-molecular weight polyphenols [107–110].

The marine red algae like Osmundea pinnatifida has been documented for its antimicrobial, antifungal, anti-leishmanial, and antioxidant [111–114] activities. Scutellarein 4′-methyl ether (Figure 1(a)) has antiallergic [115], anticancer and anticytotoxic activities in vitro and in vivo [116].

Terrestrial and marine polyphenols are similar in some respects, but different fundamentally in their chemical structures. Terrestrial polyphenols are polymers based on flavonoids or gallic acids. Marine algal polyphenols, phlorotannins, which are only known in brown algae, are restricted to polymers of phloroglucinol (1,3,5-trihydroxybenzene) [117]. Six phlorotannins have been detected by HPLC analysis in the brown seaweeds,Eisenia bicyclis and Eclonia kurome, and they are phloroglucinol (0.7%), an unknown phloroglucinol tetramer (MW 478, 3.4%), eckol (7.5%), phlorofucofuroeckol A (21.6%), dieckol (21.9%), 8,8′-bieckol (24.0%), and other unknown compounds (20.9%), in E. bicyclis, and these compounds are also present in E. kurome, respectively, at concentrations of 2.2, 0.6, 8.5, 27.6, 23.6, 6.8, and 31.7% (Figures 2(b), 2(c), 2(d), 2(e), and 2(f)). The crude phlorotannins extracted from brown algae have inhibitory effects on HAase [118]. The half maximal inhibition (IC_{50}) values of crude phlorotannins of E. bicyclis and E. kurome, two terrestrial polyphenols (catechin, EGCG), inhibit four times stronger than that by an anti-allergic drug (DSCG) [119].

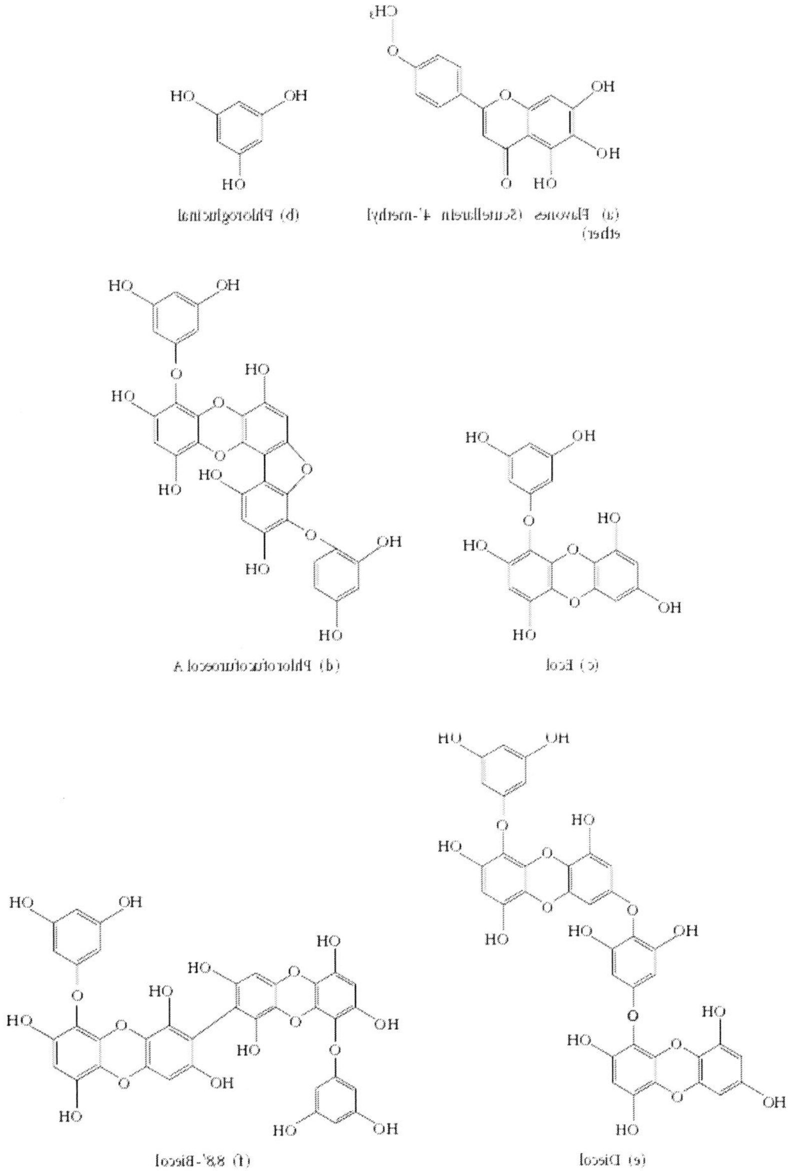

Figure 1. Anticancer polyphenolic compounds from marine floras.

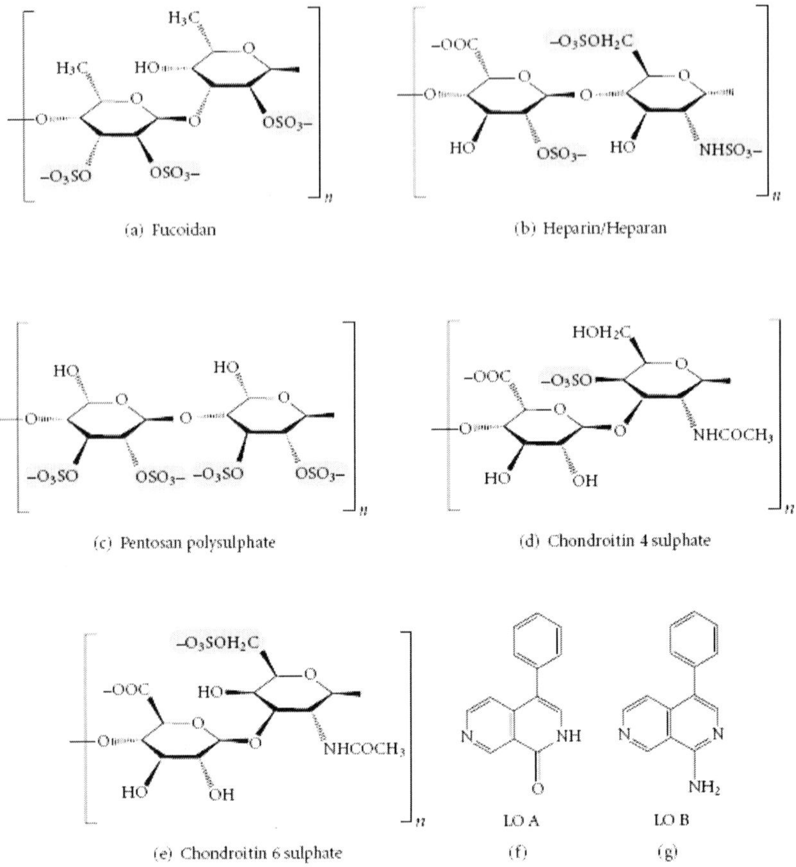

Figure 2. Anticancer polysaccharides from marine floras.

Edible seaweeds contain a range of potentially bioactive components including polyphenols and phlorotannins [120–123]. Edible seaweed like Palmaria palmate is shown to be an effective antioxidant, capable of inhibiting cancer cell proliferation [55]. The enzymatic hydrolysis of the brown seaweed Ecklonia cava yields high amount of compounds with enhanced biological activities as compared with water and organic extract counterparts [94]. Phloroglucinol and its polymers, namely, eckol (a trimer), phlorofucofuroeckol A (a pentamer), dieckol, and 8,8′-bieckol (hexamers) isolated from Eisenia bicyclis, have a potential antioxidant activity [82]. The phlorotannins isolated from Ecklonia kurome act as antiplasmin inhibitor; however, other bioactivities of phlorotannins, from a human physiological viewpoint, are still obscure [124].

Polyphenolic compounds inhibit cancer cells by xenobiotic metabolizing enzymes that alter metabolic activation of potential carcinogens, while some flavonoids can also alter hormone production and inhibit aromatase to prevent the development of cancer cells [125]. The mechanism of action of anticancer activity of phenolics is by disturbing the cellular division during mitosis at the telophase stage. Phenolics reduce the amount of cellular protein and mitotic index, and the colony formation during cell proliferation of cancer cells [126]. Several studies exhibit a close relationship between antioxidant activities and total phenolic content [127–129].

Use of phytosubstances to improve or enhance their effects with safety in foods is significantly focused in daily food. The activities of diverse constituents vary in their ability by quenching effects against active free radical oxygen by carotenes and cryptoxanthins, and polyphenols and flavonoids, by inhibition of absorption into small intestine by dietary fibres, or by regulation on efflux and influx of ions in cell membranes by minerals to inhibit tumors [130–132].

The uses of saponins are natural detergents, well known to primitive people as fish poisons. The interesting pharmacological properties associated with the Chinese drug "giwieng" are considered a panacea and other interesting biological activities such as spermicidal [133], molluscicidal [134], antimicrobial, anti-inflammatory, and cytotoxic activities [135]. Avicennia officinalis produces pharmacologically significant steroidal saponins, sapogenisis, and sapogenins. Liomonds (modified terpenes) have attracted much attention recently because of their remarkable insect antifeedent and growth-regulating activities [136]. There are many types of flavonoids such as flavones, catechins, chalcones, flavanols and isoflavonoids which exhibit antioxidant activity towards a variety of oxidizable compounds [137].

4.2. Polysaccharides

Over the last few years, medical and pharmaceutical industries have shown an increased interest in seaweed-derived polysaccharides. Polysaccharides or glycans are a group of major chemical compounds with the most common constituents of monosaccharide like D-glucose, but D-fructose, D-galactose, L-galactose, D-mannose, L-arabinose, and D-xylose are also frequently present. Some monosaccharide derivatives found in polysaccharides include the amino sugars (D-glucosamine and D-galactosamine) as well as their derivatives (N-acetylneuraminic acid and N-acetylmuramic acid) and simple sugar acids (glucuronic and iduronic acids). Polysaccharides of algal origin include alginates, agar, and carrageenans. Agar is an unbranched polysaccharide present in the cell membranes of red algae, primarily from the genera Gelidium and Gracilaria, and it is the primary structural support for the algal cell walls. Chemically, it is constituted by galactose sugar molecules.

Carrageenans are polysaccharides of galactan with alternating 1,3- and 1,4-linked galactose residues, which fill spaces between the cellulosic plant structure of seaweeds.

The active components contained in algal polysaccharides are mainly sulfated ones [63–67, 69, 70]. Most studies support that sulfated polysaccharides can enhance the innate immune response by promoting the tumoricidal activities of macrophages and natural killer cells [138–141]. Antigen-presenting cells migrate into and out of tumour tissue to present tumour antigen to T-helper cells, as well as to produce cytokines, such as interleukin-1 beta and TNF-alpha that stimulate T-helper cells. As a result, T-helper cells promote the activity of cytotoxic T-cell, which has the strong cytotoxic effect on tumour cells. Sulfated polysaccharides can enhance the adaptive immune response by promoting such process [140, 142–144]. Recent studies have implicated that sulfated polysaccharides recognize a range of cell adhesion systems. Sulfated polysaccharide can bind to CD2, CD3, and CD4 in T lymphocytes and enhance the proliferative response of T lymphocytes [145–147]. B-1, a sulfated polysaccharide isolated from the culture filtrate of marine Pseudomonas sp., induces apoptosis of human leukaemic cells (U937) [148]. PI-88, a sulfated oligosaccharide, induces apoptosis of pancreatic islet carcinoma [149]. Internalized sulfated glycosaminoglycans interfere with transcription function and subsequently induce apoptosis of murine melanoma cells [150].

Fucoidan is one of the representative sulfated polysaccharides (sulphated L-fucose) derived from cell wall of brown algae [65, 66, 151]. Fucoidan-induced apoptosis in human lymphoma HS-Sultan cell lines is accompanied by the activation of caspase-3 and down-regulation of extracellular signal-regulated kinase pathway [152]. Fucoidans have diverse biological properties, ranging from relatively simple mechanical support functions to more intricate effects on cellular processes [151] and binding proteins such as adhesion proteins [153], growth factors [154], cytokines [155], and a variety of enzymes, including coagulation proteases [156]. As a result, they can participate like glycosaminoglycans (GAGs) in cell adhesion, migration, proliferation, and differentiation. They can also modulate clinically relevant phenomena such as angiogenesis, tumor metastasis, and atherosclerosis [157]. For the past decade, fucoidans isolated from different species have been extensively studied due to their varied biological activities, including anticoagulant, antithrombotic, antivirus, antitumor, immunomodulatory, anti-inflammatory, blood lipids reducing, antioxidant, and anticomplementary activities against hepatopathy, uropathy and renalpathy, gastric protective effects, and therapeutic potential in surgery. Compared with other sulfated polysaccharides, fucoidans have been increasingly investigated in recent years to develop the drugs or functional foods [158]. The type of fucoidan, its sulphation and molecular weight, and the conformation of its sugar residues vary with the seaweed species [151, 159].

Sulphation is critical for fucoidan activity in vivo. In particular, desulphated fucoidan fails to promote angiogenesis in vitro [160] or to induce immature CD34+ cell mobilization in vivo [161]. Native fucoidan-induced mobilization is abolished in the presence of protamine [162]. The predominant sulphation pattern consists of a trisulphated disaccharide repeat similar to that found in heparin [163, 164]. Yet heparin has no effect on angiogenesis induced by HUVEC in vitro [165] and does not induce significant immature CD34+ cell mobilization [161]. Furthermore, heparan sulphate (Figure 2(b)), pentosan sulphate (Figure 2(c)), and chondroitin sulphate (Figures 2(d) and 2(e)), which exhibit anticoagulant activities, inhibit angiogenesis in vitro. Fucoidan can disrupt heparan sulphate-growth factor/cytokine complexes and can substitute for cell-surface heparan sulphates in stabilizing the growth factor/growth factor receptor interaction. Fucoidan may mediate growth factor-induced EPC differentiation by interacting with a "receptor" that promotes endothelial cell adhesion, migration, proliferation and differentiation, and that cooperates with a growth factor receptor, transducing the intracellular signals required to induce the angiogenic phenotype. This putative fucoidan receptor might contain a carbohydrate-binding domain that interacts with the fucoidan carbohydrate backbone [157].

4.2.1. Alkaloids

The term alkaloid was first proposed by Meissner in 1819 to characterize these "alkali-like" compounds found in plants [166], but it was not precisely defined [167]. With time, the definition has changed [168] to a compound that has nitrogen atom(s) in a cyclic ring. Numerous biological amines and halogenated cyclic nitrogen-containing substances are included in the term alkaloid. The latter could not be found in terrestrial plants and is specific from marine organisms including marine algae. Alkaloid chemistry and its anticancer activities have been widely studied in terrestrial plants, but the number of studies in marine plants are insignificant. Morphine was the first alkaloid extracted from a terrestrial plant in 1805 as reported by Kappelmeier [169], and hordenine was the first alkaloid isolated from marine algae in 1969 [170, 171]. Today approximately two thousand alkaloids are known. They occur abundantly in terrestrial plants and rarely in marine algae.

Among several types of compounds obtained from plants, alkaloids have traditionally been of interest due to their pronounced physiological activities in animals and humans [172]. The most famous examples of anticancer alkaloids are taxol (clinically available since 1994) from the western yew, Taxus brevifolia, and camptothecin and derivatives, currently in clinical trials, from Camptotheca acuminata [14, 173, 174]. The alkaloid taspine hydrochloride founded in Sangre de Grado plant is also considered a potential anticancer agent [175], and homoharringtonine, an alkaloid isolated from the Chinese tree Cephalotaxus harringtonia(Cephalotaxacea), has shown efficacy against various leukemias [176]. The isolation of vinca alkaloids such as vinblastine and vincristine from the Madagascar periwinkle, Catharanthus roseus G. Don. (Apocynaceae), has opened a new era of the use of alkaloids as anticancer agents. They were the first agents entered to clinical use for the treatment of cancer [177]. Vinblastine and vincristine are primarily used in combination with other cancer chemotherapeutic drugs for the treatment of a variety of cancers, including leukemias, lymphomas, advanced testicular cancer, breast and lung cancers, and Kaposi's sarcoma [177].

The alkaloids found in marine algae may be divided into three groups: Phenylethylamine alkaloids, Indole and halogenated indole alkaloids, and other alkaloids. Structurally, the alkaloids isolated from marine algae mostly belong to the phenylethylamine and indole groups. Biological activities of these alkaloids were not fully investigated. Alkaloids of marine algae are relatively rare, when compared with terrestrial plant alkaloids. Research on marine drugs has largely focused on finding drugs for cancer treatment. There are two derivatives: lophocladine A (Figure 2(f)) and lophocladine B (Figure 2(g)) isolated from a red alga Lophocladia sp., collected from Fijian Island, New Zealand [178] and their anticancer activity has been proved successfully in various cancer cell lines [168].

Coastal mangroves do contain alkaloids of anticancer activity [98]. "Rhizophrine" is an alkaloid, a major constituent of the leaves of Rhizophora mucronata and R. stylosa. Similarly the presence of acanthicifolin inAcanthus illicifolius, brugine (a sulphur containing alkaloid; Figure 3(a)) in Bruguiera sexangula, and benzoquinones (Figure 3(b)) in Aegiceras corniculatum and Kandelia kandel has been recorded.

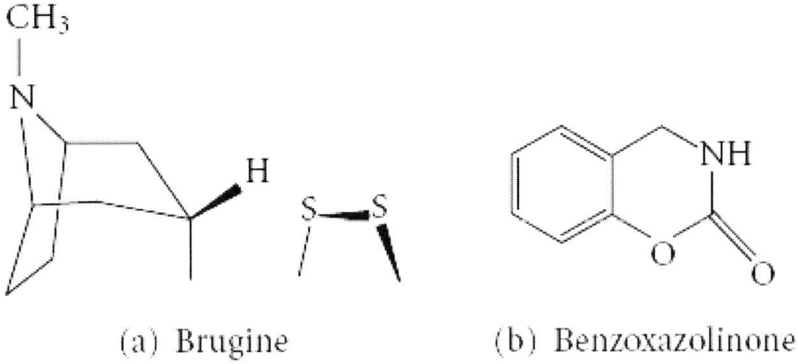

Figure 3. Anticancer alkaloids from marine floras.

5. MECHANISMS FOR THE ANTICANCER ACTIVITY OF MARINE PLANTS

DNA damage is considered to be one of the most important steps leading to cancer. A marker of mutagenic DNA damage will be useful in the estimation of cancer risk of various populations and in monitoring the effects of chemoprevention. Much of this damage is oxidative in nature. It is estimated that a typical human cell experiences about 10.000 oxidative "hits" to its DNA each day. DNA repair enzymes remove most of the damage. Oxidative lesions to DNA accumulate with age and so does the risk of cancer [4].

Antioxidants

Several mechanisms are defending against free radicals and other reactive oxygen species (ROS) in human system. Various defenses are complementary to one another because they act on different oxidants or in different cellular compartments. One important line of defense is a system of enzymes, including superoxide dismutase (SOD), glutathione peroxidase (GPx), and catalase as well as several exogenously acquired radical-scavenging substances such as vitamins E and C and carotenoids [179]. Under normal conditions, the high concentrations of SOD maintain superoxide concentrations at a level too low to allow the formation of peroxynitrite. It is also important to mention that the antioxidant reduces glutathione (GSH). GSH is ubiquitous in aerobic tissues, and although it is not a nutrient, it is synthesized from sulfhydryl-containing amino acids and is highly important in intermediary antioxidant metabolism [180].

Nutrition plays a key role in maintaining the body's enzymatic defences against free radicals. Several essential minerals including selenium, copper, manganese, and zinc are involved in the structure or catalytic activity of these enzymes [180].

Unlike other vitamins, vitamin E is not shown to be directly associated with the function of any enzyme system [181]. Its only established role is that of an antioxidant and a scavenger of free radicals, making it effective as a protector of the integrity of lipids and phospholipid membranes. As an antioxidant, vitamin E is strongly interactive with other dietary systemic antioxidants such as vitamin C and glutathione. Accumulating evidence suggests that vitamin E may have several other functions, including modulation of gene expression and inflammatory responses [182].

Vitamin C is a powerful antioxidant because it can donate a hydrogen atom and form a relatively stable ascorbyl free radical (i.e., L-ascorbate anion). As a scavenger of ROS, ascorbate is shown to be effective against the superoxide radical anion, hydrogen peroxide, the hydroxyl radical, and singlet oxygen [183, 184]. Vitamin C also scavenges reactive nitrogen oxide species to prevent nitrosation of target molecules [185]. The ascorbyl free radical can be converted back to reduced ascorbate by accepting another hydrogen atom or it can undergo further oxidation to dehydroascorbate. Dehydroascorbate is unstable but is more fat soluble than ascorbate and is taken up 10–20 times more rapidly by erythrocytes, where it will be reduced back to ascorbate by GSH or NADPH from the hexose monophosphate shunt [186]. Thus, mechanism exists to recycle vitamin C, which is similar to vitamin E.

Free radicals are a product of tissue metabolism, and the potential damage which they can cause is minimized by the antioxidant capacity and repair mechanisms within the cell. Thus in a metabolically active tissue cell in a healthy subject with an adequate dietary intake, damage to tissue will be minimal and most of the damage, if it does occur, will be repaired [187]. Despite the fact that the marine plants possess application in food and in the pharmaceutical industry, the antioxidant and anticancer activities of many types of plants are still unexplored.

Immunomodulation and Apoptosis

Apoptosis is a complex process that involves many different signaling pathways and results in a multitude of changes in the dying cells. The apoptotic machinery is triggered as a result of a shift in the balance of anti- and proapoptotic proteins. Up regulation of antiapoptotic proteins, down regulation of proapoptotic proteins, and decreased expression of caspases may lead to decreased apoptosis. Evasion of apoptosis is recognized to facilitate cancer development by blocking differentiation, promoting angiogenesis, and increasing cell motility, invasion, and metastasis [188]. Dysregulation of apoptotic signaling can play a vital role in diseases with insufficient apoptosis leading to cancer.

The proapoptotic member of the Bcl-2 family such as Bim, a BH3 induces apoptosis by binding to and inhibiting the function of antiapoptotic proteins such as Bcl-XL and Bcl-w. In addition, Bim is reportedly inducing cytochrome C release from the mitochondria [189]. The release of cytochrome C from the mitochondria is also induced by caspase 8, an initiator caspase that links the death receptor and mitochondrial pathways of apoptosis. Caspase 3 is an effector caspase that executes cell death by cleavage of proteins, vital for cell survival [190].

Induction of apoptosis is one of the active strategies to arrest proliferation of cancer cells. Radiation and chemical agents like tamoxifen, capable of inducing apoptosis, have been used to treat cancer [191, 192]. Many chemopreventive agents exert their anticarcinogenic effects by inducing apoptosis [193]. The apoptosis inducing effect of plant extracts may be attributed to up regulated immune surveillance, increased macrophage, and activations of death-inducing signal complex. Natural dietary constituents such as curcumin and resveratrol have been reported to induce apoptosis in malignant cells in vitro [194]. The marine phytochemicals also can activate the macrophages and induce apoptosis. Fucoidan from Laminaria japonica can restore the immune functions of immunosuppressed mice, and it is an immunomodulator acting directly on macrophage and T lymphocyte [195]. It can also promote the recovery of immunologic function in irradiated rats. The mechanism is associated with the arrest of lymphocyte apoptosis by fucoidan [196, 197]. Fucoidan can induce the production of interleukin-1 (IL-1) and interferon-γ (IFN-γ) in vitro. It enhances the functions of T lymphocyte, B cell, macrophage, and natural killer cell (NK cell) and also promotes the primary antibody response to sheep red blood cell (SRBC) in vivo [198]. High molecular-weight fucoidan prepared fromOkinawa mozuku promotes an increase in the proportion of murine cytotoxic T cells [199]. Fucoidan fromFucus vesiculosus has immunostimulating and maturing effects on dendritic cells (DCs), which are powerful antigen-presenting cells, via a pathway involving nuclear factor-κB (NF-κB) [200].

Nutritional Values and Anticancer Effects

Marine plants play an important role to fulfill the requirement of food and nutrition for rectifying the human ailments. Most diets that are protective against cancer are mainly made up from foods of plant origin. Higher consumption of several plant foods probably protects against cancers. The "plant-based" diets give more emphasis to those plant foods that are high in

nutrients, high in dietary fiber (and so in non-starch polysaccharides), and low in energy density. Non-starchy vegetables, and fruits, probably protect against some cancers [201].
Seaweeds are used extensively for human consumption and they contain other interesting components or traditional medicinal value with curative powers for a variety of diseases (tuberculosis, arthritis, colds, influenza, cancer, etc.). Most people unknowingly utilize seaweed products daily in the form of processed food items like processed dairy, meat, and fruit products and domestic commodities like paint, toothpaste, solid air fresheners, cosmetics, and so forth. Seaweeds are excellent source of vitamins A, Bl, B12, C, D & E, riboflavin, niacin, pantothenic acid and folic acid 3, 4 as well as minerals such as Ca, P, Na, K. Their amino acid content is well balanced, containing most of the essential amino acids needed for life and health. They have more than 54 trace elements required for human body's physiological functions in quantities greatly exceeding vegetables and other land plants [202].

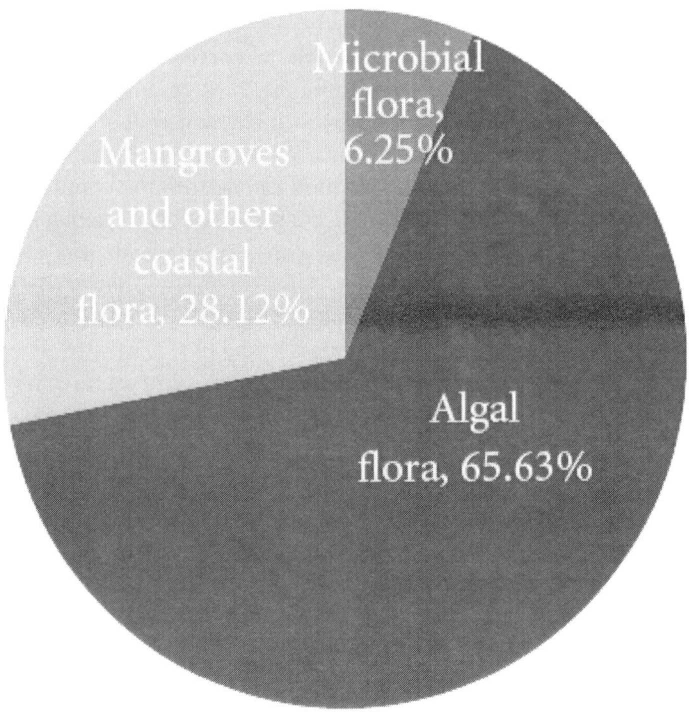

Figure 4. Relative contribution of different marine floral components to anticancer compounds.

6. CONCLUSION

Increasing global warming, malnutrition, and various environmental insults continue to increase the incidences of cancer. According to the American Cancer Society, the global burden is expected to grow as 27 million new cancer cases and 17.5 million cancer deaths simply due to the growth and aging of the population by 2050. Natural derivatives play an important role to prevent the cancer incidences as synthetic drug formulations cause various harmful side effects to human beings. Marine floras are potential source of anticancer compounds, but they are least explored (Table 1). Of the anticancer compounds extracted so far, the marine algae contribute 65.63%, the mangroves 28.12%, and the bacteria 6.25%, (Figure 4). Owing to a diverse chemical ecology, the marine organisms especially marine flora have a great promise for providing potent, cheaper, and safer anticancer drugs, which deserve an extensive investigation.

ACKNOWLEDGMENT

The authors are thankful to Professor T. Balasubramanian, Dean, Faculty of Marine Sciences, Annamalai University for providing facilities.

REFERENCES

1. A. Gurib-Fakim, "Medicinal plants: traditions of yesterday and drugs of tomorrow," Molecular Aspects of Medicine, vol. 27, no. 1, pp. 1–93, 2006.

2. B. Halliwell, "Dietary polyphenols: good, bad, or indifferent for your health?" Cardiovascular Research, vol. 73, no. 2, pp. 341–347, 2007.

3. A. D. O. Rios, L. M. G. Antunes, and M. D. L. P. Bianchi, "Bixin and lycopene modulation of free radical generation induced by cisplatin-DNA interaction," Food Chemistry, vol. 113, no. 4, pp. 1113–1118, 2009.

4. L. Langseth, Oxidants, Antioxidants, and Disease Prevention, International Life Sciences Institute Press, Washington, DC, USA, 1995.

5. H. Kikuzaki, J. Usuguchi, and N. Nakatani, "Constituents of Zingiberaceae. I. Diarylheptanoids from the rhizomes of ginger (Zingiber officinale roscoe)," Chemical and Pharmaceutical Bulletin, vol. 39, no. 1, pp. 120–122, 1991.

6. T. Masuda, "Antioxidant activity of tropical ginger extracts and analysis of the contained curcuminoids,"Journal of Agricultural and Food Chemistry, vol. 40, no. 8, pp. 1337–1340, 1992.

7. H. Kikuzaki and N. Nakatani, "Antioxidant effects of some ginger constituents," Journal of Food Science, vol. 58, pp. 1407–1410, 1993.

8. R. L. Prior, "Fruits and vegetables in the prevention of cellular oxidative damage," American Journal of Clinical Nutrition, vol. 78, no. 3, pp. 570–578, 2003.

9. Y. Cai, Q. Luo, M. Sun, and H. Corke, "Antioxidant activity and phenolic compounds of 112 traditional Chinese medicinal plants associated with anticancer," Life Sciences, vol. 74, no. 17, pp. 2157–2184, 2004.

10. C. Kaur and H. C. Kapoor, "Anti-oxidant activity and total phenolic content of some asian vegetables,"International Journal of Food Science and Technology, vol. 37, no. 2, pp. 153–161, 2002.

11. M. Namiki, "Antioxidants/antimutagens in food," Critical reviews in food science and nutrition, vol. 29, no. 4, pp. 273–300, 1990.

12. G. M. Cragg and M. R. Boyd, "Drug discovery and development at the National Cancer Institute: the role of natural products of plant origin," in Medicinal Plant Resources of the Tropical Forest, M. J. Balick, E. Elisabetsky, and S. A. Laird, Eds., pp. 101–136, Columbia University Press, New York, NY, USA, 1996.

13. G. M. Cragg, D. J. Newman, and K. M. Snader, "Natural products in drug discovery and development,"Journal of Natural Products, vol. 60, no. 1, pp. 52–60, 1997.

14. N. H. Oberlies and D. J. Kroll, "Camptothecin and taxol: historic achievement in natural products research," Journal of Natural Products, vol. 67, no. 2, pp. 129–135, 2004.

15. J. Jimeno, G. Faircloth, J. M. Fernández Sousa-Faro, P. Scheuer, and K. Rinehart, "New marine derived anticancer therapeutics—a journey from the sea to clinical trials," Marine Drugs, vol. 2, pp. 14–29, 2004.

16. K. Kathiresan and Duraisamy, "Current issue of microbiology," ENVIS Centre Newsletters, vol. 4, pp. 3–5, 2005.

17. B. Haefner, "Drugs from the deep: marine natural products as drug candidates," Drug Discovery Today, vol. 8, no. 12, pp. 536–544, 2003.

18. K. Kathiresan, M. A. Nabeel, and S. Manivannan, "Bioprospecting of marine organisms for novel bioactive compounds," Scientific Transaction Environmental Technovation, vol. 1, pp. 107–120, 2008.

19. A. Kjaervik, "Seaweed fight diabetes and thicken cat food," Gemini Magazine, vol. 4, pp. 103–107, 1993.

20. L. DeVugst and E. J. Vandamme, "Bacteriocins of lactic acid bacteria. Microbiol Genet Appl," London: Blackie Acadamic & Profession, vol. 75, pp. 140174–140179, 1994.

21. K. Kathiresan and G. Thiruneelakandan, "Prospects of lactic acid bacteria of marine origin," Indian Journal of Biotechnology, vol. 7, no. 2, pp. 170–177, 2008.

22. I. Wollowski, G. Rechkemmer, and B. L. Pool-Zobel, "Protective role of probiotics and prebiotics in colon cancer," American Journal of Clinical Nutrition, vol. 73, no. 2, pp. 451–455, 2001.

23. B. R. Goldin and S. L. Gorbach, "Probiotics for humans," in Probiotics, R. Fuller, Ed., pp. 355–376, Chapman and Hall, London, UK, 1992.

24. D. A. Devine and P. Marsh, "Prospects for the development of probiotics and prebiotics for oral applications," Journal of Oral Microbiology, vol. 1, pp. 1–11, 2009.

25. M. Kodama, T. Ogata, and S. Sato, "Bacterial production of saxitoxin," Agricultural and Biological Chemistry, vol. 52, no. 4, pp. 1075–1077, 1988.

26. M. Kodama, T. Ogata, T. Sato, and S. Sakamoto, "Possible association of marine bacteria with paralytic shellfish toxicity of bivalves," Marine Ecology Programming Service, vol. 61, pp. 203–206, 1990.

27. U. Simidu, K. Kita-Tsukamoto, T. Yasumoto, and M. Yotsu, "Taxonomy of four marine bacterial strains that produce tetrodotoxin," International Journal of Systematic Bacteriology, vol. 40, no. 4, pp. 331–336, 1990.

28. B. K. Carté, "Biomedical potential of marine natural products," BioScience, vol. 46, no. 4, pp. 271–286, 1996.

29. P. R. Jensen, C. A. Kauffman, and W. Fenical, "High recovery of culturable bacteria from the surfaces of marine algae," Marine Biology, vol. 126, no. 1, pp. 1–7, 1996.

30. R. P. Maskey, M. M. Sevvana, I. Us'on, E. Helmke, and H. Laatsch, "Gutingimycin: a highly complex metabolite from a marine streptomycete," Journal of Antibiotic, vol. 55, p. 1031, 2002.

31. E. Erba, D. Bergamaschi, S. Ronzoni et al., "Mode of action at thiocoraline, a natural marine compound with anti-tumour activity," British Journal of Cancer, vol. 80, no. 7, pp. 971–980, 1999.

32. L. Lene, "Microbial metabolites-an infinite source of novel Chemistry," Pure and Applied Chermistry, vol. 68, pp. 745–748, 1996.

33. G. A. Schiehser, J. D. White, G. Matsumoto, J. O. Pezzanite, and J. Clardy, "The structure of leptosphaerin," Tetrahedron Letters, vol. 27, no. 46, pp. 5587–5590, 1986.

34. A. J. Pallenberg and J. D. White, "The synthesis and absolute configuration of (+)-leptosphaerin,"Tetrahedron Letters, vol. 27, no. 46, pp. 5591–5594, 1986.

35. A. Guerriero, M. D. Amrosio, V. Cuomo, and F. Pietra, "A novel, degraded polyketidic lactone, leptosphaerolide, and its likely diketone precursor, leptosphaerodione, Isolation from cultures of teh marine ascomycete Leptosphaeria oeaemaris (Linder)," Helvetica Chimica Acta, vol. 74, p. 1445, 1991.

36. R. N. Lawrence, "Rediscovering natural product biodiversity," Drug Discovery Today, vol. 4, no. 10, pp. 449–451, 1999.

37. A. Abdel-Lateff, G. M. König, K. M. Fisch, U. Höller, P. G. Jones, and A. D. Wright, "New antioxidant hydroquinone derivatives from the algicolous marine fungus Acremonium sp," Journal of Natural Products, vol. 65, no. 11, pp. 1605–1611, 2002.

38. A. Abdel-Lateff, C. Klemke, G. M. König, and A. D. Wright, "Two new xanthone derivatives from the algicolous marine fungus Wardomyces anomalus," Journal of Natural Products, vol. 66, no. 5, pp. 706–708, 2003.

39. N. Thajuddin and G. Subramanian, "Cyanobacterial biodiversity and potential applications in biotechnology," Current Science, vol. 89, no. 1, pp. 47–57, 2005.

40. R. K. Jha and X. Zi-Rong, "Biomedical compounds from marine organisms," Marine Drugs, vol. 2, pp. 123–146, 2004.

41. C. S. Stevenson, E. A. Capper, A. K. Roshak et al., "Scytonemin—a marine natural product inhibitor of kinases key in hyperproliferative

inflammatory diseases," Inflammation Research, vol. 51, no. 2, pp. 112–114, 2002.

42. C. S. Stevenson, E. A. Capper, A. K. Roshak et al., "The identification and characterization of the marine natural product scytonemin as a novel antiproliferative pharmacophore," Journal of Pharmacology and Experimental Therapeutics, vol. 303, no. 2, pp. 858–866, 2002.

43. R. W. Rickards, J. M. Rothschild, A. C. Willis et al., "Calothrixins A and B, novel pentacyclic metabolites from Calothrix cyanobacteria with potent activity against malaria parasites and human cancer cells,"Tetrahedron, vol. 55, no. 47, pp. 13513–13520, 1999.

44. K. Taori, V. J. Paul, and H. Luesch, "Structure and activity of largazole, a potent antiproliferative agent from the Floridian marine cyanobacterium Symploca sp," Journal of the American Chemical Society, vol. 130, no. 6, pp. 1806–1807, 2008.

45. H. Luesch, R. E. Moore, V. J. Paul, S. L. Mooberry, and T. H. Corbett, "Isolation of dolastatin 10 from the marine cyanobacterium Symploca species VP642 and total stereochemistry and biological evaluation of its analogue symplostatin 1," Journal of Natural Products, vol. 64, no. 7, pp. 907–910, 2001.

46. R. A. Medina, D. E. Goeger, P. Hills et al., "Coibamide A, a potent antiproliferative cyclic depsipeptide from the panamanian marine cyanobacterium Leptolyngbya sp," Journal of the American Chemical Society, vol. 130, no. 20, pp. 6324–6325, 2008.

47. W. H. Gerwick, L. T. Tan, and N. Sitachitta, "Nitrogen-containing metabolites from marine cyanobacteria," in The Alkaloids, G. Cordell, Ed., pp. 75–184, Academic Press, San Diego, Calif, USA, 2001.

48. R. Banker and S. Carmeli, "Tenuecyclamides A-D, cyclic hexapeptides from the cyanobacterium Nostoc spongiaeforme var. tenue," Journal of Natural Products, vol. 61, no. 10, pp. 1248–1251, 1998.

49. B. S. Davidson, "New dimensions in natural products research: cultured marine microorganisms,"Current Opinion in Biotechnology, vol. 6, no. 3, pp. 284–291, 1995.

50. R. E. Moore, "Cyclic peptides and depsipeptides from cyanobacteria: a review," Journal of Industrial Microbiology, vol. 16, no. 2, pp. 134–143, 1996.

51. W. W. Carmichael, "Cyanobacteria secondary metabolites—the cyanotoxins," Journal of Applied Bacteriology, vol. 72, no. 6, pp. 445–459, 1992.

52. D. R. A. Mans, A. B. Da Rocha, and G. Schwartsmann, "Anti-cancer drug discovery and development in Brazil: targeted plant collection as a rational strategy to acquire candidate anti-cancer compounds,"Oncologist, vol. 5, no. 3, pp. 185–198, 2000.

53. Y. Yoshie, W. Wang, Y. P. Hsieh, and T. Suzuki, "Compositional difference of phenolic compounds between two seaweeds, Halimeda spp," Journal of Tokyo University Fisheries, vol. 88, pp. 21–24, 2002.

54. E. Furusawa and S. Furusawa, "Anticancer activity of a natural product, viva-natural, extracted from Undaria pinnantifida on intraperitoneally implanted Lewis lung carcinoma," Oncology, vol. 42, no. 6, pp. 364–369, 1985.

55. Y. V. Yuan, M. F. Carrington, and N. A. Walsh, "Extracts from dulse (Palmaria palmata) are effective antioxidants and inhibitors of cell proliferation in vitro," Food and Chemical Toxicology, vol. 43, no. 7, pp. 1073–1081, 2005.

56. H. R. Vasanthi, Biomedical and pharmacological studies of some marine algae of gulf of mannar south east coast of India, Ph.D. thesis, 2002.

57. H. R. Vasanthi, G. V. Rajamanickam, and A. Saraswathy, "Tumoricidal effect of the red algae Acanthophora spicifera on Ehrlich's ascites carcinoma in mice Seaweed Res," UtilNet, pp. 217–224, 2004.

58. I. Yamamoto and H. Maruyama, "Effect of dietary seaweed preparations on 1,2-dimethylhydrazine-induced intestinal carcinogenesis in rats," Cancer Letters, vol. 26, no. 3, pp. 241–251, 1985.

59. I. Yamamoto, H. Maruyama, and M. Moriguchi, "The effect of dietary seaweeds on 7,12-dimethyl-benz[a]anthracene-induced mammary tumorigenesis in rats," Cancer Letters, vol. 35, no. 2, pp. 109–118, 1987.

60. E. Furusawa and S. Furusawa, "Effect of pretazettine and Viva-Natural, a dietary seaweed extract, on spontaneous AKR leukemia in comparison with standard drugs," Oncology, vol. 45, no. 3, pp. 180–186, 1988.

61. E. Furusawa and S. Furusawa, "Anticancer potential of Viva-Natural, a dietary seaweed extract, on Lewis lung carcinoma in comparison with chemical immunomodulators and on cyclosporine-accelerated AKR leukemia," Oncology, vol. 46, no. 5, pp. 343–349, 1989.

62. E. Furusawa and S. Furusawa, "Antitumor potential of low-dose chemotherapy manifested in combination with immunotherapy of Viva-Natural, a dietary seaweed extract, on Lewis lung carcinoma,"Cancer Letters, vol. 50, no. 1, pp. 71–78, 1990.

63. E. Furusawa, S. Furusawa, and S. C. Chou, "Antileukemic activity of Viva-Natural, a dietary seaweed extract, on Rauscher murine leukemia in comparison with anti-HIV agents, azidothymidine, dextran sulfate and pentosan polysulfate," Cancer Letters, vol. 56, no. 3, pp. 197–205, 1991.

64. M. Ellouali, C. Boisson-Vidal, P. Durand, and J. Jozefonvicz, "Antitumor activity of low molecular weight fucans extracted from brown seaweed ascophyllum nodosum," Anticancer Research, vol. 13, no. 6, pp. 2011–2019, 1993.

65. H. Itoh, H. Noda, H. Amano, C. Zhuaug, T. Mizuno, and H. Ito, "Antitumor activity and immunological properties of marine algal polysaccharides, especially fucoidan, prepared from Sargassum thunbergii of phaeophyceae," Anticancer Research, vol. 13, no. 6, pp. 2045–2052, 1993.

66. H. Itoh, H. Noda, H. Amano, and H. Ito, "Immunological analysis of inhibition of lung metastases by fucoidan (GIV-A) prepared from brown seaweed Sargassum thunbergii," Anticancer Research, vol. 15, no. 5, pp. 1937–1947, 1995.

67. Y. Okai, S. Ishizaka, K. Higashi-Okai, and U. Yamashita, "Detection of immunomodulating activities in an extract of Japanese edible seaweed, Laminaria japonica (Makonbu)," Journal of the Science of Food and Agriculture, vol. 72, no. 4, pp. 455–460, 1996.

68. J. N. Liu, Y. Yoshida, M. Q. Wang, Y. Okai, and U. Yamashita, "B cell stimulating activity of seaweed extracts," International Journal of Immunopharmacology, vol. 19, no. 3, pp. 135–142, 1997.

69. Y. Okai, K. Higashi-Okai, S. Ishizaka, and U. Yamashita, "Enhancing effect of polysaccharides from an edible brown alga, Hijikia fusiforme (Hijiki), on release of tumor necrosis factor-α from macrophages of endotoxin-nonresponder C3H/HeJ mice," Nutrition and Cancer, vol. 27, no. 1, pp. 74–79, 1997.

70. Y. Okai, K. Higashi-Okai, S. Ishizaka, K. Ohtani, I. Matsui-Yuasa, and U. Yamashita, "Possible immunodulating activities in an extract of edible brown alga, Hijikia fusiforme (Hijiki)," Journal of Science and Food Agriculture, vol. 76, pp. 56–62, 1998.

71. B. E. Shan, Y. Yoshida, E. Kuroda, and U. Yamashita, "Immunomodulating activity of seaweed extract on human lymphocytes in vitro," International Journal of Immunopharmacology, vol. 21, no. 1, pp. 59–70, 1999.

72. C. Zhuang, H. Itoh, T. Mizuno, and H. Ito, "Antitumor active fucoidan from the brown seaweed, umitoranoo (Sargassum thunbergii)," Bioscience, Biotechnology and Biochemistry, vol. 59, no. 4, pp. 563–567, 1995.

73. D. R. Coombe, C. R. Parish, I. A. Ramshaw, and J. M. Snowden, "Analysis of the inhibition of tumour metastasis by sulphated polysaccharides," International Journal of Cancer, vol. 39, no. 1, pp. 82–88, 1987.

74. P. Vischer and E. Buddecke, "Different action of heparin and fucoidan on arterial smooth muscle cell proliferation and thrombospondin and fibronectin metabolism," European Journal of Cell Biology, vol. 56, no. 2, pp. 407–414, 1991.

75. P. Religa, M. Kazi, J. Thyberg, Z. Gaciong, J. Swedenborg, and U. Hedin, "Fucoidan inhibits smooth muscle cell proliferation and reduces mitogen-activated protein kinase activity," European Journal of Vascular and Endovascular Surgery, vol. 20, no. 5, pp. 419–426, 2000.

76. W. H. Gerwick and W. Fenical, "Ichthyotoxic and cytotoxic metabolites of the tropical brown alga Stypopodium zonale (Lamouroux) papenfuss," Journal of Organic Chemistry, vol. 46, no. 1, pp. 22–27, 1981.

77. J. A. Palermo, P. B. Flower, and A. M. Seldes, "Chondriamides A and B, new indolic metabolites from the red alga Chondria sp," Tetrahedron Letters, vol. 33, no. 22, pp. 3097–3100, 1992.

78. J. L. Fischel, R. Lemee, P. Formento et al., "Cell growth inhibitory effects of caulerpenyne, a sesquiterpenoid from the marine algae Caulerpa Taxifolia," Anticancer Research, vol. 15, no. 5, pp. 2155–2160, 1995.

79. D. Parent-Massin, V. Fournier, P. Amade et al., "Evaluation of the toxicological risk to humans of caulerpenyne using human hematopoietic progenitors, melanocytes, and keratinocytes in

culture,"Journal of Toxicology and Environmental Health A, vol. 47, no. 1, pp. 47–59, 1996.

80. P. Barbier, S. Guise, P. Huitorel et al., "Caulerpenyne from Caulerpa taxifolia has an antiproliferative activity on tumor cell line SK-N-SH and modifies the microtubule network," Life Sciences, vol. 70, no. 4, pp. 415–429, 2001.

81. J. G. Urones, M. E. M. Araujo, F. M. S. Brito Palma et al., "Meroterpenes from Cystoseira usneoides II,"Phytochemistry, vol. 31, no. 6, pp. 2105–2109, 1992.

82. T. Nakamura, K. Nagayama, K. Uchida, and R. Tanaka, "Antioxidant activity of phlorotannins isolated from the brown alga Eisenia bicyclis," Fisheries Science, vol. 62, no. 6, pp. 923–926, 1996.

83. T. Shibata, K. Fujimoto, K. Nagayama, K. Yamaguchi, and T. Nakamura, "Inhibitory activity of brown algal phlorotannins against hyaluronidase," International Journal of Food Science and Technology, vol. 37, no. 6, pp. 703–709, 2002.

84. A. R. Arment and W. W. Carmichael, "Evidence that microcystin is a thio-template product," Journal of Phycology, vol. 32, no. 4, pp. 591–597, 1996.

85. L. Shi, W. W. Carmichael, and P. J. Kennelly, "Cyanobacterial PPP family protein phosphatases possess multifunctional capabilities and are resistant to microcystin-LR," Journal of Biological Chemistry, vol. 274, no. 15, pp. 10039–10046, 1999.

86. G. Minotti, P. Menna, E. Salvatorelli, G. Cairo, and L. Gianni, "Anthracyclines: molecular advances and pharmacologie developments in antitumor activity and cardiotoxicity," Pharmacological Reviews, vol. 56, no. 2, pp. 185–229, 2004.

87. H. Sakagami, M. Kashimata, M. Toguchi et al., "Radical modulation activity of lignins from a mangrove plant, Ceriops decandra (Griff.) Ding Hou," In Vivo, vol. 12, no. 3, pp. 327–332, 1998.

88. N. S. Boopathy, K. Kathiresan, S. Manivannan, and Y. J. Jeon, "Effect of mangrove tea extract from Ceriops decandra (Griff.) Ding Hou. on salivary bacterial flora of DMBA induced Hamster buccal pouch carcinoma," Indian Journal of Microbiology. In press.

89. A. S. Kabil, S. Sharma, and S. Wahidulla, "Leishmanicidal activity of 2-Benzoaxozolinone from Acanthus illicifolius, in vitro," Planta Medica, vol. 60, pp. 187–188, 1994.

90. P. K. Minocha and K. P. Tiwari, "A triterpenoidal saponin from roots of Acanthus illicifolius,"Phytochemistry, vol. 20, no. 1, pp. 135–137, 1981.

91. S. H. Goh and I. Jantan, "A xanthone from Calophyllum inophyllum," Phytochemistry, vol. 30, no. 1, pp. 366–367, 1991.

92. M. Iinuma, H. Tosa, T. Tanaka, and S. Yonemori, "Two new xanthones in the underground part of Calophyllum inophyllum," Heterocycles, vol. 37, no. 2, pp. 833–838, 1994.

93. T. Masuda, S. Yonemori, Y. Oyama, et al., "Evolution of antioxidant activity of environmental plants: activioty of the extracts from seahore plants," Journal of Agriculture Food Chemistry, vol. 47, pp. 1749–1754, 1999.

94. S. J. Heo, P. J. Park, E. J. Park, SE. K. Kim, and Y. J. Jeon, "Antioxidant activity of enzymatic extracts from a brown seaweed Ecklonia cava by electron spin resonance spectrometry and comet assay," European Food Research and Technology, vol. 221, no. 1-2, pp. 41–47, 2005.

95. Y. Athukorala, W. K. Jung, T. Vasanthan, and Y. J. Jeon, "An anticoagulative polysaccharide from an enzymatic hydrolysate of Ecklonia cava," Carbohydrate Polymers, vol. 66, no. 2, pp. 184–191, 2006.

96. W. M. Bandaranayake, "Traditional medicinal uses of mangroves; mangrove and salt marshes," Wetlands Ecology and Management, vol. 2, pp. 133–148, 1998.

97. K. Kathiresan, "A review of studies on Pichavaram mangrove, southeast India," Hydrobiologia, vol. 430, no. 1–3, pp. 185–205, 2000.

98. K. Kathiresan and S. Z. Qasim, Biodiversity of Mangrove Ecosystems, Hindustan Publishing Corporation, New Delhi, India, 2005.

99. F. Shahidi and P. K. Wanasundara, "Phenolic antioxidants: critical review," Food Science and Nutrition, vol. 32, no. 1, pp. 67–103, 1992.

100. C. Sánchez-Moreno, J. A. Larrauri, and F. Saura-Calixto, "Free radical scavenging capacity and inhibition of lipid oxidation of wines, grape juices and related polyphenolic constituents," Food Research International, vol. 32, no. 6, pp. 407–412, 1999.

101. W. M. Bandaranayake, "Bioactivities, bioactive compounds and chemical constituents of mangrove plants," Wetlands Ecology and Management, vol. 10, no. 6, pp. 421–452, 2002.

102. G. J. Fan, B. H. Han, Y.-H. Kang, and M. K. Park, "Evaluation of inhibitory potentials of chinese medicinal plants on platelet-activating factor (PAF) receptor binding," Natural Product Sciences, vol. 7, no. 2, pp. 33–37, 2001.

103. P. D. S. Spada, G. G. N. De Souza, G. V. Bortolini, J. A. P. Henriques, and M. Salvador, "Antioxidant, mutagenic, and antimutagenic activity of frozen fruits," Journal of Medicinal Food, vol. 11, no. 1, pp. 144–151, 2008.

104. S. M. Mohsen and A. S. M. Ammar, "Total phenolic contents and antioxidant activity of corn tassel extracts," Food Chemistry, vol. 112, no. 3, pp. 595–598, 2009.

105. C. K. B. Ferrari, "Functional foods, herbs and nutraceuticals: towards biochemical mechanisms of healthy aging," Biogerontology, vol. 5, no. 5, pp. 275–289, 2004.

106. W. Bors, W. Heller, C. Michel, and M. Saran, "Flavonoids as antioxidants: determination of radical-scavenging efficiencies," Methods in Enzymology, vol. 186, pp. 343–355, 1990.

107. Y. Fujita, T. Yamane, M. Tanaka et al., "Inhibitory effect of (-)-epIgallocatechIn gallate on carcinogenesis with N-ethyl-N'-nıtro-N-nitrosoguanidine in mouse duodenum," Japanese Journal of Cancer Research, vol. 80, no. 6, pp. 503–505, 1989.

108. T. Tanaka, T. Kojima, T. Kawamori et al., "Inhibition of 4-nitroquinoline-1-oxide-induced rat tongue carcinogenesis by the naturally occurring plant phenolics caffeic, ellagic, chlorogenic and ferulic acids,"Carcinogenesis, vol. 14, no. 7, pp. 1321–1325, 1993.

109. T. Tanaka, "Cancer chemoprevention by natural products," Oncology Reports, vol. 1, no. 6, pp. 1139–1155, 1994.

110. H. Makita, T. Tanaka, H. Fujitsuka et al., "Chemoprevention of 4-nitroquinoline 1-oxide-induced rat oral carcinogenesis by the dietary flavonoids chalcone, 2-hydroxychalcone, and quercetin," Cancer Research, vol. 56, no. 21, pp. 4904–4909, 1996.

111. M. A. Rizvi and M. Shameel, "Studies on the bioactivity and elementology of marine algae from the coast of Karachi, Pakistan," Phytotherapy Research, vol. 18, no. 11, pp. 865–872, 2004.

112. H. Sabina, S. Tasneem, Y. Samreen, M. I. K. Choudhary, and R. Aliya, "Investigation of the bioactive crude extract of various seaweed

against Leishmania from the coast of Karachi, Pakistan," Pakistan Journal of Botony, vol. 37, pp. 163–168, 2005.

113. H. Sabina, M. Samreen, I. Choudhary, and R. Aliya, "In vitro activity of some seaweeds against Leishmania major," International Journal of Phycology & Phycochemistry, vol. 2, pp. 53–58, 2006.

114. H. Sabina, M. I. Choudhary, and R. Aliya, "Evaluation of antioxidant potential from Seaweeds,"International Journal of Phycology & Phycochemistry, vol. 2, pp. 213–216, 2006.

115. K. Masaru, M. Toyoda, R. Teshima, et al., "In vitro Antiallergic activity of flavonoids in Histamine release assay using rat basophilic Leukemia (RBL-2H3) cells," Journal of the Food Hygienic Society of Japan, vol. 35, pp. 497–503, 1994.

116. X. U. Shan, L. Li, Z. Liqun, et al., "Reversale effect of 4'- methylether-scutellarein on multidrug resistance of human choriocarcinoma JAR / VP 16 cell line," Shengwu Huaxue Yu Shengwu Wuli Jinzhan, vol. 33, pp. 1061–1073, 2006.

117. M. A. Ragan and K.-W. Glombitza, "Phlorotannins, brown algal polyphenols," Progress in Phycological Research, vol. 4, pp. 129–241, 1986.

118. H. Kakegawa, H. Matsumoto, and T. Satoh, "Activation of hyaluronidase by metallic salts and compound 48/80, and inhibitory effect of anti-allergic agents on hyaluronidase," Chemical and Pharmaceutical Bulletin, vol. 33, no. 2, pp. 642–646, 1985.

119. T. Shibata, K. Fujimoto, K. Nagayama, K. Yamaguchi, and T. Nakamura, "Inhibitory activity of brown algal phlorotannins against hyaluronidase," International Journal of Food Science and Technology, vol. 37, no. 6, pp. 703–709, 2002.

120. Y. Fukuyama, I. Miura, Z. Kinjyo, et al., "Eckols, novel phlorotannins with a dibenzo-p-dioxin skeltone possessing inhibitory effects on a2-macroglobulin from the brown alga Ecklonia kurome OKAMURA,"Chemistry Letters, pp. 739–742, 1985.

121. Y. Fukuyama, M. Kodama, I. Miura et al., "Structure of an anti-plasmin inhibitor, eckol, isolated from the brown alga Ecklonia kurome Okamura and inhibitory activities of its derivatives on plasma plasmin inhibitors," Chemical and Pharmaceutical Bulletin, vol. 37, no. 2, pp. 349–353, 1989.

122. Y. Fukuyama, M. Kodama, I. Miura et al., "Anti-plasmin inhibitor. V. Structures of novel dimeric eckols isolated from the brown alga Ecklonia kurome OKAMURA," Chemical and Pharmaceutical Bulletin, vol. 37, no. 9, pp. 2438–2440, 1989.

123. Y. Fukuyama, M. Kodama, I. Miura et al., "Anti-plasmin inhibitor. VI. Structure of phlorofucofuroeckol A, a novel phlorotannin with both dibenzo-1,4-dioxin and dibenzofuran elements, from Ecklonia kurome okamura," Chemical and Pharmaceutical Bulletin, vol. 38, no. 1, pp. 133–135, 1990.

124. T. Nakayama, M. Takahashi, Y. Fukuyama, and Z. Kinzyo, "An anti-plasmin inhibitor, eckol, isolated from the brown alga Ecklonia kurome OKAMURA," Agricultural and Biological Chemistry, vol. 63, pp. 3025–3030, 1989.

125. M. Zhao, B. Yang, J. Wang, Y. Liu, L. Yu, and Y. Jiang, "Immunomodulatory and anticancer activities of flavonoids extracted from litchi (Litchi chinensis Sonn.) pericarp," International Immunopharmacology, vol. 7, no. 2, pp. 162–166, 2007.

126. A. Gawron and I. Kruk, "Cytotoxic effect of xanthotoxol (8-hydroxypsoralen) on TCTC cells in vitro,"Polish Journal of Pharmacology and Pharmacy, vol. 44, no. 1, pp. 51–57, 1992.

127. X. Duan, G. Wu, and Y. Jiang, "Evaluation of the antioxidant properties of litchi fruit phenolics in relation to pericarp browning prevention," Molecules, vol. 12, no. 4, pp. 759–771, 2007. View at Publisher

128. Y. Pan, K. Wang, S. Huang et al., "Antioxidant activity of microwave-assisted extract of longan (Dimocarpus Longan Lour.) peel," Food Chemistry, vol. 106, no. 3, pp. 1264–1270, 2008.

129. B. G. Wang, W. W. Zhang, X. J. Duan, and X. M. Li, "In vitro antioxidative activities of extract and semi-purified fractions of the marine red alga, Rhodomela confervoides (Rhodomelaceae)," Food Chemistry, vol. 113, no. 4, pp. 1101–1105, 2009.

130. N. Motohashi, M. Kawase, T. Kurihara et al., "Relationship between radical intensity and biological activity of cacao husk extracts," Anticancer Research, vol. 19, no. 2, pp. 1125–1129, 1999.

131. N. Motohashi, M. Kawase, Y. Shirataki et al., "Biological activity of Feijoa peel extracts," Anticancer Research, vol. 20, no. 6 B, pp. 4323–4329, 2000.

132. Y. Shirataki, M. Kawase, S. Saito et al., "Selective cytotoxic activity of grape peel and seed extracts against oral tumor cell lines," Anticancer Research, vol. 20, no. 1A, pp. 423–426, 2000.

133. B. S. Setty, V. P. Kamboj, H. S. Garg, and N. M. Khanna, "Spermicidal potential of saponins isolated from Indian medicinal plants," Contraception, vol. 14, no. 5, pp. 571–578, 1976.

134. A. Marston and K. Hostettmann, "Review article number 6. Plant molluscicides," Phytochemistry, vol. 24, no. 4, pp. 639–652, 1985.

135. S. B. Mahato, S. K. Sarkar, and G. Poddar, "Triterpenoid saponins," Phytochemistry, vol. 27, no. 10, pp. 3037–3067, 1988.

136. C. P. Champagne, N. Morin, R. Couture, C. Gagnon, P. Jelen, and C. Lacroix, "The potential of immobilized cell technology to produce freeze-dried, phage-protected cultures of Lactococcus lactis,"Food Research International, vol. 25, no. 6, pp. 419–427, 1992.

137. R. A. Larson, "The antioxidants of higher plants," Phytochemistry, vol. 27, no. 4, pp. 969–978, 1988.

138. E. Gorelik, W. W. Bere, and R. B. Herberman, "Role of NK cells in the antimetastatic effect of anticoagulant drugs," International Journal of Cancer, vol. 33, no. 1, pp. 87–94, 1984.

139. E. Gorelik, "Augmentation of the antimetastatic effect of anticoagulant drugs by immunostimulation in mice," Cancer Research, vol. 47, no. 3, pp. 809–815, 1987.

140. J. H. Yim, E. Son, S. Pyo, and H. K. Lee, "Novel sulfated polysaccharide derived from red-tide microalgaGyrodinium impudicum strain KG03 with immunostimulating activity in vivo," Marine Biotechnology, vol. 7, no. 4, pp. 331–338, 2005.

141. G. Zhou, H. Xin, W. Sheng, Y. Sun, Z. Li, and Z. Xu, "In vivo growth-inhibition of S180 tumor by mixture of 5-Fu and low molecular λ-carrageenan from Chondrus ocellatus," Pharmacological Research, vol. 51, no. 2, pp. 153–157, 2005.

142. R. Dziarski, "Enhancement of mixed leukocyte reaction and cytotoxic antitumor responses by heparin,"Journal of Immunology, vol. 143, no. 1, pp. 356–365, 1989.

143. R. Dziarski, "Synergistic enhancement of T cell responses and interleukin-1 receptor expression by interleukin-1 and heparin or

dextran sulfate," Cellular Immunology, vol. 145, no. 1, pp. 100–110, 1992.

144. G. M. O'Sullivan, C. M. Boswell, and G. M. Halliday, "Langerhans cell migration is modulated by N-sulfated glucosamine moieties in heparin," Experimental Dermatology, vol. 9, no. 1, pp. 25–33, 2000.

145. C. R. Parish, V. McPhun, and H. S. Warren, "Is a natural ligand of the T lymphocyte CD2 molecule A sulfated carbohydrate?" Journal of Immunology, vol. 141, no. 10, pp. 3498–3504, 1988.

146. B. Miao, M. Geng, J. Li et al., "Sulfated polymannuroguluronate, a novel anti-acquired immune deficiency syndrome (AIDS) drug candidate, targeting CD4 in lymphocytes," Biochemical Pharmacology, vol. 68, no. 4, pp. 641–649, 2004.

147. B. Miao, J. Li, X. Fu, J. Ding, and M. Geng, "T-cell receptor (TCR)/CD3 is involved in sulfated polymannuroguluronate (SPMG)-induced T lymphocyte activation," International Immunopharmacology, vol. 5, no. 7-8, pp. 1171–1182, 2005.

148. M. Matsuda, T. Yamori, M. Naitoh, and K. Okutani, "Structural revision of sulfated polysaccharide B-1 isolated from a marine Pseudomonas species and its cytotoxic activity against human cancer cell lines,"Marine Biotechnology, vol. 5, no. 1, pp. 13–19, 2003.

149. J. A. Joyce, C. Freeman, N. Meyer-Morse, C. R. Parish, and D. Hanahan, "A functional heparan sulfate mimetic implicates both heparanase and heparan sulfate in tumor angiogenesis and invasion in a mouse model of multistage cancer," Oncogene, vol. 24, no. 25, pp. 4037–4051, 2005.

150. D. Berry, D. M. Lynn, R. Sasisekharan, and R. Langer, "Poly(β-amino ester)s promote cellular uptake of heparin and cancer cell death," Chemistry and Biology, vol. 11, no. 4, pp. 487–498, 2004.

151. O. Berteau and B. Mulloy, "Sulfated fucans, fresh perspectives: structures, functions, and biological properties of sulfated fucans and an overview of enzymes active toward this class of polysaccharide,"Glycobiology, vol. 13, no. 6, pp. 29–40, 2003.

152. Y. Aisa, Y. Miyakawa, T. Nakazato et al., "Fucoidan induces apoptosis of human HS-Sultan cells accompanied by activation of caspase-3 and down-regulation of ERK pathways," American Journal of Hematology, vol. 78, no. 1, pp. 7–14, 2005.

153. F. H. Bouhedja, F. Lindenmeyer, H. Lu, C. Soria, J. Jozefonvicz, and C. Boisson-Vidal, "In Vitro effects of fucans on MDA-MB231 tumor cell adhesion and invasion," Anticancer Research, vol. 22, no. 4, pp. 2285–2292, 2002.

154. H. Thorlacius, B. Vollmar, U. T. Seyfert, D. Vestweber, and M. D. Menger, "The polysaccharide fucoidan inhibits microvascular thrombus formation independently from P- and L-selectin function in vivo,"European Journal of Clinical Investigation, vol. 30, no. 9, pp. 804–810, 2000.

155. R. Sadir, F. Baleux, A. Grosdidier, A. Imberty, and H. Lortat-Jacob, "Characterization of the stromal cell-derived factor-1α-Heparin Complex," Journal of Biological Chemistry, vol. 276, no. 11, pp. 8288–8296, 2001.

156. 156. B. Richard, M. C. Bouton, S. Loyau et al., "Modulation of protease nexin-I activity by polysaccharides,"Thrombosis and Haemostasis, vol. 95, no. 2, pp. 229–235, 2006. View at MathSciNet

157. C. Boisson-Vidal, F. Zemani, G. Caligiuri et al., "Neoangiogenesis induced by progenitor endothelial cells: effect of fucoidan from marine algae," Cardiovascular and Hematological Agents in Medicinal Chemistry, vol. 5, no. 1, pp. 67–77, 2007.

158. B. Li, F. Lu, X. Wei, and R. Zhao, "Fucoidan: structure and bioactivity," Molecules, vol. 13, no. 8, pp. 1671–1695, 2008.

159. M. S. Pereira, B. Mulloy, and P. A. S. Mourão, "Structure and anticoagulant activity of sulfated fucans. Comparison between the regular, repetitive, and linear fucans from echinoderms with the more heterogeneous and branched polymers from brown algae," Journal of Biological Chemistry, vol. 274, no. 12, pp. 7656–7667, 1999.

160. F. Zemani, D. Benisvy, I. Galy-Fauroux et al., "Low-molecular-weight fucoidan enhances the proangiogenic phenotype of endothelial progenitor cells," Biochemical Pharmacology, vol. 70, no. 8, pp. 1167–1175, 2005.

161. J. D. Belcher, P. H. Marker, J. P. Weber, R. P. Hebbel, and G. M. Vercellotti, "Sulfated glycans induce rapid hematopoietic progenitor cell mobilization: evidence for selectin-dependent and independent mechanisms," Blood, vol. 96, no. 7, pp. 2460–2468, 2000.

162. E. A. Sweeney, G. V. Priestley, B. Nakamoto, R. G. Collins, A. L. Beaudet, and T. Papayannopoulou, "Mobilization of stem/progenitor cells by sulfated polysaccharides does not require selectin

presence,"Proceedings of the National Academy of Sciences of the United States of America, vol. 97, no. 12, pp. 6544–6549, 2000.

163. L. Chevolot, B. Mulloy, J. Ratiskol, A. Foucault, and S. Colliec-Jouault, "A disaccharide repeat unit is the major structure in fucoidans from two species of brown algae," Carbohydrate Research, vol. 330, no. 4, pp. 529–535, 2001.

164. B. Mulloy, "The specificity of interactions between proteins and sulfated polysaccharides," Anais da Academia Brasileira de Ciencias, vol. 77, no. 4, pp. 651–664, 2005.

165. S. Matou, D. Helley, D. Chabut, A. Bros, and A.-M. Fischer, "Effect of fucoidan on fibroblast growth factor-2-induced angiogenesis in vitro," Thrombosis Research, vol. 106, no. 4-5, pp. 213–221, 2002.

166. S. W. Pelletier, Chemistry of the Alkaloids, Van Nostrand Reinhold, New York, NY, USA, 1970.

167. G. A. Swan, An Introduction to the Alkaloids, Blackwell Scientific, Oxford, UK, 1967.

168. K. W. Bentley, The Alkaloids, Interscience, New York, NY, USA, 1957.

169. P. Kappelmeier, Die Konstitutions Erforschungder Wichtigten Opium Alkaloide, Verlag von Ferdinand Enke, Stuttgart, Germany, 1912.

170. K. C. Güven, A. Bora, and G. Sunam, "Alkaloid content of marine algae: I. Hordenine from Phyllophora nervosa," Eczacılık Bülteni, vol. 11, pp. 177–184, 1969.

171. K. C. Güven, A. Bora, and G. Sunam, "Hordenine from the alga phyllophora nervosa," Phytochemistry, vol. 9, no. 8, p. 1893, 1970.

172. T. M. Kutchan, "Alkaloid biosynthesis—the basis of metabolic engineering of medicinal plants," Plant Cell, vol. 7, no. 7, pp. 1059–1070, 1995.

173. V. J. Ram and S. Kumari, "Natural products of plant origin as anticancer agents," Drug News and Perspectives, vol. 14, no. 8, pp. 465–482, 2001.

174. D. G. I. Kingston and D. J. Newman, "Taxoids: cancer-fighting compounds from nature," Current Opinion in Drug Discovery and Development, vol. 10, no. 2, pp. 130–144, 2007.

175. J. E. Williams, "Review of antiviral and immunomodulating properties of plants of the peruvian rainforest with a particular emphasis on uña

de gato and sangre de grado," Alternative Medicine Review, vol. 6, no. 6, pp. 567–579, 2001.

176. H. M. Kantarjian, S. O'Brien, P. Anderlini, and M. Talpaz, "Treatment of chronic myelogenous leukemia: current status and investigational options," Blood, vol. 87, no. 8, pp. 3069–3081, 1996.

177. G. M. Cragg and D. J. Newman, "Plants as a source of anti-cancer agents," Journal of Ethnopharmacology, vol. 100, no. 1-2, pp. 72–79, 2005.

178. H. Gross, D. E. Goeger, P. Hills et al., "Lophocladines, bioactive alkaloids from the red alga Lophocladiasp," Journal of Natural Products, vol. 69, no. 4, pp. 640–644, 2006.

179. A. T. Diplock, J. -L. Charleux, G. Crozier-Willi et al., "Functional food science and defence against reactive oxidative," British Journal of Nutrition, vol. 80, supplement 1, pp. S77–S112, 1998.

180. A. Meister, "Glutathione metabolism and its selective modification," Journal of Biological Chemistry, vol. 263, no. 33, pp. 17205–17208, 1988.

181. R. J. Sokol, "Vitamin E.," in Present Knowledge in Nutrition, pp. 130–136, International Life Science Institute Press, Washington, DC, USA, 7th edition, 1996.

182. J. N. Hathcock, Vitamine and Mineral Safety, Council for Responsible Nutrition, 2nd edition, 2004.

183. R. C. Rose, "The ascorbate redox potential of tissues: a determinant or indicator of disease?" News in Physiological Sciences, vol. 4, pp. 190–195, 1989.

184. P. Weber, A. Bendich, and W. Schalch, "Vitamin C and human health—a review of recent data relevant to human requirements," International Journal for Vitamin and Nutrition Research, vol. 66, no. 1, pp. 19–30, 1996.

185. S. R. Tannenbaum, J. S. Wishnok, and C. D. Leaf, "Inhibition of nitrosamine formation by ascorbic acid,"American Journal of Clinical Nutrition, vol. 53, no. 1, pp. 247–250, 1991.

186. D. Hornig, "Distribution of ascorbic acid, metabolites and analogues in man and animals," Annals of the New York Academy of Sciences, vol. 258, pp. 103–118, 1975.

187. B. Halliwell, J. M. C. Gutteridge, and C. E. Cross, "Free radicals, antioxidants, and human disease: where are we now?" Journal of Laboratory and Clinical Medicine, vol. 119, no. 6, pp. 598–620, 1992.

188. I. M. Ghobrial, T. E. Witzig, and A. A. Adjei, "Targeting apoptosis pathways in cancer therapy," Ca: A Cancer Journal for Clinicians, vol. 55, no. 3, pp. 178–194, 2005.

189. L. O'Connor, A. Strasser, L. A. O'Reilly et al., "Bim: a novel member of the Bcl-2 family that promotes apoptosis," EMBO Journal, vol. 17, no. 2, pp. 384–395, 1998.

190. A. Philchenkov, "Caspases: potential targets for regulating cell death," Journal of Cellular and Molecular Medicine, vol. 8, no. 4, pp. 432–444, 2004.

191. B. A. Woynarowska, K. Roberts, J. M. Woynarowski, J. R. MacDonald, and T. S. Herman, "Targeting apoptosis by hydroxymethylacylfulvene in combination with gamma radiation in prostate tumor cells,"Radiation Research, vol. 154, no. 4, pp. 429–438, 2000.

192. W. Zhang, W. T. Couldwell, H. Song, T. Takano, J. H. C. Lin, and M. Nedergaard, "Tamoxifen-induced enhancement of calcium signaling in glioma and MCF-7 breast cancer cells," Cancer Research, vol. 60, no. 19, pp. 5395–5400, 2000.

193. V. E. Steele, "Current mechanistic approaches to the chemoprevention of cancer," Journal of Biochemistry and Molecular Biology, vol. 36, no. 1, pp. 78–81, 2003.

194. A. Liontas and H. Yeger, "Curcumin and resveratrol induce apoptosis and nuclear translocation and activation of p53 in human neuroblastoma," Anticancer Research, vol. 24, no. 2B, pp. 987–998, 2004.

195. W. T. Wang, J. H. Zhou, S. T. Xing, and H. S. Guan, "Immunomodulating action of marine algae sulfated polysaccharides on normal and immunosuppressed mice," Chinese Journal of Pharmacology and Toxicology, vol. 8, no. 3, pp. 199–202, 1994.

196. X. W. Wu, M. L. Yang, X. L. Huang, J. Yan, and Q. Luo, "Effect of fucoidan on splenic lymphocyte apoptosis induced by radiation," Chinese Journal of Radiology Medicine and Protection, vol. 23, pp. 430–432, 2003.

197. X. Wu, M. Yang, and X. Huang, "Effect of laminaria japonica polysaccharides on radioprotection and splenic lymphocyte

apoptosis," Medical Journal of Wuhan University, vol. 25, no. 3, pp. 239–252, 2004.

198. X. L. Yang, J. Y. Sun, and H. N. Xu, "An experimental study on immunoregulatory effect of fucoidan,"Chinese Journal of Marine Drugs, pp. 9–13, 1995.

199. J. Shimizu, U. Wada-Funada, H. Mano, Y. Matahira, M. Kawaguchi, and M. Wada, "Proportion of murine cytotoxic T cells is increased by high molecular-weight fucoidan extracted from Okinawa mozuku(Cladosiphon okamuranus)," Journal of Health Science, vol. 51, no. 3, pp. 394–397, 2005.

200. M. H. Kim and H. G. Joo, "Immunostimulatory effects of fucoidan on bone marrow-derived dendritic cells," Immunology Letters, vol. 115, no. 2, pp. 138–143, 2008.

201. World Cancer Research Fund, Food, Nutrition, Physical Activity, and the Prevention of Cancer: A Global Perspective, American Institute of Cancer Research, Washington, DC, USA, 2007.

202. S. B. Challan and J. C. Hamingway, in Proceedings of the 5th Seaweed Symposium, vol. 5, p. 359, 1966.

Chapter 10

Dereplication and Chemotaxonomical Studies of Marine Algae of the Ochrophyta and Rhodophyta Phyla

Robert Brkljača, Emrehan Semih Göker and Sylvia Urban *

School of Applied Sciences (Discipline of Chemistry), Health Innovations Research Institute (HIRi), RMIT University, GPO Box 2476V Melbourne, Victoria 3001, Australia

ABSTRACT

Dereplication and chemotaxonomic studies of six marine algae of the Ochrophyta and one of the Rhodophyta phyla resulted in the detection of 22 separate compounds. All 16 secondary metabolites, including four new compounds (**16–19**), could be rapidly dereplicated using HPLC-NMR and HPLC-MS methodologies in conjunction with the MarinLit database. This study highlights the advantages of using NMR data (acquired via HPLC-NMR) for database searching and for the overall dereplication of natural products.

Keywords: ochrophyta; rhodophyta; dereplication; profiling; algae; HPLC-NMR; HPLC-MS

1. INTRODUCTION

The Ochrophyta phylum contains in excess of 1800 species [1]. Recently, 17 new compounds, mostly terpenoids, were reported from the Ochrophyta phylum [2]. In contrast, marine algae belonging to the Rhodophyta phylum, are represented by over 6500 species [1] and produce a large number of halogenated secondary metabolites [3]. For example, nine new compounds were recently reported from the Rhodophyta phylum, a majority representative of bromophenols [2].

The intention of this study was to select a range of marine algae and conduct a dereplication/chemotaxonomical investigation as a means to rapidly differentiate the secondary metabolites present across different genera and between species of the same genera. For instance, marine algae of the Ochrophyta phylum such as *Cystophora retroflexa* have been reported to produce carotenoids, phlorethols and fucophlorethols [4,5,6] while *Cystophora subfarcinata* is known to produce tocotrienols and phloroglucinols [7]. The remaining Ochrophyta phylum genera and species investigated included,*Sargassum decipiens*, *Sargassum vestitum*, *Sargassum cf. fallax*, and *Halopteris pseudospicata* and importantly these have not had any marine secondary metabolites reported. However, the *Sargassum* genus is known to produce merediterpenoid, tocotrienol and terpenoid type compounds [8]. The only marine alga of the Rhodophyta phylum studied was of the*Laurencia* genus which is known to produce very different secondary metabolites from the marine brown algae [9,10,11,12].

In this study, we examined six specimens of marine brown algae belonging to the Ochrophyta phylum (*Sargassum cf. fallax*, *Sargassum decipiens* (R.Brown ex Turner) J.Agardh, *Sargassum vestitum* (R.Brown ex Turner) C.Agardh, *Cystophora retroflexa* (Labillardière) J.Agardh, *Cystophora subfarcinata* (Mertens) J.Agardh *and Halopteris pseudospicata* Sauvageau) and one marine red alga from the Rhodophyta phylum (*Laurencia* sp.), all of which were collected from Port Phillip Bay, Victoria, Australia. These marine algae were selected for phytochemical evaluation on the basis of three criteria, but in all three instances the intention was to rapidly dereplicate the secondary metabolites present and to avoid lengthy isolations. The marine algae were either selected on the basis of the observed biological activity of the crude extracts, or due to the fact that no previous secondary metabolites had been described from the species of marine alga. The final motivation for the selection was based upon the fact that our research group has previously conducted studies on other closely related*Sargassum*, *Cystophora* and *Laurencia* species and so the intention was to compare the secondary metabolites in closely related species.

Herein, we report the chemical profiling/dereplication conducted using HPLC-NMR and HPLC-MS leading to the identification of seven different structure classes. In total, 22 compounds were detected in the dichloromethane crude extracts of the marine algae studied, of which 16 could be dereplicated.

2. RESULTS AND DISCUSSION

The frozen marine algae were extracted with 3:1 methanol/dichloromethane, evaporated under reduced pressure and sequentially solvent partitioned (triturated) into dichloromethane and methanol soluble fractions, respectively. The dichloromethane and methanol crude extracts were initially analysed by off-line analytical HPLC and ^{1}H-NMR analyses and this established that the majority of the secondary metabolites were present in the dichloromethane crude extracts. Based on this, only the dichloromethane extracts were further examined by chemical profiling methodologies (HPLC-NMR & HPLC-MS).

2.1. Chemical Profiling (HPLC-NMR & HPLC-MS)

The dichloromethane crude extracts were subjected to both HPLC-NMR and HPLC-MS chemical profiling and a total of 22 compounds were detected from the seven separate marine algae. Identical HPLC-NMR and HPLC-MS conditions were employed to probe the dichloromethane crude extracts of each alga to allow for comparison between each genera and/or species. Analysis of the stop-flow WET1D proton NMR spectra and extracted UV profiles for each of the compounds concluded the presence of seven distinct chemical structure classes including phenolic acids, phenols, resorcinols, phloroglucinols, xanthophylls, tocotrienols and C_{15} halogenated acetogenins, which are known to occur in these genera or species of algae [6,7,8,13,14,15,16,17].

Twelve known (**1–5**, **11–15**, **20** and **21**) and four new (**16–19**) compounds (Figure 1) were dereplicated from the dichloromethane crude extracts of the algae. Compounds were dereplicated by analysis of the HPLC-NMR acquired data (WET1D and various combinations of gCOSY, HSQCAD, and gHMBCAD), high resolution HPLC-MS data, and use of the MarinLit database by searching parameters such as the taxonomy (usually genus), UV, MS and NMR data. While some structure classes are unique to certain genera or species, some can be present across various genera or species of algae (Table 1). For instance, in this study, phloroglucinols were detected in *S. cf. fallax*, *C. subfarcinata* and *C. retroflexa* while tocotrienols were exclusive to *S. cf. fallax*. The xanthophylls, which are known to occur in many marine brown algae [8,18], were found in high abundance in *S. vestitum* and *H. pseudospicata*. The specimen of *S. decipiens* was concluded to produce phenolic acids, phenols, and resorcinols while the specimen of *Laurencia* sp. could be deduced as containing C_{15}halogenated acetogenins. Table 2 summarises each of the components detected in the seven marine algae studied together with the search criteria used to dereplicate the structures present in the dichloromethane crude extracts. The amount of compound present in each of the crude extracts was estimated on the basis of the limit of detection (LOD) methodology recently reported for our HPLC-NMR system [19]. In this study, the LOD for five key NMR experiments was established for a given set of parameters. These LODs and the parameters utilized were reviewed, and on this basis, the approximate amount of each compound present in the crude extract for each of the HPLC-NMR analyses undertaken was estimated (seeTable 2). In HPLC-NMR analyses, it is imperative to supress signals arising from the HPLC solvents (HDO signal arising from D_2O and the CH_3CN peak) in order to maximise signal intensity and obtain better quality NMR spectra. Unfortunately, during this process NMR signals of the compound of interest which occur within this suppression region are also inadvertently suppressed.

Table 1. Chemotaxonomic comparison of the seven marine algae studied and the chemical classes present in each.

Alga	Chemical Class(es) Present	Compounds Present *
C. subfarcinata	Phloroglucinols	**18, 19**
C. retroflexa	Phloroglucinols	**11-13, 16, 18, 20, 21**
S. cf. fallax	Phlroglucinols, tocotrienols	**12, 14, 15, 17, 20, 21**
S. decipiens	Phenols, phenolic acids, resorcinols	**1–4**
S. vestitum	Xanthophylls	**5**
H. pseudospicata	Xanthophylls	**5**
Laurencia sp.	Polyhalogenated C_{15} acetogenins	-

* Retention times for compounds present are provided in Table 2.

Table 2. Identification of chemical structure classes present in seven marine algae studied (ordered on the basis of HPLC-NMR retention time, R_t).

Peak #	R_t (min)	Compound	Structure Class	Marine Alga (~Amount Present in μg)	UV (nm)	MarinLit Search Parameters	New/Known
1	2.29	(**2**)	Phenolic acid	*S. decipiens* (500–1000)	240, 302	Compound not in MarinLit database	Known
2	2.44	(**3**)	Phenol	*S. decipiens* (500–1000)	236, 301	Compound not in MarinLit database	Known
3	3.42	(**11**)	Phloroglucinol	*C. retroflexa* (750–1000)	235, 285	Molecular formula, UV ± 5	Known
4	3.55	(**1**)	Phenolic acid	*S. decipiens* (<100)	235, 301	Molecular formula, UV ± 10	Known
5	4.45	(**16**)	Phloroglucinol	*C. retroflexa* (750–1000)	235, 285	Compound not in MarinLit database	New
6	5.00	n.a.	C_{15} acetogenin	*Laurencia* sp. (<25)	220, 237	Genus, UV ± 5, 1 triplet methyl group	Not Identified
7	6.05	n.a.	Unknown	*Laurencia* sp. (500–1000)	220, 240, 255	Unable to dereplicate using any parameters	Not Identified
8	6.70	n.a.	C_{15} acetogenin	*Laurencia* sp. (<25)	220, 237	Genus, UV ± 5, 1 triplet methyl group	Not Identified
9	7.87	(**4**)	Resorcinol	*S. decipiens* (<10)	229, 276, 281	Compound not in MarinLit database	Known
10	9.98	(**12**)	Phloroglucinol	*C. retroflexa* (500–1000), *S. cf. fallax* (<250)	230, 285	Molecular formula, UV ± 5	Known
11	12.95	(**13**)	Phloroglucinol	*C. retroflexa* (250–750)	230, 285	Molecular formula, UV ± 5	Known
12	13.65	(**17**)	Phloroglucinol	*S. cf. fallax* (<250)	215, 228, 285	Compound not in MarinLit database	New
13	14.53	(**5**)	Xanthophyll	*S. vestitum* (<100), *H. pseudospicata* (<100)	450	Molecular formula	Known
14	15.50	(**20**)	Phloroglucinol	*C. retroflexa* (<500), *S. cf. fallax* (<100)	212, 228, 285	Compound not in MarinLit database	Known [13]
15	20.15	(**21**)	Phloroglucinol	*C. retroflexa* (<250), *S. cf. fallax* (<50)	230, 285	Compound not in MarinLit database	Known [13]
16	21.62	(**14**)	Phloroglucinol	*S. cf. fallax* (<100)	212, 228, 285	Molecular formula, UV ± 5	Known
17	22.96	(**18**)	Phloroglucinol	*C. retroflexa* (<100), *C. subfarcinata* (<50)	228, 285	Compound not in MarinLit database	New
18	23.16	n.a.	Phloroglucinol	*C. retroflexa* (<100)	238, 288	Genus, UV ± 5	Not Identified
19	26.71	n.a.	Xanthophyll	*S. vestitum* (<5), *H. pseudospicata* (<5)	450	Insufficient data to search MarinLit Database	Not Identified
20	30.27	n.a.	Xanthophyll	*S. vestitum* (<5), *H. pseudospicata* (<5)	450	Insufficient data to search MarinLit Database	Not Identified
21	33.40	(**19**)	Phloroglucinol	*C. subfarcinata* (<50)	213, 228, 285	Compound not in MarinLit database	New
22	60.80	(**15**)	Tocotrienol	*S. cf. fallax* (<10)	212, 300	Class, UV ± 5, contains only singlet aromatic/vinyl CH_3 groups, aromatic ring	Known

n.a. indicates that a structure could not be concluded.

2.2. Identification of Phenols, Phenolic Acids and Resorcinols

The specimen of *S. decipiens* was concluded to contain compounds **1–4**, which represent three different structure classes (phenols, phenolic acids and resorcinols). While the phenols and phenolic acids displayed similar UV absorbances (300 nm), the resorcinol exhibited unique UV absorbances (276 and 281 nm). The compound eluting at R_t = 3.55 min was dereplicated from the MarinLit database using the molecular formula and UV absorbances as search parameters. This yielded four possible compounds, but analysis of the NMR data obtained from HPLC-NMR supported only one of these structures. In this way, the compound eluting at R_t = 3.55 min could be identified as 6-tridecylsalicylic acid (**1**) which had been previously reported from the marine brown alga *Caulocystis cephalornithos* [20].

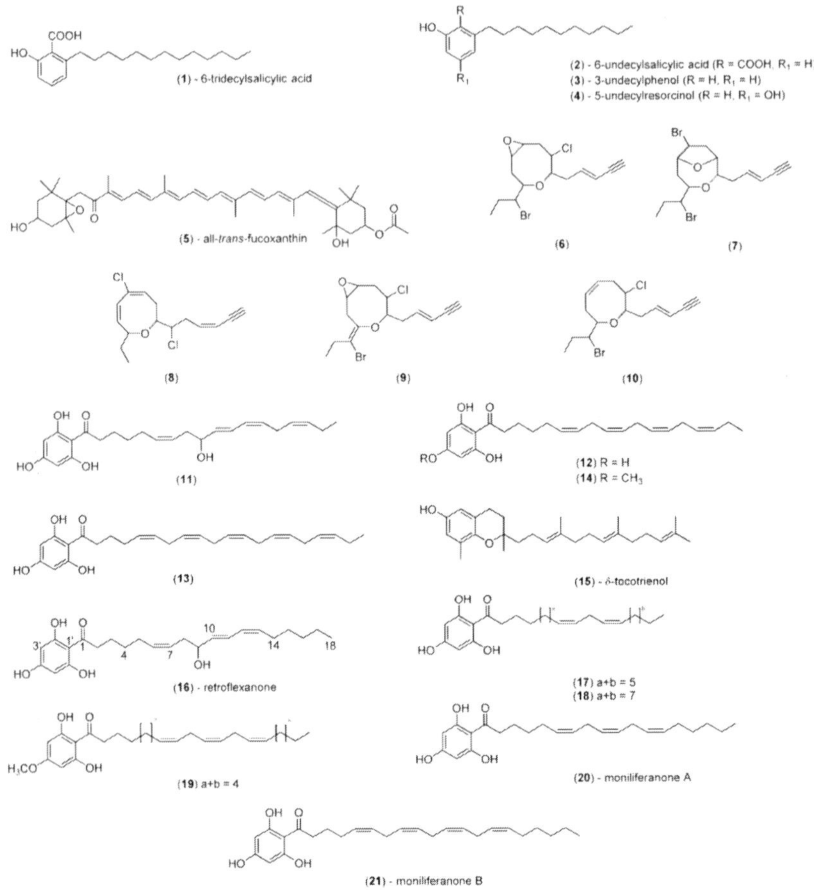

Figure 1. Compounds and range of structure classes as dereplicated by HPLC-NMR and HPLC-MS in conjunction with the MarinLit database.

The remaining compounds eluting at R_t = 2.29, 2.44 and 7.87 min did not yield any matches in the MarinLit database when using various combinations of UV, mass and molecular formulae, and, when only UV data was searched this resulted in far too many possible structure classes. On the basis of the WET1D NMR spectra and UV profiles of the remaining three compounds (R_t = 2.29, 2.44 and 7.87 min) it could be concluded that they were closely related to 6-tridecylsalicylic acid (**1**). The marine brown alga *C. cephalornithos*, which is known to produce 6-tridecylsalicylic acid (**1**), also produces a variety of structurally related analogues [20,21]. Comparison of the data obtained from HPLC-NMR and HPLC-MS to the data for the compounds reported from *C. cephalornithos*, allowed for the compounds eluting at R_t = 2.29, 2.44 and 7.87 min to be identified as undecylsalicylic acid (**2**), 3-undecylphenol (**3**) and 5-undecylresorcinol (**4**) respectively. It is important to point out that these compounds do not appear separately in the MarinLit database and care must be taken in such dereplication exercises. This is the first study conducted on *S. decipiens* and compounds **1–4** have not been reported from the *Sargassum*genus. This highlights the importance of profiling different genera and species as a means of extending knowledge on marine biodiversity. The HPLC-NMR and HPLC-MS data of the compounds identified were consistent with the data reported previously [20,21,22,23].

2.3. Identification of Xanthophylls

The dichloromethane crude extracts of *S. vestitum* and *H. pseudospicata* were found to contain an abundance of xanthophylls. The main compound in the dichloromethane crude extract of each of these two algae (compound eluting at R_t= 14.53 min) was identified as all-*trans*-fucoxanthin (**5**), the main pigment found in marine brown algae. This pigment was identified using the MarinLit database by searching the molecular formula obtained by high resolution HPLC-MS, which yielded only one structure. The UV profile, WET1D, gCOSY and HSQCAD NMR spectra of **5** were found to be in agreement with the structure of all-*trans*-fucoxanthin [24,25] A ROESYAD NMR experiment conducted in stop-flow HPLC-NMR mode confirmed that the configuration for all of the double bonds was *trans* (Figure 2).

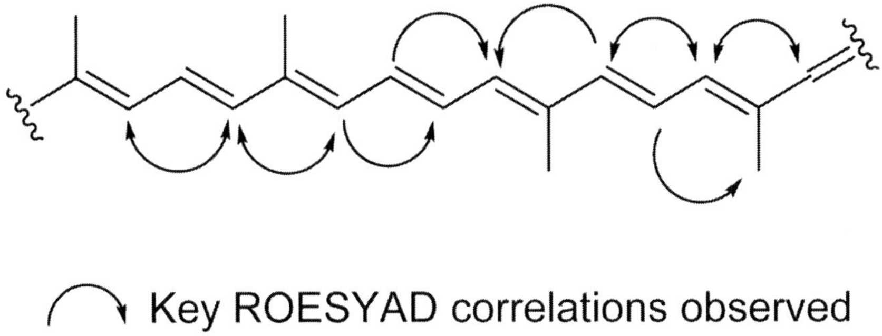

Figure 2. key ROESYAD correlations confirming the all *trans* configuration in all-*trans*-fucoxanthin (**5**).

A further two structurally related compounds eluting at R_t = 26.71 and 30.27 min were also detected in the dichloromethane crude extract of both *S. vestitum* and *H. pseudospicata*, but in much lower quantities. Identification was not possible due to the insufficient quantities present to obtain HPLC-NMR data, and due to the fact that the compounds did not ionize in either positive or negative ESI high resolution HPLC-MS. However, these compounds could be deduced to be two xanthophyll structural analogues based upon comparison of their UV profiles to all-*trans*-fucoxanthin (**5**) (Figure 3). This is the first report of all-*trans*-fucoxanthin (**5**) and other xanthophylls occurring in the *Halopteris* genus [8].

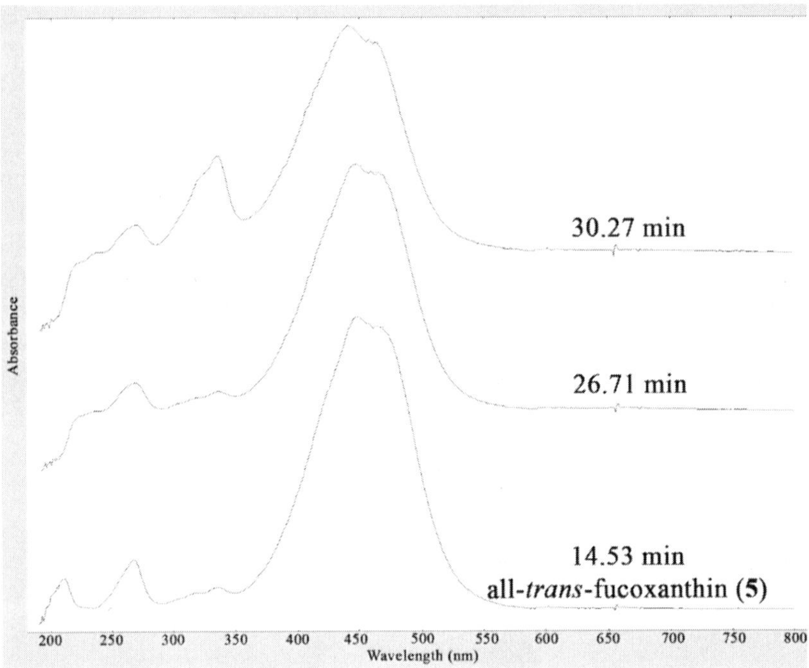

Figure 3. UV profiles (obtained from HPLC-NMR) of the three related xanthophylls present in the dichloromethane crude extracts of *H. pseudospicata and S. vestitum*showing their similarity.

2.4. Identification of Halogenated C_{15} Acetogenins

Profiling of a specimen of *Laurencia* sp. yielded three compounds (eluting at R_t = 5.00, 6.05 and 6.70 min), which displayed similar WET1D NMR spectra (Figure 4) confirming that they were structurally related. WET1D and gCOSY

NMR data were obtained for the compounds eluting at R_t = 5.00 and 6.70 min, while WET1D, gCOSY, HSQCAD and gHMBCAD NMR data was obtained for the compound eluting at R_t = 6.05 min.

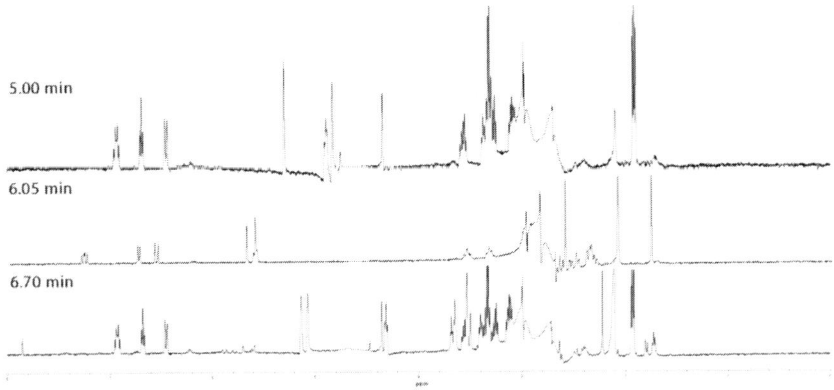

Figure 4. WET1D NMR spectra (75% CH_3CN/D_2O, 500 MHz) of compounds eluting atR_t = 5.00, 6.05 and 6.70 min from the dichloromethane crude extract of *Laurencia* sp.

Based upon the HPLC-NMR WET1D spectra (Figure 4), it was clear that the compounds eluting at R_t = 5.00 and 6.70 min were structural analogues, whereas the compound eluting at R_t = 6.05 min was a closely related structural derivative. A MarinLit search was conducted for the compound eluting at R_t = 5.00 min using the genus, UV and the presence of a single triplet methyl in the WET1D proton NMR spectrum obtained from stop-flow HPLC-NMR. This yielded nine possible structures including five polyhalogenated C_{15} acetogenins (**6–10**) (Figure 1). The WET1D NMR data for the compound eluting at R_t = 5.00 min supported the presence of olefinic protons (δ 6.93, dt, J = 7.5, 10.0 Hz; 6.69, t, J = 8.0 Hz; 6.46, d, J = 10.0 Hz), and the presence of halogens was deduced based on the presence of several deshielded methines (δ 5.30, s; 4.90, m; 4.84, s; 4.76, s; 4.35, s). Unfortunately, due to suppression of the methine signals in the D_2O suppression region, it was not possible to confirm the total number of halogens present. Furthermore, the compound eluting at R_t = 5.00 min did not ionize in either positive or negative ESI high resolution HPLC-MS, making it impossible to determine a molecular formula. It could only be proposed that the compounds eluting at R_t = 5.00 min and R_t = 6.70 min are of the polyhalogenated C_{15}acetogenin structure class, but the exact nature of the ring size could not be concluded.

The WET1D NMR spectrum for the compound eluting at R_t = 6.05 min showed slight differences suggesting it was a structural variant, further supported by the UV profile (220, 237 nm for the compounds eluting at R_t = 5.00 and 6.70 min), which also differed, and the absence of any absorbances in the UV profile suggested very little conjugation (220, 240 and 255 nm). Only partial HSQCAD and gHMBCAD NMR data could be obtained for this component and this hindered the ability to dereplicate the compound. Similar to the compounds eluting at R_t = 5.00 and 6.70 min, the compound eluting at R_t= 6.05 min did not ionize in ether positive or negative ESI high resolution HPLC-MS. Various searches conducted of the MarinLit database using different combinations of data (taxonomy, UV and NMR) did not aid in dereplicating a general structure class, and so the compound eluting at R_t = 6.05 min remains unidentified. Off-line isolation would be necessary to unequivocally deduce the structures of these three compounds.

2.5. Identification of Phloroglucinols and Tocotrienols

The dichloromethane crude extracts of *S. cf. fallax*, *C. subfarcinata* and *C. retroflexa* yielded a total of eleven phloroglucinols (**11–14**, **16–21**) and one tocotrienol (**15**). These two structure classes display similar UV absorbances, with the phloroglucinols typically displaying an absorbance at 285 nm and the tocotrienols at 300 nm, however, differences are observed in the WET1D NMR spectra. This represents the first instance of phloroglucinols and tocotrienols being reported from *C. retroflexa* and *S. cf. fallax*. The known phloroglucinols (**11–14**) and tocotrienol (**15**) were all dereplicated with use of the MarinLit database utilising the search parameters as indicated in Table 2, and by comparison of the NMR data obtained by HPLC-NMR. One of the phloroglucinols (compound eluting at R_t = 23.16 min) could not be identified due to insufficient quantities present to permit sufficient HPLC-NMR data acquisition and also due to there being no observed molecular ion in the high resolution HPLC-MS. However, based on the similarities of the UV absorbances and WET1D NMR data to **11**, it was concluded to represent a phloroglucinol containing an alcohol substituent in the terpene side chain. δ-tocotrienol (**15**) did not ionize in the high resolution HPLC-MS analysis, but a search of the MarinLit database together with consideration of the WET1D NMR data, resulted in δ-tocotrienol (**15**) being identified. The HPLC-NMR and HPLC-MS data of the known compounds was consistent with the data previously reported [26,27,28,29].

As well as compounds **11–15**, a series of new phloroglucinols were also determined. A MarinLit search conducted on these phloroglucinols using combinations of taxonomy, UV, molecular formulae and NMR data did not result in any confirmed structures, supporting the fact that these represented new phloroglucinols.

High resolution HPLC-MS yielded a molecular formula of $C_{24}H_{34}O_5$ for **16** (observed 401.2337 [M − H]$^-$, calcd. for $C_{24}H_{33}O_5$, 401.2328) and stop-flow HPLC-NMR enabled for WET1D proton, gCOSY, HSQCAD and gHMBCAD NMR data to be obtained (Table 3). Three double bonds were concluded to be present based on the degrees of unsaturation and inspection of the WET1D NMR spectrum (δ_H 7.30, 1H; 6.80, 1H; 6.48, 1H; 6.32, 1H; 6.28, 1H; 6.23, 1H). A diagnostic methine at δ_H 4.96 was observed which suggested the presence of an alcohol substituent, together with a diagnostic methylene at δ_H3.89, which is typical of the methylene group attached adjacent to the ketone functionality. The gCOSY and gHMBCAD NMR data was able to secure the spin system from this diagnostic methylene (δ_H 3.89, H-2) to the first olefinic proton (δ_H6.32, H-6). Further interpretation of the gCOSY NMR data secured the spin system from H-6 (δ_H 6.32) to H-14 (δ_H 3.00). The proton at position H-14 lies on the edge of the suppression region of the acetonitrile signal, which prevented any gCOSY NMR correlations from the proton being observed. Fortunately, in the gHMBCAD NMR spectrum, key correlations were observed from this methylene which allowed for the carbon at position C-15 to be assigned (δ_C 29.9). The terminal methyl group (δ_H 1.72, H-18) displayed a key gHMBCAD NMR correlation to the carbon at position C-16 (δ_C 32.0), confirming its assignment. The protons at positions H-5, H-15 and H-16 could not be assigned as these signals resided in the acetonitrile suppression region. The configuration of the double bonds was established by consideration of the NMR coupling constants and on biosynthetic grounds. Compound **16** represents a structure analogue of the known phloroglucinol **11**, which is known to have a 6*Z* configuration [28].The co-occurrence of **11** and **16** led to the conclusion that their double bond configuration about position 6/7 would be the same when considering their biosynthesis. As such, the structure for **16** was proposed as 9-hydroxy-1-(2,4,6-trihydroxyphenyl)octadeca-6*Z*,10*E*,12*Z*-trien-1-one, attributed the trivial name retroflexanone (**16**). The configuration of the single stereogenic center at position C-9 remains undefined.

Based upon the molecular formula of the phloroglucinols eluting at R_t = 13.65, 22.96 and 33.40 min, the number of double bonds present in each compound could be concluded. Unfortunately, NMR and MS data alone is not sufficient to determine the placement of the double bond within the structures. This meant that only *tentative* structures could be proposed, which are represented as **17–19**, respectively. To establish the position of the double bonds in the terpene side chain, off-line approaches such as chemical derivatization or degradation are required. The double bonds were assigned on the basis that olefinic protons that correspond to a *cis* geometry appear as a narrow multiplet in the proton NMR spectrum [28] which was also observed for the known compounds (**12–14**) during this study.

Table 3. NMR data (500 MHz, 75% CH_3CN/D_2O, suppression of HDO and CH_3CN at δ_H 4.64 and 2.82 ppm, respectively) for retroflexanone (**16**) obtained via stop-flow HPLC-NMR.

Retroflexanone (16)				
Position	δ_H (*J* in Hz)	δ_C [a], Type	gCOSY	gHMBCAD
1		207.2, s		
2	3.89, t (7.0)	44.2, t	3	1, 3, 4
3	2.48, p (7.0)	25.1, t	2, 4	1, 2, 4, 5
4	2.23, m	29.9, t	3	2, 3, 5, 6
5	SS	27.8, t		
6	6.32, m	132.6, d	7	
7	6.23, m	126.2, d	6, 8	
8	3.12, m	35.8, t	7 [w], 9	6, 7, 9
9	4.96, dt (6.5, 7.0)	72.6, d	8, 10	11
10	6.48, dd (7.0, 15.0)	136.6, d	9, 11	12
11	7.30, dd (15.0, 11.0)	126.4, d	10, 12	
12	6.80, t (11.0)	128.8, d	11, 13 [w]	
13	6.28, m	133.3, d	12, 14	
14	3.00, m [b]	ND		12, 13, 15
15	SS	29.9, t		
16	SS	32.0, t		
17	2.13, m	23.0, t	18	16
18	1.72, t (6.5)	14.3, q	17	16, 17
1′		105.2, s		
2′		165.0, s *		
3′	6.72, s	95.7, d		1′, 2′, 5′
4′		ND *		
5′	6.72, s	95.7, d		1′, 3′, 6′
6′		165.0, s *		
2′-OH	ND			
4′-OH	ND			
6′-OH	ND			

[a] carbon assignments based on HSQCAD and gHMBCAD NMR experiments; [b] signal assigned based on correlations in gCoSY experiment; * signals for C-2′ and C-6′are interchangeable with C4′; [w] indicates weak or long range correlation; SS Signal suppressed; ND Not Detected.

Phloroglucinols **20** and **21** (compounds eluting at R_t = 20.15 and 15.50 min) do not appear in the MarinLit database, however, a recent study conducted by the research group describes the first report of these phloroglucinols occurring in *C. monilifera* and *C. subfarcinata* [13].

2.6. Anti-Microbial Activity

The crude extracts of *S. cf. fallax*, *S. vestitum*, *C. subfarcinata*, *H. pseudospicata* and *C. retroflexa* were assessed for their anti-microbial activity against six bacteria and three fungi (Table 4). The crude extracts of the algae showed varying selectivity and activity across the micro-organisms tested, with *S. vestitum*, *C. subfarcinata* and *C. retroflexa* showing the most promising activity. The crude extracts of the two marine algae specimens containing the xanthophylls (*S. vestitum* and *H. pseudospicata*) displayed different biological activity suggesting that the active component(s) was unlikely to be the xanthophylls but other chemical component(s). However, all-*trans*-fucoxanthin (**5**) has been reported to display anti-inflammatory, anti-oxidant and anti-tumor activity [30,31,32,33]. The crude extracts of *S. cf. fallax*, *C. subfarcinata*, *C. retroflexa* all showed similar anti-microbial activities which can potentially be attributed to the presence of the phloroglucinols. Phloroglucinols have been demonstrated to possess various anti-microbial activities [34,35,36]. The crude extracts of *S. decipiens* and *Laurencia* sp. were not evaluated for their biological activity.

3. EXPERIMENTAL SECTION

3.1. Marine Alga Material

S. cf. fallax was collected at low tide on January 3, 2003 from St Paul's Beach, Sorrento, Port Phillip Bay, Victoria, Australia.*C. subfarcinata*, *S. vestitum* and *H. pseudospicata* were collected at low tide on January 22, 2006 from the Borough of Queenscliff (near Point Lonsdale), Port Phillip Bay, Victoria, Australia. *Laurencia* sp., *S. decipiens* and *C. retroflexa* were collected by SCUBA on 21 April 2010 from Governor Reef (near Indented Head), Port Phillip Bay, Victoria, Australia. The marine algae were identified by Dr. Gerald Kraft (The University of Melbourne) and voucher specimens (designated the code numbers 2003-06, 2006-11, 2006-12, 2006-13, 2010-04, 2010-08 and 2010-09, respectively) are deposited at the School of Applied Sciences (Discipline of Applied Chemistry), RMIT University, Melbourne, Australia.

3.2. Extraction

Each of the frozen marine algae were extracted with 3:1 methanol/dichloromethane (1 L). The crude extracts were then decanted and concentrated under reduced pressure and sequentially solvent partitioned (triturated) into dichloromethane and methanol soluble extracts, respectively.

Table 4. Anti-microbial activity of the crude extracts obtained from *S. cf. fallax, C. subfarcinata, C. retroflexa, S. vestitum* and *H. pseudospicata* showing zones of inhibition (mm).

Crude	Microorganism Concentration (mg/mL)	*E. coli* ATCC 25922	*S. aureus* ATCC 25923	*S. aureus* *MRSA* 344/2-32	*P. aeruginosa* ATCC 27853	*S. pyogenes* 345/1	*B. subtilis* *ATCC 19659*	*C. albicans* ATCC 10231 or 14053*	*T. mentagrophytes* *ATCC 28185*	*C. resinae*
S. vestitum (3:1 MeOH/DCM)	50	ND [a]	NT [b]	NT [b]	3	NT [b]	ND [a]	3 *	2	ND [a]
H. pseudospicata (3:1 MeOH/DCM)	50	ND [a]	NT [b]	NT [b]	ND [a]	NT [b]	ND [a]	ND [a]	ND [a]	ND [a]
S. cf. fallax (3:1 MeOH/DCM)	50	ND [a]	NT [b]	NT [b]	ND [a]	NT [b]	2	ND [a]*	ND [a]	ND [a]
C. subfarcinata (3:1 MeOH/DCM)	50	ND [a]	NT [b]	NT [b]	1	NT [b]	ND [a]	3*	ND [a]	ND [a]
C. retroflexa (DCM)	50	ND [a]	2	3	5	ND [a]	NT [b]	ND [a]	NT [b]	NT [b]
C. retroflexa (MeOH)	50	1	4	6	1	ND [a]	NT [b]	ND [a]	NT [b]	NT [b]

[a] indicates no zone of inhibition detected; [b] indicates not tested; * indicates tested against ATCC 14053. Please note: S. *deciptans* and *Laurencia* sp. were not evaluated for biological activity.

3.3. Biological Evaluation

For details on the biological evaluation of the dichloromethane and methanol crude extracts of *C. retroflexa* please refer to [37]. The 3:1 MeOH/DCM crude extracts of *S. cf. fallax, C. subfarcinata, S. vestitum* and *H. pseudospicata* were assessed for anti-microbial activity at the University of Canterbury, Christchurch, New Zealand. A standardized inoculum was prepared by transferring a loop of bacterial/fungal cells, from a freshly grown stock slant culture, into a 10 mL vial of sterile water. This was vortexed and compared to a 5% $BaCl_2$ in water standard to standardize the cell density. This gave a cell density of 108 colony-forming units per millilitre. Ten millilitres of the standardized inoculum was then added to 100 mL of Mueller Hinton or potato dextrose agar (at between 40 and 50 °C) and mixed by swirling, giving a final cell density of 107 colony forming units per millilitre. Five millilitres of this was poured into sterile 85 mm petri dishes. The suspensions were allowed to cool and solidify on a level surface to give a "lawn" of bacteria/fungi over the dish. The crude extract was pipetted onto 6 millimeter diameter filter paper disks and the solvent evaporated. These disks were then placed onto the prepared seeded agar dishes (with appropriate solvent and positive controls) and incubated. Active anti-microbial samples displayed a zone of inhibition outside the disk, which was measured in mm as the radius of inhibition for each bacteria/fungi. The six organisms were *Escherícha coli* (ATCC 25922), *Bacillus subtilis* (ATCC 19659) and *Pseudomonas aeruginosa* (ATCC27853) for the bacteria and, *Candida albicans* (ATCC 14053), *Trichophyton mentagrophytes* (ATCC 28185) and*Cladosporium resinae* for the fungi.

3.4. Chemical Profiling

Chemical profiling was carried out on the dichloromethane soluble extracts of the marine algae employing HPLC-NMR and HPLC-MS methodologies. The dichloromethane extracts were dissolved in HPLC-NMR grade CH_3CN and filtered through a 0.45 PTFE membrane filter (Grace Davison Discovery Sciences, Columbia, MD, USA). *S. decipiens*: 109.1 mg dissolved in 1090 µL (5005 µg per HPLC-NMR injection); *C. retroflexa*: 185.6 mg dissolved in 2230 µL (4161 µg per HPLC-NMR injection); *S. cf. fallax*: 166.5 mg dissolved in 1665 µL (5000 µg per HPLC-NMR injection); *S. vestitum*: 342.8 mg dissolved in 3430 µL (4997 µg per HPLC-NMR injection); *H. pseudospicata*: 61.6 mg dissolved in 615 µL (5008 µg per HPLC-NMR injection); *Laurencia* sp.: 216.2 mg dissolved in 2160 µL (5005 µg per HPLC-NMR injection); *C. subfarcinata*: 741.9 mg dissolved in 7420 µL (4999 µg per HPLC-NMR injection).

3.5. HPLC-NMR & HPLC-MS Conditions

For details of the HPLC-NMR conditions please refer to [37]. For both on-flow and stop-flow HPLC-NMR modes, 50 µL injections of the dichloromethane extracts were injected onto an Agilent Eclipse Plus C_{18} (150 × 4.6) 5 µ column using a solvent composition of 75% CH_3CN/D_2O at a flow rate of 1 mL/min. During HPLC-NMR analyses, the HDO and CH_3CN signals are suppressed at 4.64 and 2.82 ppm, respectively. In the stop-flow HPLC-NMR mode, WET1D, gCOSY, HSQCAD and gHMBCAD NMR experiments were acquired. HRESILCMS was carried out on an Agilent 6540 Series TOF system in either the positive or negative ionization mode (ESI operation conditions of 12 L/min N2, 325 °C drying gas temperature, and 3500 V capillary voltage) equipped with an Agilent 1260 Infinity Binary Pump, Agilent 1290 Infinity Autosampler and Agilent 1260 DAD detector (Agilent, Santa Clara, CA, USA). The instrument was calibrated using the "Agilent Tuning Mix" with purine as the reference compound and the Hewlett-Packard standard HP0921. The separations were carried out using an Agilent Eclipse Plus C_{18} (4.6 × 150) 5 µ column using a solvent composition of 75% CH_3CN/H_2O at a flow rate of 1 mL/min.

3.6. On-Line (HPLC-NMR & HPLC-MS) Partial Characterization of Compounds

1-(2,4,6-trihydroxyphenyl)-hexadecadien-1-one (unknown double bond positions) (**17**): HPLC-NMR WET1D NMR (500 MHz, 75% CH_3CN/D_2O, suppression of HDO and CH_3CN at t δ_H 4.64 and 2.82 ppm, respectively) obtained from stop-flow mode δ 6.71 (2H, s, H-3'/H-5'), 6.22 (4H, m, C**H**C**H**), 3.89 (2H, t, *J* = 8.0, H-2), 3.62 (2H, m, CHC**H**$_2$CH), 2.11 (m, CH_2)*, 1.77 (3H, t, *J* = 8.0; HRESILCMS; *m/z* 359.2226 (calcd for $C_{22}H_{31}O_4$, 359.2222).

1-(2,4,6-trihydroxyphenyl)-octadecadien-1-one (unknown double bond positions) (**18**): HPLC-NMR WET1D NMR (500 MHz, 75% CH_3CN/D_2O, suppression of HDO and CH_3CN at t δ_H 4.64 and 2.82 ppm, respectively) obtained from stop-flow mode δ 6.70 (2H, s, H-3'/H-5'), 6.20 (4H, m, C**H**C**H**), 3.87 (2H, t, *J* = 7.5, H-2), 3.61 (2H, dd, *J* = 6.0, 7 Hz, CHC**H**$_2$CH), 2.46 (2H, m, H-3), 2.11 (m, CH_2)*, 1.71 (3H, t, *J* = 7.0; HRESILCMS; *m/z* 387.2539 (calcd for $C_{24}H_{35}O_4$, 387.2535).

1-(2,6-dihydroxy-4-methoxyphenyl)-octadecatrien-1-one (unknown double bond positions) (**19**): HPLC-NMR WET1D NMR (500 MHz, 75% CH_3CN/D_2O, suppression of HDO and CH_3CN at t δ_H 4.64 and 2.82 ppm, respectively) obtained from stop-flow mode δ 6.82 (2H, s, H-3'/H-5'), 6.21 (6H, m, C**H**C**H**), 3.91 (2H, t, *J* = 7.0, H-2), 3.66 (4H, m, CHC**H**$_2$CH), 2.49 (2H, m, H-3), 2.25 (2H, m, H-4), 2.10, (m, CH_2)*, 1.70 (3H, t, *J* = 6.5; HRESILCMS; *m/z* 399.2539 (calcd for $C_{25}H_{35}O_4$, 399.2535).

Please refer to the supplementary information file containing UV profiles, HPLC-NMR data including tabulated NMR data and the high resolution HPLC-MS chromatograms for all remaining compounds (these are listed in order of retention time).

4. CONCLUSIONS

This study has demonstrated the importance and ability of HPLC-NMR in conjunction with high resolution HPLC-MS and databases such as MarinLit to rapidly dereplicate the identity of secondary metabolites from a range of marine algae. The chemical diversity between, and within, marine algae genera was highlighted (See Table 1 and Table 2). The phloroglucinols (**11–14, 16–21**) are an example of compounds that can be found occurring across different species of the same genus (*Cystophora*), while the xanthophylls (**15**) provide an example of compounds that can extend over different genera (*Halopteris* and *Sargassum*). The application of HPLC-NMR to investigate either genera or species of marine algae which were previously not studied (*S. decipiens, S. vestitum, S. cf. fallax*, and *H. pseudospicata*) and to rapidly identify structure classes present, without the need for traditional and lengthy isolation procedures is noteworthy. Finally, this study also highlights the advantage of using HPLC-NMR over HPLC-MS data for dereplication, especially when compounds do not easily ionize during HPLC-MS analyses. In such cases, crucial NMR data, which can be acquired via HPLC-NMR, provides important structural features and connectivity, which can enable a compound to be dereplicated. Unlike HPLC-MS, HPLC-NMR also allows for the differentiation of structural isomers.

ACKNOWLEDGMENTS

The Marine And Terrestrial Natural Product (MATNAP) research group would like to thank Roderick Watson (MAFRI), Rick Tinker, Daniel Dias and Priyanka Reddy for their assistance with the collection of the marine algae; Gerald Kraft (The University of Melbourne) for the taxonomic identification of the marine algae; Nerida Thurbon (School of Applied Sciences (Discipline of Biotechnology and Biological Sciences), Science Engineering and Health, RMIT University) for providing access to the micro-organisms to conduct the anti-microbial assays and for her invaluable technical support; Gill Ellis (University of Canterbury, Christchurch, New Zealand) for conducting some of the anti microbial biological testing; Sally Duck (School of Chemistry, Faculty of Science, Monash University) for conducting the high resolution mass spectrometric analyses (HPLC-MS). Robert Brkljača would like to acknowledge his Australian Postgraduate Award (APA) scholarship that has supported his studies. Emrehan Göker was a recipient of the School of Applied Sciences Vacation scholarship that supported his BSc (AppSc) (honours) studies on *C. retroflexa*.

AUTHOR CONTRIBUTIONS

Experimental work for *S. cf. fallax*, *C. subfarcinata*, *S. vestitum*, *H. pseudospicata*, *Laurencia* sp., and *S. decipiens* was conducted by R. Brkljača. Experimental work for *C. retroflexa* was conducted by E. S. Göker. Manuscript was prepared by R. Brkljača and S. Urban.

SUPPLEMENTARY INFORMATION

HPLC-NMR and HPLC-MS data and UV profiles for the crude extracts of the seven marine algae are included (these are listed in order of retention time). This material is available free of charge via MDPI Website.

CONFLICTS OF INTEREST

The authors declare no conflict of interest.

REFERENCES

1. Guiry, M.D.; Guiry, G.M. AlgaeBase. Available online: http://www.algaebase.org (accessed on 6 March 2015).
2. Blunt, J.W.; Copp, B.R.; Keyzers, R.A.; Munro, M.H.; Prinsep, M.R. Marine natural products. Nat. Prod. Rep. 2015, 32, 116–211.
3. Choi, H.; Pereira, A.R.; Gerwick, W.H. The Chemistry of Marine Algae and Cyanobacteria. In Handbook of Marine Natural Products; Fattorusso, E., Gerwick, W.H., Taglialatela-Scafati, O., Eds.; Springer: London, England, UK, 2012.
4. Sailler, B.; Glombitza, K.-W. Halogenated phlorethols and fucophlorethols from the brown alga Cystophora retroflexa.Nat. Toxins 1999, 7, 57–62.
5. Sailler, B.; Glombitza, K.-W. Phlorethols and fucophlorethols from the brown alga Cystohpora retroflexa. Phytochemistry1999, 50, 869–881.
6. Czeczuga, B.; Taylor, F.J. Carotenoid content in some species of the brown and red algae from the coastal area of New Zealand. Biochem. Syst. Ecol. 1986, 15, 5–8.
7. Laird, D.W.; Bennett, S.; Bian, B.; Sauer, B.; Wright, K.; Hughes, V.; van Altena, I.A. Chemical investigation of seven Australasian Cystophora species: New chemistry and taxonomic insights. Biochem. Syst. Ecol. 2010, 38, 187–194.
8. MarinLit Database. Available online: http://pubs.rsc.org/marinlit/ (accessed on 6 March 2015).
9. Kazlauskas, R.; Murphy, P.T.; Wells, R.J.; Daly, J.J.; Oberhansli, W.E. Heterocladol, a halogenated selinane sesquiterpene of biosynthetic significance from the red alga Laurencia filiformis: Its isolation, crystal structure and absolute configuration. Aust. J. Chem. 1977, 30, 2679–2687.
10. Capon, R.; Ghisalberti, E.L.; Jefferies, P.R.; Skelton, B.W.; White, A.H. Sesquiterpene metabolites from Laurencia filiformis. Tetrahedron 1981, 37, 1613–1621.

11. Capon, R.J.; Ghisalberti, E.L.; Mori, T.A.; Jefferies, P.R. Sesquiterpenes from Laurencia spp. J. Nat. Prod. 1988, 51, 1302–1304.

12. Dias, D.A.; White, J.M.; Urban, S. Laurencia filiformis: Phytochemical profiling by conventional and HPLC-NMR approaches. Nat. Prod. Commun. 2009, 4, 157–172.

13. Brkljača, R.; Urban, S. Dereplication (HPLC-NMR & HPLC-MS) and structural identification studies of marine brown algae of the genus Cystophora. Phytochemistry 2015. submitted for publication.

14. Suzuki, M.; Takahashi, Y.; Matsuo, Y.; Guiry, M.D.; Masuda, M. Scanlonenyne, a novel halogenated C15 acetogenin from the red alga Laurencia obtusa in Irish waters. Tetrahedron 1997, 53, 4271–4278.

15. San-Martin, A.; Darias, J.; Soto, H.; Contreras, C.; Herrera, J.S.; Rovirosa, J. A new C15 acetogenin from the marine alga Laurencia claviformis. Nat. Prod. Lett. 1997, 10, 303–311.

16. Suzuki, M.; Nakano, S.; Takahashi, Y.; Abe, T.; Masuda, M. Bisezakyne-A and -B, halogenated C15 acetogenins from a Japanese Laurencia species. Phytochemistry 1999, 51, 657–662.

17. Aydogmus, Z.; Imre, S.; Ersoy, L.; Wray, V. Halogenated secondary metabolites from Laurencia obtusa. Nat. Prod. Res.2004, 18, 43–49.

18. Takaichi, S. Carotenoids in Algae: Distributions, Biosyntheses and Functions. Mar. Drugs 2011, 9, 1101–1118.

19. Brkljača, R.; Urban, S. Limit of detection studies for application to natural product identification using high performance liquid chromatography coupled to nuclear magnetic resonance spectroscopy. J. Chromatogr. A 2015,1375, 69–75.

20. Kazlauskas, R.; Mulder, J.; Murphy, P.T.; Wells, R.J. New metabolites from the brown alga Caulocystis cephalornithos.Aust. J. Chem. 1980, 33, 2097–2101.

21. Narkowicz, C.K.; Blackman, A.J. Further acetogenins from Tasmanian collections of Caulocystis cephalornithosdemonstrating chemical variability. Biochem. Syst. Ecol. 2006, 34, 635–641.

22. Spencer, G.F.; Tjarks, L.W.; Kleiman, R. Alkyl and phenylalkyl anacardic acids from Knema elegans seed oil. J. Nat. Prod. 1980, 43, 724–730.

23. Asakawa, Y.; Masuya, T.; Tori, M.; Campbell, E.O. Long chain alkyl phenols from the liverwort Schistochila appendiculata. Phytochemistry 1987, 26, 735–738.

24. Englert, G.; Bjornland, T.; Liaaen-Jensen, S. 1D and 2D NMR studies of some allenic carotenoids of the fucoxanthin series. Magn. Reson. Chem. 1990, 28, 519–528.

25. Haugan, J.A.; Englert, G.; Glinz, E.; Liaaen-Jensen, S. Algal carotenoids. 48. Structural assignments of geometrical isomers of fucoxanthin. Acta Chem. Scand. 1992, 46, 389–395.

26. Ohnmacht, S.; West, R.; Simionescu, R.; Atkinson, J. Assignment of the 1H and 13C NMR of tocotrienols. Magn. Reson. Chem. 2008, 46, 287–294.

27. Gregson, R.P.; Kazlauskas, R.; Murphy, P.T.; Wells, R.J. New metabolites from the brown alga Cystophora torulosa.Aust. J. Chem. 1977, 30, 2527–2532.

28. Kazlauskas, R.; King, L.; Murphy, P.T.; Warren, R.G.; Wells, R.J. New metabolites from the Brown Algal GenusCystophora. Aust. J. Chem. 1981, 34, 439–447.

29. Amico, V.; Currenti, R.; Oriente, G.; Piatelli, M.; Tringali, C. A phloroglucinol derivative from the brown alga Zonaria tournefortii. Phytochemistry 1981, 20, 1451–1453.

30. Kim, S.-K.; Pangestuti, R. Biological activities and potential health benefits of fucoxanthin derived from marine brown algae. Adv. Food Nutr. Res. 2011, 64, 111–128.

31. Tan, C.-P.; Hou, Y.-H. First evidence for the anti-inflammatory activity of fucoxanthin in high-fat-diet-induced obesity in mice and the antioxidant functions in PC12 cells. Inflammation 2014, 37, 443–450.

32. Kim, K.-N.; Heo, S.-J.; Kang, S.-M.; Ahn, G.; Jeon, Y.-J. Fucoxanthin induces apoptosis in human leukemia HL-60 cells through a ROS-mediated Bcl-xL pathway. Toxicol. Vitro 2010, 24, 1648–1654.

33. Xia, S.; Wang, K.; Wan, L.; Li, A.; Hu, Q.; Zhang, C. Production, charaterization, and antioxidant activity of fucoxanthin from the marine diatom Odontella aurita. Mar. Drugs 2013, 11, 2667–2681.

34. Wisespongpand, P.; Kuniyoshi, M. Bioactive phloroglucinols from the brown alga Zonaria diesingiana. J. Appl. Phycol.2003, 15, 225–228.

35. Gerwick, W.; Fenical, W. Phenolic lipids from the related marine algae of the order Dictyotales. Phytochemistry 1982,21, 633–637.

36. Ravi, B.N.; Murphy, P.T.; Lidgard, R.O.; Warren, R.G.; Wells, R.J. C18 terpenoid metabolites of the brown algaCystophora moniliformis. Aust. J. Chem. 1982, 35, 171–182.

37. Brkljača, R.; Urban, S. Chemical profiling (HPLC-NMR & HPLC-MS), isolation, and identification of bioactive meroditerpenoids from the southern Australian marine brown alga Sargassum paradoxum. Mar. Drugs 2015, 13, 102–127.

Chapter 11

Chemical Profiling (HPLC-NMR & HPLC-MS), Isolation, and Identification of Bioactive Meroditerpenoids from the Southern Australian Marine Brown Alga*Sargassum paradoxum*

Robert Brkljača and Sylvia Urban *

School of Applied Sciences (Discipline of Chemistry), Health Innovations Research Institute (HIRi) RMIT University, GPO Box 2476V Melbourne, Victoria 3001, Australia

ABSTRACT

A phytochemical investigation of a southern Australian marine brown alga, *Sargassum paradoxum*, resulted in the isolation and identification of four new (**5**, **9**, **10**, and **15**) and nine previously reported (**1**, **2**, **6–8**, and **11–14**) bioactive meroditerpenoids. HPLC-NMR and HPLC-MS were central to the identification of a new unstable compound, sargahydroquinal (**9**), and pivotal in the deconvolution of eight (**1**, **2**, **5–7**, and **10–12**) other meroditerpenoids. In particular, the complete characterization and identification of the two main constituents (**1** and **2**) in the crude dichloromethane extract was achieved using stop-flow HPLC-NMR and HPLC-MS. This study resulted in the first acquisition of gHMBCAD NMR spectra in the stop-flow HPLC-NMR mode for a system solely equipped with a 60 μL HPLC-NMR flow cell without the use of a cold probe, microcoil, or any pre-concentration.

Keywords: *Sargassum*; profiling; dereplication; HPLC-NMR; HPLC-MS; bioassay-guided; biological activity; meroditerpenoid

1. INTRODUCTION

Terpenoids and phenolic compounds represent the largest group of secondary metabolites reported from marine brown algae [1]. Marine brown algae belonging to the *Sargassum* genus (Sargassaceae, Fucales) number in excess of 300 species [2] located throughout most regions of the world [3,4], and are known to produce secondary metabolites such as meroterpenoids [1,5]. Meroditerpenoids are metabolites of mixed biogenesis containing terpenoid and non-terpenoid derived fragments. Meroditerpenoids derived from algae of the genus *Sargassum* are comprised of a polyprenyl chain attached to either a *p*-benzoquinone or hydroquinone moiety [6,7,8]. Variations of the meroditerpenoid structures occur mainly in the terpene side chain and include the addition of exocyclic double bonds, carboxylic acids, alcohols, or aldehyde functional groups [1,7,9]. Meroditerpenoids have been reported to display a range of biological activities including antibacterial, antioxidant, and antitumor activities [6,7,10,11,12].

We recently examined a specimen of the marine brown alga *Sargassum paradoxum* (R. Brown ex Turner) Hooker and Harvey, collected from Port Phillip Bay, Victoria, Australia. This alga was selected for chemical investigation on the basis of the crude extract antimicrobial activity and that no previous chemistry had been reported from this particular *Sargassum*species [1,13]. Previous studies conducted by our research group on another closely related *Sargassum* species (*S. fallax*) resulted in the isolation of three new meroditerpenoids [7]. This also provided the motivation for studying this *Sargassum*species in that a comparison of the two species could potentially allow for chemotaxonomic markers to be identified. Herein we report the chemical profiling study conducted using HPLC-NMR and HPLC-MS together with the bioassay-guided isolation and structure determination of one new meroditerpenoid with a hydroquinone moiety paradoxhydroquinone (**5**) and two new meroditerpenoids possessing a *p*-benzoquinone moiety, paradoxquinol (**10**) and paradoxquinone (**15**). A new unstable meroditerpenoid, sargahydroquinal (**9**), was identified on the basis of the HPLC-NMR and HPLC-MS studies conducted. Revisions in the proton and/or carbon NMR chemical shift assignments for three of the meroditerpenoids (**1**, **2**, and **13**) have also been documented. In all, 14 meroditerpenoids (Figure 1) were detected in the crude extract of *S. paradoxum* and, of these, 13 could be identified using a combination of on-line (HPLC-NMR and HPLC-MS) and off-line (conventional isolation and structure elucidation) methodologies.

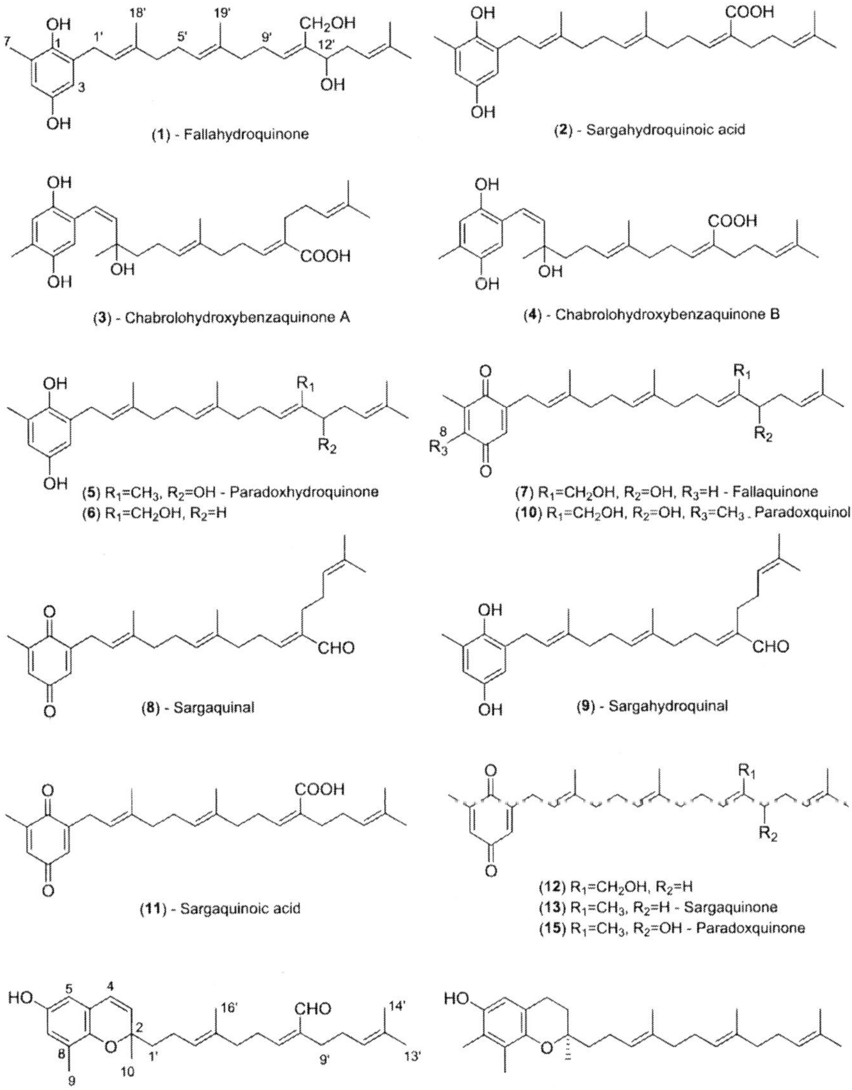

Figure 1. Structures of meroditerpenoids.

2. RESULTS AND DISCUSSION

The frozen marine alga was extracted with 3:1 methanol/dichloromethane, evaporated under reduced pressure, and sequentially solvent partitioned (triturated) into dichloromethane- and methanol-soluble fractions, respectively. While both the dichloromethane- and methanol-soluble fractions displayed some antimicrobial activity, the dichloromethane extract was slightly more selective in its activity (Section 2.3). ^{1}H NMR and analytical HPLC analyses indicated that the dichloromethane extract contained a series of structurally related compounds. On the basis of these observations, only the dichloromethane extract was further examined.

2.1. Chemical Profiling (HPLC-NMR & HPLC-MS)

The dichloromethane extract was subjected to both HPLC-NMR and HPLC-MS chemical profiling and a total of 10 peaks (A–J) were detected (Figure 2). Analysis of the stop-flow WET1D proton NMR spectra showed the presence of characteristic proton NMR signals in the aromatic and olefinic regions, together with various upfield proton NMR signals (Figure 2). Examination of the UV profile extracted for each of the peaks detected by PDA showed the presence of two distinct UV chromophores at λ_{max} 255 and 290 nm, typical of *p*-benzoquinones and hydroquinones that are known to occur in this genera of algae [1,13].

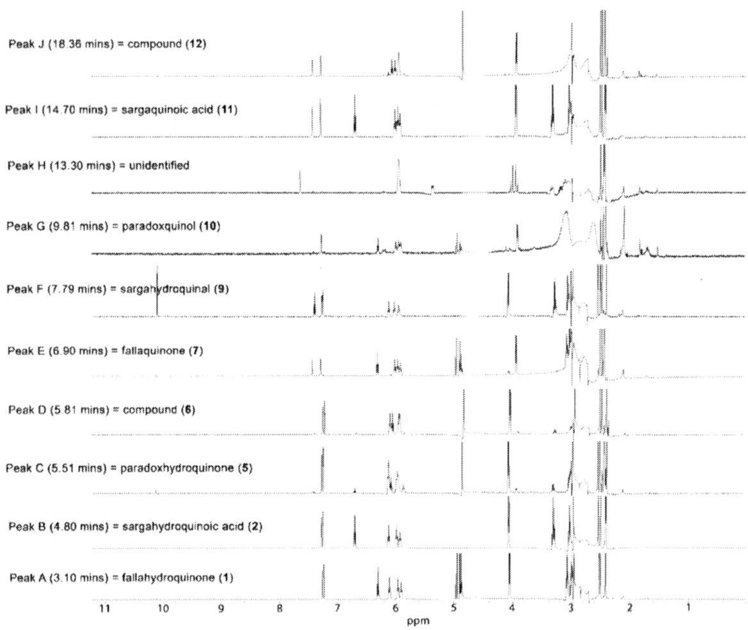

Figure 2. Stop-flow Wet1D proton NMR spectra (500 MHz, 75% CH_3CN/D_2O, suppression of HDO and CH_3CN at t δ_H 4.64 and 2.82 ppm, respectively) of peaks A–J resulting from analysis of the dichloromethane crude extract of *S. paradoxum*.

The two main peaks that were present in the dichloromethane crude extract of *S. paradoxum* (peaks A and B in Figure 2) were completely identified and characterized by HPLC-NMR and HPLC-MS. Both compounds displayed a UV maxima at 290 nm, supporting the presence of a hydroquinone moiety [14].

The HPLC-NMR stop-flow WET1D proton NMR spectrum of peak A (Figure 2) showed two *meta*-coupled protons at δ_H7.22 and 7.25, indicating the presence of an aromatic moiety displaying an AB splitting pattern as well as deshielded proton signals at δ_H 4.95, 4.88, and 4.87. Complete analysis of the 1D and 2D NMR data (Table 1) obtained via stop-flow HPLC-NMR, and the high resolution ESI MS obtained for this peak via HPLC-MS analysis (*m/z* 427.2846 $[M - H]^-$), allowed for the structure to be unequivocally elucidated as the previously described meroditerpenoid fallahydroquinone (**1**) [7].

The HPLC-NMR stop-flow WET1D proton NMR spectrum of peak B (Figure 2) supported the presence of a *meta*-coupled aromatic AB system (δ_H 7.23 and 7.26). Also present was a deshielded olefinic proton resonance (δ_H 6.69). The gHMBCAD NMR spectrum obtained in the stop-flow HPLC-NMR mode showed a signal at δ_C 170.9 ppm, confirming a carboxylic acid functional group (Table 1). Complete analysis of the 1D and 2D NMR data obtained via stop-flow HPLC-NMR and the high-resolution ESI MS obtained via HPLC-MS (*m/z* 425.2694 $[M - H]^-$) suggested the previously described meroditerpenoid sargahydroquinoic acid (**2**) [8]. While a direct comparison of the proton NMR chemical shifts obtained via stop-flow HPLC-NMR to the NMR data reported in the literature is impeded by the expected chemical shifts differences that occur for spectra acquired using off-line conventional deuterated NMR solvents compared to HPLC-NMR solvents, the majority of the proton NMR signals for this compound varied from the literature data by a consistent factor. However, the proton chemical shift for position H-10′ (δ_H 6.69) differed to that reported for sargahydroquinoic acid (**2**) (δ_H 6.02) [8]. To confirm the 10′/11′ double bond configuration, single irradiation nOe NMR experiments were carried out whilst in the stop-flow HPLC-NMR mode. The proton at δ_H 6.69 was irradiated and a key nOe enhancement observed to the methylene protons at δ_H 3.02 (H-12′). This provided confirmation that peak B (Figure 2) has a 10′*Z* double bond configuration, which corresponds to the structure assigned to sargahydroquinoic acid. Further confirmation of the 10′*Z* double bond configuration came from comparison to the meroditerpenoids chabrolohydroxybenzaquinone A (**3**) and C (**4**), which were isolated as co-occurring double bond isomers from the soft coral *Nephthea charoli* [15]. These compounds show that there is a characteristic difference in the carbon chemical shift of the C-12′ methylene (δ_C 26.7 ppm and 34.5 ppm for the 10′*E* and 10′*Z* isomers, respectively) [15]. This γ effect is particularly valuable for distinguishing *E* and *Z* isomers of trisubstitued alkenes. Since the carbon for the C-12′ methylene in (**2**) displayed a carbon chemical shift at δ_C 35.3, this provided further confirmation for the 10′*Z* configuration.

Table 1. NMR data (500 MHz, 75% CH_3CN/D_2O, suppression of HDO and CH_3CN at δ_H 4.64 and 2.82 ppm, respectively) for fallahydroquinone (**1**) and sargahydroquinoic acid (**2**) obtained via stop-flow HPLC-NMR.

	Fallahydroquinone (1)				Sargahydroquinoic Acid (2)				
Position	δ_C [a], Type	δ_H (*J* in Hz)	gCOSY	gHMBCAD	δ_C [a], Type	δ_H (*J* in Hz)	gCOSY	gHMBCAD	nOe
1	146.0, C				146.0, C				
2	ND [b]				130.4, C				
3	114.4, CH	7.22, d (3.0)			114.4, CH	7.23, d (3.0)	1′	1, 4, 5	
4	ND [b]				150.6, C				
5	115.6, CH	7.25, d (3.0)	7		115.6, CH	7.26, d (3.0)	7	1, 3	
6	126.9, C				126.9, C				
7	ND [b]	2.96, s	5	1, 5, 6	ND [b]	2.96, s		1, 5, 6	
1′	29.3, CH_2	4.05, d (7.5)	2′, 18′	1, 3, 2′, 3′	29.3, CH_2	4.06, d (7.0)	3, 2′, 18′	1, 2, 3, 2′, 3′	
2′	123.4, CH	6.10, t (7.5)	1′, 18′		123.4, CH	6.10, t (7.0)	1′, 18′	1′, 4′, 18′	
3′	137.0, C				137.1, C				
4′	40.2, CH_2	SS [c]			40.2, CH_2	2.91, m			
5′	ND [b]	2.94, m			ND [b]	2.94, m	6′, 19′	3′, 4′, 6′, 7′	
6′	125.4, CH	5.96, t (7.0)	5′, 19′		125.6, CH	5.97, t (7.0)	5′, 19′	8′, 19′	
7′	135.6, C				135.4, C				
8′	40.1, CH_2	SS [c]			39.6, CH_2	2.91, m	9′		
9′	ND [b]	3.01, m	10′	10′, 11′	28.4, CH_2	3.30, dt (7.0, 7.5)	10′	7′, 8′, 10′, 11′	
10′	130.7, CH	6.30, t (7.0)	9′		142.6, CH	6.69, t (7.5)	9′	8′, 12′, 20′	9′, 12′
11′	140.3, C				132.5, C				
12′	75.7, CH	4.87, t (7.5)	13′	10′, 11′	35.3, CH_2	3.02, m		10′, 11′, 13′, 14′, 20′	
13′	35.4, CH_2	3.06, dd (7.0, 7.5)	12′, 14′, 16′, 17′	12′, 14′, 15′	28.3, CH_2	2.91, m	17′		
14′	121.6, CH	5.90, dd (7.0)	13′		124.3, CH	5.91, t (7.0)	13′, 16′, 17′	16′	
15′	134.1, C				133.1, C				
16′	18.0, CH_3	2.41, s		14′, 15′, 17′	17.7, CH_3	2.39, s	14′	14′, 15′, 17′	
17′	25.9, CH_3	2.49, s	13′	14′, 15′, 16′	25.7, CH_3	2.49, s	14′	14′, 15′, 16′	
18′	16.2, CH_3	2.52, s	1′	2′, 3′, 4′	16.2, CH_3	2.53, s	1′, 2′	1′, 2′, 3′, 4′	
19′	16.1, CH_3	2.41, s			15.9, CH_3	2.41, s	6′	6′, 7′, 8′	
20a′	57.8, CH_2	4.95, d (12.5)		10′	170.9, C				
20b′		4.88, d (12.0)							
1-OH		ND [b]				ND [b]			
4-OH		ND [b]				ND [b]			
12′-OH		ND [b]							
20′-OH		ND [b]				ND [b]			

[a] Carbon NMR assignments made on the basis of gHSQCAD and gHMBCAD NMR experiments; [b] Signal not detected due to signal suppression; [c] Signal suppressed.

The HPLC-NMR stop-flow WET1D proton NMR spectra of peaks C and D resembled that of peak A [fallahydroquinone (**1**)] (Figure 2), both of which eluted closely. Upon closer examination, it was evident that peak D was a meroditerpenoid that contained one alcohol functional group, due to the presence of a deshielded methylene proton at δ_H 4.84. Examination of the high resolution-ESI MS obtained via HPLC-MS for peaks C and D indicated that these were isobaric and that they both possessed a UV maxima at 290 nm, supportive of a hydroquinone moiety [14]. On the basis of the mass difference and the proton NMR differences it was proposed that peak D contained a terminal alcohol moiety but, unlike fallahydroquinone (**1**), did not contain a secondary alcohol functional group; this led to peak D being identified as the previously reported compound 2-[11-(hydroxymethyl)-3,7,15-trimethyl-2,6,10,14-hexadecatetraen-1-yl]-6-methyl-1,4-benzenediol

(**6**) [16]. This represents the first report of **6** occurring as a natural product. Due to suppression of the HDO peak, no deshielded proton resonances could be observed for peak C; however, in consideration of the slight elution time difference, and the identical molecular masses, it was suspected that peak C contained an oxymethine group. While in stop-flow HPLC-NMR, the closely eluting compounds showed diffusion, and the oxymethine signal at δ_H 4.84 could clearly be distinguished via on-flow HPLC-NMR as being present in peak D and absent in peak C (see Supplementary Information file). The structure of peak C was proposed to be the new merodirerpenoid 2-[12-hydroxy-3,7,11,15-tetramethyl-2,6,10,14-hexadecatetraen-1-yl]-6-methyl-1,4-benzenediol, attributed the trivial name paradoxhydroquinone (**5**). Although subsequent off-line isolation of peaks C and D afforded an inseparable mixture, identification of these peaks was possible via the chemical profiling approach since individual WET1D proton and gCOSY NMR data could be obtained separately for each peak. This highlights an important feature of HPLC-NMR: typically co-eluting secondary metabolites that are difficult to obtain separately by conventional off-line isolation approaches can be obtained as separate entities via stop-flow HPLC-NMR.

Peak E was determined to be the previously described meroditerpenoid fallaquinone (**7**) [7], based on the observed UV maxima, together with the stop-flow WET1D proton NMR spectrum and the high-resolution ESI MS obtained via HPLC-MS, which showed the presence of an ion at *m/z* 425.2694 $[M - H]^-$.

On the basis of the HPLC-NMR stop-flow WET1D proton NMR spectrum of peak F and the UV profile (λ_{max} 290 nm), this compound also possessed a hydroquinone moiety [14]. The high-resolution ESI MS ion *m/z* of 409.2745 $[M - H]^-$obtained via HPLC-MS suggested a molecular formula of $C_{27}H_{38}O_3$. The stop-flow WET1D proton NMR spectrum showed a distinct proton signal at δ_H 10.07, s, confirming the presence of an aldehyde moiety. The MarinLit database indicated that sargaquinal (**8**), which possesses a *p*-benzoquinone moiety and an aldehyde functional group, had been previously reported from the *Sargassum* genus [17]. Peak F was proposed as being the new meroditerpenoid (possessing a hydroquinone moiety), attributed the name sargahydroquinal (**9**). During subsequent off-line bioassay-guided isolation, sargahydroquinal (**9**) oxidized into sargaquinal (**8**) before any off-line data could be obtained. Owing to the low abundance of sargahydroquinal (**9**) in the crude dichloromethane extract, only the stop-flow WET1D proton NMR and gCOSY data were obtained in the HPLC-NMR mode for sargahydroquinal (**9**) and are provided in Table 2. By comparison of the off-line data for sargaquinal (**8**) to peak F, the structure of sargahydroquinal (**9**) could be established. The configuration of the double bonds for sargaquinal (**8**) have been reported as 2′*E*, 6′*E*, and 10′*E* [17]. A bsNOESY NMR experiment carried out for sargaquinal (**8**) revealed nOe enhancements between the olefinic protons at positions H-2′ and H-6′ to the methylene protons at positions H-4′ and H-8′, along with the olefinic proton at position H-10′ showing a nOe enhancement to the aldehyde proton at position H-20′. On biosynthetic grounds, the same configuration was attributed to the double bonds in sargahydroquinal (**9**).

Table 2. NMR data (500 MHz, 75% CH_3CN/D_2O, suppression of HDO and CH_3CN at t δ_H 4.64 and 2.82 ppm, respectively) for sargahydroquinal (**9**) obtained via stop-flow HPLC-NMR.

	Sargahydroquinal (9)	
Position	δ_H (*J* in Hz)	gCOSY
1		
2		
3	7.23, d (2.5)	
4		
5	7.25, d (2.5)	
6		
7	2.94, s	
1′	4.05, d (7.5)	2′, 18′
2′	6.10, t (7.5)	1′
3′		
4′	2.70-3.00, m	
5′	2.96, m	6′
6′	6.00, t (7.0)	5′
7′		
8′	2.98, m	9′
9′	3.26, dt (7.0, 8.0)	8′, 10′
10′	7.37, t (7.0)	9′
11′		
12′	2.70-3.00, m	
13′	2.70-3.00, m	
14′	5.92, t (7.0)	16′
15′		
16′	2.37, s	14′
17′	2.48, s	
18′	2.52, s	1′, 2′
19′	2.35, s	
20′	10.07, s	
1-OH	ND [a]	
4-OH	ND [a]	

[a] Signal not detected.

The UV profile (λ_{max} 255 nm) observed for peak G in the HPLC-NMR and HPLC-MS analyses confirmed a *p*-benzoquinone moiety [14]. The HPLC-NMR stop-flow WET1D proton NMR spectrum of peak G showed close resemblance to fallaquinone (**7**), except that an aromatic proton NMR resonance was absent. Comparison of the mass of peak G to fallaquinone (**7**), observed from ESI MS obtained via HPLC-MS analysis, showed a difference of 14 mass units, indicating that one of the aromatic proton signals had been replaced by a methyl substituent. The structure of peak G was therefore proposed to be the new meroditerpenoid 5-[12*R*-hydroxy-11-(hydroxymethyl)-3,7,15-trimethyl-2,6,10,14-hexadecatetraen-1-yl]-2,3-dimethyl-1,4-benzoquinone, attributed the trivial name paradoxquinol (**10**).

Peak I showed close similarities to sargahydroquinoic acid (**2**) and was identified as the previously reported sargahydroquinoic acid (**11**) [7,17], the benzoquinone counter part of **2**.

Peak J possessed a *p*-benzoquinone moiety from the UV chromophore at 263 nm [14]. Analysis of the HPLC-NMR stop-flow WET1D NMR data showed close resemblance to **6**. On the basis of the molecular ion deduced from the high-resolution ESI MS (409.2742 $[M - H]^-$) obtained via HPLC-MS, in consultation with a SciFinder search, peak J was identified as previously described meroditerpenoid 2-[11-(hydroxymethyl)-3,7,15-trimethyl-2,6,10,14-hexadecatetraen-1-yl]-6-methyl-1,4-benzoquinone (**12**) [16,17]. Although subsequent off-line isolation afforded **12** and **15** as an inseparable mixture, identification of these compounds was possible via the chemical profiling approach since individual WET1D and gCOSY NMR data could be obtained separately for **12**, which could then be related back to the mixture.

2.2. Off-Line Bioassay-Guided Isolation

Following the chemical profiling (HPLC-NMR and HPLC-MS) conducted on the dichloromethane crude extract, a bioassay-guided isolation approach was undertaken to deduce the nature of the bioactive constituent(s) responsible for the crude extract bioactivity. The off-line isolation also allowed for any further identification and characterization of the meroditerpenoids concluded on the basis of the chemical profiling analysis as well as identifying any additional minor constituents not detected by HPLC-NMR.

A portion of the dichloromethane extract was fractionated by silica gel flash chromatography and selected fractions were evaluated for antimicrobial activity. Fractions for further purification were selected based on the observed antimicrobial activity, analysis of the ^1H NMR spectra, and the analytical HPLC chromatograms. Purification was conducted using reversed phase HPLC resulting in the isolation of 12 meroditerpenoids, eight (**1**, **2**, **5**–**7**, and **10**–**12**) of which were previously detected by HPLC-NMR and HPLC-MS analyses, and four of which were additional meroditerpenoids (**8** and**13**–**15**) that were not observed in the chemical profiling. Nine known meroditerpenoids (**1**, **2**, **6**–**8**, and **11**–**14**) were isolated and identified by direct comparison of their NMR spectroscopic and mass spectrometry data with that reported in the literature [7,8,16,17,18,19]. The off-line study also confirmed the structures of **1**, **2**, **5**–**7**, and **9**–**12** as deduced by HPLC-NMR and HPLC-MS.

Fallahydroquinone (**1**) was isolated as an unstable yellow oil. Analysis of the 2D NMR data showed that the carbon NMR chemical shifts for positions C-2 and C-6, reported as occurring at δ_C 125.4 and 127.8, respectively, should be reassigned to δ_C 127.8 (C-2) and δ_C 125.4 (C-6), respectively. In addition, the proton NMR signals for the position H-4′ and H-8′ protons reported at δ_H 2.01 and 2.08, respectively, should also be reversed. The specific rotations of the previously reported meroditerpenoids fallahydroquinone (**1**) and fallaquinone (**7**) were compared to literature values [7]. While the specific rotation for fallahydroquinone (**1**) was comparable in sign and magnitude, the specific rotation of fallaquinone (**7**) differed to that reported. The purity of fallaquinone (**7**) in this study was higher than that obtained in the original isolation. It was concluded that the impurities present were sufficient to cause the specific rotation to vary in sign and magnitude. The accuracy of the specific rotations was considered given the low quantities isolated. The relevant compounds isolated in this study were of high purity, and did not display small specific rotations. That both the specific rotation of both fallahydroquinone (**1**) and fallaquinone (**7**) are of the same sign and magnitude is consistent with the fact that the former oxidizes to the latter with retention of configuration.

Sargahydroquinoic acid (**2**) was isolated as an unstable oil. Analysis of the 2D NMR data showed that the carbon NMR chemical shifts for positions C-9′ and C-13′, reported as occurring at δ_C 27.8 and 28.3, respectively, should be reassigned to δ_C 28.3 (C-9′) and δ_C 27.8 (C-13′), respectively.

Comparison of the 2D NMR data of sargaquinone (**13**) with the literature data indicated discrepancies with some of the carbon NMR chemical shift assignments. The carbon NMR chemical shifts for positions C-3, C-5, C-3′, and C-15′ were either incorrectly assigned or not assigned. These carbon NMR chemical shifts have been unequivocally established as occurring at δ_C 132.3, 133.2, 140.0 and 131.3, respectively.

Sargahydroquinal (**9**) and one other unidentified peak (peak H) (Figure 2) degraded during the off-line isolation, which meant that it was not possible to conduct a complete 2D NMR or antimicrobial activity evaluation on these constituents.

Paradoxhydroquinone (**5**) was isolated off-line as an inseparable mixture with 2-[11-(hydroxymethyl)-3,7,15-trimethyl-2,6,10,14-hexadecatetraen-1-yl]-6-methyl-1,4-benzenediol (**6**) in a ratio of approximately 3:5. While complete 2D NMR characterization was conducted on the mixture, these components were obtained as separate entities via stop-flow HPLC-NMR. By analysis of the data obtained from both chemical profiling and off-line isolation, the compounds could be identified. In the first instance, the previously reported compound 2-[11-(hydroxymethyl)-3,7,15-trimethyl-2,6,10,14-hexadecatetraen-1-yl]-6-methyl-1,4-benzenediol (**6**) could be confirmed [16]. The comparison of the aromatic proton signals of **5** with those of the known meroditerpenoids isolated supported the presence of a hydroquinone moiety. The structure of**5** as proposed by chemical profiling was confirmed by analysis of the gHMBCAD NMR spectrum, which indicated that the proton signal at δ_H 3.97 (H-12′) showed correlations with the carbons at δ_C 126.2 (C-10′), 120.2 (C-14′), and 11.7 (C-20′) (Table 3). The oxymethine group was concluded to be located at position 12′ on the basis of the HMBC NMR correlation observed from the singlet methyl group at position H-20′ (δ_H 1.61, s) to the carbon at δ_C 77.3 (C-12′), which is directly coupled to the signal at δ_H 3.97. The compound was identified as the new meroditerpenoid 2-[12-hydroxy-3,7,11,15-tetramethyl-2,6,10,14-hexadecatetraen-1-yl]-6-methyl-1,4-benzenediol, and attributed the trivial name paradoxhydroquinone (**5**). Unfortunately, **5** and **6** oxidized to **15** and **12** before any NOESY NMR experiments could be carried out. Therefore a bsNOESY NMR experiment was carried out on **15** and **12**, respectively, and the results related back to **5** and **6**. On biosynthetic grounds, the configuration of the double bonds was therefore confirmed as 2′*E*, 6′*E*, and 10′*E* for**5**, and 2′*E*, 6′*E*, and 10′*Z* for **6**.

Paradoxquinol (**10**), unlike many of the previously isolated meroditerpenoids, which show the presence of an AB aromatic system, only displayed a single aromatic proton NMR signal at δ 6.46, s (H-3), suggesting further substitution of the *p*-benzoquinone ring. The gHMBCAD NMR spectrum confirmed the structure of **10** as proposed by chemical profiling. The two deshielded methyl groups [δ_H 2.03 (s, H-7) and 2.00 (s, H-8)] showed correlations to carbons at δ_C 140.6 (C-5), 141.5 (C-6), and 187.7 (C-1), and δ 140.6 (C-5), 141.5 (C-6), and 187.9 (C-4), respectively (Table 4). Further analysis of the HMBC NMR data confirmed the position of attachment for the terminal and the secondary alcohol moieties as positions 20′ and 12′, respectively, and confirmed **10** as the new meroditerpenoid 5-[12*R*-hydroxy-11-(hydroxymethyl)-3,7,15-trimethyl-2,6,10,14-hexadecatetraen-1-yl]-2,3-dimethyl-1,4-benzoquinone, attributed the trivial name paradoxquinol (**10**). A single irradiation nOe NMR experiment confirmed the configuration of the double bond at position C-10′ as 10′*E* (irradiation of H-10′ showed a key enhancement to H-12′). Although this represents the first occurrence in a marine alga of a meroditerpenoid containing the position 8 methyl, this biosynthetic feature has been reported in terrestrial natural products [20,21]. It is suggested that the biosynthetic pathway of **10** is reminiscent to that of γ-tocotrienol (**16**).

Table 3. ^{1}H and ^{13}C NMR data (500 MHz, $CDCl_3$) data for paradoxhydroquinone (**5**).

		Paradoxhydroquinone (5)		
Position	δC [a], Type	δH (*J* in Hz)	gCOSY	gHMBCAD
1	146.4, C			
2	127.6, C			
3	114.0, CH	6.46, d (2.5)	5, 1′	1, 4, 5, 1′
4	149.0, C			
5	115.5, CH	6.50, d (2.5)	3, 7	1, 3, 4, 7
6	125.5, C			
7	16.0, CH_3	2.18, s	5	1, 5, 6
8				
1′	30.0, CH_2	3.28, d (7.0)	3, 2′, 4′$_w$, 18′$_w$	1, 2, 3, 2′, 3′
2′	122.0, CH	5.26, t (7.0)	1′, 4′, 18′	1′, 4′, 18′
3′	138.1, C			
4′	39.5, CH_2	2.08, m	1′$_w$	5′, 18′
5′	26.1, CH_2	2.13, m		4′, 7′
6′	124.4, CH	5.09, m		4′, 5′, 19′
7′	135.1, C			
8′	39.2, CH_2	2.01, m		6′, 7′, 9′, 19′
9′	26.1, CH_2	2.10, m	8′	7′, 10′, 11′
10′	126.2, CH	5.37, t (6.5)	9′, 20′	12′, 20′
11′	136.6, C			
12′	77.3, CH	3.97, dd (6.0, 7.0)	13a′, 13b′	10′, 14′, 20′
13a′	34.2, CH_2	2.20, m	12′, 16′, 17′	
13b′		2.28, ddd (7.0, 8.0, 14.0)	12′, 16′, 17′	12′, 14′, 15′
14′	120.2, CH	5.09, m	16′, 17′	
15′	134.7, C			
16′	18.0, CH_3	1.63, s	14′	14′, 15′, 17′
17′	25.9, CH_3	1.72, s	13b′, 14′	14′, 15′, 16′
18′	16.2, CH_3	1.75, s	1′, 2′	2′, 3′, 4′
19′	16.1, CH_3	1.59, s	5′, 6′	7′, 8′
20′	11.7, CH_3	1.61, s	10′	10′, 11′, 12′
1-OH		ND [b]		
4-OH		ND [b]		
12′-OH		ND [b]		

[a] Carbon NMR assignments made on the basis of gHSQCAD and gHMBCAD NMR experiments. [b] Signal not detected.

Paradoxquinone (**15**) was isolated off-line as an inseparable mixture with 2-[11-(hydroxymethyl)-3,7,15-trimethyl-2,6,10,14-hexadecatetraen-1-yl]-6-methyl-1,4-benzoquinone (**12**) in a ratio of approximately 3:5. While complete NMR characterization was conducted on the mixture, the latter of these was identified as a separate entity via stop-flow HPLC-NMR. By analysis of the data obtained from both chemical profiling and off-line isolation, the latter of these compounds could be identified as the known meroditerpenoid 2-[11-(hydroxymethyl)-3,7,15-trimethyl-2,6,10,14-hexadecatetraen-1-yl]-6-methyl-1,4-benzoquinone (**12**). This compound had previously been reported as a derivative of a natural product; however, this represents the first report of its natural occurrence [17]. The ^{1}H NMR spectrum of paradoxquinone (**15**) was similar to that of paradoxhydroquinone (**5**). Minor differences were observed for the aromatic protons (6.46, bs and 6.54, bs) and the terminal methyl group at position H-7 (δ_H 2.05, s) (Table 4). Complete analysis of the 2D NMR spectra resulted in the compound being identified as the new meroditerpenoid 2-[12-hydroxy-3,7,11,15-tetramethyl-2,6,10,14-hexadecatetraen-1-yl]-6-methyl-1,4-benzoquinone, attributed the trivial name paradoxquinone (**15**). For compound **12**, nOe enhancements were observed from each of the olefinic protons at positions H-2′, H-6′, and H-10′ to the methylene protons at H-4′, H-8′, and H-12′. For compound **15**, nOe enhancements were observed from the olefinic protons at positions H-2′ and H-6′ to the methylene protons at H-4′ and H-8′, together with an enhancement from the olefinic proton at H-10′ to the oxymethine proton at H-12′. The configuration of the double bonds was therefore confirmed as 2′*E*, 6′*E*, and 10′*E* for **15**, and 2′*E*, 6′*E*, and 10′*Z* for **12**.

The chirality of secondary allylic alcohols can be elucidated via the exciton chirality method (usually by preparation of a benzoate derivative) or by NMR spectroscopy of the diastereoisomeric Mosher or modified Mosher esters [22,23,24,25]. In the former methodology, the absolute configuration of acyclic secondary alcohols have been assigned by interpretation of the Cotton effects observed at two wavelength regions (~220 and ~240–260 nm, respectively) [22,24].

The CD spectra of fallahydroquinone (**1**), fallaquinone (**7**), and paradoxquinol (**10**) were recorded and Cotton effects observed in the circular dichroism spectra noted. The CD spectra of fallahydroquinone (**1**), fallaquinone (**7**), and paradoxquinol (**10**) all showed the presence of positive Cotton effects at 260, 247, and 245 nm, respectively, of Δε +2.0, +2.3, and +2.4 as well as at 224, 220, and 220 nm of Δε +1.8, +1.0, and +6.4, respectively. On the basis of the similarities in the CD spectra, these compounds were concluded to have the same (undefined) absolute configuration. Subsequent to these analyses, fallahydroquinone (**1**), fallaquinone (**7**), and paradoxquinol (**10**) completely degraded, which precluded any further attempts to address the absolute configuration by conversion to the corresponding Mosher esters.

Table 4. ^{1}H and ^{13}C NMR data (500 MHz, $CDCl_3$) data for paradoxquinol (**10**) and paradoxquinone (**15**).

Position	δC [a], Type	δH (J in Hz)	gCOSY	gHMBCAD	δC [a], type	δH (J in Hz)	gCOSY	gHMBCAD
1	187.7, C				188.0, C			
2	148.1, C				148.5, C			
3	132.1, CH	6.46, s	1′		132.3, CH	6.46, bs	5, 1′	1, 4, 5
4	187.9, C				188.0, C			
5	140.6, C *				133.2, CH	6.54, bs	3, 7	1, 3, 4
6	141.5, C *				145.9, C			
7	12.4, CH_3	2.03, s		1, 5, 6	16.0, CH_3	2.05, s	5	1, 5, 6
8	12.1, CH_3	2.00, s		4, 5, 6			3, 2′, 18′	1, 2, 3, 2′, 3′
1′	27.4, CH_2	3.12, d (7.0)	3, 2′, 18′	1, 2, 3, 2′, 3′	27.5, CH_2	3.13, d (7.5)	1′, 18	1′, 4′, 18′
2′	118.2, CH	5.15, t (7.0)	1′, 18′	4′	118.1, CH	5.15, t (7.5)		
3′	139.5, C				139.8, C			2′, 3′, 5′, 18′
4′	39.5, CH_2	2.06, m		2′, 5′, 6′, 18′	39.6, CH_2	2.07, m	6′, 18′$_w$, 19′$_w$	3′, 4′, 6′, 7′
5′	26.3, CH_2	2.12, m	6′	4′, 6′	26.2, CH_2	2.11, m	5′	4′, 5′, 19′
6′	124.4, CH	5.11, m	5′, 19′	4′, 8′	124.2, CH	5.10, m		
7′	134.7, C				135.1, C			6′, 7′, 10′
8′	39.5, CH_2	2.06, m		19′	39.3, CH_2	2.02, m	10′, 20′$_w$	7′, 10′, 11′
9′	26.0, CH_2	2.21, m	10′		26.2, CH_2	2.11, m	9′, 20′	9′, 12′, 20′
10′	130.5, CH	5.53, t (7.0)	9′	12′, 20′	126.1, CH	5.38, t (7.0)		
11′	138.9, C				136.7, C		13a′	10′, 11′, 13′, 14′, 20′
12′	76.9, CH	4.16, dd (5.5, 7.5)	13a′, 13b′	10′	77.2, CH	3.97, dd (5.5, 7.5)	12′, 17′	
13a′	35.1, CH_2	2.26, m	12′, 14′		34.2, CH_2	2.20, m	12′, 17′	11′, 12′, 14′, 15′
13b′		2.43, ddd (7.5, 8.5, 14.5)	12′, 13a′, 14′	12′, 14′		2.27, m	17′	
14′	119.9, CH	5.11, m	16′, 17′		120.3, CH	5.09, m		
15′	135.4, C				134.6, C			14′, 15′
16′	18.1, CH_3	1.65, s	13a′, 13b′	14′, 15′, 17′	18.0, CH_3	1.63, s		14′, 15′, 16′
17′	25.9, CH_3	1.73, s	13a′, 13b′, 14′	14′, 15′, 16′	25.9, CH_3	1.72, s		2′, 3′
18′	16.1, CH_3	1.62, s	1′, 2′	2′, 3′, 4′	16.1, CH_3	1.61, s		7′
19′	16.1, CH_3	1.60, s	5′, 6′	6′, 7′, 8′	16.1, CH_3	1.61, s		10′, 11′
20′	58.5, CH_2	4.26, d (3.5)		10′, 11′, 12′	11.7, CH_3	1.61, s		
12′-OH		ND [b]				ND [b]		
20′-OH		ND [b]						

[a] Carbon NMR assignments made on the basis of gHSQCAD and gHMBCAD NMR experiments. [b] Signal not detected. * Indicates signals interchangeable

The compounds isolated from *S. paradoxum* in this study also occur in many other *Sargassum* species. However, two of the compounds—fallahydroquinone (**1**) and fallaquinone (**7**)—have only been reported from one other *Sargassum* species (*S. fallax*) [7]. On this basis, it is proposed that the presence of these two compounds could potentially be used as chemotaxonomic biomarkers for *S. paradoxum* and *S. fallax*.

2.3. Antimicrobial Studies

Fallahydroquinone (**1**) and fallaquinone (**7**) have been previously reported to display slight antitumor activity [7]. Sargahydroquinoic acid (**2**) and sargaquinoic acid (**11**) display similar antitumor [7,26] and peroxynitrite-scavenging activity [27], as well as antiplasmodial activity against malaria parasites [28]. Sargahydroquinoic acid (**2**) also shows insecticidal activity [29], selective vasodilatation effects [30], the ability to stimulate adipocyte differentiation [31], and radical scavenging activity [6]. Sargaquinoic acid (**11**) shows weak antimicrobial activity [7], the ability to promote neurite outgrowth [32], the ability to induce cell apoptosis [33], antioxidant activity

[34], and cholinesterase inhibition activity [35]. Sargaquinal (**8**) displays antiplasmodial activity against malaria parasites [28]. A range of activities have been reported for sargaquinone (**13**) including radical scavenging [36], anti-inflammatory activity [37], activity against P-388 cells [7,38], and ichthyotoxicity to certain species of fish [39]. Antileishmanial activity has been reported for 9-(6-hydroxy-2,8-dimethyl-2*H*-1-benzopyran-2-yl)-6-methyl-2-(4-methyl-3-penten-1-yl)-2,6-nonadienal (**14**) [19].

Antimicrobial evaluation of the crude extracts, selected silica column fractions, and the isolated merodîterpenoids was carried out against five bacteria and one fungus. Eleven of the isolated meroditerpenoids (**1–2**, **5–7**, **9–13**, and **15**), together with a commercially available antibiotic and antifungal agent, were tested at 1 mg/mL, with all displaying varying degrees of zones of inhibition in the antimicrobial assays (Table 5). Compared to the antibiotic ampicillin, the isolated compounds were far less potent against *S. aureus* and *S. pyogenes*. However, compounds **2**, **7**, **8**, and **13** were more potent against *P. aeruginosa* than ampicillin. In recent years, concern has grown around *P. aeruginosa* with regards to its prevalence and multidrug resistance [40]; therefore, the importance of identifying possible drug leads against these bacteria remains highly relevant. There was no difference in activity between compounds with the hydroquinone or the *p*-benzoquinone moieties. The activity observed for sargaquinone (**13**), the simplest of the meroditerpenoids isolated, suggests that the unsubstituted meroditerpenoid skeleton is responsible for the activity against *P. aeruginosa*. The addition of an alcohol group at position 12′ or 20′ (**1**, **5**, **6**, **12**, and **15**) appears to reduce the activity against *P. aeruginosa*, but increases the activity against *S. pyogenes*. Finally, incorporation of a carboxylic acid at position C-20′ (**2** and **11**) gives rise to activity against *S. aureus* and *S. aureus* MRSA.

3. EXPERIMENTAL SECTION

3.1. General Experimental Procedures

All organic solvents used were analytical reagent (AR or GR), UV spectroscopic, or HPLC grades with milli-Q water also being used. Optical rotations were carried out using a 1.5-mL cell on a Rudolph Research Analytical Autopol IV automatic polarimeter, set to the Na 589 nm wavelength. UV/VIS spectra were recorded on an Agilent CARY 60 spectrophotometer, using ethanol. CD spectra were obtained on a Jasco 815 Circular Dichroism spectrometer in ethanol. FTIR spectra were recorded as a film using a NaCl disk on a Perkin-Elmer Spectrum One FTIR spectrometer. ^{1}H (500 MHz), ^{13}C (125 MHz), and 1D nOe spectra were acquired in $CDCl_3$ on a 500 MHz Agilent DD2 NMR spectrometer with referencing to solvent signals (δ 7.26 and 77.0 ppm). Two-dimensional NMR experiments recorded included gradient correlation spectroscopy (gCOSY), heteronuclear single-quantum correlation spectroscopy with adiabatic pulses (HSQCAD), gradient heteronuclear multiple-bond spectroscopy with adiabatic pulses (gHMBCAD), and band selective 2D nuclear overhauser enhancement spectroscopy (bsNOESY) experiments. ESI mass spectra were obtained on a Micromass Platform II mass spectrometer equipped with a LC-10AD Shimadzu solvent delivery module (50% CH_3CN/H_2O at a flow rate of 0.2 mL/min) in both the positive and negative ionization modes using cone voltages between 20 and 30 V. Silica gel flash chromatography was carried out using Davisil LC35Å silica gel (40–60 mesh) with a 20% stepwise solvent elution from 100% petroleum spirits (60–80 °C) to 100% dichloromethane to 100% ethyl acetate and finally to 100% methanol. HPLC-NMR was carried out on a 500 MHz Agilent DD2 NMR spectrometer equipped with a Varian $^1H[^{13}C]$ pulsed field gradient flow probe with a 60-μL active volume flow cell coupled to a Varian Prostar 210 solvent delivery system, a Prostar 430 Autosampler, and a Prostar 335 PDA detector. The HPLC-NMR analyses were carried out using CORBA communication and operated with VnmrJ software. The 2H resonance observed from the D_2O was used to obtain a field-frequency lock. The resonances from the HOD and the methyl of the acetonitrile were suppressed using the water enhanced through transverse gradients (WET) solvent suppression experiment [41]. The residual HOD resonance of D_2O was referenced to 4.64 ppm. For both on-flow and stop-flow HPLC-NMR modes, 50-μL injections (4995 μg) of the dichloromethane extract were injected onto an Agilent Eclipse Plus C_{18} (150 × 4.6) 5-μ column using a solvent composition of 75% CH_3CN/D_2O at a flow rate of 1 mL/min. In the stop-flow HPLC-NMR mode WET1D, gCOSY, HSQCAD, gHMBCAD, and 1D nOe NMR experiments were acquired. HRESIMS was carried out on an Agilent 6200 Series TOF system (ESI operation conditions of 8 L/min N2, 325 °C drying gas temperature, and 3500 V capillary voltage) equipped with an Agilent 1200 Series LC solvent delivery module (100% CH_3OH at a flow rate of 0.3 mL/min) in either the positive or negative ionization modes. The instrument was calibrated using the "Agilent Tuning Mix" with purine as the reference compound and the Hewlett–Packard standard HP0921. HRESILCMS was carried out on the same system and conditions using an Agilent Eclipse Plus C_{18} (4.6 × 150) 5-μ column using a solvent composition of 75% CH_3CN/H_2O at a flow rate of 1 mL/min. All analytical HPLC analyses and method development were performed on a Dionex P680 solvent delivery system equipped with a PDA100 UV detector (operated using "Chromeleon" software). Analytical HPLC analyses were carried out using either a gradient method 0–2 min 10% CH_3CN/H_2O; 14–24 min 75% CH_3CN/H_2O; 26–30 min 100% CH_3CN; and 32–40 min 10% CH_3CN/H_2O or an isocratic method (either 100%, 95%, 90%, or 85% CH_3CN/H_2O) on an Alltech Alltima HP C_{18} (250 × 4.6) 5-μ column at a flow rate of 1.0 mL/min. Semi-preparative HPLC was carried out on a Varian Prostar 210 solvent delivery system equipped with a Prostar 335 PDA detector (operated using "Star Workstation" software) using an isocratic method (either 100%, 95%, 90%, or 85% CH_3CN/H_2O) and an Alltech Alltima C_{18} (250 × 10) 5-μ column at a flow rate of 3.5 mL/min.

3.2. Biological Evaluation

Crude extracts, enriched fractions, and compounds isolated from the marine alga, together with the standard antibiotic (ampicillin, Sigma-Aldrich, Castle Hill, Australia) and antifungal (carbendazim, Sigma-Aldrich, Castle Hill, Australia) compounds, were evaluated against six microorganisms (five bacteria and one fungus) at concentrations of 50, 25, or 1 mg/mL (see Table 5). Each microorganism was prepared by creating a 0.5 McFarlane solution suspension. Lawn cultures were prepared on either Mueller–Hinton or Brain Heart Infusion Agar (BHIA) (used for *S. pyogenes*). Then 20 μL of the crude extracts, enriched fractions, pure compounds or the standard compounds (ampicillin and carbendazim) were pipetted onto 6 mm diameter filter paper disks and their solvents evaporated. These disks were then placed onto the prepared lawn cultures and incubated at 37 °C overnight. Active antimicrobial samples displayed a zone of inhibition outside the disk, which was measured in mm as the radius of inhibition for each bacteria/fungi. The five test bacteria were*Eschericha coli* (ATCC 25922), *Staphylococcus aureus* (ATCC 25923), *Staphylococcus aureus* MRSA (344/2-32), *Pseudomonas aeruginosa* (ATCC 27853), and *Streptococcus pyogenes* (345/1). The test fungus was *Candida albicans* (ATCC 10231).

3.3. Marine Alga Material

The marine brown alga was collected by SCUBA at a depth of 3 m on 21 April 2010 from Governor Reef near Indented Head, Port Phillip Bay, Victoria, Australia and then stored at −80 °C. The alga was identified as *Sargassum paradoxum* (R. Brown ex Turner) Hooker and Harvey by Dr. Gerald Kraft (Honorary Principal Fellow), Faculty of Science, School of Botany, The University of Melbourne, Australia. A voucher specimen (designated the code number 2010–12) is deposited at the School of Applied Sciences (Discipline of Applied Chemistry), RMIT University.

3.4. Chemical Profiling

Chemical profiling was carried out on the dichloromethane soluble extract of the alga employing HPLC-NMR and HPLC-MS methodologies. Details of these analyses are provided in Section 3.1. The dichloromethane extract (77 mg) was dissolved in HPLC-NMR grade CH_3CN (771 μL) and filtered through a 0.45 PTFE membrane filter (Grace Davison Discovery Sciences).

Table 5. Antimicrobial activity of the crude extract, selected silica column fractions, and pure compounds obtained from *S. paradoxum*, together with commercial standard antibiotic and antifungal compounds, showing zones of inhibition (mm).

	Microorganism	*E. coli*	*S. aureus*	*S. aureus MRSA*	*P. aeruginosa*	*S. pyogenes*	*C. albicans*
	Concentration (mg/mL)	ATCC 25922	ATCC 25923	344/2-32	ATCC 27853	345/1	ATCC 10231
Dichloromethane extract	50	ND [g]	2	1	ND [g]	5	ND [g]
Methanol extract	50	ND [g]	1	1	10	3	4
Silica fraction **1** [a]	25	ND [g]	ND [g]	ND [g]	ND [g]	ND [g]	ND [g]
Silica fraction **4** [b]	25	ND [g]	ND [g]	ND [g]	ND [g]	1	ND [g]
Silica fraction **6** [c]	50	ND [g]	ND [g]	1	ND [g]	1	ND [g]
Silica fraction **10** [d]	25	ND [g]	ND [g]	1	4	3	ND [g]
Silica fraction **13** [e]	50	ND [g]	ND [g]	1	ND [g]	3	ND [g]
Silica fraction **17** [f]	50	ND [g]	ND [g]	ND [g]	ND [g]	ND [g]	ND [g]
Fallahydroquinone (**1**)	1	ND [g]	ND [g]	ND [g]	ND [g]	1	ND [g]
Sargahydroquinoic acid (**2**)	1	ND [g]	1	1	2	3	ND [g]
Paradoxhydroquinone (**5**) & compound (**6**)	1	ND [g]	ND [g]	ND [g]	ND [g]	3	ND [g]
Fallaquinone (**7**)	1	ND [g]	ND [g]	ND [g]	4	ND [g]	ND [g]
Sargaquinal (**8**)	1	ND [g]	ND [g]	ND [g]	3	1	ND [g]
Paradoxquinol (**10**)	1	ND [g]	ND [g]	ND [g]	ND [g]	1	ND [g]
Sargaquinoic acid (**11**)	1	ND [g]	1	1	1	3	ND [g]
Paradoxquinone (**15**) & compound (**12**)	1	ND [g]	ND [g]	ND [g]	ND [g]	2	ND [g]
Sargaquinone (**13**)	1	ND [g]	ND [g]	ND [g]	5	ND [g]	ND [g]
Ampicillin (antibiotic)	1	ND [g]	15	3	2	20	NT [h]
Carbendazim (antifungal)	1	NT [h]	NT [h]	NT [h]	NT [h]	NT [h]	ND [g]

[a] 100% to 80% petroleum spirits (60–80 °C)/dichloromethane; [b] 20% petroleum spirits (60–80 °C)/dichloromethane; [c] 80% dichloromethane/ethyl acetate; [d] 20% dichloromethane/ethyl acetate; [e] 80% ethyl acetate/methanol; [f] 100% methanol; [g] Indicates no zone of inhibition detected; [h] Indicates not tested.

3.5. Extraction and Isolation

The frozen marine alga (88 g, wet weight) was extracted with 3:1 methanol/dichloromethane (2 L). The crude extract was then decanted and concentrated under reduced pressure and sequentially solvent partitioned (triturated) into dichloromethane- and methanol-soluble extracts, respectively. Approximately 450 mg of the dichloromethane extract was subjected to flash silica gel column chromatography (20% stepwise elution from petroleum spirits (60–80 °C) to dichloromethane to ethyl acetate and finally to methanol). The 40% petroleum spirits/dichloromethane silica gel column fraction was subjected to reversed phase HPLC (100% CH_3CN) to yield sargaquinone (**13**) (2.5 mg, 0.02%). The 80% dichloromethane/ethyl acetate silica gel fraction was subjected to reversed-phase HPLC (95% CH_3CN/H_2O) to yield paradoxquinone (**15**) and 2-[11-(hydroxymethyl)-3,7,15-trimethyl-2,6,10,14-hexadecatetraen-1-yl]-6-methyl-1,4-benzoquinone (**12**) as an inseparable mixture (6.0 mg, 0.04%), and sargaquinal (**8**) (3.0 mg, 0.02%). The 40% dichloromethane/ethyl acetate to 60% dichloromethane/ethyl acetate silica gel column fractions were combined and subjected to Sephadex LH-20 size exclusion column chromatography using 100% methanol. The third fraction resulting from this analysis was subjected to reversed phase HPLC (85% CH_3CN/H_2O) to yield fallaquinone (**7**) (1.3 mg, 0.01%) and paradoxquinol (**10**) (0.2 mg, 0.001%). The remaining half of the dichloromethane extract was purified separately using reversed-phase HPLC (90% CH_3CN/H_2O) to yield fallahydroquinone (**1**) (7.3 mg, 0.05%), sargahydroquinoic acid (**2**) (17.6 mg, 0.11%), paradoxhydroquinone (**5**) and 2-[11-(hydroxymethyl)-3,7,15-trimethyl-2,6,10,14-hexadecatetraen-1-yl]-6-methyl-1,4-benzenediol (**6**) as an inseparable mixture (6.5 mg, 0.04%), sargaquinoic acid (**11**) (13.1 mg, 0.08%), and 9-(6-hydroxy-2,8-dimethyl-2*H*-1-benzopyran-2-yl)-6-methyl-2-(4-methyl-3-penten-1-yl)-2,6-nonadienal (**14**) (0.4 mg, 0.005%). The percentage yields are reported on the basis of the dry mass of the alga extracted (refer to the supporting information for details of the bioassay-guided isolation scheme adopted).

3.6. On-Line (HPLC-NMR & HPLC-MS) Characterization of Compounds

2-[12*S*-Hydroxy-11-(hydroxymethyl)-3,7,15-trimethyl-2,6,10,14-hexadecatetraen-1-yl]-6-methyl-1,4-benzenediol (fallahydroquinone) (**1**): HPLC-NMR WET1D NMR (500 MHz, 75% CH_3CN/D_2O, suppression of HDO and CH_3CN at t δ_H4.64 and 2.82 ppm, respectively) obtained from stop-flow mode (see Table 1); HRESILCMS *m/z* 427.2846 (calcd for $C_{27}H_{39}O_4$, 427.2849).

12-(2,5-Dihydroxy-3-methylphenyl)-6,10-dimethyl-2-(4-methyl-3-penten-1-yl)-(2*Z*,6*E*,10*E*)-2,6,10-dodecatrienoic acid (sargahydroquinoic acid) (**2**): HPLC-NMR WET1D NMR (500 MHz, 75% CH_3CN/D_2O, suppression of HDO and CH_3CN at t δ_H 4.64 and 2.82 ppm respectively) obtained from stop-flow mode (see Table 1); HRESILCMS *m/z* 425.2694 (calcd for $C_{27}H_{37}O_4$, 425.2692).

2-[12-Hydroxy-3,7,11,15-tetramethyl-2,6,10,14-hexadecatetraen-1-yl]-6-methyl-1,4-benzenediol (paradoxhydroquinone) (**5**): HPLC-NMR WET1D NMR (500 MHz, 75% CH_3CN/D_2O, suppression of HDO and CH_3CN at t δ_H 4.64 and 2.82 ppm, respectively) obtained from stop-flow mode δ 7.26 (1H, d, *J* = 3.0, H-5), 7.22 (1H, d, *J* = 3.0, H-3), 6.11 (1H, t, *J* = 7.0, H-2′), 6.06 (1H, t, *J* = 7.0, H-10′), 5.96 (2H, m, H-6′/H-14′), 4.06 (2H, d, *J* = 7.0, H-1′), 3.30 (1H, dd, *J* = 7.0, 7.0, H-12′), 2.95–3.04 (m), 2.96 (3H, s, H-7), 2.94 (2H, m, H-5′/H-13′*), 2.53 (3H, s, H-18′), 2.49 (3H, s, H-17′), 2.42 (3H, s, H-16′), 2.41 (3H, s, H-20′*), 2.37 (3H, s, H-19′*), ND (1-OH, 4-OH, 12′-OH) *signals interchangeable; HRESILCMS *m/z* 411.2899 (calcd for $C_{27}H_{39}O_3$, 411.2899).

2-[11-(Hydroxymethyl)-3,7,15-trimethyl-2,6,10,14-hexadecatetraen-1-yl]-6-methyl-1,4-benzenediol (**6**): HPLC-NMR WET1D NMR (500 MHz, 75% CH_3CN/D_2O, suppression of HDO and CH_3CN at t δ_H 4.64 and 2.82 ppm, respectively) obtained from stop-flow mode δ 7.25 (1H, d, *J* = 3.0, H-5), 7.22

(1H, d, *J* = 3.0, H-3), 6.10 (1H, t, *J* = 7.0, H-2′), 6.06 (1H, t, *J* = 7.5, H-10′), 5.95 (2H, m, H-6′/H-14′), 4.84 (2H, s, H-20′), 4.05 (2H, d, *J* = 7.0, H-1′), 2.95–3.04 (m), 2.97 (3H, s, H-7), 2.95 (2H, m, H-9′), 2.93 (2H, m, H-5′/H-13′*), 2.52 (3H, s, H-18′), 2.48 (3H, s, H-17′), 2.41 (6H, s, H-16′/H19′) ND (1-OH, 4-OH, 20′-OH) *signals interchangeable; HRESILCMS *m/z* 411.2899 (calcd for $C_{27}H_{39}O_3$, 411.2899).

5-[12*S*-Hydroxy-11-(hydroxymethyl)-3,7,15-trimethyl-2,6,10,14-hexadecatetraen-1-yl]-6-methyl-1,4-benzoquinone (fallaquinone) (**7**): HPLC-NMR WET1D NMR (500 MHz, 75% CH_3CN/D_2O, suppression of HDO and CH_3CN at t δ_H 4.64 and 2.82 ppm, respectively) obtained from stop-flow mode δ 7.42 (1H, bs, H-5), 7.28 (1H, bs, H-3), 6.30 (1H, t, *J* = 7.5, H-10′), 6.00 (1H, t, *J* = 7.0, H-2′), 5.95 (1H, t, *J* = 6.5, H-6′), 5.91 (1H, t, *J* = 6.5, H-14′), 4.95 (1H, d, *J* = 12.0, H-20a′), 4.89 (1H, d, *J* = 12.5, H-20b′), 4.87 (1H, dd, *J* = 6.0, 7.0, H-12′), 3.93 (2H, d, *J* = 7.0, H-1′), 2.95–3.10 (m), 3.08 (2H, m, H-13′), 3.03 (2H, m, H-9′), 2.96 (2H, m, H-5′), 2.50 (3H, s, H-17′), 2.46 (3H, s, H-18′), 2.42 (6H, s, H-16′/H-19′) ND (12′-OH, 20′-OH); HRESILCMS *m/z*425.2694 (calcd for $C_{27}H_{37}O_4$, 425.2692).

6,10-dimethyl-12-(5-methyl-3,6-dihydroxy-1,4-cyclohexadien-1-yl)-2-(4-methyl-3-pentenyl)-(2*E*,6*E*,10*E*)-2,6,10-dodecatrienal (sargahydroquinal) (**9**): UV (75% CH_3CN/D_2O) λ_{max} 238, 292; HPLC-NMR WET1D NMR (500 MHz, 75% CH_3CN/D_2O, suppression of HDO and CH_3CN at t δ_H 4.64 and 2.82 ppm, respectively) obtained from stop-flow mode (seeTable 2); HRESILCMS *m/z* 409.2745 (calcd for $C_{27}H_{37}O_3$, 409.2743).

5-[12*S*-Hydroxy-11-(hydroxymethyl)-3,7,15-trimethyl-2,6,10,14-hexadecatetraen-1-yl]-2,3-dimethyl-1,4-benzoquinone (paradoxquinol) (**10**): HPLC-NMR WET1D NMR (500 MHz, 75% CH_3CN/D_2O, suppression of HDO and CH_3CN at t δ_H4.64 and 2.82 ppm, respectively) obtained from stop-flow mode δ 7.27 (1H, s, H-3), 6.29 (1H, t, *J* = 7.0, H-10′), 5.99 (1H, m, H-2′), 5.92 (2H, m, H-6′/H-14′), 4.95 (1H, d, *J* = 12.0, H-20a′), 4.88 (1H, d, *J* = 13.0, H-20b′), 4.87 (1H, dd, *J* = 6.0, 7.5, H-12′), 3.92 (2H, d, *J* = 7.5, H-1′), 2.95-3.10 (m), 2.49 (3H, s, H-18′), 2.45 (3H, s, H-17′), 2.41 (6H, s, H-16′/H-19′) ND (12′-OH, 20′-OH); HRESILCMS *m/z* 439.2850 (calcd for $C_{28}H_{39}O_4$, 439.2849).

6,10-Dimethyl-12-(5-methyl-3,6-dioxo-1,4-cyclohexadien-1-yl)-2-(4-methyl-3-pentenyl)-(2*Z*,6*E*,10*E*)-2,6,10-dodecatrienoic acid (sargaquinoic acid) (**11**): HPLC-NMR WET1D NMR (500 MHz, 75% CH_3CN/D_2O, suppression of HDO and CH_3CN at t δ_H 4.64 and 2.82 ppm, respectively) obtained from stop-flow mode δ 7.42 (1H, d, *J* = 1.5, H-5), 7.28 (1H, d, *J* = 1.5, H-3), 6.69 (1H, t, *J* = 7.5, H-10′), 6.00 (1H, t, *J* = 7.0, H-2′), 5.95 (1H, t, *J* = 6.5, H-6′), 5.91 (1H, t, *J* = 6.5, H-14′), 3.93 (2H, d, *J* = 7.0, H1′), 3.31 (2H, dt, *J* = 7.5, 8.0, H-9′), 3.02 (2H, m, H-12′), 2.95–3.10 (m), 2.97 (2H, m, H-5′), 2.49 (3H, s, H-17′), 2.46 (3H, s, H-

18′), 2.41 (3H, s, H-19′), 2.40 (3H, s, H-16′) ND (20′-OH); HRESILCMS *m/z* 423.2542 (calcd for $C_{27}H_{35}O_4$, 423.2536).

2-[11-(Hydroxymethyl)-3,7,15-trimethyl-2,6,10,14-hexadecatetraen-1-yl]-6-methyl-1,4-benzoquinone (**12**): HPLC-NMR WET1D NMR (500 MHz, 75% CH_3CN/D_2O, suppression of HDO and CH_3CN at t δ_H 4.64 and 2.82 ppm, respectively) obtained from stop-flow mode δ 7.41 (1H, bs, H-5), 7.27 (1H, bs, H-3), 6.05 (1H, t, *J* = 7.5, H-10′), 6.00 (1H, t, *J* = 7.5, H-2′), 5.94 (2H, m, H-6′/H-14′), 4.84 (2H, s, H-20′), 3.93 (2H, d, *J* = 7.5, H1′), 2.95–3.10 (m), 2.49 (3H, s, H-17′), 2.46 (3H, s, H-18′), 2.41 (6H, s, H-16′/H-19′) ND (20′-OH); HRESILCMS *m/z* 409.2742 (calcd for $C_{27}H_{37}O_3$, 409.2743).

3.7. Off-Line Characterization of Compounds

(2′*E*,6′*E*,10′*Z*)-2-[12*S*-Hydroxy-11-(hydroxymethyl)-3,7,15-trimethyl-2,6,10,14-hexadecatetraen-1-yl]-6-methyl-1,4-benzenediol (fallahydroquinone) (**1**): unstable yellow oil; [α]25D +45.1 (*c* 0.035, $CHCl_3$); CD (EtOH) λ_{max} (Δε) 202 (+6.1), 221 (+1.6), 224 (1.8), 243 (−0.2), 260 (+2.0), 275 (+0.5), 290 (+0.6); UV (EtOH) λ_{max} (log ε) 252 (3.60), 288 (3.58); IR ν_{max} 3391, 2925, 2855, 1652, 1607, 1470, 1381, 1197, 1037 cm^{-1}. All off-line NMR spectroscopic and mass spectrometric data were identical to those reported in the literature; however, some carbon and proton NMR chemical shift reassignments have been made [7].

(2′*E*,6′*E*,10′*Z*)-12-(2,5-Dihydroxy-3-methylphenyl)-6,10-dimethyl-2-(4-methyl-3-penten-1-yl)-2,6,10-dodecatrienoic acid (sargahydroquinoic acid) (**2**): yellow oil which darkened with time. All off-line NMR spectroscopic and mass spectrometric data were identical to those reported in the literature [7,8].

(2′*E*,6′*E*,10′*Z*)-2-[12-Hydroxy-3,7,11,15-tetramethyl-2,6,10,14-hexadecatetraen-1-yl]-6-methyl-1,4-benzenediol (paradoxhydroquinone) (**5**): dark yellow oil; ^{1}H and ^{13}C NMR (500 MHz, $CDCl_3$) (see Table 3); ESIMS *m/z* 411 $[M - H]^-$; HRESIMS *m/z* 411.2898 (calcd for $C_{27}H_{39}O_3$, 411.2899).

(2′*E*,6′*E*,10′*Z*)-2-[11-(Hydroxymethyl)-3,7,15-trimethyl-2,6,10,14-hexadecatetraen-1-yl]-6-methyl-1,4-benzenediol (**6**): dark yellow oil. All off-line NMR spectroscopic and mass spectrometric data were identical to those reported in the literature [16]. Acquisition of the 1D and 2D NMR data has resulted in the first complete assignment of this compound and is provided in the supporting information.

(2′*E*,6′*E*,10′*Z*)-5-[12*S*-Hydroxy-11-(hydroxymethyl)-3,7,15-trimethyl-2,6,10,14-hexadecatetraen-1-yl]-6-methyl-1,4-benzoquinone (fallaquinone) (**7**): unstable yellow oil which darkened with time; [α]25D +31.4 (*c* 0.065, $CHCl_3$); CD (EtOH) λ_{max} (Δε) 206 (+1.8), 220 (+1.0), 238 (+2.1), 247 (+2.3), 262 (+1.6), 270 (+1.9), 286 (+0.1), 294 (+0.3); UV (EtOH) λ_{max} (log ε) 254 (4.10); IR ν_{max} 3392, 2924, 2855, 1652, 1614, 1510, 1436, 1378, 1295, 1195, 1156 cm^{-1}. All off-line NMR spectroscopic and mass spectrometric data were identical to those reported in the literature [7].

(2′*E*,6′*E*,10′*Z*)-6,10-Dimethyl-12-(5-methyl-3,6-dioxo-1,4-cyclohexadien-1-yl)-2-(4-methyl-3-pentenyl)-2,6,10-dodecatrienal (sargaquinal) (**8**): yellow oil which darkened with time; ^{1}H NMR (500 MHz, $CDCl_3$) δ 9.34 (1H, s, H-20′), 6.54 (1H, bs, H-5), 6.45 (1H, bs, H-3), 6.43 (1H, t, *J* = 7.5, H-10′), 5.15 (2H, t, *J* = 7.5, H-2′, H-6′), 5.09 (1H, m, H-14′), 3.12 (2H, d, *J* = 7.5, H1′), 2.45 (2H, dt, *J* = 7.0, 7.5, H-9′), 2.26 (2H, t, *J* = 7.5 Hz, H-12′), 2.17 (2H, m, H-8′), 2.14 (2H, m, H-5′), 2.07 (2H, m, H-4′), 2.06 (3H, s, H-7), 2.03 (2H, m, H-13′), 1.66 (3H, s, H-16′), 1.63 (3H, s, H-18′), 1.62 (3H, s, H-19′), 1.57 (3H, s, H-17′); ^{13}C NMR (125 MHz, $CDCl_3$) δ 195.2 (CH, C-20′), 188.0 (C, C-1, C-4), 155.0 (CH, C-10′), 148.4 (C, C-2), 146.0 (C, C-6), 143.2 (C, C-11′), 139.7 (C, C-3′), 133.9 (C, C-7′), 133.2 (CH, C-5), 132.4 (C, C-15′), 132.2 (CH, C-3), 125.1 (CH, C-6′), 123.6 (CH, C-14′), 118.2 (CH, C-2′), 39.5 (CH_2, C-4′), 38.3 (CH_2, C-8′), 27.5 (CH_2, C-1′), 27.4 (CH_2, C-9′), 27.0 (CH_2, C-13′), 26.4 (CH_2, C-5′), 25.7 (CH_3, C-16′), 24.3 (CH_2, C-12′), 17.7 (CH_3, C-17′), 16.0 (CH_3, C-7, C-18′, C-19′).

(2′*E*,6′*E*,10′*Z*)-5-[12*S*-Hydroxy-11-(hydroxymethyl)-3,7,15-trimethyl-2,6,10,14-hexadecatetraen-1-yl]-2,3-dimethyl-1,4-benzoquinone (paradoxquinol) (**10**): unstable yellow oil which darkened with time; [α]25D +48.5 (*c* 0.0125, $CHCl_3$); CD (EtOH) λ_{max} (Δε) 218 (+6.2), 220 (+6.4), 235 (−4.2), 245 (+2.4), 255 (+1.2); UV (EtOH) λ_{max} (log ε) 232 (4.17), 254 (4.32); IR ν_{max} 3401, 2924, 2853, 1652, 1511, 1456, 1249 cm^{-1}; ^{1}H and ^{13}C NMR (500 MHz, $CDCl_3$) (see Table 4); ESIMS *m/z* 439 $[M - H]^-$; HRESIMS *m/z* 439.2850 (calcd for $C_{28}H_{39}O_4$, 439.2849).

(2′*E*,6′*E*,10′*Z*)-6,10-Dimethyl-12-(5-methyl-3,6-dioxo-1,4-cyclohexadien-1-yl)-2-(4-methyl-3-pentenyl)-2,6,10-dodecatrienoic acid (sargaquinoic acid) (**11**): yellow oil which darkened with time. All off-line NMR spectroscopic and mass spectrometric data were identical to those reported in the literature [7,17].

(2′*E*,6′*E*,10′*Z*)-2-[11-(Hydroxymethyl)-3,7,15-trimethyl-2,6,10,14-hexadecatetraen-1-yl]-6-methyl-1,4-benzoquinone (**12**): dark yellow oil. All off-line NMR spectroscopic and mass spectrometric data were identical to those reported in the literature [16,17]. Acquisition of the 1D and 2D NMR data has resulted in the first complete assignment of this compound and is provided in the supporting information.

(2′*E*,6′*E*,10′*Z*)-2-Methyl-6-(3,7,11,15-tetramethyl-2,6,10,14-hexadecatetraenyl)-1,4-benzoquinone (sargaquinone) (**13**): dark yellow oil. All off-line NMR spectroscopic and mass spectrometric data were identical to those reported in the literature; however, some carbon NMR chemical shift reassignments have been made [18].

(3′*E*,7′*Z*)-9-(6-Hydroxy-2,8-dimethyl-2*H*-1-benzopyran-2-yl)-6-methyl-2-(4-methyl-3-penten-1-yl)-2,6-nonadienal (**14**): dark yellow oil; UV (90% CH_3CN/H_2O) λ_{max} 232, 273s, 334; IR ν_{max} 3351, 2961, 2925, 2853, 2718, 1725, 1684, 1640, 1610, 1508, 1456, 1376, 1250 cm^{-1}. All off-line NMR spectroscopic and mass spectrometric data were identical to those reported in the literature [19].

(2′*E*,6′*E*,10′*Z*)-2-[12-Hydroxy-3,7,11,15-tetramethyl-2,6,10,14-hexadecatetraen-1-yl]-6-methyl-1,4-benzoquinone (paradoxquinone) (**15**): yellow oil which darkened with time; ^1H and ^{13}C NMR (500 MHz, $CDCl_3$) (see Table 4); ESIMS *m/z*409 $[M - H]^-$; HRESIMS *m/z* 409.2755 (calcd for $C_{27}H_{37}O_3$, 409.2743).

4. CONCLUSIONS

The study of the marine brown alga *S. paradoxum* successfully implemented the use of HPLC-NMR and HPLC-MS, in combination with the use of databases, to rapidly dereplicate, identify, and deduce the structures of nine meroditerpenoids (**1**, **2**, **5–7**, and **9–12**). In particular, chemical profiling was an invaluable tool for the on-line identification of sargahydroquinal (**9**), which rapidly degraded when an off-line bioassay-guided isolation was employed, as well as for the meroditerpenoids **5**, **6**, and **12**, which could be resolved and identified as individual components via stop-flow HPLC-NMR. This study reports, for the first time, the complete 1D and 2D NMR characterization and identification of two known (**1** and**2**) natural products via stop-flow HPLC-NMR and HPLC-MS. The bioassay-guided isolation approach confirmed the identity of the compounds responsible for the dichloromethane crude extract antimicrobial activity. Subsequent biological evaluation of the isolated meroditerpenoids indicated that there were no significant differences in antimicrobial activity for 11 of the meroditerpenoids isolated. Off-line bioassay-guided isolation also permitted the first complete NMR characterization of 2-[11-(hydroxymethyl)-3,7,15-trimethyl-2,6,10,14-hexadecatetraen-1-yl]-6-methyl-1,4-benzenediol (**6**) and 2-[11-(hydroxymethyl)-3,7,15-trimethyl-2,6,10,14-hexadecatetraen-1-yl]-6-methyl-1,4-benzoquinone (**12**) to be carried out. It is proposed that the presence of fallahydroquinone (**1**) and fallaquinone (**7**) could be used as potential chemotaxonomic markers for both *S. paradoxum* and *S. fallax*, which have only been reported from these two species of*Sargassum*.

ACKNOWLEDGMENTS

The Marine and Terrestrial Natural Product (MATNAP) research group would like to thank G. Kraft (The University of Melbourne, Victoria, Australia) for the taxonomic identification of the marine alga; R. Watson from the Victorian Marine Sciences Consortium (VMSC) for the collection of the specimen; N. Thurbon (School of the School of Applied Sciences (Discipline of Biotechnology and Biological Sciences)), RMIT University for providing access to the microorganisms for the antimicrobial assays as well as for her invaluable technical support; S. Duck (School of Chemistry, Faculty of Science, Monash University) for conducting the high-resolution mass spectrometric and HPLC-MS analyses; J. Niere for her useful NMR discussions and guidance; and D. Giang for his assistance with some of the preliminary fractionations and isolation. Robert Brkljača would also like to acknowledge his Australian Postgraduate Award (APA) scholarship that supported his PhD studies.

AUTHOR CONTRIBUTIONS

All experimental work was conducted by R. Brkljača. Manuscript was prepared by R. Brkljača and S. Urban.

SUPPLEMENTARY INFORMATION

Complete HPLC-NMR and HPLC-MS analysis profiles of the crude extract of *S. paradoxum* are included. NMR spectroscopic and mass spectrometric data obtained from the HPLC-NMR and HPLC-MS analyses have been provided for the merediterpenoids (**1**, **2**, **5**–**7**, and **9**–**12**). The off-line NMR spectroscopic and mass spectrometric data obtained for the new meroditerpenoids (**5**, **10**, and **15**) and for compounds **6** and **12**, which have been characterized completely for the first time, have also been made available. This material is available free of charge via the Internet at http://pubs.acs.org.

CONFLICTS OF INTEREST

The authors declare no conflict of interest.

REFERENCES

1. MarinLit Database; Royal Society of Chemistry: Cambridge, UK, 2014.

2. Guiry, M.D.; Guiry, G.M. AlgaeBase; World-Wide Electronic Publication: National University of Ireland, Galway, Ireland, 2014; Available online: http://www.algaebase.org (accessed on 1 December 2014).

3. Phillips, N. Biogeography of Sargassum (Phaeophyta) in the Pacfic basin. Taxon. Ecomonic Seaweeds 1995, 5, 107–144.

4. Dixon, R.R.M.; Mattio, L.; Huisman, J.M.; Payri, C.E.; Bolton, J.J.; Gurgel, C.F.D. North meets south—Taxonomic and biogeographic implications of a phylogenetic assessment of Sargassum subgenera Arthrophycus and Bactrophycus(Fucales, Phaeophyceae). Phycologia 2014, 53, 15–22.

5. Liu, L.; Heinrich, M.; Myers, S.; Dworjanyn, S.A. Towards a better understanding of medicinal uses of the brown seaweed Sargassum in traditional chinese medicine: A phytochemical and pharmacological review. J. Ethnopharmacol.2012, 142, 591–619.

6. Jung, M.; Jang, K.H.; Kim, B.; Lee, B.H.; Choi, B.W.; Oh, K.-B.; Shin, J. Meroditerpenoids from the brown algaSargassum siliquastrum. J. Nat. Prod. 2008, 71, 1714–1719.

7. Reddy, P.; Urban, S. Meroditerpenoids from the southern australian marine brown alga Sargassum fallax.Phytochemistry 2009, 70, 250–255.

8. Segawa, M.; Shirahama, H. New plastoquinones from the brown alga Sargassum sagamianum var. yezoense. Chem. Lett.1987, 16, 1365–1366.

9. Kim, M.C.; Kwon, H.C.; Kim, S.N.; Kim, H.S.; Um, B.H. Plastoquinones from Sargassum yezoense; chemical structures and effects of the activation of peroxisome proliferator-activated receptor gamma. Chem. Pharm. Bull. 2011, 59, 834–838.

10. Horie, S.; Tsutsumi, S.; Takada, Y.; Kimura, J. Antibacterial quinone metabolites from the brown alga, Sargassum sagamianum. Bull. Chem. Soc. Jpn. 2008, 81, 1125–1130.

11. Culioli, G.; Ortalo-Magne, A.; Valls, R.; Hellio, C.; Clare, A.S.; Piovetti, L. Antifouling activity of meroditerpenoids from the marine brown alga Halidrys siliquosa. J. Nat. Prod. 2008, 71, 1121–1126.

12. Foti, M.; Piattelli, M.; Amico, V.; Ruberto, G. Antioxidant activity of phenolic meroditerpenoids from marine algae. J. Photochem. Photobiol. B 1994, 26, 159–164.

13. SciFinder; American Chemical Society: Washington, DC, USA, 2014.

14. Scott, A.I. Interpretation of the Ultraviolet Spectra of Natural Products; Pergamon Press Ltd.: London, UK, 1964.

15. Sheu, J.-H.; Su, J.-H.; Sung, P.-J.; Wang, G.-H.; Dai, C.-F. Novel meroditerpenoid-related metabolites from the formosan soft coral Nephthea chabrolii. J. Nat. Prod. 2004, 67, 2048–2052.

16. Sato, A.; Shindo, T.; Hasegawa, K.; Ushiyama, S. Preparation of 2-(11-Hydroxymethyl-3,7,15-Trimethyl-2,6,10,14-Hexadecatetraenyl)-6-Methyl-1,4-Benzoquinone or -1,4-Benzenediol or Their Acyl Derivatives as 5-Lipoxygenase Inhibitors. Kokai Tokkyo Koho Japan H02-290826, 1990.

17. Kusumi, T.; Shibata, Y.; Ishitsuka, M.; Kinoshita, T.; Kakisawa, H. Structures of new plastoquinones from the brown alga Sargassum serratifolium. Chem. Lett. 1979, 8, 277–278.

18. Amico, V.; Cunsolo, F.; Piattelli, M.; Ruberto, G. Tetraprenyltoluquinols from the brown alga Cystoseira jabukae.Phytochemistry 1985, 24, 1047–1050.

19. Kimura, J.; Horie, C.; Marushima, H.; Matsumoto, Y.; Sanjoba, C.; Osada, Y. Antileishmanial Agents Containing p-Benzoquinone Derivative. JP 2012-502793, 2012.

20. Silva, D.H.S.; Pereira, F.C.; Zanoni, M.V.B.; Yoshida, M. Lipophyllic antioxidants from Iryanthera juruensis fruits.Phytochemistry 2001, 57, 437–442.

21. Barr, R.; Crane, F.L. Comparative studies on plastoquinones. III. Distribution of plastoquinones in higher plants.Plant Physiol. 1967, 42, 1255–1263.

22. Gonnella, N.C.; Nakanishi, K. General method for determining absolute configurations of acyclic allylic alcohols. J. Am. Chem. Soc. 1982, 104, 3775–3776.

23. Kobayashi, M.; Ito, M.; Koyama, T.; Ogura, K. Stereochemistry of the carbon to carbon bond formation in the biosynthesis of polyprenyl chains with Z double bonds. Studies with undecaprenyl-pyrophosphate synthetase. J. Am. Chem. Soc. 1985, 107, 4588–4589.

24. Lamshoft, M.; Schmickler, H.; Marner, F.-J. Determination of the absolute configuration of hydroxyiridals by chiroptical and NMR spectroscopic methods. Eur. J. Org. Chem. 2003, 2003, 727–733.

25. Sunazuka, T.; Shirahata, T.; Yoshida, K.; Yamamoto, D.; Harigaya, Y.; Nagai, T.; Kiyohara, H.; Yamada, H.; Kuwajima, I.; Omura, S. Total synthesis of pinellic acid, a potent oral adjuvant for nasal influenza vaccine. Determination of the relative and absolute configuration. Tetrahedron Lett. 2002, 43, 1265–1268.

26. De la Mare, J.-A.; Lawson, J.C.; Chiwakata, M.T.; Beukes, D.R.; Edkins, A.L.; Blatch, G.L. Quinones and halogenated monoterpenes of algal origin show anti-proliferative effects against breast cancer cells in vitro. Investig. New Drugs2012, 30, 2187–2200.

27. Seo, Y.; Lee, H.-J.; Park, K.E.; Kim, Y.A.; Ahn, J.W.; Yoo, J.S.; Lee, B.-J. Peroxynitrite-scavenging constituents from the brown alga Sargassum thunbergii. Biotechnol. Bioprocess Eng. 2004, 9, 212–216.

28. Afolayan, A.F.; Bolton, J.J.; Lategan, C.A.; Smith, P.J.; Beukes, D.R. Fucoxanthin, tetraprenylated toluquinone, and toluhydroquinone metabolites from Sargassum heterophyllum inhibit the in vitro growth of the malaria parasitePlasmodium falciparum. J. Biosci. 2008, 63, 848–852.

29. Cespedes, C.L.; Torres, P.; Marin, J.C.; Arciniegas, A.; de Vivar, A.R.; Perez-Castorena, A.L.; Aranda, E. Insect growth inhibition by tocotrienols and hydroquinones from Roldana barba-johannis. Phytochemistry 2004, 65, 1963–1975.

30. Park, B.-G.; Shin, W.-S.; Um, Y.; Cho, U.; Park, G.-M.; Yeon, D.-S.; Kwon, S.-C.; Ham, J.; Choi, B.W.; Lee, S. Selective vasodilatation effect of sargahydroquinoic acid, an active constituent of Sargassum micracanthum, on the basilar arteries of rabbits. Bioorg. Med. Chem. Lett. 2008, 18, 2624–2627.

31. Kim, S.-N.; Choi, H.Y.; Lee, W.; Park, G.-M.; Shin, W.-S.; Kim, Y.K. Sargaquinoic acid and sargahydroquinoic acid from Sargassum yezoense stimulate adipocyte differentiation through PPARα/γ activation in 3T3-L1 cells. FEBS Lett.2008, 582, 3465–3472.

32. Kamei, Y.; Tsang, C.K. Sargaquinoic acid promotes neurite outgrowth via protein kinase A and MAP kinases-mediated signaling pathways in PC12D cells. Int. J. Dev. Neurosci. 2003, 21, 255–262.

33. Hur, S.; Lee, H.; Kim, Y.; Lee, B.-H.; Shin, J.; Kim, T.-Y. Sargaquinoic acid and sargachromenol, extracts of Sargassum sagamianum, induce

apoptosis in HaCaT cells and mice skin: Its potentiation of UVB-induced apoptosis. Eur. J. Pharmacol. 2008, 582, 1–11.

34. Silva, D.H.S.; Zhang, Y.; Santos, L.A.; Bolzani, V.S.; Nair, M.G. Lipoperoxidation and cyclooxygenases 1 and 2 inhibitory compounds from Iryanthera juruensis. J. Agric. Food Chem. 2007, 55, 2569–2574.

35. Choi, B.W.; Ryu, G.; Park, S.H.; Kim, E.S.; Shin, J.; Roh, S.S.; Shin, H.C.; Lee, B.-H. Anticholinesterase activity of plastoquinones from Sargassum sagamianum: Lead compounds for Alzheimer's disease therapy. Phytother. Res. 2007,21, 423–426.

36. Nahas, R.; Abatis, D.; Anagnostopoulou, M.A.; Kefalas, P.; Vagias, C.; Roussis, V. Radical-scavenging activity of aegean sea marine algae. Food Chem. 2007, 102, 577–581.

37. Tziveleka, L.-A.; Abatis, D.; Paulus, K.; Bauer, R.; Vagias, C.; Roussis, V. Marine polyprenylated hydroquinones, quinones and chromenols with inhibitory effects on leukotriene formation. Chem. Biodivers. 2005, 2, 901–909.

38. Voutquenne, L.; Lavaud, C.; Massiot, G.; Sevenet, T.; Hadi, H.A. Cytotoxic polyisoprenes and glycosides of long-chain fatty alcohols from Dimocarpus fumatus. Phytochemistry 1999, 50, 63–69.

39. Gerwick, W.H.; Fenical, W.; Norris, J.N. Chemical variation in the tropical seaweed Stypopodium zonale (dictyotaceae).Phytochemistry 1985, 24, 1279–1283.

40. Master, R.N.; Clark, R.B.; Karlowsky, J.A.; Ramirez, J.; Bordon, J.M. Analysis of resistance, cross-resistance and antimicrobial combinations for Pseudomonas aeruginosa isolates from 1997 to 2009. Int. J. Antimicrob. Agents 2011, 38, 291–295.

41. Smallcombe, S.H.; Patt, S.L.; Keifer, P.A. WET solvent suppression and its applications to LC NMR and high-resolution NMR spectroscopy. J. Magn. Reson. Ser. A 1995, 117, 295–303.

Chapter 12

Bioactive Dehydrotyrosyl and Dehydrodopyl Compounds of Marine Origin

Manickam Sugumaran [1,*] and William E. Robinson [2]

[1]*Department of Biology, University of Massachusetts Boston, Boston, MA 02125, USA*

[2]*Environmental, Earth and Ocean Sciences Department, University of Massachusetts Boston, Boston, MA 02125, USA*

ABSTRACT

The amino acid, tyrosine, and its hydroxylated product, 3,4-dihydroxyphenylalanine (dopa), plays an important role in the biogenesis of a number of potentially important bioactive molecules in marine organisms. Interestingly, several of these tyrosyl and dopa-containing compounds possess dehydro groups in their side chains. Examples span the range from simple dehydrotyrosine and dehydrodopamines to complex metabolic products, including peptides and polycyclic alkaloids. Based on structural information, these compounds can be subdivided into five categories: (a) Simple dehydrotyrosine and dehydrotyramine containing molecules; (b) simple dehydrodopa derivatives; (c) peptidyl dehydrotyrosine and dehydrodopa derivatives; (d) multiple dehydrodopa containing compounds; and (e) polycyclic condensed dehydrodopa derivatives. These molecules possess a wide range of biological activities that include (but are not limited to) antitumor activity, antibiotic activity, cytotoxicity, antioxidant activity, multidrug resistance reversal, cell division inhibition, immunomodulatory activity, HIV-integrase inhibition, anti-viral, and anti-feeding (or feeding deterrent) activity. This review summarizes the structure, distribution, possible biosynthetic origin, and biological activity, of the five categories of dehydrotyrosine and dehydrodopa containing compounds.

Keywords: marine alkaloids; bioactive peptides; dehydrotyrosine; dehydrodopa; dehydrotopa

1. INTRODUCTION

The origin of almost all antibiotics used today can be traced back to naturally occurring compounds isolated from bacteria and fungi. While the majority of our current antibiotics are considered "semisynthetic" (*i.e.*, modified versions of natural products that are synthetically mass produced), there is only a limited number of totally man-made antibiotic compounds that have proven to be effective in combating bacterial pathogens, such as the broad-spectrum quinolones and sulfonamides, and the Gram-positive targeted oxazolidinones [1]. Because of this, the search for new antibiotics still relies initially on the identification of natural products. Moreover, development of bacterial resistance to a large number of the currently prescribed antibiotics, particularly multi-drug resistance (MDR), has caused serious concern among health care professionals [2,3]. Many experts agree that the lack of development of new antibiotics to replace the ones that are currently ineffective is currently a major threat to human health, and in the years to come. Therefore, there is an urgent need to develop new antibiotics, especially for controlling MDR bacteria that are often found in hospitals and nursing homes located in high population density areas. More broadly, there is also a pressing need for new anti-fungal, anti-viral and anti-tumor compounds.

Marine organisms seem to be a particularly likely source of new antimicrobial and antitumor compounds. Although over 70% of the Earth's surface is covered by oceans, only about 15% of the approximately 1.8 to 2.0 million species that have currently been named, live in the marine environment [4]. In contrast, biodiversity appears to be far greater in the oceans than on land, since the oceans currently support 32 phyla, whereas only 12 phyla are present on land [4]. Marine waters are therefore a potentially rich source of undiscovered natural products. Marine metabolites and other natural products have to work in saline environments, thus, to some extent, pre-adapting them to human physiological conditions. Nevertheless, their aqueous environment causes rapid dilution, which could greatly reduce their effectiveness. To avoid such dilution problems, many aquatic organisms have evolved efficient and more potent metabolites that exhibit higher toxicity/biological activity even at extremely low concentrations. Hence, marine metabolites could potentially work in physiological saline at concentrations much below the levels needed by compounds of terrestrial origin.

Within the marine environment, marine invertebrates should prove to be a rich source of bioactive compounds. Over 95% of all animals are invertebrates, with over 33 invertebrate phyla [5]. Nevertheless, over 90% of the marine invertebrate species are yet to be described [5]. We would argue that the diversity of invertebrate community structure, organism-to-organism interactions, intricate food webs (predator-prey as well as competition), broad range of reproductive strategies, and host-parasite relationships would make invertebrates a potentially rich source of bioactive compounds. Lacking the complicated immune system of higher animals, marine invertebrates successfully manage to evade and fight infection using a plethora of host defense mechanisms including the use of antibiotic peptides. With such advantages, it is clear that marine invertebrate compounds deserve more attention in the development of newer and more effective antibiotics and other important bioactive compounds.

However, a large-scale, animal collection, tissue homogenization and activity-screening approach to examining possible bioactive compounds in invertebrates is a poor strategy, and is unlikely to be repeatedly successful. René Dubos, credited with the discovery of the first naturally occurring antibiotic gramicidin, was also the first to advocate for a deliberate, systematic approach for searching for antibacterial compounds [6]. The conventional ways to find new antibiotic compounds, although more systematic than the "shotgun" approach, rely on screening techniques employing libraries of both synthetic and naturally occurring compounds. Yet such screening techniques have not generated the much-needed arsenal of chemicals to combat different disease-causing bacteria. We advocate a different systematic strategy—use known structural data on specific groups of bioactive compounds that have been isolated from marine invertebrates to identify likely antibiotics, and then use chemical modification and synthesis to enhance antibiotic potency. Unfortunately, current knowledge of groups of bioactive compounds is patchy and incomplete, thereby limiting the number of systematic studies that can be sustained.

One particularly rich group of bioactive compounds is the dopa/topa-containing compounds in marine invertebrates (and more specifically, dehydrotyrosyl/dopa compounds). Even a cursory glance at the literature of compounds possessing dehydrotyrosyl/dopyl units reveals that these compounds are widely and uniquely distributed in marine invertebrates, possess unusual biological properties, and often exhibit antibiotic activities. Such compounds have been found in a very diverse (and apparently unrelated) number of phyla, including the Porifera (sponges), Cnidaria (coelenterates), Mollusca (bivalves), Arthropoda (insects) and Urochordata (ascidians). This latter group is of particular interest to us. Ascidians (also called tunicates or simply sea squirts; subphylum Tunicata, Class Ascidiacea) are sessile marine filter-feeding invertebrates that exhibit features in their free-swimming larval stage that are characteristic of the vertebrates, including gill slits, notocord and dorsal nerve cord, yet are considered to be a highly divergent offshoot from the other members of the Chordata [7]. As we will discuss later, a number of species of tunicates contain various, low molecular weight, dopa- or topa-containing peptides (or modified peptides) in their blood cells or other body tissues including styelins from *Styela clava* [8], plicatamide from *Styela plicata* [9], halocyamines from *Halocynthia roretzi* [10], lamellarins from *Didemnum chartaceum* [11], ferreascidin from *Pyura stolonifera* [12] and tunichromes from eleven species of tunicates [13–19]. Although there is a wealth of information on invertebrate bioactive compounds, to date these data have been stumbled upon (a stochastic process) rather than systematically investigated (a scientific process). Our aim is to review what is known about this group of compounds, highlight chemical relationships within the group, and suggest promising avenues for future research. This is the first step in the approach we advocate to systematically search for new dehydrotyrosyl/dopyl compounds in marine species to add to the existing list of potentially new antibiotic compounds to tackle the multiple drug-resistance problem. Adding the structures of newly discovered dehydrotyrosyl/dopyl compounds to the list of currently known compounds will better enable researchers to then address the structure-activity relationships.

Dopa- and topa-containing compounds often possess dehydro groups in their side chains. Examples span the range from simple dehydrotyrosine and dehydrodopamines to complex metabolic products, including peptides and polycyclic alkaloids. Structural information allows these compounds to be divided into five categories: (a) simple dehydrotyrosine- and dehydrotyramine-containing compounds; (b) simple dehydrodopa derivatives; (c) simple peptidyl dehydrotyrosine and dehydrodopa derivatives; (d) multiple dehydrodopa-containing compounds; and (e) polycyclic condensed dehydrodopa derivatives. We will address each of these in turn.

2. Simple Dehydrotyrosine Derivatives: Tuberine, Erbastatin, p-Hydroxycinnamaldehyde, Lasoidine, Botryllamide, Hamigeramine, Hamigeroxalamic Acid, Tridentatols, Anthosamines, Cyclo-Arg-Dehydrotyrosine and Rigidins

The first dehydrotyrosine derivative that was shown to possess biological activity was tuberine [20]. Tuberine (**1**) possessed mild antibiotic properties. The related erbstatin (**2**) was isolated by Umezawa *et al.* [21] (Figure 1) from the culture broth of *Streptomyces amnkusaensis*. These authors demonstrated its potential to inhibit tyrosine-specific protein kinase activity. Leem *et al.* [22] identified *p*-hydroxy cinnamaldehyde (**3**) as an antibacterial substance from the saw fly,*Acantholyda parki*. The tetrapeptide lasoidine A, (**4**) isolated by Marchand *et al.* in 1969 [23] from an African buckthorn plant (family Rhamnaceae), contains a dehydrotyrosine residue. However, the first group of marine compounds possessing dehydrotyrosine unit is botryllamides [24]. They were isolated from two species of ascidians, *Botryllus* sp. from Philippines and *Botryllus schlosseri* from the Great Barrier Reef of Australia. They showed mild cytotoxicity against the human colon cancer cell line HCT-116. Henrich *et al.* [25] used a different species of *Botryllus* (*B. tyreus*) and isolated a number of botryllamides (**5–14**) all possessing dehydrotyramine units (Figure 2). These compounds are apparently derived from a tyrosyl tyrosine dipeptide by modification. Botryllamides proved to be effective inhibitors of the ATP binding cassette (ABC) transporter called ABCG2 that is associated with multi drug resistance [25]. They were selective in inhibiting ABCG2 (also known as breast cancer resistant protein, BCRP) and not the two other types of transporters (ABCB1 encoding P-glycoprotein, P-gp; or ABCC1 encoding multidrug associated protein 1, MDR-1) [26].

From the Mediterranean sponge, *Hamigera hamigera*, Hassan *et al.* [27] isolated two compounds called hamigeramine (**15**) and hamigeroxalamic acid (**16**) whose structures are shown in Figure 3. As is evident, they are simple dehydrotyramine derivates. Due to the low amount of the isolated materials, the authors could not perform quantitative studies, but qualitative studies reveal that these two compounds, along with other unidentified compounds, exhibit fish feeding deterrent activity.

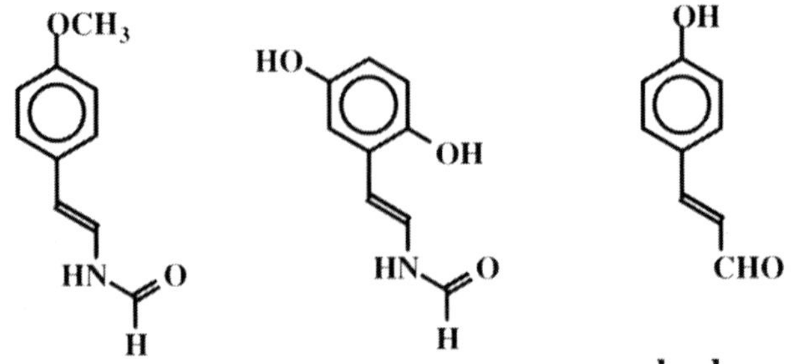

Tuberin (1) Erbstatin (2) *p*-hydroxy cinnamaldehyde (3)

Lasoidine A (4)

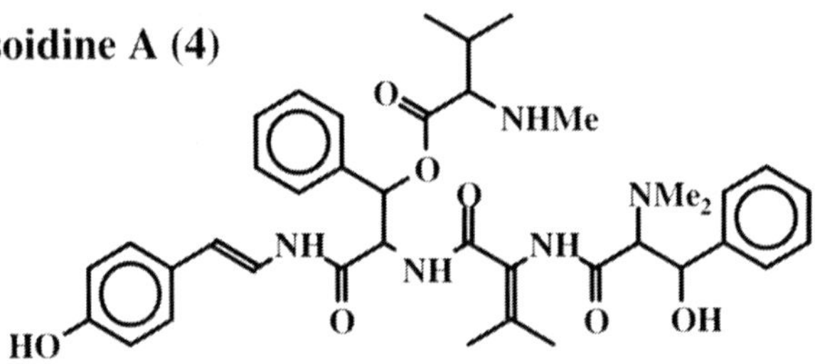

Figure 1. Structures of some simple dehydro compounds.

In 1996, Lindquist *et al.* isolated a group of dithiocarbamate related compounds from the marine hydroid, *Tridentata marginata* [28]. They named these compounds tridentatols A, B, and C (**17**, **18** and **19**). In addition, they also isolated a precursor molecule, tridentatol D (**20**), which did not possess any biological activity. The structures of these molecules are shown in Figure 4. Methylation of tridentatol D (**20**) could give rise to tridentatol A (**17**) and cyclization of tridentatol D (**20**) will generate tridentatol C (**19**). Tridentatol B (**18**) is the *cis* isomer of tridentatol A (**17**) that might be formed during the dehydrogenation reaction of a precursor molecule. The *cis* isomer exhibited more potent antioxidant activity against LDL oxidation caused by copper ions than the naturally occurring antioxidant Vitamin E in bioassays [29]. Moreover, these compounds also exhibited deterrent activity as well as protection against solar UV radiation damage [30]. Subsequently, Lindquist [31] isolated five more tridentatol derivates from the same organism and showed that four of them are sulfated derivatives of the tridentatols A–D (**21**–**24**). The sulfated compounds do not possess fish deterrent activity. Upon crushing the marine hydroid, the free forms that possess fish deterrent activity are rapidly released [31].

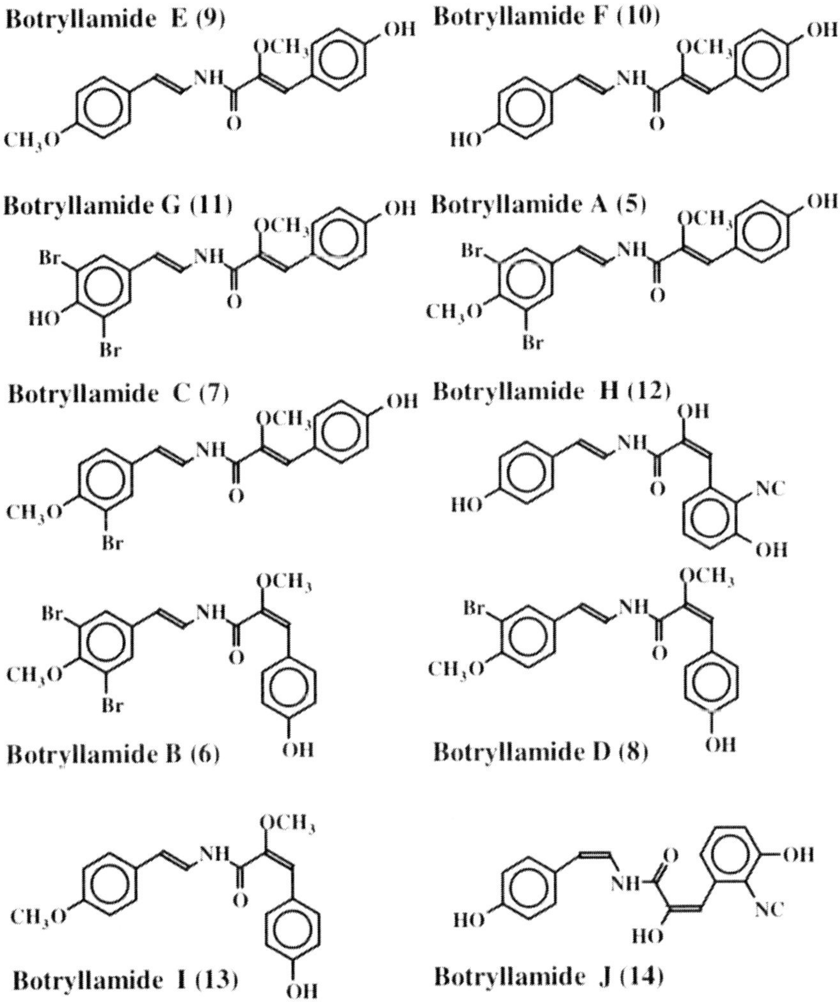

Figure 2. Structures of botryllamides.

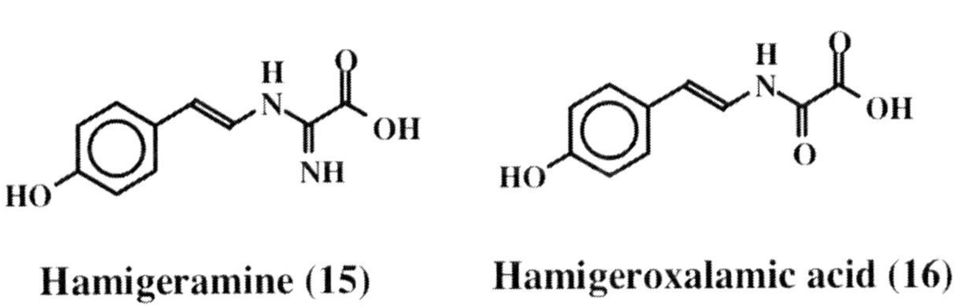

Figure 3. Structures hamigeramine and hemigeroxalamic acid.

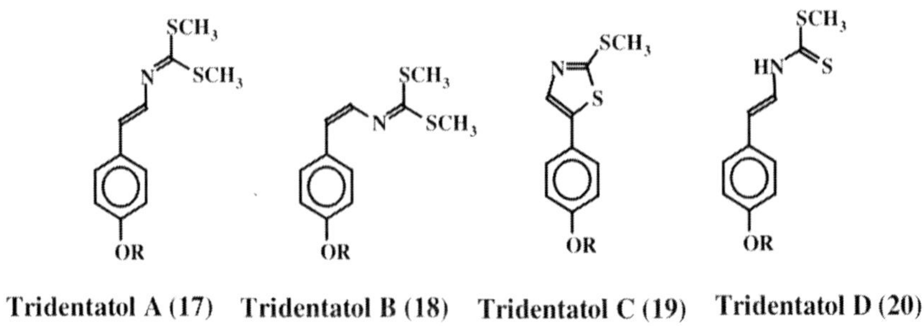

Figure 4. Structures of tridentatols (R = H, **17–20**; R = OSO_3Na are tridentatols E–H,**21–24**).

During their extended series of studies on the chemical cues that alter larval settlement and metamorphosis, Tsukamoto*et al.* [32] isolated new pipecolate derivatives called anthosamines A (**25**) and B (**26**) and a new diketopiperazine, cyclo-L-arginine-dehydrotyrosine (**27**), from a marine sponge that belong to the Clionidae class, *Anthosigmella* aff. *raromicrosclera*(Figure 5). These compounds possess dehydrotyrosine units and induce larval metamorphosis in ascidian *Halocynthia roretzi.* Anthosamine A (**25**) and B (**26**) exhibit reversible isomerization between amine and iminium ion forms. The amine form predominately occurs in the aprotic solvent while the iminium ion predominates in the protic solvents. The dehydrotyrosine group is conserved in the iminium form and is lost during conversion to the bicyclic amine form (Figure 5).

Rigidin A (**28,** Figure 6), a pyrrolepyrimidine alkaloid containing a dehydrotyramine unit was isolated from the Okinawan marine tunicate, *Eudistoma* cf. *rigida* [33]. This compound exhibited antagonistic activity against calmodulin. The biological activities of the related compounds, rigidin B (**29**), C (**30**) and D (**31**), which were isolated from a different species of tunicate, *Cystodytes* sp., are yet to be determined [34].

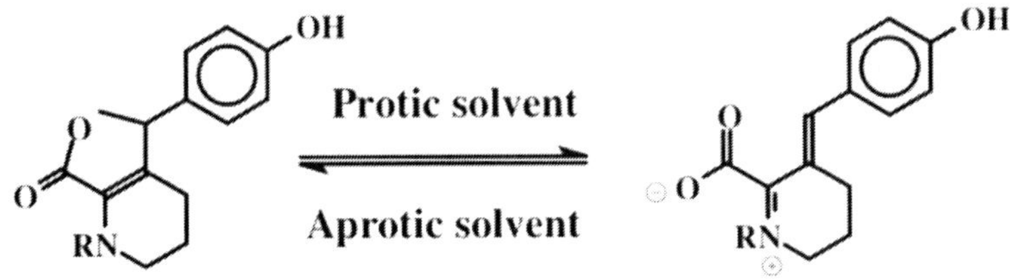

Anthosamine A (25, R = H) Anthosamine B (26, R = methyl)

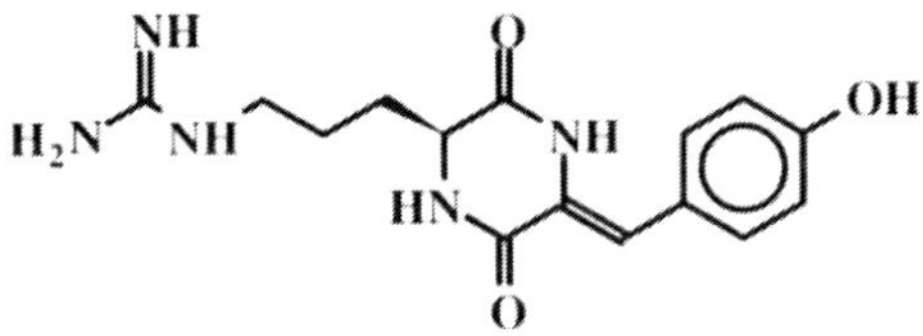

Cyclo (L-Arginine) dehydro tyrosine (27)

Figure 5. Structures of anthosamines (**25**, **26**) and cyclo arginine dehydrotyrosine (**27**).

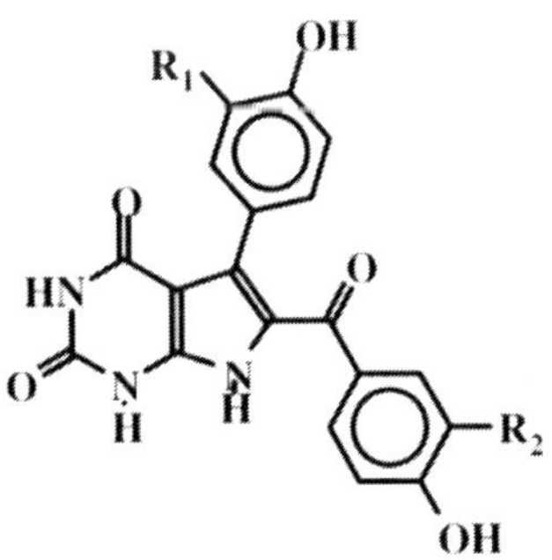

Rigidin A, 28, $R_1 = R_2 = H$

Rigidin B, 29, $R_1 = H; R_2 = CH_3$

Rigidin C, 30, $R_1 = CH_3; R_2 = H$

Rigidin D, 31, $R_1 = R_2 = CH_3$

Figure 6. Structures of Rigidins (**28–31**).

3. Simple Dehydrodopa Derivatives: 1,2-Dehydro-*N*-acetyldopamine, Narain, Jaspisin, Isojaspisin, Tubastrine, Orthidine and Wondonin A and B, Leucettamines

1,2-Dehydro-*N*-acetyldopamine (dehydro NADA, **32**) is one of the most thoroughly studied dehydro compounds. Although this compound is of arthropod origin, given the fact that most of this review is devoted to dehydrodopa derivatives, and that a vast majority of marine metabolites possess the basic structure of this compound, it is important to discuss the biochemistry of this novel compound. Andersen and his associates first isolated dehydro NADA (**32**) from the sclerotized cuticle of locusts and beetles [35,36]. Subsequently, Andersen and Roepstorff isolated this compound as a component of insect cuticle [37]. Since then its chemical synthesis, biogenesis, and potential biological reactions via oxidative transformations have been extensively studied by one of our research laboratories [38–45]. Although this simple compound is very widely used in insects as the major crosslinking agent to make protein-protein adducts, protein-chitin adducts and chitin-chitin adducts, during cuticular hardening process, it is also known to possess antioxidant properties [39]. This compound is very labile and easily undergoes both enzymatic and nonenzymatic oxidation forming dimers.Figure 7 for instance shows the phenoloxidase mediated dimerization of dehydro NADA. Several modifications of this simple structure are widely manifested in marine organisms, as we shall see later.

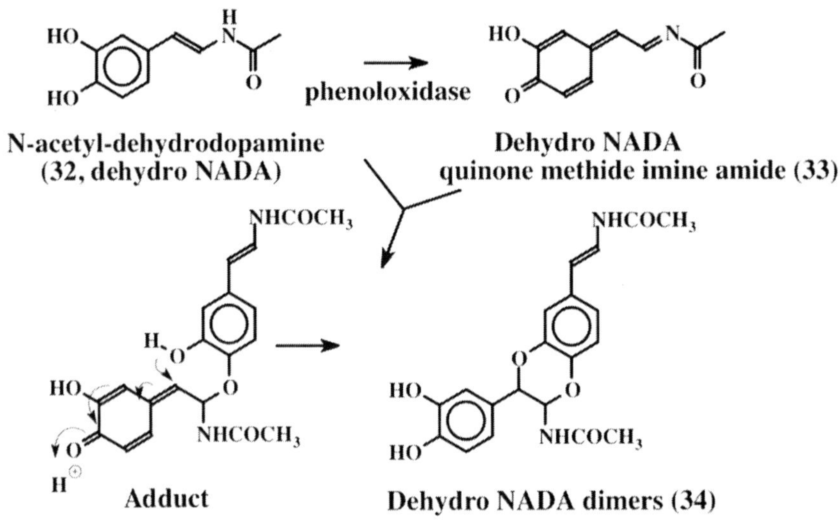

Figure 7. 1,2-Dehydro-*N*-acetyldopamine and its dimer formation. Dehydro NADA (**32**) is oxidized by phenoloxidase to quinone methide imine amide (**33**) which adds on to the parent compound forming dimers via a transient intermediate. The reaction yields all four possible stereoisomers (**34**). The reaction of the quinone methide imine amide with *N*-acetyldopamine will produce saturated dimers (**35**, not shown in the figure).

The cast-off shell (exuviae) of the cicada of *Cryptotympana* sp. (Cicadidae) is used as a crude Chinese traditional medicine called "Zentai", which is used as an antifebrile, a spasmolytic and as an antiphlogistic. It is also known to possess sedative and sympathetic ganglionic blocking activities. Since insect cuticle is mostly made of polymeric proteins and chitin and to lesser extent catecholamines, the suspected bioactive compound is most likely the catecholamine derivative. Accordingly, several groups of workers have isolated bioactive catecholamine compounds from insect cuticle.

Noda *et al.* [46] first isolated a mixture of saturated dehydro NADA dimers (**35**) as the principle component of the drug. Following this work, Tada *et al.* [47] isolated the same compounds from a different species (*Cryptotympana tuslulata*) and showed that they possessed strong tyrosinase inhibitory activity and could be used as potential cosmetic skin whitening agents. Subsequently, Xu *et al.* [48] isolated both the saturated (**35**) and the unsaturated dimers (**34**) from the exuviae of cicadae available from their region. The unsaturated dimer (**34**) was far more effective in inhibiting reactive oxygen species (ROS) generation, inducible nitric oxide (NO) production and nuclear factor NF-kB activity in biological assays. This compound also induced pro-inflammatory molecules such as inducible nitric oxide synthase (iNOS), interleukin (IL)-6, tumor necrosis factor (TNF)-a and cyclooxygnease (COX)-2 in lipopolysaccharide (LPS) induced cells [48]. Thus both the saturated and unsaturated dimers seem to possess antioxidant and anti-inflammatory properties. However, the "dehydrodopa" derivatives isolated from marine organisms possess even more interesting properties.

The first compound to be identified in this group is tubastrine [49]. It is a guanido dihydroxystyrene compound (**36**) whose structure is shown in Figure 8. It was isolated from the bright orange-red coral, *Tubastrea aurea* in a polar extract, which also possessed antiviral activity against herpes simplex virus and vesicular stomatitis virus. Subsequently, Sperry and Crews [50] isolated this compound along with its saturated analog from the marine sponge, *Petrosia* cf. *contignata.* In a bioassay directed survey, Barenbrock and Kock [51] identified tubastrine (**36**) as the active compound from several ascidians that showed inhibition of epidermal growth factor receptor using a protein tyrosine kinase assay. Tubastrine was isolated as the principle inhibitory compound from the ascidian, *Dendrodoa grossularia* [51]. Recently, Pearce *et al.* [52] identified tubastrine (**36**) and a number of its dimeric products called orthidines (**37–41**), from the ascidian, *Aplidium orthium* (Figure 8).

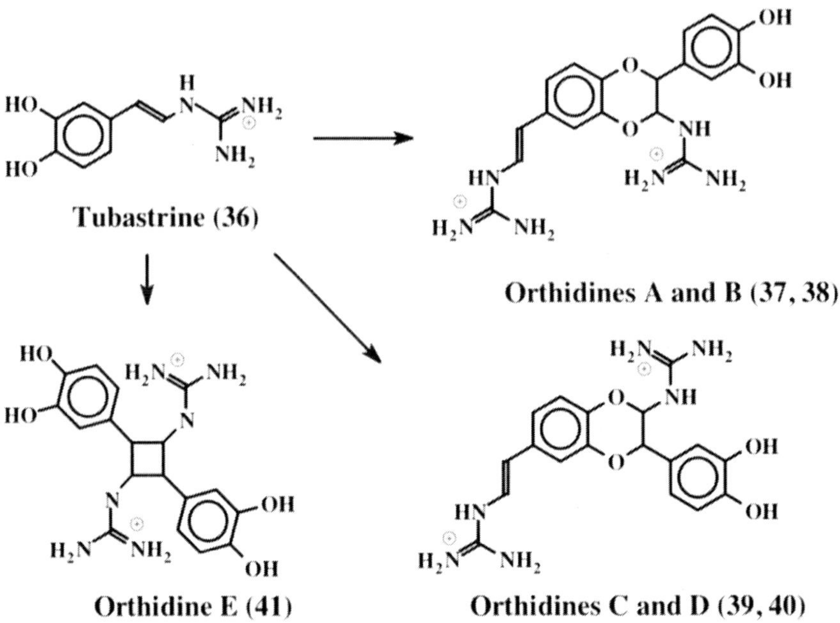

Figure 8. Structures of tubastrine and orthidines. Orthidines (**37–41**) are dimers of tubastrine (**36**) formed by a similar mechanism shown in Figure 7 for the dimerization of dehydro NADA (**32**).

The four benzodioxan dimers (orthidines A–D; **37–40**) are the same kind that were characterized for dehydro NADA (**32**). The cyclobutane ring containing dimer (orthidine E, **41**) is unique and has not been identified in any other system so far. Tubastrine (**36**) and its dimers (**37–41**) exhibited *in vivo* and *in vitro* anti-inflammatory activities. These compounds drastically reduced the superoxide production by neutrophils *in vivo* in a murine model of gouty inflammation. Accordingly the *in vitro* production of superoxide by PMA-stimulated human neutrophils was inhibited by tubastrine analogs in a dose dependent fashion with an IC_{50} value ranging from 10–36 μM [52].

Jaspisin (**42**) was another dehydrodopa related compound that was isolated from the marine sponge, *Jaspis* sp. [53]. It is the sodium salt of (*E*)-5,6-dihydroxystyryl sulfate (Figure 9) and inhibited the fertilization of sea urchin gametes by blocking the exoplasmic membrane fusion with a minimum inhibition concentration of about 60 μM. The same authors also isolated and reported [54] the structure of the (*Z*) isomer, isojaspisin (**43**, Figure 9). Jaspisin (**42**) inhibited the fusion of acrosome reacted sperm with the plasma membrane of the egg [55]. However, it did not inhibit the acrosome reaction in sperm or the egg cortical reaction. It proved to be a powerful antihatching substance inhibiting the hatching enzyme from sea urchin, a zinc dependent metaloendoprotease [55].

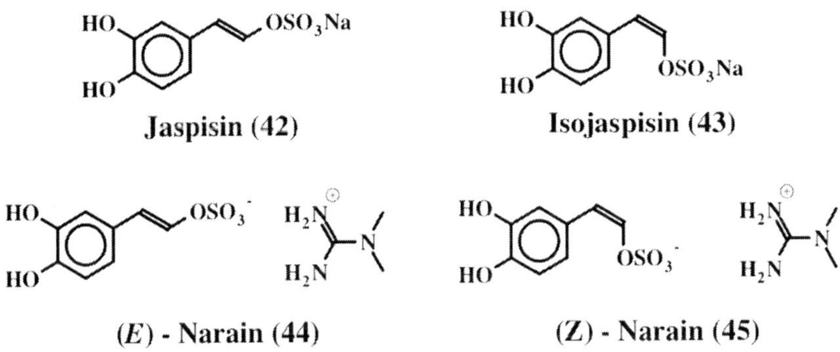

Figure 9. Structures of Jaspisin related compounds.

Narains (*E* and *Z* isomers, **44**, **45**) are *N*,*N*-dimethylguanidium salts of dihydroxystyryl sulfates (Figure 9) isolated from a *Jaspis* sp. which induce larval metamorphosis in the ascidian *Halocynthia roretzi* [56]. Analogous to the dimers of dehydro NADA (**32**) and tubastrine (**36**), narains (and jaspisins) also form dimers (Figure 10). These dimers (**46**) also induce larval metamorphosis in ascidians *Halocynthia roretzi* and *Ciona savignyi* [57]. A slightly different dimer which has lost one sulfate unit was isolated from an association of the sponges, *Poecillastra wondoensis* and *Jaspis* sp., and named wondonins A and B (**47**, Figure 11). These compounds exhibited antiangiogenic activity against human umbilical vein endothelial cells [58].

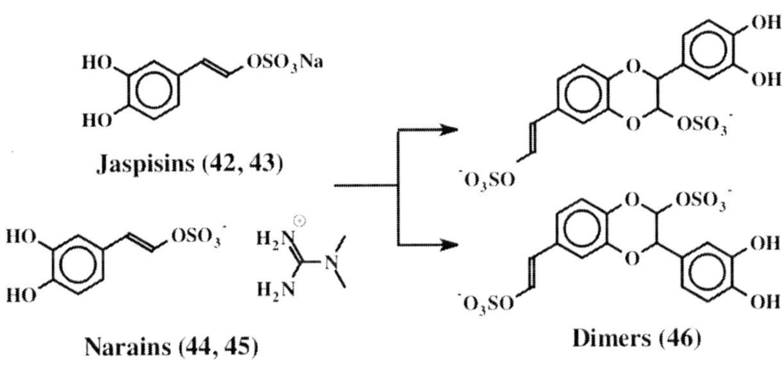

Figure 10. Dimerization of jaspisin.

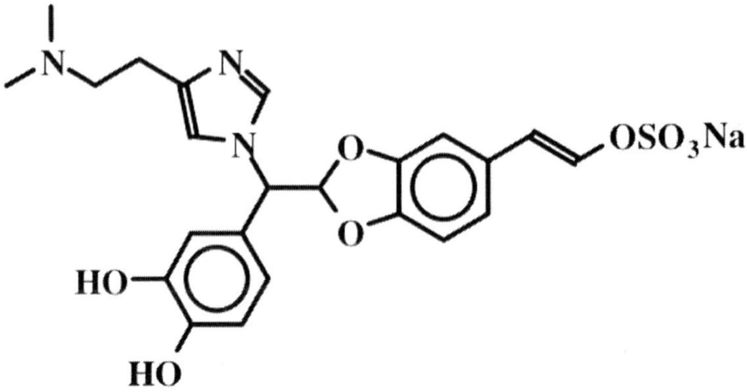

Wondonins A and B (47)

Figure 11. Structure of wondonins.

Three new imidazole alkaloids (**48**, **49** and **50**) were isolated from a Palauan sponge, *Leucetta microraphis* [59]. Although leucettamine B (**49**) was inactive, leucettamine A (**48**, structure not shown), a compound possessing extra benzylic group, showed potent inhibition of leukotriene B4 receptor binding activity with a Ki of 1.3 μM. In contrast, leucettamine C (**50**) exhibited only a mild antibiotic activity against *Eschericia coli*, *Staphylococcus aureus*, *Bacillus subtilis* and *Candida albicans*[60]. Recently, several derivatives of leucettamine B (**49**) were synthesized and shown to inhibit protein kinase activity [61]. Polyandrocarpamine A and B (**51**, **52**), are related to leucettamines. They were isolated from a Fijian ascidian [62]. Polyandrocarpamine A (**51**) exhibits selective cytotoxicity against central nervous system cell line (SF 268) with a GI value of about 65 μM [63]. The structures of these molecules are shown in Figure 12.

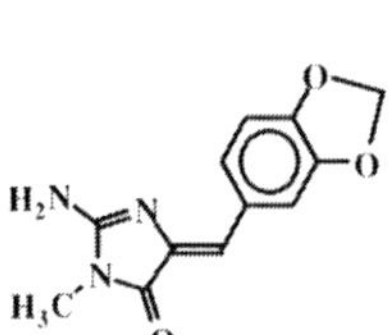

Leucettamine B (49)

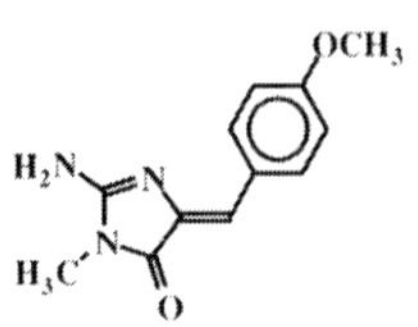

Leucettamine C (50)

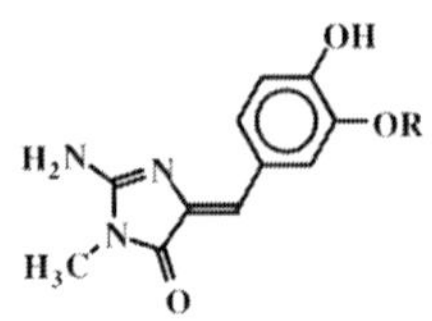

Polyandrocarpamine A (51, R = CH 3)

Polyandrocarpamine B (52, R = H)

Figure 12. Structures of polyandrocarpamines and leucettamines.

4. SIMPLE PEPTIDYL DEHYDROTYROSINE AND DEHYDRODOPA DERIVATIVES: CLIONAMIDE, MORULIN PM, AND PLICATAMIDE

The first peptide possessing a single dehydrodopa unit to be isolated from any organism was that of clionamide (**53**) extracted from the sponge *Cliona celata* [64]. It was shown to have the structure 6-bromotryptophan-dehydrotopamine (**53**). It exhibited only a mild antibiotic activity in comparison with the potency of the crude *Cliona* extracts. Subsequent studies provided a number of additional peptidyl dehydrodopa compounds that may explain this discrepancy (discussed in the next two sections).

Morulin PM (**54**) was isolated as an unusual post translationally modified peptide possessing both topa and 6-bromotryptophan residues from the morula cells of the vanadium accumulating ascidian, *Phallusia mammillata* by Taylor *et al.* [65]. Structural studies revealed that the *C*-terminal residue of the peptide possess a dehydrotopamine residue. Presence of both dehydrotopamine unit and 6-bromotryptophan in the same peptide indicates the likelihood of antibacterial activity for this compound. However, test results have not supported this hypothesis so far, although more systematic studies may resolve this issue. In this regard, it is interesting to note that the octapeptide called plicatamide (**55**), possessing the structure Phe-Phe-His-Leu-His-Phe-His-dehydrodopamine, was isolated from the tunicate, *Styela plicata*, and shown to possess powerful antibiotic activity against *Staphylococcus aureus* [9,66]. Both wild type and methicillin resistant *S. aureus*strains exhibited massive efflux of potassium ions upon exposure to plicatamide. Within seconds bacterial strains exposed to plicatamide ceased to consume molecular oxygen and became nonviable. Plicatamide (**55**) was also shown to be a potent hemolytic agent against human erythrocytes but had no effect on ovine erythrocytes [66]. Its relatively small size, combined with the rapid impact on ion channels [66], make plicatamide a powerful lead compound to develop potential antibiotic compounds in future.

While not a member of the peptidyl dehydrotyrosine and dehydrodopa derivatives category of compounds, styelins are a small group of dopa-containing peptides isolated from ascidians (*Styela* sp.) that exhibit antimicrobial activities against several kinds of bacteria and yeasts, and show cytotoxic activities against eukaryotic cells as well [67]. The hemocytes of*Styela clava* possess a 32 amino acid antimicrobial peptide, called styelin D, having multiple dopa units (but no dehydrodopa units) [8,67]. Styelin D inhibited the growth of both Gram-positive and Gram-negative bacteria and exhibited hemolytic and cytotoxic properties against eukaryotic cells. A much smaller tetra peptide possessing both dehydrotryptophan and dopa units, has been isolated and characterized from the hemocytes of the solitary ascidian,*Halocynthia roretzi* [10,68]. The remaining group of styelins (A, B, C and E), all isolated from *Styela clava*, form pores in bacteria causing leaching of nutrients and eventual cell death [67]. Two other dopa- and topa-containing peptides, halocyamines [10] and ferreascidin [12], have also been isolated from tunicates.

5. PEPTIDES WITH MULTIPLE DEHYDRODOPA UNITS: TUNICHROMES, POLYPHENOLIC PROTEIN AND CELENAMIDES

Tunichromes were the first members of this group to be isolated. Tunichromes have been isolated solely from ascidians. They are small, modified peptides that have been extracted and characterized from blood cell lysates and tissues of the phlebobranch *Ascidia nigra* (**An-1**, **An-2**, **An-3; 56**, **57**, **58**) [13–16], the stolidobranch *Molgula manhattensis* (**Mm-1**, **Mm-2; 59,60**) [16], and the phlebobranch *Phallusia mammillata* (**Pm-1**, **Pm-2**, **Pm-3; 61**, **62**, **63)** [17]. In addition, they have been identified by thin layer chromatography of hemocyte extracts in seven additional Phlebobranch species [18]. The structures of these peptidyl derivatives are presented in Figure 13 and Table 1. More recently, a modified pentapeptide tunichrome (**Sp-1; 64**) has been isolated from the hemocytes of the stolidobranch ascidian *Styela plicata* [19].

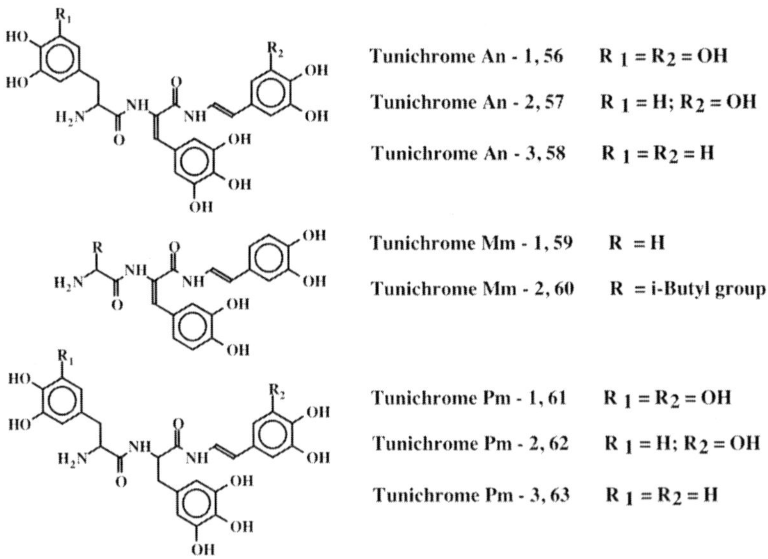

Figure 13. Structures of some tunichromes.

Table 1. Structure of some tunichromes and related compounds.

No.	Compound	Structure	References
1	Tunichrome An-1, **56**	Topa-DeTopa-DeTopamine	[14,15]
2	Tunichrome An-2, **57**	Dopa-DeTopa-DeTopamine	[14,15]
3	Tunichrome An-3, **58**	Dopa-DeTopa-DeDopamine	[14,15]
4	Tunichrome Mm-1, **59**	Gly-DeDopa-DeDopamine	[16]
5	Tunichrome Mm-2, **60**	Leu-DeDopa-DeDopamine	[16]
6	Tunichrome Pm-1, **61**	Topa-Topa-DeTopamine	[17]
7	Tunichrome Pm-2, **62**	Dopa-Topa-DeTopamine	[17]
8	Tunichrome Pm-3, **63**	Dopa-Topa-DeDopamine	[17]
9	Tunichrome Sp-1, **64**	Dopa-Dopa-Gly-Pro-DeDopamine	[19]
10	Plicatamide, **55**	Phe-Phe-His-Leu-His-Phe-His-DeDopamine	[9,66]
11	Morulin Pm, **54**	Polypeptide with 6-BrTrp & DeDopamine	[65]
12	Clionamide, **53**	6-BrTrp-DeTopamine	[64]
13	Celenamide A, **65**	Leu-DeTopa-6-BrTrp-DeDopamine	[69–71]
14	Celenamide B, **66**	Val-DeTopa-6-BrTrp-DeDopamine	[69–71]
15	Celenamide C, **67**	Leu-DeTopa-6-BrTrp-DeTyramine	[69–71]
16	Celenamide D, **68**	Leu-DeTopa-DeTopa-DeDopamine	[69–71]
17	Celenamide E, **69**	DeTopa-6-BrTrp-DeDopamine	[69–71]

Common to all tunichromes is the presence of dehydrodopamine units. Many other peptides from tunicates, though not part of the tunichrome family of compounds, also possess dehydrodopamine units (for structure, refer to Table 1). In addition, two groups of peptides isolated from the sponge *Cliona celata*, the bromotryptophan containing dipeptide clionamide (**53**, discussed in section 4) [64] and the tri- and tetrapeptide celenamides (**65–69**) [69–71], most of which contain dehydrodopamine/topamine units.

Several antibacterial peptides including styelins, clavanins, halocyamines and plicatamide have been isolated from ascidians. Many of them possess dopyl units [8,10,66–68,72–76]. Due to extreme instability and low availability, tunichromes have not been generally tested for antibiotic properties. Preliminary results, using a novel extraction protocol that maintains stability of the native compounds [77], indicate that tunichrome mixtures isolated from *Ascidia nigra*, exhibit antimicrobial activity against Gram-negative bacteria [78]. Future studies will confirm whether this antibiotic activity is widespread among the multiple dehydrodopa-containing peptides.

Asidians possessing tunichromes accumulate large amounts of trace metals such as vanadium and/or iron [16,79–81]. In*Ascidia ahodori*, vanadium comprised as much as 2% of the dry weight of the hemocytes [82]. It was originally postulated that tunichromes were involved in metal accumulation [17,79–81]. However, this hypothesis is not in harmony with the finding that the metals are located in separate blood cells from the tunichromes [83]. Studies carried out in our laboratory suggest that tunichromes are associated either with cross-linking, wound healing and/or tunic formation [78]. In this regard, it is important to point out that the monomeric unit found in tunichromes, namely dehydrodopamine, is the very same compound that is involved in the sclerotization and hardening of insect cuticle [44,45]. During cuticular hardening in insects and most arthropods, structural proteins and carbohydrate polymer chitin are cross-linked and rendered insoluble by the covalent interaction with reactive intermediates generated from sclerotizing precursors such as *N*-acetyldopamine and *N*-β-alanyldopamine, generally called *N*-acyldopamines (**70**). These two precursors are enzymatically converted to quinones (**71**), quinone methides (**72**) and dehydro *N*-acyldopamines (**73**) prior to cross-linking [44,45]. Upon enzymatic oxidation, dehydro *N*-acyldopamines (**73**) generate quinone methide imine amides (**74**) as initial two-electron oxidation products. These reactive intermediates then react non-enzymatically with chitin and protein to form protein-protein, protein-chitin and chitin-chitin adducts and cross-links that are necessary for hardening and gluing the cuticle. The course of sclerotization reactions employed by insects is depicted in Figure 14.

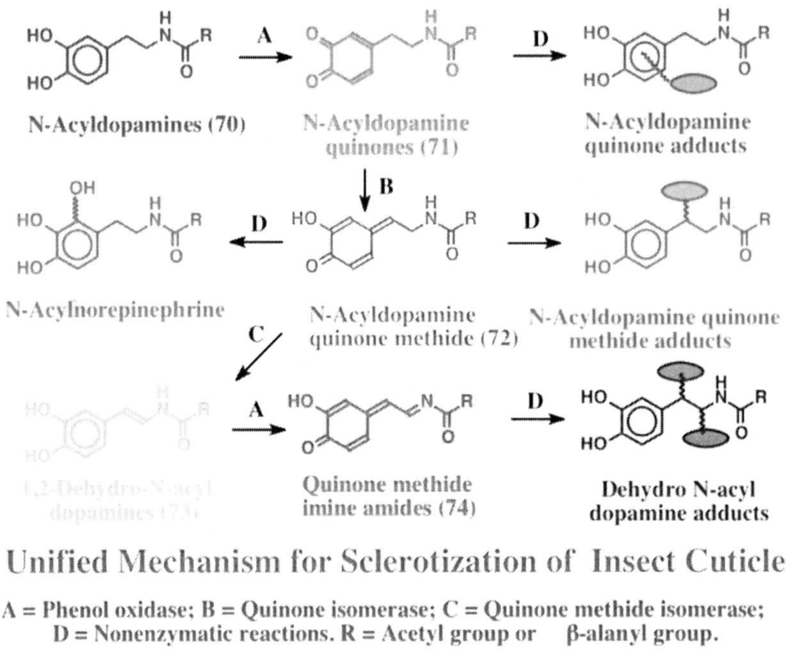

Figure 14. Mechanism associated with the sclerotization of insect cuticle.

Marine bivalves use a similar multiple dopyl-containing protein called polyphenolic protein (MW 130 kDa) under oxidative conditions to crosslink byssal threads in order to attach themselves and bind to solid surfaces [84–86]. Polyphenolic protein is composed of a decapeptide sequence containing a tyrosine and a dopa, which is repeated as many as 75 times [84]. With more than one dehydrodopa and/or dehydrodopamine units, tunichromes are likely to exhibit similar reactions, and hence may be involved in tunic formation and wound healing, which are similar to the processes involved in the hardening of insect cuticle [78].

6. Polycyclic Condensed Dehydrodopa Derivatives: Halitulin, Storniamides, Purpurones, Ningalins, Baculiferins, Lamellarin, Dictyodendrins, Polycitrins, Polycitones and Lukainols

Kashman *et al.* [87], who have examined the chemistry and bioactivity of a number of marine sponges, found that the extract of the sponge, *Haliclona tulearensis* (family Chalinidae) possessed cytotoxic activity and isolated an active component, which they named halitulin (**75**, Figure 15). This compound exhibited an IC_{50} value of: (a) 25 μg/mL against P-388 murine leukemia cell line; (b) 12 μg/mL against A-549 human lung carcinoma cells; (c) 12 μg/mL against HT-29 human colon carcinoma cells; and (d) 25 μg/mL against MEL-28 human melanoma cell line. In addition to possessing a pyrrole entity, halitulin also, interestingly enough, possess fused dehydrodopamine units [87].

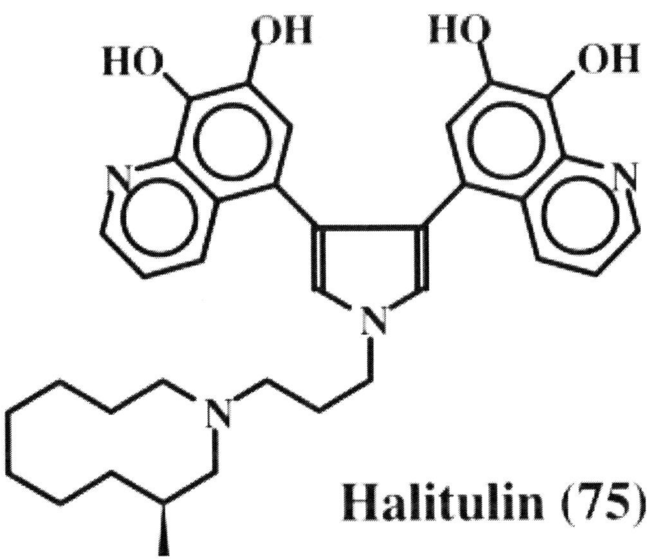

Figure 15. Structure of halitulin.

Marine sponges of the genus *Cliona* (family Clionidae) have turned out to be rich sources of dehydrodopa containing compounds (see previous discussions in Sections 4 and 5). Clionidae are burrowing organisms that live on calcareous substrates such as coral shells and rocks. They cause serious damage to coral beds and oyster reefs, since they can bore into calcareous structures easily. As mentioned earlier, clionamide (**53**, Section 4) and celenamides (**65–69**, Section 5) were two groups of compounds that were initially isolated from *Cliona celata.* Subsequently Palermo *et al.* [88] isolated storniamides A–D (**76–79**, Figure 16) through a bioassay guided fractionation procedure, and identified them to be a new group of pyrrole alkaloids exhibiting antibiotic activity against several Gram-positive bacteria. Bogar's group [89] further studied these compounds and showed that they possess cytotoxicity against leukemia cell lines. In addition, they also identified multi drug resistance (MDR) reversal activity. Furstner *et al.* [90] also reported that storniamide A (**76**) possesses a DNA cleaving property, in addition to MDR reversal activity. Storniamides are probably biosynthesized by free radical coupling of the dipeptide, tyr-tyr followed by oxidative decarboxylation of the *C*-terminal carboxylic group. Dehydrotyrosyl-dehydrotyramine dimeric peptide thus formed, upon condensation with *p*-hydroxyphenylacetaldehyde (produced by monoamine oxidation of tyramine) will produce the basic stroniamide skeleton.

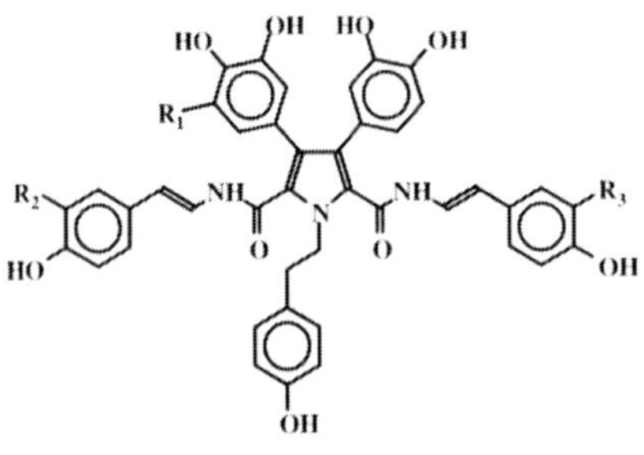

	R_1	R_2	R_3
Storniamide A, 76,	OH	H	H
Storniamide B, 77,	OH	H	OH
Storniamide C, 78,	H	OH	OH
Storniamide D, 79,	OH	OH	OH

Figure 16. Structures of Storniamides.

A purple colored pentacylic dehydrodopa derivative called purpurone (**80**, Figure 17), was isolated from the Indopacific sponge of the genus *Iotrochota*, which was shown to inhibit ATP citrate lyase activity with an IC_{50} value of 25 mg/mL [91]. ATP citrate lyase is essential for the synthesis of acetyl CoA and hence reduction in the production of acetyl CoA could drastically affect both lipogenesis and choleterogenesis. Therefore, purpurone (**80**) could be a valuable drug to lower low-density lipoproteins, which are produced from fatty acid and cholesterol. Since purpurone was liberated by acid hydrolysis, it is probably present as a sugar and/or protein conjugate. Purpurone (**80**) has also been isolated from a south sea marine sponge of the same genus, *Iotrochota*, by a bioactivity-guided protocol aimed at identifying antioxidant compounds by Liu *et al.* [92].

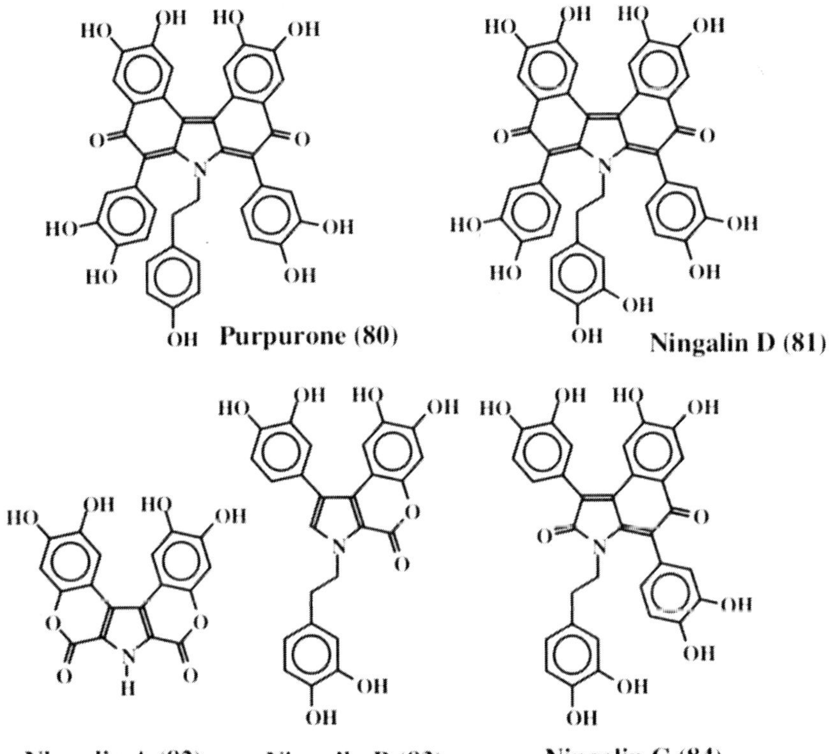

Purpurone (80) Ningalin D (81)

Ningalin A (82) Ningalin B (83) Ningalin C (84)

Figure 17. Structures of purpurone and ningalins.

A hydroxylated derivative of purpurone was subsequently isolated from a western Australian unidentified ascidian belonging to the genus *Didemnum* and named ningalin D (**81**) [93]. These authors also isolated a number of biogenetically related compounds that were like purpurone from the same organism (ningalins A, B, and C; **82–84**, Figure 17). Both ningalins, as well as their derivatives, exhibited marked cytotoxicity against several cancer cell lines. In addition, they also exhibited significant MDR reversal activity at non-cytotoxic concentrations [94,95]. Recently a group of about five different compounds that are derivatives of purpurone and ningalins were isolated from the Chinese marine sponge, *Iotrochota* *baculifera* and shown to possess anti HIV-1 activity [96]. Since ningalins resemble a number of lamellarins, it was proposed that ningalins might serve as the biosynthetic precursor for a number of lamellarins [93].

Lamellarins are a group of over seventy different polycyclic condensed aromatic compounds [11]. Faulker and his group first reported the isolation and characterization of four lamellarins from the prosobranch mollusc, *Lamellaria* sp. in 1985 and named them lamellarin A–D [97]. Subsequently, four additional members of this group (E–H) were isolated form the didemnid ascidian *Didemnum chartaceum* [98]. Since then, as many as seventy different, yet structurally closely related, polycyclic aromatic condensed compounds have been isolated from a variety of marine organism possessing a wide range of biological activities that include (yet not limited to) cytotoxicity, antibiotic activity, antitumor activity, antioxidant activity, MDR reversal activity, HIV integrase inhibition, human aldose reductase inhibition, cell division inhibition, immunomodulatory activity, and feeding deterrent activity [11]. Since an excellent review article is available solely on all lamellarins [11], it is unnecessary to review the structure function aspect of lamellarins again here. Lamellarins fall broadly under three structural categories shown in Figure 18. The majority of the lamellarins possess either Type 1a or 1b structures (**85**, **86**). These compounds contain the dehydrodopamine unit. The last structure (*i.e.*, unfused lamellarins, **87**) lacks the dehydrodopamine unit but possesses instead dehydrotyramine unit. Only a few compounds (about four) belong to this category. Interestingly, a number of related compounds possessing only dehydrotyramine units are also identified from marine organisms and the rest of this section deals with such compounds. Even though they are not dehydrodopamine containing molecules, since they are all polycyclic condensed molecules similar to lamellarins, they are listed here for simplicity's sake.

Warabi *et al.* [99] isolated five compounds, which they named dictyodendrins (A–E; **88**–**92**), from the sponge*Dictyodendrilla verongiformis*, as potent inhibitors of telomerase. Structures of some of these compounds along with two related compounds (**93**, **94**) [100] are shown in Figure 19. Telomerase, which adds repeats of TTAGGG units called telomeres, to the 3'-end of chromosomes, is inhibited by these compounds at 50 μg/mL level. Since telomerase is found nearly in 90% of cancer cells but not in any significant amount in normal cells, this finding could pave the way to the development of new kinds of anticancer drugs.

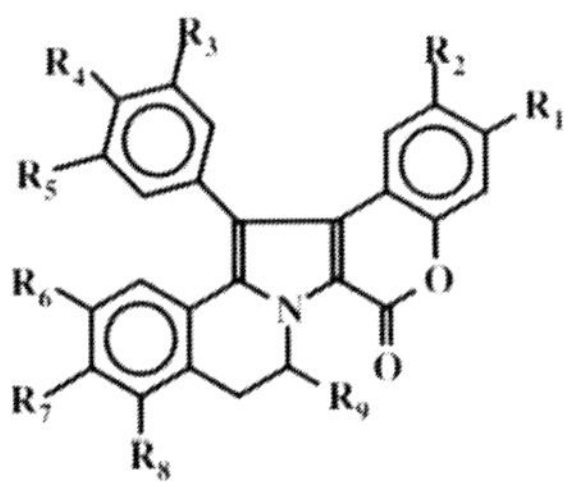

Lamellarin Type 1a (85)

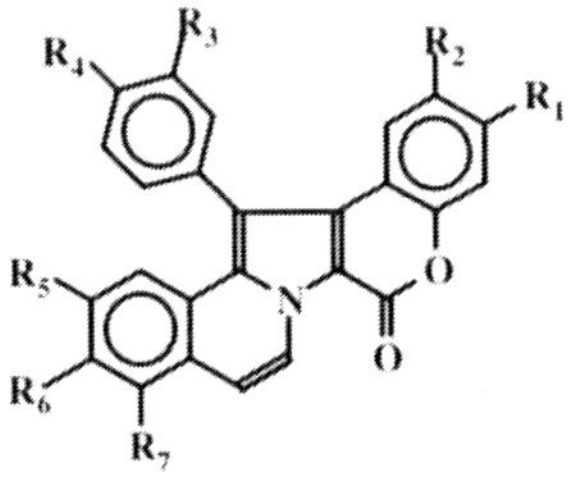

Lamellarin Type 1b (86)

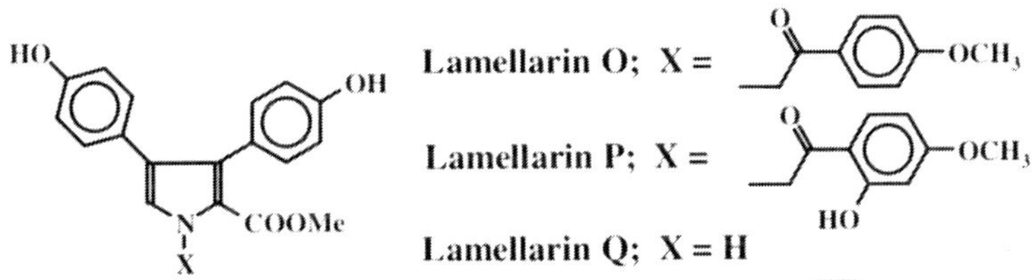

unfused lamellarins (87)

Figure 18. Structures of lamellarins.

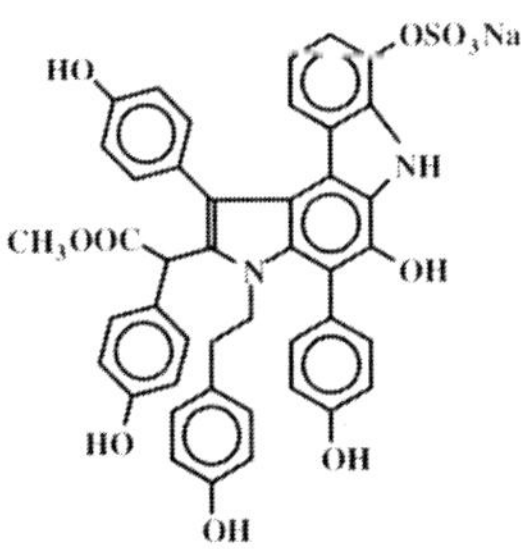

Dictyodendrin A (88)

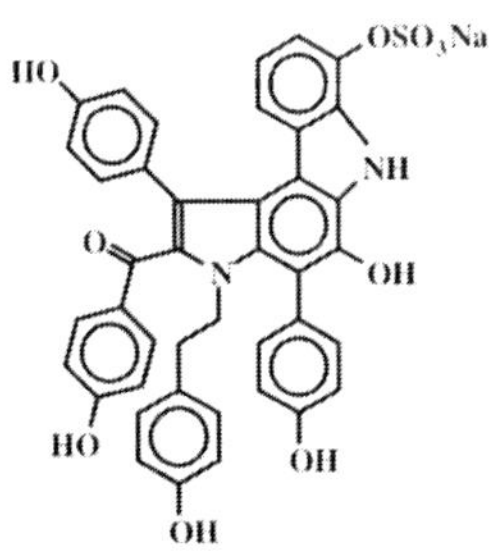

Dictyodendrin B (89)

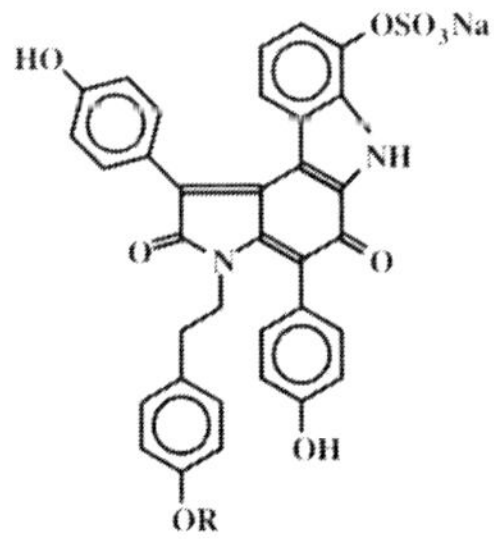

Dictyodendrin (90, 91)
(C = H; D = OSO 3Na)

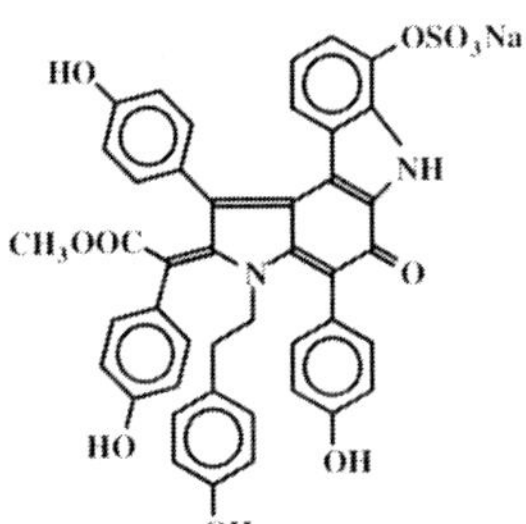

Dictyodendrin E (92)

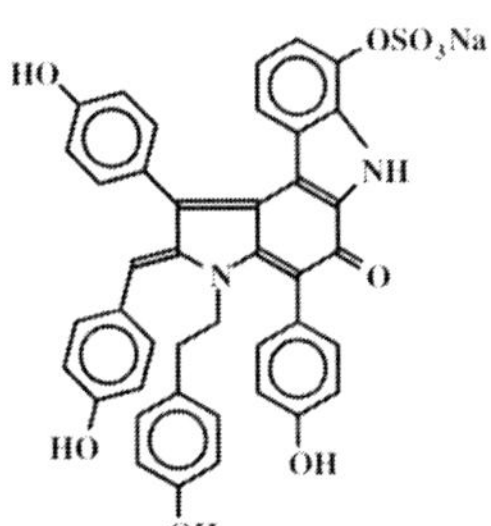

Dictyodendrin X (93)

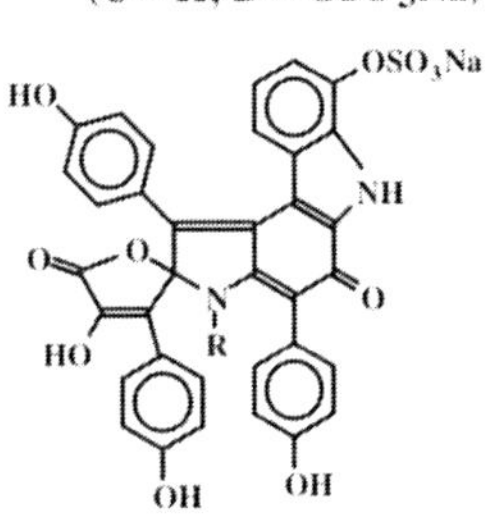

Dictyodendrin Y (94)

Figure 19. Structures of dictyodendrins.

Rudi *et al.* [101] isolated polycitrin A (**95**) and polycitone A (**96**) (Figure 20) from the ascidian, *Polycitor* sp. in 1994 and showed that the penta-*O*-methyl derivative of polycitone A (**96**) could inhibit SV40 transformed fibroblast cells at concentrations as low as 10 μg/mL. Subsequently, this group was able to demonstrate the inhibition of retroviral reverse transcriptases (isolated from human immunodeficiency virus, murine leukemia virus, and mouse mammary tumor virus) as well as cellular DNA polymerase (DNA polymerase B and *E. coli* DNA polymerase I) activities by polycitone A (**96**) [102]. Furthermore, they also isolated polycitone B (**97**) and prepolycitrin A from the ascidian, *Polycitor africanus* [103].

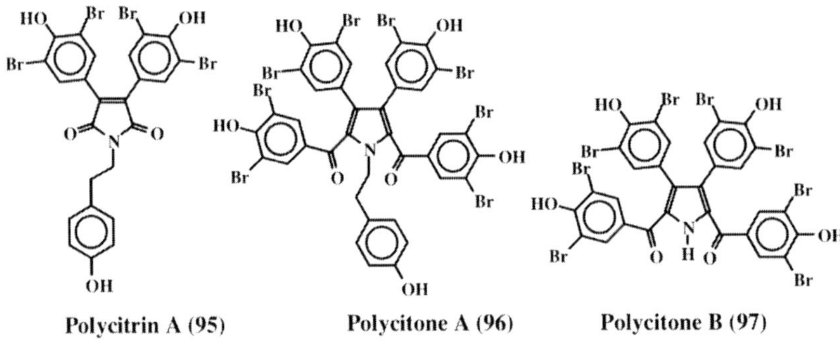

Figure 20. Structure of polycitrin A (**95**) and polycitones (**96, 97**).

From the extracts of a Pacific tunicate, Scheuer *et al.* [104] isolated lukianol A and B (**98, 99**; Figure 21). Both compounds exhibited toxicity against a human epidermatoid carcinoma cell line. Lukianol A (**98**) possessed a minimum inhibitory concentration of 1 μg/mL and lukianol B (**99**) possessed a minimum inhibitory concentration of 100 μg/mL. Subsequently, Boger *et al.* [89] synthesized and tested lukianol A (**98**) and other related synthetic compounds on a group of cancer cell lines. The results indicated that these compounds possessed IC_{50} values ranging from 1–20 μM. Although lukianol A did not possess any MDR reversal activity on the cellular P-glycoprotein efflux pump, one of its synthetic precursors showed a reasonable MDR reversal activity at non-cytotoxic concentrations. In this regard, it is interesting to note that the pyrroles possessing phenolic substituents seem to be associated with cytotoxicity, whereas phenolic ethers tend to exhibit MDR reversal activity. Gupton's group [105,106] synthesized one of the key intermediate of lukianol A (**98**) and demonstrated its potent cytotoxicity against a number of cancer cell lines with ED_{50} values ranging from of 3–20 μM. In the lymphocytic leukemia cell lines, this compound also inhibited both DNA synthesis and protein synthesis by inhibiting a number of key enzymes such as DNA polymerase a, some RNA polymerases, ribonucleotide reductase, dihydrofolate reductase, phosphoribosyl pyrophosphate transferase and IMP dehydrogenase [105,106]. Even compounds with only one aryl group showed cytotoxicity at the same level as the diaryl pyrrole [105,106].

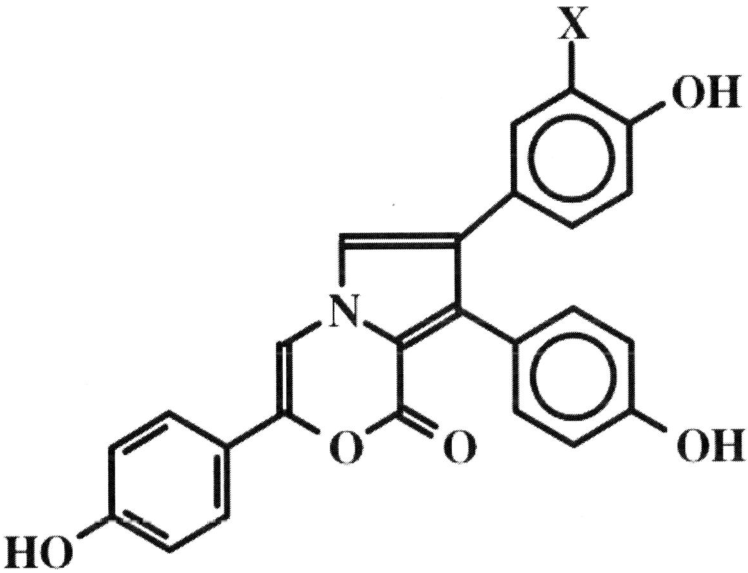

Lukianol A (98, X = H)
Lukianol B (99, X = I)

Figure 21. Structure of lukianols.

7. BIOGENESIS OF DEHYDRO COMPOUNDS

From the foregoing discussion it is evident that unusually large numbers of dehydrotyrosine and dehydrodopa compounds are biosynthesized in marine organisms. In spite of accumulation of such a vast knowledge on the isolation and characterization of a plethora of these molecules, the information on their biosynthetic pathways is pretty scarce. Therefore, one can only hypothesize on their biosynthetic mechanism(s), based on what little is known about the biosynthesis of dehydrotyrosine and dehydrodopa compounds. From the structures, it is evident that these compounds arise by the introduction of the double bond in the side chain of the saturated derivatives of the parent compounds *viz.*, tyrosine and dopa. Examination of the biosynthetic literature on the fate of tyrosine and dopa reveals that two different routes make dehydrotyrosine and dehydrodopa derivatives. The introduction of the double bond in peptidyl tyrosine units can be achieved by the action of the recently identified enzyme, tyrosine side chain oxidase [107]. This enzyme, first identified in the biosynthesis of the antibiotic compound, chondrochloren (**100**, **101**) produced by *Chondromyces crocatus*, causes oxidative decarboxylation of an acyltyrosine peptide (**102**) (synthesized by nonribosomal peptide synthesis) to a dehydrotyramine containing compound (Figure 22).

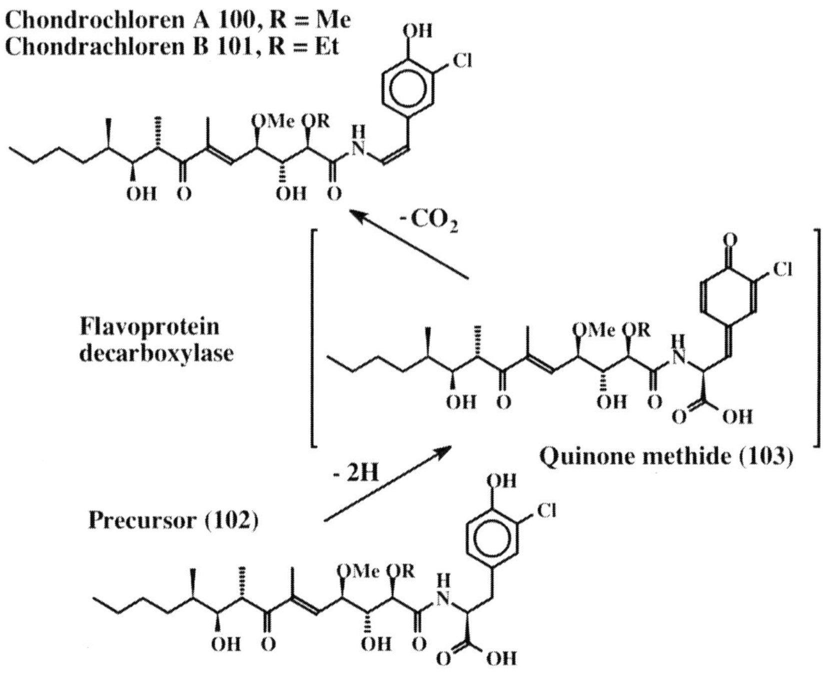

Figure 22. Formation of dehydrotyramine.

Isolation and expression of the gene in *E. coli* and examining the gene product revealed that it is a FAD-dependent oxidative decarboxylase [107]. It seems to oxidize tyrosine precursor (**102**) to a transient quinone methide (**103**) by extracting two hydrogen atoms from the 1,6 position (from the phenolic group and the methylene group, as shown inFigure 22). The resultant quinone methide (**103**) spontaneously loses the carboxyl group and undergoes isomerization to a dehydrotyramine-containing compound (**100**, **101**). If the carboxyl group is blocked by acylation, such as peptide bond formation, the carboxyl group will remain intact. Loss of a proton from the neighboring methylene group in such molecules and simultaneous aromatization of the quinone methide nucleus, results in the generation of dehydrotyrosine units. On the other hand, if the carboxyl group is unprotected, it will suffer a rapid and spontaneous nonenzymatic decarboxylation reaction accompanied by the aromatization of the quinone methide nucleus that generates dehydrotyramines. A direct hydroxylation of dehydrotyrosines and dehydrotyramines by a tyrosinase type enzyme can lead to the dehydro derivatives of dopa and dopamine. Alternatively, dehydrodopa and dehydrodopamines can also be made from their saturated analogs by a different route. The amino acid tyrosine is converted to dopa in a number of biological systems by the action of a specific tyrosine hydroxylase as well as by tyrosinase. While tyrosine hydroxylase reaction stops at the production of dopa, the tyrosinase acts further on the resultant dopa generating dopaquinone as the transient two-electron oxidant product. Dopaquinone is highly unstable and undergoes rapid intramolecular cyclization producing leucochrome initially, which gets further oxidized nonenzymatically to produce a series of compounds that finally result in the polymerization and production of melanin pigments [44,45,108]. This reaction, which is useful for the biosynthesis of melanin polymer, is not very helpful for producing dehydro derivatives of dopa and dopamine. Protecting the amino group by acylation deactivates the amino group reactivity and prevents the intramolecular cyclization of protected dopaquinones. Such compounds, upon oxidation by tyrosinase, can generate dehydrodopa derivatives. For instance, the deaminated dopa, dihydrocaffeic acid (**104**), upon oxidation by tyrosinase produces both dihydroesculetin (**105**, a cyclized product) and traces of caffeic acid (desaturated product) as shown in Figure 23 [109]. If the carboxyl group is also prevented from exhibiting intramolecular cyclization reaction—say by amide formation or esterification—the resultant dihydrocaffeate derivates (**106**) solely exhibit side chain desaturation reaction when oxidized by tyrosinase [109,110]. The reaction was shown to occur by the spontaneous isomerization of tyrosinase produced quinone (**107**) to quinone methide (**108**) and subsequent aromatization of the quinone methide with the introduction of the double bond in the side chain leading to the caffeic acid derivatives (**109**) (Figure 23).

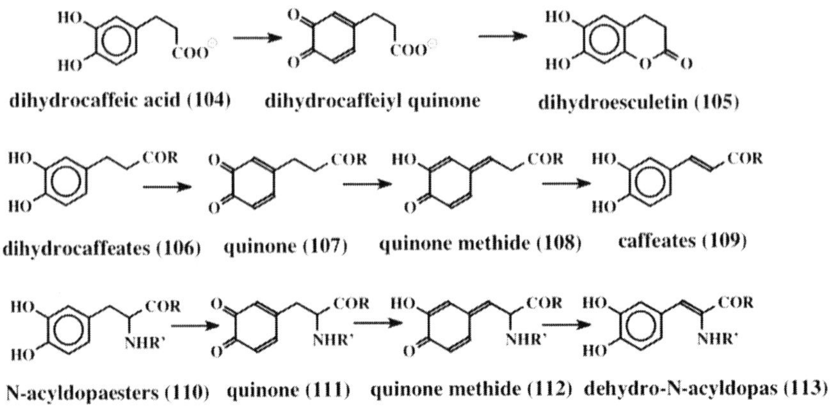

Figure 23. Oxidative transformation of protected dopa compounds. Deaminated dopa (dihydrocaffeic acid), upon oxidation to quinone, undergoes intramolecular cyclization, producing a dihydroesculetin type structure that is prevalent in lamellarins and other compounds (top line). If the carboxyl group is protected, the resultant quinone undergoes isomerization to quinone methide and then produces dehydro compounds (middle line). The same reaction is also exhibited by *N*-acyldopa esters, as shown on the last line.

Dopa derivatives also exhibit this reaction when both the carboxyl and amino groups are protected by acylation and amide formation. Accordingly, the tyrosinase generated quinones from both *N*-acetyldopa methyl ester and ethyl esters **(110)** exhibit spontaneous isomerization reaction to produce dehydrodopa derivatives (**113**) via quinone (**111**) and quinone methide intermediates (**112**) [111,112]. Thus peptidyl dopa derivatives can be converted to dehydro dopa units by simple tyrosinases that are present ubiquitously in biological systems without the need for any other enzymes. On the other hand, if the carboxyl (or carbonyl) group is absent to assist the quinone-to-quinone methide conversion, as in the case of 1,2-dehydro-*N*-acyldopamine production, there is a need for additional enzymatic catalysts [113–115]. If the carboxyl group in dopa is decarboxylated to dopamine, direct introduction of the double bond into its side chain is rather difficult. However, this reaction is achieved by the use of tyrosinase and quinone isomerases [44,45]. Unprotected simple dopamine will generate only melanin type molecules as mentioned earlier. But if the amino group is protected by acylation, *N*-acyldopamines thus formed, upon oxidation by tyrosine will produce *N*-acyldopamine quinones that are quite stable. We have identified two separate isomerases—one that acts on *N*-acyldopamine quinone producing quinone methide [113,114] and the other, which acts on the resultant quinone methide producing the side chain desaturated product—dehydrodopamine [115]. Thus if the carboxyl group is removed from dopa, one has to have two additional enzymes to cause the isomerization of the quinone and the quinone methide (shown in Figure 14). Finally, dehydrodopamine can also arise from the decarboxylation of amino protected dopaquinone derivatives after quinone methide formation, much like the tyrosyl peptide to dehydrotyramine peptide route discussed above.

Examination of the structures of a number of condensed compounds indicates that coumarin type molecules are also formed routinely in ningalins and lamellarins. This condensation can occur by intramolecular cyclization of *N*-protected dopyl compounds to form the six-membered ring [109]. We have shown such a facile cyclization as early as 1989 in the case of dihydrocaffeic acid (Figure 23 top line). Finally, enzymology of the biosynthetic process of all these naturally occurring compounds is practically untouched and might yield rich details for future investigators. All our attempts to identify the isomerases in ascidians have so far fallen short of confirming their presence in tunicates. More biochemical studies are necessary to throw light on this process.

8. CONCLUSIONS

Dehydrotyrosyl and dehydrodopyl compounds have been isolated from a broad range of invertebrate phyla (Table 2). These compounds are generally either peptides or small proteins. All have been isolated from organisms that are sedentary as adults. Furthermore, each of these compounds is bioactive to some degree, most likely due to the highly reactive catechol group(s). However, different types of bioactivity have been reported for different compounds, including antibiotic and other defense activities, enzyme inhibition, free radical mediation, wound repair, and structural crosslinking of components of exoskeletons. All of these varied processes can be, in theory, attributed to reactive catechols. Surprisingly, these diverse compounds appear quite common in two widely separated Phyla—the simple metazoan sponges (Phylum Porifera) and, at the opposite extreme, the bilateral eumetazoan deuterostome ascidians (Phylum Chordata, subphylum Urochordata). Examples have also been isolated from intermediate phyla, including the radially symmetrical Phylum Cnidaria (hydroids), and the bilateral protostome Phylum Mollusca (bivalves). Even more surprising, several of the same dopa-containing compounds have been isolated from members of different phyla (Table 2). The simple dehydrodopa compound tubastrine has been found in a sponge, a coelenterate and an ascidian. In the ascidian, not only has the monomeric tubastrine (**36**) been identified, but a dimeric form (named orthidine, **37–41**) has also been isolated. In addition, the tri-peptide tunichromes, which are widespread in the ascidians, are structurally similar to the bromotryptophan-containing dipeptide clionamide (**53**) and to the tri- and tetra-peptide celenamides (**65–69**), both of which are found in sponges. Finally, the more complex, polycyclic condensed dehydrodopa compound purpurone (**80**) was originally isolated from a sponge, but has also turned up in an ascidian as a hydroxylated derivative, ningalin D (**81**). A second polycyclic dehydrodopa family, the lamellarins, was isolated from both a snail and an ascidian.

Table 2. Dehydrotyrosyl and dehydrodopyl compounds found in various groups of marine invertebrates. The five categories are explained in the text. The same compound isolated from different groups of animals is highlighted in red.

Category	Sponges	Coelenterates	Molluscs	Ascidians
1	Hamigeramine (**15**); Hamigeroxalamic acid (**16**); Anthosamine A & B (**25**, **26**); Cyclo-L-arginine-dehydrotyrosine (**27**)	Tridentatols A–D (**17–20**)		Botryllamide (**5–14**); Rigidin A–D (**28–31**)
2	*Tubastrine* (36); Jaspisin (**42**); Isojaspisin (**43**); Narains (**44**, **45**); Wondonins (**47**); Leucettamine A–C (**48–50**)	*Tubastrine* (36)		*Tubastrine* (36); *Orthidines* (37–41); Polyandrocarpamine A & B (**51**, **52**)
3	Clionamide (**53**)			Morulin PM (**54**); Plicatamide (**55**); Styelin A–D
4	Celenamides (**65–69**)		Polyphenolic protein	Tunichromes (**56–64**)
5	*Purpurone* (80); Halitulin (**75**); Storniamide A–D (**76–79**); Dictyodendrin A–E (**88–92**)		Lamellarin A–D	*Ningalin D* (81); Ningalin A–C (**82–84**); Lamellarin E–H; Polycitrin A (**95**); Polycitone A & B (**96**, **97**); Lukianol A & B (**98**, **99**)

Given this widespread distribution of dehydrotyrosyl and dehydrodopyl compounds among the invertebrate phyla, and the discovery of the same compounds in widely separate phyla, it appears that the ability to synthesize this group of compounds arose very early in evolutionary history, and has been retained by a variety of animals because of its selective advantage. It is also possible that bacterial symbionts could form a potential source of these compounds. It is likely that examples of these compounds have been found in sponges, hydroids, bivalves and ascidians simply because scientists happened to have looked for them in these groups. If this is the case, then it is very likely that similar compounds are present in other phyla that have yet to be examined. Since all of the organisms that have been successfully assayed to date are sedentary organism, the search for additional compounds should probably begin with members of the fouling communities, including additional hydroids, sedentary polychaete worms, barnacles, bryozoans, and ectoprocts. In addition, one major phylum that has yet to be tested is the ecdhinoderms (seastars, brittle stars, sea urchins, sea cucumbers,*etc.*).

A careful "deconstruction" of all the compounds mentioned in this review indicates that they all start the same way, perhaps from peptidyltyrosine and/or peptidyldopa units. They are most likely synthesized primarily by two different routes. The first involves post-translational modification of simple peptides obtained by traditional ribosomal synthesis. The second employs nonribosomal peptidyl assembly followed by post-translational modification of the resultant small peptide. Both routes are likely to function. Additional post-translational modifications are necessary to produce the final compounds in many cases. Neither the mechanisms nor the sites of synthesis of these compounds have yet been explored.

As a final note, compiling the list of compounds we have reported on in this review (e.g., Table 2) was not a trivial task, given the morass of common names published in the literature. Nomenclature was not based on structural attributes (e.g., tyrosyl or dopyl based), making literature searches difficult. We could very easily have missed additional related compounds in our searches. We highly recommend that authors carefully consider structurally based nomenclature and use structurally based key words (e.g., dehydrotyrosine, dehydrodopa, *etc.*) when publishing newly discovered natural products.

We have reviewed the widespread occurrence of dehydrotyrosyl and dehydrodopyl containing compounds in marine invertebrate phyla, and have highlighted the structural similarities among them. Furthermore, we have speculated that all of these compounds originate via common pathways. Now that we better understand the interrelationships among these compounds, more in-depth structural comparisons relative to a specific type of bioactivity is now possible. For example, all of these structures should be compared in the context of antimicrobial activity. This will allow us to suggest structural modifications (reactive and nonreactive side groups, hydroxylations, methylations, *etc.*) that could be used to optimize antimicrobial activity. These suggested changes can be tested following synthesis of model compounds in the laboratory. At the same time, we should not avoid a further search for new lead dehydrotyrosyl and dehydrodopyl compounds in additional species of sponges, coelenterates, molluscs and ascidians, as well as in other marine phyla that have so far been overlooked. This will provide us with additional structures to include in our scheme of possible structural similarities.

REFERENCES

1. Von Nussbaum, F; Brands, M; Hinzen, B; Weigand, S; Häbich, D. Antibacterial natural products in medicinal chemistry—Exodus or revival. Angew Chem Int Ed Engl 2006, 45, 5072–5129.

2. Slama, TG. Gram-negative antibiotic resistance: There is a price to pay. Crit Care 2008, 12, 1–7.

3. Nikaido, H. Multidrug resistance in bacteria. Annu Rev Biochem 2009, 78, 119–146.

4. McKinney, ML; Schoch, RM; Yonavjak, L. Environmental Science: Systems and Solutions, 4th ed; Jones and Bartlett Publishers: Sudbury, MA, USA, 2007.

5. Brusca, RC; Brusca, GJ. Invertebrates; Sinauer Associates: Sunderland, MA, USA, 1990.

6. Van Epps, HL. René Dubos: Unearthing antibiotics. J Exp Med 2006, 203, 259.

7. Zeng, L; Swalla, BJ. Molecular phylogeny of the protochordates: Chordate evolution. Can J Zool 2005, 83, 24–33.

8. Taylor, SW; Craig, AF; Fischer, WH; Park, M; Lehrer, RI. Styelin D, an extensively modified antimicrobial peptide from ascidian hemocytes. J Biol Chem 2000, 275, 38417–38426.

9. Tincu, JA; Craig, AG; Taylor, SW. Plicatamide: A lead to the biosynthetic origins of the tunichromes. Biochem Biophys Res Commun 2000, 270, 421–424.

10. Azumi, K; Yokosawa, H; Ishii, S. Halocyamines: Novel antibacterial tetrapeptide-like structures isolated from the hemocytes of the solitary ascidian halocynthia roretzi. Biochemistry 1990, 29, 159–165.

11. Fan, H; Peng, J; Hamann, MT; Hu, JF. Lamellarins and related pyrrole derived alkaloids from marine organisms. Chem Rev 2008, 108, 264–287.

12. Dorsett, LC; Hawkins, CJ; Grice, JA; Lavin, MF; Merefield, PM; Parry, DL; Ross, IL. Ferreascidin: A highly aromatic protein containing 3,4-

dihydroxypphenylalanine from the blood cells of a stolidobranch ascidian. Biochemistry 1987,26, 8078–8082.

13. Macara, IG; McLeod, GC; Kustin, K. Isolation, properties and structural studies on a compound from tunicate blood cells that may be involved in vanadium accumulation. Biochem J 1979, 181, 457–465.

14. Bruening, RC; Oltz, EM; Furukawa, J; Nakanishi, K. Isolation and structure of tunichrome B-1, a reducing blood pigment from the tunicate Ascidia nigra L. J Am Chem Soc 1985, 107, 5298–5300.

15. Bruening, RC; Oltz, EM; Furukawa, J; Nakanishi, K; Kustin, K. Isolation of tunichrome B-1, a reducing blood pigment of the sea squirt Ascidia nigra. J Nat Prod 1986, 49, 193–204.

16. Oltz, EM; Bruening, RC; Smith, MJ; Kustin, K; Nakanishi, K. The tunichromes. A class of reducing blood pigments from sea squirts: Isolation, structures and vanadium chemistry. J Am Chem Soc 1988, 110, 6162–6172.

17. Bayer, E; Schiefer, G; Waidelich, D; Scippa, S; De Vincentiis, M. Structure of the tunichrome of tunicates and its role in concentration of vanadium. Angew Chem Int Ed Engl 1992, 31, 52–54.

18. Parry, DL; Brand, SG; Kustin, K. Distribution of tunichromes in the Ascidiacea. Bull Mar Sci 1992, 50, 302–306.

19. Tincu, JA; Taylor, SW. Tunichrome Sp-1: New pentapeptide tunichrome from the hemocytes of Styela plicata. J Nat Prod2002, 65, 377–378.

20. Okuma, K; Anzai, S; Suzuki, S. A new antibiotic, tuberine, V: Biological activities of tuberine analogs. J Antibiot 1962,15, 202–209.

21. Umezawa, H; Imoto, M; Sawa, T; Isshiki, K; Matsuda, N; Uchida, T; Iinuma, H; Hamada, M; Takeuchi, T. Studies on a new epidermal growth factor-receptor kinase inhibitor, erbstatin, produced by MH435-hF3. J Antibiot 1986, 39, 170–173.

22. Leem, JY; Jeong, IM; Park, KT; Park, HY. Isolation of p-hydroxycinnamaldehyde as an antibacterial substance from the saw fly, Acantholyda parki S. FEBS Lett 1999, 442, 53–56.

23. Marchand, J; Pais, M; Monseur, X; Jarreau, FX. Alcaloides peptidiques—VII. Les lasiodines A et B, alcoloides duLasidiscus marmoratus. C.H. Wright (Rhamnacees). Tetrahedron 1969, 25, 937–954.

24. McDonald, LA; Swersey, JC; Ireland, CM; Carroll, AR; Coll, JC; Bowden, BF; Fairchild, CR; Cornell, L. Botryllamides A–D. New brominated tyrosine derivatives from styelid ascidians of the genus. Botryllus Tetrahedron 1995, 51, 5237–5244.

25. Henrich, CJ; Robey, RW; Takada, K; Bokesch, HR; Bates, SE; Shukla, S; Ambudkar, SV; McMohan, JB; Gustafson, KR. Botryllamides: Natural product inhibitors of ABCG2. ACS Chem Biol 2009, 4, 637–647.

26. Takada, K; Imamura, N; Gustafson, KR; Henrich, CJ. Synthesis and structure-activity relationship of botryllamides that block the ABCG2 multidrug transporter. Bioorg Med Chem Lett 2010, 20, 1330–1333.

27. Hassan, W; Edrada, R; Ebel, R; Wray, V; Proksch, P. New alkaloids from the Mediterranean sponge Hamigera hamigera.Mar Drugs 2004, 2, 88–100.

28. Lindquist, N; Lobkovsky, E; Clardy, J. Tridentatols A–C, novel natural products of the marine hydroid Tridentata marginata. Tetrahedron Lett 1996, 37, 9131–9134.

29. Johnson, MK; Alexander, KE; Lindquist, N; Loo, G. Potent antioxidant activity of a dithiocarbamate related compound from a marine hydroid. Biochem Pharmacol 1999, 58, 1313–1319.

30. Stachowicz, JJ; Lindquist, N. Chemical defense among hydroids on pelagic Sargassum: Predator deterrence and absorption of solar UV radiation by secondary metabolites. Mar Ecol Prog Ser 1997, 155, 115–126.

31. Lindquist, N. Tridentatols D–H, nematocyst metabolites and precursors of the activated chemical defense in the marine hydroid Tridentata marginata (Kirchenpauer 1864. J. Nat. Prod 2002, 65, 681–684.

32. Tsukamoto, S; Kato, H; Hirota, H; Fusetani, N. Pipecolate derivates, anthosamines A and B inducers of larval metamorphosis in ascidians, from a marine sponge, Anthosigmella aff. raromicrosclera. Tetrahedron 1995, 51, 6687–6694.

33. Kobayashi, J; Cheng, JF; Kikuchi, Y; Ishibashi, M; Yamamura, S; Ohizumi, Y; Ohta, T; Nozoe, S. Rigidin, a novel alkaloid with calmodulin antagonistic activity from the okinawan marine tunicate Eudistoma cf. rigida. Tetrahedron Lett 1990, 31, 4617–4620.

34. Tsuda, M; Nozawa, K; Shimbo, K; Kobayashi, J. Rigidins B–D, New pyrrolopyrimidine alkaloids from a tunicate Cystodytes species. J Nat Prod 2003, 66, 292–294.

35. Andersen, SO; Roepstorff, P. Sclerotization of insect cuticle—II Isolation and identification of phenolic dimers from sclerotized insect cuticle. Insect Biochem 1981, 11, 25–31.

36. Andersen, SO; Jacobsen, JP; Roepstorff, P. Studies of the sclerotization of insect cuticle—The structure of dimeric products formed by incubation of N-acetyldopamine with locust cuticle. Tetrahedron 1980, 36, 3249–3252.

37. Andersen, SO; Roepstorff, P. Sclerotization of insect cuticle—III. An unsaturated derivative of N-acetyldopamine and its role in sclerotization. Insect Biochem 1982, 12, 269–276.

38. Sugumaran, M; Dali, H; Semensi, V; Hennigan, B. Tyrosinase catalyzed unusual oxidative dimerization of 1,2-dehydro-N-acetyldopamine. J Biol Chem 1987, 262, 10546–10549.

39. Sugumaran, M; Hennigan, B; Semensi, V; Dali, H. On the nature of nonenzymatic and enzymatic oxidation of the putative sclerotizing precursor, 1,2-dehydro-N-acetyldopamine. Arch Insect Biochem Physiol 1988, 8, 89–100.

40. Sugumaran, M; Schinkmann, K; Bedell-Hogan, D; Dali, H. Mechanism of activation of 1,2-dehydro-N-acetyldopamine for cuticular sclerotization. Arch Insect Biochem Physiol 1990, 14, 93–109.

41. Sugumaran, M; Semensi, V; Kalyanaraman, B; Bruce, JM; Land, EJ. Evidence for the formation of a quinone methide during the oxidation of the insect cuticular sclerotizing precursor, 1,2-dehydro-N-acetyldopamine. J Biol Chem 1992,267, 10355–10361.

42. Sugumaran, M. Oxidation chemistry of 1,2-dehydro-N-acetyldopamines: Direct evidence for the formation of 1,2-dehydro-N-acetyldopamine quinone. Arch Biochem Biophys 2000, 378, 404–410.

43. Abebe, A; Zheng, D; Evans, J; Sugumaran, M. Reexamination of the mechanisms of oxidative transformations of the insect cuticular sclerotization precursor, 1,2-dehydro-N-acetyldopamine. Insect Biochem Mol Biol 2010, 40, 650–659.

44. Sugumaran, M. Unified mechanism for sclerotization of insect cuticle. Adv Insect Physiol 1998, 27, 229–334.

45. Sugumaran, M. Chemistry of cuticular sclerotization. Adv Insect Physiol 2010, 39, 151–209.

46. Noda, N; Kubota, S; Miyata, Y; Miyahara, K. Optically active N-acetyldopamine dimer of the crude drug "Zentai", the cast-off shell of the Cicada Cryptotympana sp. Chem Pharm Bull 2000, 48, 1749–1752.

47. Tada, T; Ohnishi, K; Suzuki, K; Tomita, H; Okamori, M; Katuzaki, H; Komiya, T; Imai, K. Potential cosmetic whitening agents from insect cuticle: Tyrosinase inhibitory activity of N-acetyldopamine dimers from the exuviae of Cicada,Cryptotympana tuslulata FABR. J Oleo Sci 2002, 51, 355–358.

48. Xu, MZ; Lee, WS; Han, JM; Oh, HW; Park, DS; Tian, GR; Jeong, TS; Park, HY. Antioxidant and anti-inflammatory activities of N-acetyldopamine dimers from periostracum Cicadae. Bioorg Med Chem 2006, 14, 7826–7834.

49. Sakai, R; Higa, T. Tubastrine, a new guanidinostyrene from the coral Tubastrea aurea. Chem Lett 1987, 127–128.

50. Sperry, S; Crews, P. Dihydrotubastrines: phenethylguanidine analogues from the Indo-Pacific marine sponge, Petrosiacf. contignata. J Nat Prod 1998, 61, 859–861.

51. Barenbrock, JS; Kock, M. Screening enzyme—inhibitory activity in several ascidian species from Orkney Islands using protein tyrosine kinase (PTK) bioassay—guided fractionation. J Biotechnol 2005, 117, 225–232.

52. Pearce, AN; Chia, EW; Berridge, MV; Maas, EW; Page, MJ; Harper, JL; Webb, VL; Copp, BR. Orthidines A–E, tubastrine, 3,4-dimethoxyphenylethyl-β-guanidine, and 1,14-sperminedihomovanillamide: Potential anti-inflammatory alkaloids isolated from the New Zealand ascidian Aplidium orthium that act as inhibitors of neutrophil respiratory burst. Tetrahedron 2008, 64, 5748–5755.

53. Ohta, S; Kobayashi, H; Ikegami, S. Jaspisin, a novel styryl sulfate from the marine sponge, Jaspis species. Biosci Biotechnol Biochem 1994, 58, 1752–1753.

54. Ohta, S; Kobayashi, H; Ikegami, S. Isojaspisin, a novel styryl sulfate from a marine sponge, Jaspis sp., that inhibits hatching of sea urchin embryos. Tetrahedron Lett 1994, 35, 4579–4580.

55. Ikegami, S; Kobayashi, H; Myotoishi, Y; Ohta, S; Kato, KH. Selective inhibition of exoplasmic membrane fusion in echinoderm gametes with jaspisin, a novel antihatching substance isolated from a marine sponge. J Biol Chem 1994,269, 23262–23267.

56. Tsukamoto, B; Kato, H; Hirota, H; Fusetani, N. Narains: N,N-dimethylguanidinium styryl sulfates, metamorphosis inducers of ascidian larvae from a marine sponge, Jaspis sp. Tetrahedron Lett 1994, 35, 5874–5874.

57. Tsukamoto, B; Kato, H; Hirota, H; Fusetani, N. 3,4-Dihydroxystyrene dimers, inducers of larval metamorphosis in ascidians, from a marine sponge, Jaspis sp. Tetrahedron 1994, 48, 13583–13592.

58. Shin, J; Rho, JR; Seo, Y; Lee, HS; Cho, KW; Kwon, HJ; Sim, CJ. Wondonins A and B, new bis(dihydroxystyryl)imidazoles from a two sponge association. Tetrahedron Lett 2001, 42, 1965–1968.

59. Chan, GW; Mong, S; Hemling, ME; Freyer, AJ; Offen, PH; DeBrosse, CW; Sarau, HM; Westley, JW. New leukotriene B4receptor antagonist: Leucettamine A and related imidazoles alkaloids from the marine sponge Leucetta microraphis. J Nat Prod 1993, 56, 116–121.

60. Crews, P; Clark, DP; Tenney, K. Variation in the alkaloids among Indo-Pacific Leucetta sponges. J Nat Prod 2003, 66, 177–182.

61. Debdab, M, Renault, S, Lozach, O, Meijer, L, Paquin, L, Carreaux, F, Bazuraeu, JP. Synthesis and preliminary biological evaluation of new derivatives of the marine alkaloid leucettamine B as kinase inhibitors. Eur J Med Chem2010, 45, 805–810.

62. Davis, RA; Aalbersberg, W; Meo, S; Moreira da Rocha, R; Ireland, CM. The isolation and synthesis of polyandrocarpamines A and B. Two new 2-aminoimidazolone compounds from the Fijian ascidian, Polyandrocarpasp. Tetrahedron 2002, 58, 3263–3269.

63. Davis, RA; Baron, PS; Neve, JE; Cullinane, C. A microwave-assisted stereoselective synthesis of polyandrocarpamines A and B. Tetrahedron Lett 2009, 50, 880–882.

64. Andersen, RJ; Stonard, RJ. Clionamide, a major metabolite of the sponge Cliona celata Grant. Can J Chem 1979, 57, 2325–2328.

65. Taylor, SW; Kammerer, B; Nicholson, GJ; Pusecker, K; Walk, T; Bayer, E; Scippa, S; De Vincentiis, M. Morulin Pm: A modified polypeptide containing TOPA and 6-bromotryptophan from the morula cells of the

ascidian Phalusia mammillata. Arch Biochem Biophys 1997, 348, 278–288.

66. Tincu, JA; Menzel, LP; Azimov, R; Sands, J; Hong, T; Waring, AJ; Taylor, SW; Lehrer, RI. Plicatamide, an antimicrobial octapeptide from Sytela plicata hemocytes. J Biol Chem 2003, 278, 13546–13553.

67. Tincu, JA; Taylor, SW. Antimicrobial peptides from marine invertebrates. Antimicrob Agents Chemother 2004, 48, 3645–3654.

68. Azumi, K; Yoshimizu, M; Suzuki, S; Ezura, Y; Yokosawa, H. Inhibitory effect of halocyamine, an antimicrobial substance from ascidian hemocytes, on the growth of fish viruses and marine bacteria. Experientia 1990, 46, 1066–1068.

69. Stonard, RJ; Andersen, RJ. Celenamides A and B linear peptide alkaloids from the sponge Cliona celala. J Org Chem1980, 45, 3687–3691.

70. Stonard, RJ; Andersen, RJ. Linear peptide alkaloids from the sponge Cliona celata (Grant). Celenamides C and D. Can J Chem 1980, 58, 2121–2126.

71. Palermo, JA; Brasco, MFR; Cabezas, E; Balzaretti, V; Seldes, AM. Celenamide E, a tripeptide alkaloid from the Patagonian sponge Cliona chilensis. J Nat Prod 1998, 61, 488–490.

72. Lee, IH; Cho, Y; Lehrer, RI. Effects of pH and salinity on the antimicrobial properties of clavanins. Infect Immun 1997,65, 2898–2903.

73. Lee, IH; Cho, Y; Lehrer, RI. Styelins, broad-spectrum antimicrobial peptides from the solitary tunicate Styela clava.Comp Biochem Physiol B Biochem Mol Biol 1997, 118, 515–521.

74. Lehrer, RI. Plicatamide, an antimicrobial octapeptide from Styela plicata hemocytes. J Biol Chem 2003, 278, 13546–13553.

75. Lehrer, RI; Lee, IH; Menzel, L; Waring, A; Zhao, C. Clavanins and styelins, alpha-helical antimicrobial peptides from the hemocytes of Styela clava. Adv Exp Med Biol 2001, 484, 71–76.

76. Lehrer, RI; Tincu, JA; Taylor, SW; Menzel, LP; Waring, AJ. Natural peptide antibiotics from tunicates: Structures, functions and potential uses. Integr Comp Biol 2003, 43, 313–322.

77. Taylor, SW; Ross, MM; Waite, HJ. Novel 3,4-di- and 3,4,5-trihydroxyphenylalanine containing polypeptides from the blood cells of the ascidians Ascidia ceratodes and Molgula manhattensis. Arch Biochem Biophys 1995, 324, 228–240.

78. Cai, M; Sugumaran, M; Robinson, WE. The crosslinking and antibacterial properties of tunichromes. Comp Biochem Physiol B Biochem Mol Biol 2008, 151, 110–117.

79. Oltz, EM; Pollack, S; Delohery, T; Smith, MJ; Ojika, M; Lee, S; Kustin, K; Nakanishi, K. Distribution of tunichrome and vanadium in sea squirt blood cells sorted by flow cytometry. Experientia 1989, 45, 186–190.

80. Smith, MJ; Kim, D; Horenstein, B; Nakanishi, K; Kustin, K. Unraveling the chemistry of tunichromes. Acc Chem Res1991, 24, 117–124.

81. Taylor, SW; Kammerer, B; Bayer, E. New perspectives in the chemistry and biochemistry of the tunichromes and related compounds. Chem Rev 1997, 97, 333–346.

82. Michibata, H; Terada, T; Anada, N; Yamakawa, K; Numakunai, T. The accumulation and distribution of vanadium, iron, and manganese in some solitary ascidians. Biol Bull 1986, 171, 672–681.

83. Kustin, K; Robinson, WE; Smith, MJ. Tunichromes, vanadium, and vacuolated blood cells in tunicates. Invert Reprod Develop 1990, 17, 129–139.

84. Waite, HJ. Evidence for a repeating 3,4-dihydroxyphenylalanine- and hydroxyproline-containing decapeptide in the adhesive protein of the mussel, Mytilus edulis L. J Biol Chem 1983, 258, 2911–2915.

85. Waite, HJ. Nature's underwater adhesive specialist. Int J Adhes Adhes 1987, 7, 9–14.

86. Waite, HJ. The phylogeny and chemical diversity of quinone tanned glues and varnishes. Comp Biochem Physiol B 1990,97, 19–29.

87. Kashman, Y; Koren-Goldshlager, G; Gravalos, MDG; Schleyer, M. Halitulin, a new cytotoxic alkaloid from the marine sponge Haliclona tulearensis. Tetrahedron Lett 1999, 40, 997–1000.

88. Palermo, JA; Brasco, MFR; Seldes, AM. Storniamides A–D: Alkaloids from a Patagonian Sponge Cliona sp. Tetrahedron1996, 52, 2727–2734.

89. Boger, D; Boyce, C; Labroli, M; Sehon, C; Jin, Q. Total Syntheses of Ningalin A, Lamellarin O, Lukianol A, and Permethyl Storniamide A Utilizing Heterocyclic Azadiene Diels–Alder Reactions. J Am Chem Soc 1999, 121, 54–62.

90. Furstner, A; Krause, H; Thiel, O. Efficient relay syntheses and assessment of the DNA-cleaving properties of the pyrrole alkaloid derivatives permethyl storniamide A, lycogalic acid A dimethyl ester, and the halitulin core.Tetrahedron 2002, 58, 6373–6380.

91. Chan, GW; Francis, T; Thureen, DR; Offen, PO; Pierce, NJ; Westley, JW; Randall, K; Johnson, RK; Faulkner, JD. Purpurone, an inhibitor of ATP-citrate lyase: A novel alkaloid from the marine sponge Iotrochota sp. J Org Chem 1993,58, 2544–2546.

92. Liu, Y; Ji, H; Dong, J; Zhang, S; Lee, KJ; Mathew, S. Antioxidant alkaloid from the South China sea marine sponge,Iotrochota sp. Z Naturforsch C 2008, 63, 636–638.

93. Kang, H; Fenical, W. Ningalins A–D: Novel aromatic alkaloids from a western Australian ascidian of the genusDidemnum. J Org Chem 1997, 62, 3254–3262.

94. Boger, DL; Soenen, DR; Boyce, CW; Hedrick, MP; Jin, Q. Total synthesis of Ningalin B utilizing a heterocyclic azadiene Diels-Alder reaction and discovery of a new class of potent multidrug resistant (MDR) reversal agents. J Org Chem 2000, 65, 2479–2483.

95. Tao, H; Hwang, I; Boger, DL. Multidrug resistance reversal activity of permethyl ningalin B amide derivatives. Bioorg Med Chem Lett 2004, 14, 5979–5981.

96. Fan, H; Li, Z; Shen, S; Zeng, Y; Yang, Y; Xu, M; Bruhn, T; Nhrun, H; Morschhauser, J; Bringmann, G; Lin, W. Baculiferins A–O, O-sulfated pyrrole alkaloids with anti-HIV-1 activity, from the Chinese marine sponge Iotrochota Baculifera. Bioorg Med Chem 2010, 18, 5466–5474.

97. Andersen, RJ; Faukner, DJ; He, C; Van Duyne, GD; Clardy, J. Metabolites of the marine prosobranch molluskLamellaria sp. J Am Chem Soc 1985, 107, 5492–5495.

98. Lindquist, N; Fenical, W; Van Duyne, GD. Clardy, New alkaloids of the lamellarin class from the marine ascidian, Didemnum chartaceum (Sluiter, 1909. J. Org. Chem 1988, 53, 4570–4574.

99. Warabi, K; Matsunaga, S; van Soest, RWM; Fusetani, N. Dictyodendrins A–E, the first telomerase inhibitory marine natural products from the

sponge Dictyodendrilla verongiformis. J Org Chem 2003, 68, 2735–2770.

100. Sato, A; Morishita, T; Shiraki, T; Yoshioka, S; Horikoshi, H; Kuwano, H; Hanakawa, H; Hata, T. Aldose reductase inhibitors from a marine sponge, Dictyodendrilla sp. J Org Chem 1993, 58, 7632–7634.

101. Rudi, A; Goldberg, I; Stein, Z; Frolow, F; Benayahu, Y; Schleyer, M; Kashman, Y. Polycltone A and polycitrins A and B: New alkaloids from the marine ascidian, Polycitor sp. J Org Chem 1994, 59, 999–1003.

102. Loya, S; Rudi, A; Kashman, Y; Hizi, A. Polycitone A, a novel and potent general inhibitor of retroviral reverse transcriptases and cellular DNA polymerases. Biochem J 1999, 344, 85–92.

103. Rudi, A; Evan, T; Akin, M; Kashman, Y. Polycitone B and prepolycitrin A: Two novel alkaloids from the marine ascidian Polycitor africanus. J Nat Prod 2000, 63, 832–833.

104. Yoshida, W; Lee, K; Carroll, A; Scheuer, P. A complex pyrrolo-oxazinone and its derivate isolated from tunicates. Helv Chim Acta 1992, 75, 1721–1725.

105. Gupton, J; Krumpe, K; Burnham, B; Webb, T; Shuford, J; Siberoski, J. The application of vinylogous iminium salt derivatives to a regiocontrolled and efficient relay synthesis of lukianol A and related marine natural products.Tetrahedron 1999, 55, 14515–14522.

106. Gupton, JT. Pyrrole natural products with antitumor properties. Top Heterocycl Chem 2006, 2, 53–92.

107. Rachid, S; Revemann, O; Dauth, C; Kazmaier, U; Muller, R. Characterization of a novel type of oxidative decarboxylase involved in the biosynthesis of the styryl moiety of chondrochloren from an acylated tyrosine. J Biol Chem 2010, 285, 12482–12489.

108. Sugumaran, M. Comparative biochemistry of eumelanogenesis and the protective roles of phenoloxidase and melanin in insects. Pigment Cell Res 2002, 15, 2–9.

109. Sugumaran, M; Dali, H; Kundzicz, H; Semensi, V. Unusual intramolecular cyclization and side chain desaturation of carboxyethyl-o-benzoquinone derivatives. Bioorg Chem 1989, 17, 443–453.

110. Sugumaran, M; Semensi, V; Dali, H; Saul, SJ. Nonenzymatic transformations of enzymatically generated N-acetyl dopamine

quinone and isomeric dihydrocaffeiyl methylamide quinone. FEBS Lett 1989, 255, 345–349.

111. Rzepecki, LM; Waite, JH. α,β-dehydro-3,4-dihydroxyphenylalanine derivatives: Rate and mechanism of formation.Arch Biochem Biophys 1991, 285, 27–36.

112. Sugumaran, M; Ricketts, D. Model sclerotization studies. 3. Cuticular enzyme catalyzed oxidation of peptidyl model tyrosine and dopa derivatives. Arch Insect Biochem Physiol 1995, 28, 17–32.

113. Saul, SJ; Sugumaran, M. A novel quinone: Quinone methide isomerase generates quinone methides in insect cuticle.FEBS Lett 1988, 237, 155–158.

114. Saul, SJ; Sugumaran, M. 4-Alkyl-o-quinone/2-hydroxy-p-quinone methide isomerase from the larval hemolymph ofSarcophaga bullata. I. Purification and characterization of enzyme-catalyzed reaction. J Biol Chem 1990, 265, 16992–16999.

115. Saul, SJ; Sugumaran, M. N-acetyldopamine quinone methide/1,2-dehydro-N-acetyldopamine tautomerase. A new enzyme involved in sclerotization of insect cuticle. FEBS Lett 1989, 255, 340–344.

Index